APPORTIONMENT IN PRIVATE LAW

This collection of essays investigates the way in which modern private law apportions responsibility between multiple parties who are (or may be) responsible for the same legal event. It examines both doctrines and principles that share responsibility between plaintiffs and defendants, on the one hand, and between multiple defendants, on the other.

The doctrines examined include those 'originating' doctrines which operate to create shared liabilities in the first place (such as vicarious and accessorial liability); and, more centrally, those doctrines that operate to distribute the liabilities and responsibilities so created. These include the doctrine of contributory (comparative) negligence, joint and several (solidary) liability, contribution, reimbursement, and 'proportionate' liability, as well as defences and principles of equitable 'allowance' that permit both losses and gains to be shared between parties to civil proceedings. The work also considers the principles which apportion liability between multiple defendants and insurers in cases in which the cause, or timing, of a particular loss is hard to determine.

The contributions to this volume offer important perspectives on the law in the UK, USA, Canada, Australia and New Zealand, as well as a number of civilian jurisdictions. They explicate the main rules and trends and offer critical insights on the growth and distribution of shared responsibilities from a number of different perspectives – historical, comparative, empirical, doctrinal and philosophical.

Volume 30 in the series Hart Studies in Private Law

Apportionment in Private Law

Edited by
Kit Barker
and
Ross Grantham

• HART •
OXFORD • LONDON • NEW YORK • NEW DELHI • SYDNEY

HART PUBLISHING

Bloomsbury Publishing Plc

Kemp House, Chawley Park, Cumnor Hill, Oxford, OX2 9PH, UK

HART PUBLISHING, the Hart/Stag logo, BLOOMSBURY and the Diana logo are trademarks of Bloomsbury Publishing Plc

First published in Great Britain 2019

A catalogue record for this book is available from the British Library.

Library of Congress Cataloging-in-Publication data

Names: Barker, Kit, editor. | Grantham, Ross, editor.

Title: Apportionment in private law / edited by Kit Barker, Ross Grantham.

Description: Oxford, UK ; Portland, Oregon : Hart Publishing, 2019. | Series: Hart studies in private law | Includes bibliographical references and index.

Identifiers: LCCN 2018049646 (print) | LCCN 2018050022 (ebook) | ISBN 9781509917495 (EPub) | ISBN 9781509917501 (hardback)

Subjects: LCSH: Correality and solidarity. | Joint tortfeasors. | Negligence, Comparative. | Negligence, Contributory. | BISAC: LAW / Contracts. | LAW / Comparative.

Classification: LCC K958 (ebook) | LCC K958 .A67 2018 (print) | DDC 346.03—dc23

LC record available at https://lccn.loc.gov/2018049646

ISBN: HB: 978-1-50991-750-1
ePDF: 978-1-50991-751-8
ePub: 978-1-50991-749-5

Typeset by Compuscript Ltd, Shannon

To find out more about our authors and books visit www.hartpublishing.co.uk. Here you will find extracts, author information, details of forthcoming events and the option to sign up for our newsletters.

PREFACE

The range of cases in which private law is required to decide how to apportion legal responsibility between multiple parties has increased significantly through the twentieth and the early part of the twenty-first century. This is partly a result of expanded doctrines of vicarious and accessorial liability, partly of more liberal, pro-claimant adjustments to causation rules, and partly of new liabilities for public authority omissions in tort; all of which developments have collectively served to widen the pool of persons now potentially responsible for one and the same harm. The creation of more and more shared responsibility for harm has in turn triggered the development of more sophisticated and sensitive mechanisms for apportioning it between those considered legally responsible – doctrines of contributory (comparative) negligence, indemnity, contribution, reimbursement, solidary (joint and several) liability and – most recently – 'proportionate liability'. In the same way, as the scope of restitutionary and 'disgorgement' liabilities has increased with the development of unjust enrichment doctrine, private law has cultivated means for adjusting defendants' gain-based liabilities, so as to take account of harms defendants have themselves been caused, gains they have conferred on claimants, or contributions they have made to the profits for which they are being held accountable. This is done in part through the restitutionary defence of change of position, and through sophisticated, but still highly opaque mechanisms of 'equitable allowance'.

Collectively, these mechanisms of apportionment are often understood to reflect a general shift away from stark ideologies of 'all or nothing' in civil liability, towards more sensitive allocations of legal responsibility that respond both to the relative causal contribution and relative fault of responsible parties. In fact, however, the motivations for recent developments have been more complex, reflecting a mix of both moral and powerful, political impulses. The introduction across many common law jurisdictions of regimes of 'proportionate liability', for example, although often clothed in the language of fairness, has almost universally been the product of aggressive political lobbying on the part of powerful defendant interest groups – the insurance industry in particular – at times of economic downturn and market failure. The result of these political interventions has been the introduction of extensive and often highly complex statutory modifications to basic apportionment regimes across many jurisdictions in a relatively short time-period. This has wrought a fundamental change in the balance of risk between plaintiffs and wrongdoers, casting more and more of it back upon plaintiffs themselves.

This collection of essays examines both the doctrinal origins and modern dynamics of apportionment in private law, drawing on the experience of experts who have been central to the debates about them in the United States, United Kingdom, Canada, Australia, New Zealand, and European Continental legal systems. It considers some of the doctrines that give rise to shared liabilities in the first place (vicarious liability; accessorial liability), as well as those that now regulate apportionment between plaintiffs and defendants (contributory negligence, change of position, equitable allowance) and between defendants (contribution, solidary and proportionate liability). The aim is to better understand the modern dynamics, situating them in their moral, historical, and political contexts. We hope hereby to contribute to important modern debates about reform.

ACKNOWLEDGEMENTS

This book was born as the result of a symposium jointly hosted by the Australian Centre of Private Law in the TC Beirne School of Law, The University of Queensland and the Queensland Supreme Court Library in Brisbane on 15 August 2017. Some of the papers were presented on that day and others were solicited independently by the editors in order to complement and broaden the themes explored on that occasion.

We would like to express our gratitude to all those who travelled and participated in the very lively and productive day of discussion in Brisbane, and to the Supreme Court Library for making the Court Library's excellent facilities available to us. For chairing proceedings and providing judicial support for the event, we would like to thank The Hon Justice PD McMurdo, The Hon Justice David Jackson, The Hon Justice Hugh Fraser, The Hon Justice Peter Applegarth and The Hon Justice Roger Derrington. For their assistance in staging the event, we would like to say a special thank you to David Bratchford and Megan Reeve of the Supreme Court Library, Jane Gay and Therese Yat. We would also like to thank Bill Asquith and Sinead Moloney of Hart Publishing for their enthusiasm for the project.

Kit Barker and Ross Grantham

May 2018

CONTENTS

TABLE OF CASES

Austria

Australia

Belgium

Canada

France

Germany

Hong Kong

New Zealand

United Kingdom

United States of America

TABLE OF LEGISLATION

Austria

Australia

Canada

China

European Union

Germany

New Zealand

Russia

United Kingdom

United State of America

LIST OF CONTRIBUTORS

Kit Barker is Professor of Law at the TC Beirne School of Law, The University of Queensland, Australia.

David Cheifetz is a former, senior practitioner at the Ontario and British Columbia Bars in Canada.

Simone Degeling is Professor of Law at UNSW, Australia.

Joachim Dietrich is Professor of Law at Bond University, Australia.

James Goodkamp is Professor of the Law of Obligations at the University of Oxford and a Fellow of Keble College, Oxford. He is also a barrister at 7 King's Bench Walk, London.

Ross Grantham is Professor of Commercial Law at the TC Beirne School of Law, The University of Queensland, Australia.

Lewis Klar QC is Professor Emeritus at the University of Alberta, Canada.

Helmut Koziol is Vice-Director of the European Centre of Tort and Insurance Law, Honorary Professor of Private Law at the University of Graz and a former Professor of Law at the University of Vienna.

Barbara McDonald is Professor of Law at the University of Sydney Law School, Australia.

Geoff McLay is Professor of Law at Victoria University of Wellington, New Zealand, and a former New Zealand Law Commissioner.

Rob Merkin QC is the Lloyd's Professor of Commercial Law at the University of Exeter, England.

Donal Nolan is Professor of Private Law at the University of Oxford and the Francis Reynolds and Clarendon Fellow and Tutor in Law at Worcester College, Oxford.

Jenny Steele is Professor of Law at York Law School, England.

Warren Swain is Professor of Law at the Faculty of Law, the University of Auckland, New Zealand.

Richard Wright is University Distinguished Professor and Professor of Law at Chicago-Kent College of Law, Illinois Institute of Technology, USA.

PART I

Frameworks, Ethics and Politics

1

Apportionment in Private Law: Nothing, All, or Something in Between?

KIT BARKER*

I. Introduction

One aspect of the increased complexity of private law in the late twentieth and early twenty-first centuries is the rise in the incidence and intricacy of rules designed to apportion responsibility between multiple parties for losses and gains that are legally attributable to more than one of them. As Tony Weir observed in 2004 in an article to which the title of this chapter pays tribute, the law has moved, within a relatively short timeframe, from a formal stance in which civil liability is an 'all-or-nothing' business to one in which it is 'shared' through a set of compromise solutions.[1] Tort plaintiffs whose own careless conduct might previously have led their claims to fail by virtue of strict causation rules, or through the application of the total defence of contributory negligence can hence now often recover something for their injuries. Defendants who, under the old system, were held 100 per cent liable in damages for indivisible injuries for which they were responsible in common with other parties, can obtain contribution or reimbursement (indemnity) from those other parties.[2] Similarly, in the field of gain-based private law claims, there has been a gradual transition from rules in which causes of action are relatively hard to establish, but 'total' on success, to ones in which the basic preconditions to establishing a claim are less exacting, but the resulting liabilities are more often partial. Defendants can thus now offset against their liabilities for unjust enrichment the losses they have themselves been (or may be) caused by innocent changes in their position[3] and they can – through the operation of

* I am grateful to Richard Wright and Ross Grantham for helpful comments upon an earlier draft. All remaining defects are most definitely my own.

[1] T Weir, 'All or Nothing' (2004) 78 *Tul L Rev* 511.

[2] As can their insurers through the process of subrogation.

[3] See generally, C Mitchell, P Mitchell, S Watterson, *Goff and Jones The Law of Unjust Enrichment*, 9th edn (London, Sweet & Maxwell, 2016) ch 27; J Edelman and E Bant, *Unjust Enrichment*, 2nd edn (Oxford, Hart Publishing, 2016) ch 14.

'equitable allowances' or conditions attached to orders for rescission – offset the value of contributions they have themselves made to gains obtained (or claimed by) a plaintiff.

Most recently and perhaps most controversially, there has been a widely-documented drift in some (but not all) common law jurisdictions away from systems of 'solidary' (joint and several) liability towards 'proportionate' liability,[4] so that multiple defendants responsible for the same indivisible injury are no longer even in principle liable to a plaintiff for the whole damage caused, but only for such proportion of it as a court finds them to be responsible, relative to other responsible parties.[5] This is another, modern, 'sharing' solution, albeit one of a very different type and one which, unlike the previous examples, designedly operates to the prejudice of plaintiffs, so as to redistribute the burden of procedural hurdles, evidential difficulties and insolvency risks away from defendants and their insurers. It can leave a significant proportion of those suffering indivisible loss caused by multiple defendants with gaps in their compensation. Whilst such individuals were previously guaranteed full recovery, provided only that they could identify and sue at least *one* of those responsible, they must now accept only partial compensation in any case in which it proves impossible to successfully sue *all* of them.

Weir avoided speculating upon the explanations or justifications for these trends. Apportionment, he sagely observed, is a 'twisted path'[6] that itself invites mixed reactions and is born of mixed motivations. There are only limited commonalities across different legal systems and the criteria underpinning courts' decisions of how to apportion responsibility (for example, parties' 'relative fault' and the 'causal potency' of their conduct) are notoriously difficult to apply in practice, even when they are agreed upon. This can result in uncertainty and potentially prejudice out-of-court settlements. The high degree of variation in the form of the relevant legislation within some federal legal systems can also result in different regimes applying to litigants, depending simply on their postcode.[7] Although 'sharing' solutions are often presented as if they are always more logical, morally sophisticated and 'fair', this is also only true in some instances. As Richard Wright shows in the next chapter, the language of ethical superiority is often pure rhetoric. Much depends on who is sharing what, with whom, and why. On occasions, it is true, the sharing of losses and gains is indeed a response to intuitions concerning parties' proper respective moral responsibility for the consequences

[4] K Barker and J Steele, 'Drifting Towards Proportionate Liability: Ethics and Pragmatics' (2015) 74 *CLJ* 49.

[5] These parties need not, in many jurisdictions, even be joined to the relevant proceedings – a fact which can seriously complicate the job of making reliable assessments.

[6] Weir (n 1) 527.

[7] This is a particular, acknowledged problem in the US and Australia.

of their conduct.[8] On other occasions, however, as in the case of recent proportionate liability reforms, 'shared liability' is simply a synonym for 'less' liability for defendants and constitutes the product of the successful lobbying efforts of particularly powerful defendant groups that have managed to gain the ear of governments.

It cannot be assumed, therefore, that the idea of 'sharing' has any particular moral valence and recent commentaries have begun to count the costs, as well as benefits, of 'partial' solutions – particularly those in which the divisions and compromises are discretionary rather than 'pre-set,' and even more so when they result in the under-compensation of those who have been wronged. Some are accordingly now pressing for a return to more clear-cut, 'digital' (on-off) rules, at least in some instances.[9] With notable exceptions, few empirical studies have been done to determine the actual effects of the changes in apportionment rules that have occurred in terms of the rates or distributions of recovery; economic analysis of the rules is often complex and inconclusive[10] and commentators and courts remain unclear even about their precise rationale. It is hence still a matter of contention whether the rules instantiate norms of corrective[11] or distributive justice;[12] whether they are principled or pragmatic in nature; and whether the benefits of their apparent technical subtleties outweigh the burden of the uncertainties they bring. When it comes to reform, commentators are also divided as to whether the best response to the fractured chaos of recent proportionate liability

[8] This is truest of the defence of contributory (comparative) negligence, although even here, the ethics are disputed. See Section III(B).

[9] Weir himself (n 1, 518) questioned the proprietary of allowing contribution between tortfeasors responsible for the same damage on the basis of its practical complications. Others recently advocating the restoration of 'total' rules include R Stevens, 'Should Contributory Negligence be Analogue or Digital?' in A Dyson, J Goudkamp and F Wilmot-Smith (eds), *Defences in Tort* (Oxford, Hart Publishing, 2015) ch 13, 253–54 (rejecting the defence of contributory negligence to tort claims), a wide range of academic commentators critical of the recent proportionate liability reforms (on which see Section VI below) and Australian governments reintroducing 100% deductions for contributory negligence in some cases (see Section V(A) below).

[10] For this conclusion in relation to proportionate liability rules (and reference to the literature), see Barker and Steele (n 4) 70; McLay, ch 13. See similarly, regarding comparative negligence, R Wright, 'Principled Adjudication: Tort Law and Beyond' (1999) 7 *Canterbury Law Review* 265, 284–86, 'Allocating Liability' (1988) 21 *UC Davis Law Review* 1141, 1169–79; I Gilead, 'Introduction to Economic Analysis of Loss Division' in K Oliphant (ed), *Aggregation and Divisibility of Damage* (Wien, Springer, 2009) 449, 464; M Faure, 'Economic Analysis of Contributory Negligence' in U Magnus and M Martín-Casals (eds), *Unification of Tort Law: Contributory Negligence* (The Hague, Kluwer Law International, 2004) 233.

[11] Corrective justice has variously been said to justify the solidary liability of multiple defendants for the same harm (R Wright, 'Allocating Liability Among Multiple Responsible Causes: A Principled Defense of Joint and Several Liability for Actual Harm and Risk Exposure' (1987–8) 21 *UC Davis L Rev* 1141); contribution between defendants (Cheifetz, ch 10); the contributory negligence defence (A Beever, *Rediscovering the Law of Negligence* (Oxford, Hart Publishing, 2007) 340–45) and various restitutionary defences including change of position (R Grantham and C Rickett, A Normative Account of Defences to Restitutionary Liability' (2008) 67 *CLJ* 92; Grantham, ch 8).

[12] Barker and Steele (n 4) 65–66 (in respect of contributory negligence rules).

legislation in Australia and the United States is to try to tidy it up and make it uniform, repeal it completely, or replace it with more targeted solutions designed to protect defendants against 'excessive' exposure, such as capping their liabilities in particular spheres of risk, or even cutting back on their primary legal duties altogether in respect of certain types of harm. Caught mid-stream, reformers are uncertain of their footing and questioning whether it is better, when in blood stepped in so far, to return, or go o'er.[13]

II. Aims and Overview

The aim of this book is to tackle some of these difficult modern debates across a variety of different common law and civilian jurisdictions, from a number of different perspectives – historical, doctrinal, empirical, and theoretical. In doing so, it canvases a wide variety, but by no means all, apportionment doctrines and readers should look elsewhere for comprehensive statements of the rules.[14] The book is divided into four parts, replicated in the later structure of this chapter. There is significant connection and overlap between the different parts.

Part 1 ('Frameworks, Ethics and Politics') maps some of the legal, ethical and political frameworks within which modern apportionment exercises take place. It provides some terminological and analytical guidance to the field; explores the rationale(s) of some of the different types of apportionment rule and gives an overview of the ways in which different legal systems (common law and civilian[15]) deal with the allocative questions they throw up.

Part 2 ('Originating Doctrines') interrogates some of the most important substantive rules that give rise to 'shared' liabilities, focusing in particular on the doctrines of 'vicarious' and 'accessorial' liability. Although these doctrines do not, strictly speaking, govern the *proportion* in which different parties are held liable for events brought about by them all, the reasons *why* such defendants share liability must, I argue, influence the way that liability is subsequently distributed between them. Unfortunately, as the contributions to this Part illustrate, the reasons for vicarious and accessorial liabilities are various, contested and unstable, which currently makes it hard either to predict the incidence of the liabilities themselves, or to make many generalisations about the way in which they should be apportioned.

[13] An inexact reformulation of Macbeth's rather more serious dilemma: Act 3, Scene 4, lines 142–44.

[14] See, amongst other works, D Cheifetz, *Apportionment of Fault in Tort* (Aurora, Canada Law Book, 1981); *Restatement of Torts (Third) Apportionment of Liability* (American Law Institute, St Paul, 2000); C Mitchell, *The Law of Contribution and Reimbursement* (Oxford, Oxford University Press, 2003); Oliphant (n 10); WVH Rogers (ed), *Unification of Tort Law: Multiple Tortfeasors* (The Hague, Kluwer Law International, 2004); K Magnus and Martín-Casals (n 10); I Gilead, M Green, B Koch (eds), *Proportional Liability: Analytical and Comparative Perspectives* (Berlin, De Gruyter, 2013).

[15] See Koziol, ch 3.

Parts 3 and 4 of the book then provide a detailed assessment of key apportionment rules. Part 3 ('Plaintiff-Defendant Apportionment') focuses on devices that apportion gains and losses between plaintiffs and defendants – the modern defence of contributory (comparative) negligence, the restitutionary defence of change of position, and the principles governing awards for breach of fiduciary duty, where losses and gains are hard to assess with certainty and where courts apportion the risks of the uncertainties through quantification rules. Part 4 ('Apportionment Between Defendants') finishes with an examination of principles regulating the liability inter se of multiple defendants who are (or may be) responsible for the same, indivisible harm. These include the doctrines of contribution, solidary ('joint and several') and 'proportionate' liability, together with some exceptional causation rules developed in the United Kingdom in the context of asbestos-related claims, that allow the risk of some, very specific types of causal uncertainty to be distributed between defendants, so as to partialise their liability. This part takes in many of the recent debates concerning proportionate liability reform and provides an important insurer's perspective on cases involving uncertain risks.

III. Frameworks, Ethics and Politics

'Partial' solutions are nothing new. Weir refers to their presence in Roman systems.[16] He also hints at the strong probability that, before contributory negligence ceased to be a total defence to tort claims in the UK in 1945, civil juries regularly made informal apportionments of responsibility behind closed doors[17] by fixing damages in ways that achieved compromise between careless plaintiffs and wrongdoing defendants. This sidestepping of the old, blunt 'all-or-nothing' rule may therefore have been formalised by the legislative change, but was probably hiding in the system long before this date. Actions for contribution and reimbursement are also ancient, dating back in equity to at least 1629, but probably much earlier at common law.[18] What is more modern is their wider availability to tortfeasors and others liable for the same damage[19] and the emergence around them of a new intellectual architecture (unjust enrichment), importing fresh thinking

[16] Weir (n 1), 547–49.

[17] ibid, 549.

[18] *Fleetwood v Charnock* (1629) Nelson 10 (equitable contribution between co-sureties). Mitchell (n 14) 68 cites David Ibbetson for the view that there was a common law example as early as 1380.

[19] Originally, contribution and reimbursement actions were confined to guarantors and co-sureties of the same debt, trustees under a common liability for breach of trust, and company directors liable for breach of equitable duties to the company. In England, the extension to tortfeasors liable for the same damage occurred in 1935 with the Law Reform (Marred Women and Tortfeasors) Act, 25 & 26 Geo 5 (1935). Further extensions occurred under the Civil Liability (Contribution) Act 1978, which extends contribution rights to all persons liable in respect of the same damage.

about their rationale, availability and quantification.[20] The same architecture is responsible for re-invigorating debate about equitable allowances for wrongdoing fiduciaries, which have been in evidence since the early eighteenth century.[21] Even the modern restitutionary defence of change of position probably only formalises the expression of instincts for allocative fairness that were previously given more isolated and invisible effect through technical devices, such as tracing rules.[22] The spirit of compromise is hence not new, but modern apportionment rules strike a different set of compromises to those which have been struck in the past; and they purport to bring a new visibility, legitimacy, science and sense to the process that was formerly lacking.

A. Terminology – A Short Primer

In this book, the term 'apportionment' is used to refer to any legal mechanism for dividing responsibility for either losses *or* gains between plaintiffs and defendants in private law actions.[23] This is a very broad definition. In Australia, references to 'the apportionment legislation' are usually very specific allusions to the statutory rules enacting what is now known in the United Kingdom as the partial defence of 'contributory negligence.' In the United States and Canada, that, same defence is called 'comparative' negligence', in order to distinguish it from the 'absolute' version still operating in a minority of jurisdictions.[24]

Jurisdictional variations in terminology are highlighted in the following chapters, but it may nonetheless assist to provide a short primer of the main concepts of 'sharing' and 'division' used in the book, referencing their cross-jurisdictional equivalents and variations. Even then, it must be accepted that the meanings specified below are not exclusive; and that the patterns of language used to refer to apportionment issues are more varied still than the table suggests.

[20] Mitchell (n 14); *Goff and Jones* (n 3) ch 19. For doubts about the inclusion of contribution within the taxonomy (due in part to uncertainties about the latter's scope) see Cheifetz, ch 10, n 87 and text.

[21] J Heydon, M Leeming, P Turner, *Meagher, Gummow and Lehane's Equity, Doctrines and Remedies* 5th edn, (Chatswood, LexisNexis Butterworths, 2015) [5-280] cites *Brown v Litton* (1711) 1 P Wms 140, 24 ER 329 as the earliest example.

[22] eg, the rule that a wrongdoer who mixes his own money with that of P and then spends part of the mixture is presumed to spend his own money first (so that he is obliged to bear its loss), whereas an innocent is regarded as spending both P's and his own money in the proportions in which they contributed it (pari passu). See *Goff and Jones* (n 3) 214–19.

[23] The term is also used to refer both to rules that apportion *after* D's liability has been established (eg, the defence of contributory negligence) and rules limiting the amount of P's initial claim (eg, rules apportioning the risk of causal uncertainties, or limiting recoverable gains and losses, such as rules of remoteness, mitigation of loss, and the principles regulating accounts of profit).

[24] The absolute version still exists in 5 US jurisdictions (Alabama, Maryland, North Carolina, Virginia and the District of Columbia), although usually only where P is adjudged at least 50% responsible for his injury.

Concept	Definition and Variations
1. Joint Liability	The liability of D1 and D2 to P for one and the same wrong. Note: historically, this term had a procedural connotation, referring only to the subset of those above who might be joined in the same lawsuit.
2. Several Liability	The liability of D1 and D2 to P for separate wrongs. Note: In the *US Restatement of Torts (Third)*, this term is now used to mean 'proportionate liability' as defined below.
3. Concurrent Liability	The liability of D1 and D2 to P for one and the same, indivisible harm.
4. Vicarious Liability	The liability of D1 to P on behalf of D2. Note: Although D1 is liable on D2's behalf, D2 also remains liable to P. For this reason, some prefer to describe vicarious liability as the liability of D1 'for D2's wrong'.
5. Accessorial Liability	The liability of D1 to P for D1's involvement in the wrong of D2.
6. Solidary Liability	The liability of D1 to P for 100% of an indivisible harm for which multiple defendants (D1, D2 … D*x*) are legally responsible. Note: In the UK, US, NZ and Canada, the term 'joint and several' liability is used.
7. Contribution	The process via which a D who is liable on a solidary basis to P exercises a right to claim a proportion of the value of that liability from (an)other D(s) liable in respect of the same, indivisible harm.
8. Indemnity/ Reimbursement	The process via which a D who is liable on a solidary basis to P exercises a right to claim the whole value of that liability from another D liable in respect of the same indivisible harm.
9. Proportionate Liability	The liability of a D to P for (only) such proportion of an indivisible harm caused to P as D is considered personally responsible, relative to other Ds legally responsible for the same harm. Note: the US language is now 'several' liability – see (2) above.
10. Contributory Negligence	The defence according to which D's liability for a loss suffered by P is reduced so as to reflect the relative responsibility of D and P for that loss. Note: In the US and Canada, this defence is referred to as 'comparative negligence', the term 'contributory' negligence being reserved for the absolute version of the defence persisting in only a small number of US jurisdictions.
11. Change of Position	The defence to a restitutionary claim by P to a benefit obtained by D, which permits D to reduce his or her liability on account of some change in D's position.

B. Ethics

The ethics of apportionment are complex and contested. Sometimes, as the following section on 'Politics' suggests, they have probably even been purposely confused by governments and lobbyists, who have been anxious to portray the raft of modern proportionate liability reforms as a logical extension of the same sort of ethics as is at work in the defence of contributory (comparative) negligence. That analogy cannot be accepted, since the decision to reduce a plaintiff's damages on account of some contribution she may have made to her own harm is a different kind of decision to the decision that she should only be entitled to recover in part from a defendant because *other defendants* are *also* responsible for the same, indivisible harm.[25] Whilst in the former case, D clearly has a viable argument about his own moral responsibility compared to that of P ('your failure to wear a seatbelt probably made some difference to the injury I culpably caused you') in the latter he has only an argument about the *additional* responsibility to P of other wrongdoers ('don't *just* blame me – I am not the *only* one that did it').

The difference is so obvious that it would be extraordinary if the arguments had genuinely been confused by governments enacting modern proportionate liability reforms. Every parent knows that the fact that his or her child (Joanne) was not the only one to be throwing stones at the school windows is no reason for not holding her fully accountable for a breakage she has caused. If no other child is caught, or has the pocket-money to pay, it is very hard to see why Joanne's pocket money should not be docked until the school's damage is fully made good.[26] As against the innocent school, the uncertainty about precisely what contribution to the damage Joanne's own stone made amongst others is no answer. She must bear the risk. As against other children who are caught, the position is different.

Note that the same sort of uncertainty about the 'precise causal contribution' of D's action to P's harm is present in both the seatbelt (contributory negligence) and the broken window (solidary liability) examples – that uncertainty exists in *any case* in which two or more parties are found to have caused one and the same 'indivisible' injury. That does not, however, mean that one is morally required to deal with the uncertainty in the same way in both cases. There is a perfectly good moral reason to assign the entire risk of the uncertainty to Joanne in the second instance, rather than to the school, because the school's own conduct is not implicated in

[25] Barker and Steele (n 4) 67–68.

[26] It has rightly been pointed out to me by Richard Wright that this example is not the strongest one that can be used to show that solidary liability is ethically justified, since the damage caused by the separate stones being thrown simultaneously at the broken window by the various children in Joanne's case is only 'practically,' not theoretically indivisible. An even stronger case might therefore be one in which several children are pushing simultaneously on a school door, the combined pressure of them all being sufficient to break it, but the individual contributions of each of them being necessary for that result. It follows from the text that I regard both cases of practical and theoretical indivisibility as ones in which solidary liability is ethically justified.

any way in the damage. Where, by contrast, P has failed to wear a seat belt and is therefore careless, the case for assigning some proportion of the risk of the uncertainty to her is stronger. This is so even though P and D are, admittedly, not in a state of exact moral *equivalence*, because P's conduct presented only a risk to herself, whereas D's conduct was a breach of his legal *duty to P*.

There are many, myself included, who have been persuaded by these arguments to conclude that there is no convincing moral case for departing from the basic 'total' solidary liability rule in cases involving multiple parties who are responsible for the same damage, so that the recent wave of proportionate liability reforms is simply a mistake. That conclusion is endorsed by many, but not necessarily all contributors to this book.[27]

For Richard Wright, the moral correctness of solidary liability flows from the premises of corrective justice – one does not lose the responsibility to set right harm that one has wrongfully caused simply because others have also caused it.[28] So stated, the ethical case for the total liability rule appears to be indisputable. The only question, to my mind, is whether corrective justice *itself* justifies that rule. My hesitation stems from the fact that in all cases of solidary liability, the damage suffered by P is itself, by definition, 'indivisible' and this can only mean that, although we know that it would not have happened 'but for' the actions of each of the defendants, we do not – and cannot – know the precise nature and extent of the contribution any of them made to it. 'Indivisibility' of damage is itself a confession of the *impossibility* of precise causal judgement as to parts. The effect of the total liability rule is then surely to assign to all defendants the risk of the uncertainty regarding division. This is most certainly justified morally, given the relative moral positions of an innocent plaintiff and guilty defendants, but the decision to distribute the risk in this way operates covertly *within* the judgement (underpinning the corrective justice view) that each and every one of them caused the *whole* of the damage. In other words, the total liability of each defendant could be regarded as an instantiation of the ethics of localised distributive, not corrective justice.[29]

[27] For a hint that the scheme may be more acceptable in respect of economic than physical injury, see McLay, ch 13. Contrast Wright, ch 2; McDonald, ch 11 and Dietrich, ch 5. The great weight of academic commentary and that of independent law reform bodies has been against the reforms: see Barker and Steele (n 4) 51, nn 4, 5, 19, 31, 41, 46, 47.

[28] Wright (n 11). Wright now prefers the language of 'interactive' not 'corrective' justice: R Wright, 'The Principles of Justice' (2000) 75 *Notre Dame L Rev* 1859.

[29] I take no hard stance on this here. The point turns on whether corrective justice is understood formally, or substantively. If you take the formal view, then the fact that basic causal rules distribute the risks of uncertainty does not mean that, when those rules are satisfied, one is not doing corrective justice when one requires one of a number of wrongdoers found to have caused the damage to pay for all of it. Others taking a more substantive approach to the definition of corrective justice may not agree. In any event, there is no dispute that justice demands the result. The question is simply what type of justice is at stake. On localised distributive justice, see S Perry, 'The Moral Foundations of Tort Law' (1991) *Iowa Law Review* 77 449; J Gardner, 'What is Tort Law For? Part 2. The Place of Distributive Justice' in J Oberdiek (ed), *Philosophical Foundations of the Law of Torts* (Oxford, OUP, 2014) ch 16, 346–50.

Somewhat surprisingly, similar doubts have recently been voiced about the ethics of the defence of contributory negligence. Later in this volume, Lewis Klar[30] suggests that, although the partial defence has long been recognised in Canada, there may actually be no moral justification for it, at least in cases in which P's own carelessness is a cause only of her injury, not the accident itself. A similar view is taken by Professor Stevens[31] on the basis that what P does to put only herself at risk is not D's 'business'[32] – P does not owe D any duty not to hurt herself (the point made above); and risk-taking is a personal liberty. If P is the real cause of the injury, then she should recover nothing, but otherwise she should recover in full. No partial solution discounting D's liability is warranted. The same argument would clearly also rule out any reduction in a plaintiff's damages on account of her unreasonable failure to mitigate her loss.

No definitive response to this argument can be provided here. It is premised on the view that: (a) all-or-nothing causal judgements are all that is possible ('part causation' is 'conceptually meaningless'), and (b) that splitting the risk of any uncertainty in respect of who (P or D) caused an indivisible injury suffered by P is morally unacceptable. The former proposition is undoubtedly correct, but it does not, I suggest, rule out the possibility of splitting the risks of causal uncertainties between plaintiffs and defendants in contributory negligence cases. 'Part causation' is indeed a meaningless idea, but 'causation of a part' is not. The problem is once again that, in cases involving 'indivisible' injury (imagine a broken skull and associated brain damage resulting from an un-seat-belted passenger's head impacting the windscreen of a vehicle in an accident culpably caused by D), we necessarily cannot separate out different 'parts' of the damage caused by P and D. We only know that 'but for' the failure of each of them, the impact with the screen and the *total indivisible* harm would not have happened. Imposing total liability on D for all the consequences of the accident in such an instance therefore carries a risk of attributing responsibility to him for one (unprovable) part of P's total injury that D *may not* have caused and which cannot in practice be determined. There is a risk, in other words, of imposing upon D a duty to pay for a part – that he *may* not actually have caused – of formally 'indivisible' damage (which he probably *has*, according to the customary 'but for' test). Does this risk of an unwarranted amount of liability not make P's careless conduct his 'business' after all? Could it not justify a defence discounting the liability so as to account for the risk?

There is still, of course, the powerful point made by Klar and Stevens alike that P is innocent of any wrong in the seatbelt case, whereas D is not, so that it is improper to assign the risk of the uncertainty to P, not D. There is, they say, no moral equivalence between the two. But this does not rule out the use of other criteria for distributing the risk between P and D which are not based – or not solely based – on whether P and D have violated each other's prior rights. Indeed,

[30] See ch 6.
[31] Stevens (n 9).
[32] ibid, 254.

the fact that legislatures have almost universally seen fit to permit apportionment in these instances suggests that they take the view that the parties' relative *capacity* to avoid harm is a salient distributive criterion.

The debate about the ethics of using distributive criteria to apportion responsibility between tortfeasors and their victims finds a parallel in modern debates about the form of the new defence of change of position to restitutionary claims. Here, distributive criteria clearly do operate, but there have been attempts to limit them. For example, courts have to date resisted the idea that a defendant should have a defence to a claim for the return of a mistaken payment just because this would cause her hardship. She must have suffered, or stand to suffer, a provable detriment that she would not otherwise have suffered, had she not entertained a genuine belief in her entitlement to the sum in question. The defence hence generally requires prejudice provably connected to circumstances and beliefs surrounding the payment's receipt which make it unjust to require restitution.[33] It is not simply a product of the defendant's relative wealth, poverty, or new circumstances that have given her a particularly pressing need for the money paid. At the same time, bad faith disqualifies her from the defence and, depending on the jurisdiction, her fault may also do so.[34] In some American jurisdictions, she loses the defence and must pay in full if she is more at fault in respect of the original payment than the plaintiff,[35] mirroring the way in which the comparative negligence defence now operates in most States in loss-based claims. In New Zealand, courts take the most flexible approach of all by 'weighing the equities' between the parties and apportioning D's loss proportionately between them, as we shall see in Section V below. All of these approaches carry some risk of uncertainty, but the last has been thought by the Privy Council to do so to an intolerable degree.[36]

Before moving on from ethics, we should further consider the concern about uncertainty, because it is often asserted that a key aspect of any ethical solution to 'sharing' problems is that rules should not only be 'fair', but clear and predictable. It is not impossible for solutions to be both, but the more numerous and open-textured the criteria that bear upon apportionment decisions, and the more flexible their structuring in judicial reasoning, the more clarity and predictability suffer. The perennial question is – how fundamental is the uncertainty problem and where does the proper balance between certainty and justice lie?[37]

[33] The exact formulations differ slightly between jurisdictions. Compare *Lipkin Gorman (a firm v Karpnale Ltd)* [1991] 2 AC 548 (HL), 577–80; *David Securities Pty Ltd v Commonwealth Bank of Australia* (1992) 175 CLR 353 (HCA), 385; *Australian Financial Services & Leasing Pty Ltd v Hills Industries Ltd* [2014] HCA 14 [23], [67], [81], [157]; *Restatement of Restitution and Unjust Enrichment (Third)* (American Law Institute, St Paul, 2011) §65; Judicature Act 1908 (NZ) s 94B; *National Bank of New Zealand Ltd v Waitaki International Processing (NI) Ltd* [1999] 2 NZLR 211, 227–30.

[34] See further Section V(B) below.

[35] *Restatement of Restitution* (n 33) §65, comment a.

[36] *Dextra Bank & Trust Co Ltd v Bank of Jamaica* [2002] 1 All ER (Comm) 193 (PC).

[37] J Goudkamp, 'Apportionment of Damages for Contributory Negligence: A Fixed or Discretionary Approach?' (2015) 35 *Legal Studies* 621.

Those who focus on fairness will insist that the introduction of partial contributory negligence and change of position defences has made it possible for judges to give more sensitive expression to the reasons that underpinned older all-or-nothing (usually 'no recovery') rules. This may produce less predictable solutions, they will say, but it is also less arbitrary and more rational. For example, if the reason for initially inhibiting restitutionary causes of action was the fear that innocent defendants might be unduly prejudiced by having to pay money back, then a solution that allows recovery, but which eliminates any resulting prejudice through a change of position defence has greater moral legitimacy than one that denies the plaintiff's claim entirely for fear of the unproven consequence.[38] The duty of rationality that judges have is to give the most accurate and sensitive effect possible to the reasons that they have, and these reasons are more accurately expressed in these instances by partial, than by all-or-nothing rules.

Those who, by contrast, favour certainty still have a legitimate argument. Certainty is important both to markets and to the autonomy of individual citizens. Nonetheless, it is, I suggest, a second order value in civil adjudication that only really kicks in once judges' duties to formulate rules rationally has been met. Judges' (and legislatures') *first* duty is to give rules the form that most closely respects the reasons for having those rules – to reason rationally in accordance with the reasons that they have. Their *second* duty is then to make the operation of those rules as clear and predictable as possible. If one applies this approach to private law disputes, then the unpredictabilities that attend modern apportionment rules are certainly undesirable and should be minimised as far as possible, but they are not a reason for not engaging in partial apportionment exercises at all, if these constitute a rational moral practice.

C. Politics

Despite the dominant language of ethics, politics have been the driving force in most recent changes to apportionment rules.[39] Weir himself credibly suggested that the English contribution legislation was a product of determined lobbying by liability insurers[40] and the same is true both of the legislation introducing the defendant-friendly version of the defence of contributory negligence that now applies in most US jurisdictions[41] and of recent proportionate liability reforms. This explains the inconsistency between proportionate liability provisions in different jurisdictions in the United States and Australia; and it explains why

[38] See, eg, *Lipkin* (n 33) 581 (Lord Goff).

[39] Wright, ch 2; Barker and Steele (n 4).

[40] Weir (n 1) 519.

[41] G Schwartz, 'Contributory Negligence under United States Law' in Magnus and Martín-Casals (n 10) 223 (noting that the modified version has almost universally been introduced by legislation, not judicial decision); *Restatement of Torts* (n 14) §7, Reporter's Note to comment a. See Section V(A) below.

proportionate liability is exclusively the product of legislative, not judicial activity. None of the relevant legislation resulted from the recommendations of an independent law reform commission.

What are the pressures on defendants that have produced these lobbying efforts? Recent economic downturn and the over-exposure of liability insurers to investment risk are two immediate factors. However, background pressure has also been created by a general increase in the 'shared' liability of 'peripheral' defendants (and their insurers) resulting from the expansion of substantive liability doctrines such as vicarious liability, accessorial liability and tort liability for omissions during the latter part of the twentieth century. Such 'peripheral' defendants (public authorities and professional advisers are perhaps the most significant group) are now responsible, where once they were not, for indivisible damage more 'immediately' brought about by other wrongdoers, including fraudsters, unreliable contractors and reckless (or even criminal) employees, many of whom are insolvent or hard for plaintiffs to bring to judgment. A significant proportion of the new, shared liabilities are for pure economic loss and 'peripheral' defendants often end up paying most of the bill. The modern agenda of proportionate liability reform is hence at least in part a reflection of the raw desire of such defendants (and their insurers) to deflect the impact of these additional, shared responsibilities for the conduct of others, and to throw their risk back upon plaintiffs as a group. The term 'peripheral' defendants, it should be noted, is one chosen by defendants themselves to minimise the sense of their responsibility, despite the law having concluded them to be legally responsible for the damage caused.

The strategy has clearly worked effectively in some countries, but it is very unsophisticated, because it is unlikely that the solidary liability rule itself played a significant role in bringing about the economic pressures alleged by defendants.[42] The pressures are also not uniform amongst defendant groups, so that, even if one accepted that they were real and required intervention, there would be no case for implementing proportionate liability as a generalised scheme. It would be far more rational to cap the liabilities of particular defendant groups, where they can prove that their liabilities are so seriously prejudicial to society as a whole that plaintiffs should go partially uncompensated.

There is now a sense in Australia that proportionate liability reformers may have pushed things too far, too fast and in such a random way as to cause trouble for themselves as well as plaintiffs by creating unmanageable complication and uncertainty in the system. The point about pragmatics is that they change all the time. Such pressures as were being experienced by insurers have eased. As Barbara McDonald explains in chapter eleven, the modern debate in Australia has hence ironically become one about how to achieve uniformity and predictability in a scheme that, from a moral point of view, made little sense in the first place and which was precipitated by a short-term crisis that has since receded.

[42] P Cane, 'Reforming Tort Law in Australia: A Personal Perspective' (2003) *MULR* 649, 660–63.

The problem with attempting any radical repeal or change to the new schemes so as to restore greater equity and compensation to plaintiffs, is that the schemes work to the benefit of the very 'peripheral defendant' governments who would be asked to scrap them. The pragmatics of self-interest therefore weigh upon future progress like a dead hand.

IV. Originating Doctrines

Part 2 of the book analyses two, originating doctrines that give rise to the shared liability of multiple defendants for the same harm – vicarious and accessorial liability. Both doctrines have grown considerably during the twentieth and twenty first centuries and therefore form part[43] of the story of increased shared liability for 'peripheral' defendants outlined above. The former doctrine theoretically creates liability for D1 *on behalf* of D2 (D1 being liable for D2's wrong on account of the *status* of the relationship between them), whereas the latter imposes liability on D1's for his or her *involvement in* the wrong of D2. The precise rationales of the doctrines are, however, still not fully understood.[44]

Warren Swain's historical analysis of vicarious liability in chapter four makes this particularly clear, tracking as it does the evolution of the doctrine from Roman times to the modern day. He shows how the rationale of the principle has never been settled, having variously been stated in terms of practical convenience, social policy, command, authority, agency, or (most recently) 'enterprise risk'. Within these ideas, there are some that are clearly capable of grounding strict moral responsibility for the deeds of others, including consent, control, risk-creation and the obtaining of benefits from others' acts, but there are also references to broader, instrumental policies of deterrence, compensation and efficient loss-spreading. Modern 'tests' of vicarious liability reflect not just the fluid reality of modern employment relationships, but also the mixed reasons that have historically underpinned courts' decisions. Recent cases imposing liability on schools and churches for criminal acts of physical or sexual abuse have exposed the tensions between these theories.[45] Exceptional instances aside (in which the institution authorises, or acquiesces in the abuse), the only reasons really sustaining liability in such instances relate to the special risks created by certain types of job (where there is an especially 'close connection' between

[43] Probably a minor part. The more significant pressures appear to have flowed from the increase in tort liabilities for omission and pure economic loss.

[44] As regards vicarious liability, see the frank admission of the High Court of Australia in *Sweeney v Boylan Nominees Trading as Quirks Refrigeration* [2006] HCA 19, [11] (Gleeson CJ, Gummow, Hayne, Heydon and Crennan JJ).

[45] *Bazley v Curry* (1999) 174 DLR (4th) 45; *Lister v Hesley Hall Ltd* [2002] 1 AC 215 (HL); *Various Claimants v Catholic Child Welfare Society* [2012] UKSC 56; *New South Wales v Lepore* (2003) 195 ALR 412 (HCA); *Prince Alfred College v ADC* [2016] HCA 37.

it and the abuse[46]), the need to compensate victims who lack effective remedies against impecunious criminal offenders, or the desire to incentivise institutions to safeguard vulnerable persons. Only the first of these (the creation of risks of abuse) has any chance of attracting criteria of attribution that have anything like clear edges and the resulting liability then actually seems to flow from the institution's own conduct, not to be 'vicarious' at all.[47]

Until recently, accessorial liability has also lacked a coherent jurisprudence.[48] Several different doctrines operate under its broad umbrella (including joint tortfeasorship, liability for inducing a breach of contract, and accessorial liability in equity), but it has nonetheless forcefully been argued that differences in rules' origins should not preclude their rationalisation within the same organisational framework.[49] In chapter five, Joachim Dietrich, one of the architects of this idea, unravels some of the doctrine's key mysteries, including the tricky question whether accessories' liabilities are for the *same*, or different wrong(s); solidary or proportionate; and necessarily always the same for accessory and principal alike. These matters are especially complicated in equity by virtue of the fact that equitable accessorial liability can be gain- as well as loss-based. As regards the underlying principles grounding the doctrine, these appear to lie in the existence of a common design between defendants (ie, in their combined intentions), or in purposive actions of the accessory which induce, assist or otherwise have a (loosely-defined) relevant causal impact on the commission of the principal wrong.

The uncertainties underpinning the normative foundations of both vicarious and accessorial liability are not just problematic for the doctrines themselves, but also for decisions about how the shared liabilities they create are to be apportioned. The reason why D1 shares D2's liability for harm suffered by P must bear upon the way the liability is then allocated between D1 and D2. If, for example, D1 is liable to P for harm caused by D2 because D1 has *agreed* to protect P against the risk of D2's actions, there is a good reason to make his liability total (solidary). He has consented to making D2's responsibility his own. If, by contrast, D1 and D2 are independent tortfeasors whose separate wrongs happen to coincide to bring about one and the same damage to P, then the case for D1 being only partly liable to P (a solution I personally reject for reasons already given and which Dietrich also rejects) is more arguable. If D1 and D2 are parties

[46] *Bazley* (n 45); *Lister* (n 45). The test in Australia is now formulated slightly differently, in terms of whether the job provided the 'occasion' for the abuse: *Prince Alfred* (n 45) [80].

[47] C Beuermann, 'Vicarious Liability and Conferred Authority Strict Liability' (2013) 20 *Torts Law Journal* 265.

[48] See now J Dietrich and P Ridge, *Accessories in Private Law* (Cambridge, Cambridge University Press, 2016); P Davies, *Accessory Liability* (Oxford, Hart Publishing, 2015).

[49] Dietrich and Ridge (n 48), J Dietrich, 'Dealing with Complexity: Different Approaches to Explaining Accessory Liability' in K Barker, K Fairweather, R Grantham (eds), *Private Law in the 21st Century* (Oxford, Hart Publishing, 2017) ch 10.

to a 'common design' that harms P, the case is more like the case in which D1 has consented to making D2's responsibility his own, although it is not on an exact par. If D1 *intended* to harm P through his assistance, when D2, the principal wrongdoer, intended P no harm, or if D1 is in breach of a *fiduciary duty* to P, there might be deterrent reasons to make D1 solidarily liable to P, even if D2 is not. Indeed, there might even be a reason to bar D1 claiming a contribution from D2.

There are some signs that the norms underpinning shared liabilities do indeed affect the way in which apportionment schemes later divide those liabilities between defendants. For example, under most American and Australian statutory systems, proportionate liability for indivisible harm is excluded and liability remains solidary whenever D1 acted intentionally or fraudulently with regard to P, where his liability was vicarious, or where it arose from his partnership with D2. In both countries, D1's liability is also solidary where he was acting 'in concert' with D2. In some Australian jurisdictions, the same is true where D1 and D2 were joint tortfeasors liable in respect of the same wrong.[50] In the United States, there is an additional exception preserving solidary liability for the case where D1 had a duty to P to protect P against the risk of D2's wrongdoing, as for example, where D1 is a professional adviser engaged to protect P against fraudulent debtors.[51] That is *not* currently provided for in Australia, but almost certainly should be, given the argument set out above.

The main point, then, is that there is a clear normative connection between the reasons for the existence of shared liabilities in private law and the way they should be shared, but that it is difficult to reach clear or consistent conclusions on how apportionment should work whilst there is uncertainty concerning the rationale of 'originating doctrines' themselves. Although there appears to be a broad consensus that vicarious liabilities should always be total (solidary) whatever the reasons why they exist, conclusions regarding accessorial liabilities may yet to be fully worked through.

V. Plaintiff-Defendant Apportionment

Part 3 of the Book focuses on three, important mechanisms for apportioning losses and gains between plaintiffs and defendants – the doctrine of contributory (comparative) negligence, the restitutionary defence of change of position and the rules governing the quantification of equitable accounts in cases involving breach of fiduciary duty.

[50] This is the case in Queensland and South Australia.

[51] *Restatement of Torts* (n 14) §14. Contrast the result in *Hunt & Hunt Lawyers v Mitchell Morgan Nominees Pty Ltd* [2013] HCA 10, critically discussed by McDonald in ch 11.

A. Loss-Based Claims and the Defence of Contributory Negligence

The partial defence of contributory negligence is now widely accepted, despite the reservations expressed above about its ethics. In the UK, Australia, New Zealand, Canada and virtually all European countries,[52] partial reductions in awards are available even where P was more responsible for his injury than D, whereas in most US jurisdictions this is only the case where P was no more responsible than D.[53] If P is adjudged more responsible than D, the defence bars P's claim completely. This reversion to an absolute bar is now also permitted (but not mandated) in Australia, which causes logical problems considered further below. The precise scope of the doctrine and the criteria according to which it apportions responsibility are also unclear; and we have, until recently, had no clear view of the actual impact of the defence on plaintiffs' awards.

The concern about apportionment criteria is highlighted by Klar in chapter six. Although two are regularly cited – the relative 'causative potency' of P and D's conduct and their relative fault[54] – doubts have been expressed about each. The latter was regarded by Lord Denning as requiring an impractical inquiry into matters that were likely to be hotly contested and hard to resolve.[55] Others go further, claiming that the relative fault criterion is literally impossible to apply because it requires one to compare incommensurables – the breach of D's duty to P and P's want of regard for his own welfare.[56] Comparative fault is nonetheless regularly used to determine allocations in all jurisdictions. In Canada, it is the only criterion formally used. This either means that courts are simply ignoring the incommensurability objection, or (perhaps more likely) that they are crudely comparing *other* aspects of P and D's behaviour that *are* commensurable, such as their relative knowledge and capacity to avoid the harm in question.

The other factor – 'causal potency' – is rejected by Klar on the basis that 'part causation' is a meaningless idea.[57] This is clearly true. For reasons explained above, wherever indivisible damage is brought about by both P and D, what is at stake is the allocation of the *risk of the uncertainty* about causation, not any genuine attempt to assess the relative causal contribution of P and D's conduct. All that the 'causal potency' criterion does in those jurisdictions in which it operates is hence to assign the risk of the uncertainty in accordance with the extent to which P or

[52] Magnus & Martín-Casals (n 10) 259–60.
[53] *Restatement of Torts* (n 14) §7, Reporter's Note to comment a.
[54] *Podrebersek v Australian Iron and Steel Pty Ltd* (1985) 59 ALR 529, 532–33; J Goudkamp, 'Apportionment of Damages for Contributory Negligence: Appellate Review, Relative Blameworthiness and Causal Potency' (2015) 19 *Edinburgh Law Review* 367.
[55] *Froom v Butcher* [1976] 1 QB 286, 296.
[56] Stevens (n 9) 259.
[57] See further J Goudkamp and L Klar, 'Apportionment of Damages for Contributory Negligence: The Causal Potency Criterion' (2016) 53 *Alberta Law Review* 1.

D's conduct *increased the probability* of P's injury. Given that this is presumably already taken into account in adjudging the extent to which P and D are each regarded as being at fault in respect of that injury, the criterion does indeed seem normatively redundant, although it perhaps helps to single out one component of that inquiry for separate consideration.

The other factors that Klar identifies as being relevant to relative fault in Canada are the nature of D's duty, the number of faulty acts of D and P respectively, their nature, and their temporal sequencing. The *Third Restatement of Torts* adds references to the parties' intentions and their awareness of the risks created by their conduct.[58] Occasional allusions are made in European jurisdictions to the parties' relative financial resources and ability to obtain insurance cover,[59] but this is rare and common law jurisdictions tend to ignore such factors. References to the nature and purpose of D's duty are sensible as they connect the apportionment decision back to the original basis of D's liability – if D's primary duty was to protect P against the risk of his (P's) own conduct, then D must take responsibility for the consequences of P's acts. The sequencing idea is much more controversial, appearing, as it does, to hark back to the old 'last opportunity' or 'last clear chance' rule' that has been abolished in most (but oddly not all) Canadian jurisdictions. If the sequencing of acts is at all relevant, it seems to be more logically relevant to causation (Klar's suggestion), remoteness of damage, or 'causal potency' (understood now to mean the probability that the act might cause the relevant injury, as part of the relative fault inquiry). The first two of these concepts are relevant to D's basic liability, not to the defence, and the last is a criterion that Canadian law has supposedly abandoned. It is therefore hard to dissent from Klar's conclusion that references to last chance doctrine and the sequencing of P and Ds' acts should be dropped in the context of the modern comparative defence.

Whilst the partialism of the contributory negligence defence was always designed to be fairer to plaintiffs, it has not gone unscathed by recent Australian reforms, which now expressly provide for the possibility of 100 per cent reductions.[60] This is part of the larger raft of measures aimed at paring back defendants' liabilities. As courts have been swift to point out,[61] 100 per cent deductions are logically inconsistent with the idea that the modern defence operates on a 'comparative responsibility' basis. For this reason, it has been hinted that the new measures must be understood as having impliedly 'modified' the original legislative schemes so as to permit courts to use a different, *non-comparative* method.[62]

[58] *Restatement of Torts* (n 14) §8.

[59] Magnus and Martin-Casals (n 10) 273.

[60] Civil Liability Act 2003 (Qld), s 24; Civil Liability Act 2002 (NSW), s 5S; Wrongs Act 1958 (Vic), s 63; Civil Law (Wrongs) Act 2002 (ACT), s 47; Wrongs Act 1954 (Tas), s 4(1).

[61] *Wynbergen v Hoyts Corporation Pty Ltd* (1997) 149 ALR 25, 29; *Reeves v Commissioner of Police of the Metropolis* [2000] 1 AC 360 (HL), 372; *Anderson v Newham College of Further Education* [2002] EWCA Civ 505; *Buyukardicli v Hammerson UK Properties plc* [2002] EWCA Civ 683; *Pitts v Hunt* [1991] 1 QB 24 (CA).

[62] *French v QBE Insurance (Australia) Limited* [2011] QSC 105, [197] (Fryberg J).

This yields a system akin to the one that exists in most US jurisdictions, save in so far as there is no set point at which the decision to switch from the partial to the complete defence must be made. Courts are therefore at liberty in Australia to apply the defence 'absolutely' wherever they consider this to be 'just and equitable.'

If these reforms were intended as a less-than-subtle legislative hint to judges that they should now revert to a 'total' version of the defence on a regular basis, that signal has for the most part been wisely ignored. There have been only 12 reported cases since the reforms were enacted in which a 100 per cent deduction has been considered appropriate by a court[63] and in each and every instance, the failure of the plaintiff's claim was justified primarily on the basis that P had not proven any breach of duty, or causation. In practice, the provisions' most significant impact is therefore likely to lie in appeal-proofing first instance judgments made on other grounds and in driving down the level of out-of-court settlements.

Australian legislatures have also introduced provisions that reverse the onus of proof in respect of contributory negligence in cases involving plaintiff intoxication (or reliance by a plaintiff upon an intoxicated party). Provisions of the latter kind mandate minimum deductions of 25 per cent or 50 per cent from a plaintiff's award.[64] The effect can be arbitrary and penalise plaintiffs far more harshly than any criminal fine. It can also leave seriously injured victims without the long-term support they need. The financial impact of P getting into a car with a seriously drunk driver on her damages for paraplegia (a minimum 50 per cent cut in the award) could be staggering. If the objective of governments was really to deter recklessness around alcohol and enforce road safety laws (rather than just to reduce defendants' awards), then they have probably not only picked an inefficient tool, but have shot themselves in the foot economically, since many of the long-term disabled caught by the provisions will now have to look to the state for support, not to wrongdoing defendants and their insurers.

A problem with speculations of this type and indeed with any attempt to work out the impact of the modern defence upon plaintiffs overall is the lack of empirical evidence. We need information on three, key matters: first, what deductions do courts make in practice in which types of case; secondly, how have out-of-court settlements been affected; and thirdly, how has the availability of the partial defence

[63] *Adams v State of New South Wales* [2008] NSWSC 1257, [133]; *Zilio v Lane* [2009] NSWDC 26 [227]; *Russell v Lozanes* [2011] NSWDC 149, [111]; *Thompson v New South Wales Land & Housing Corporation* [2011] NSWSC 94, [71]]; *Richardson v Mt Druitt Workers Club* [2011] NSWSC 31, [26]; *Davis v Swift* [2013] NSWDC 99, [57]; *Vourvahakis v Marrickville Metro Shopping Centre Pty Ltd* [2013] NSWDC 73, [70]; *Jacobe v QSR Pty Ltd (t/as Kentucky Fried Chicken Lakemba)* [2014] NSWDC 150, [120]; *Lim v Cho* (NSWDC, unrep, 5 July 2017) (aff'd [2018] NSWCA 145); *Knibbs v Sheteh* [2017] NSWDC 119, [278]; *Burke v State of Queensland* [2013] QDC 186, [25] (aff'd [2014] QCA 200); *Contor v Bickey* [2016] QSC 91, [35]. A 100% award was set aside in *MacKenzie v Nominal Defendant* [2005] NSWCA 180.

[64] See, eg, Civil Liability Act 2003 (Qld) ss 48, 49.

affected courts' use of other, absolute ones? Goudkamp and Nolan's pioneering recent work has greatly advanced our understanding of the first question[65] and is continued in this volume with a penetrating critical analysis of the incidence and size of deductions in cases involving professional defendants. Their findings suggest that although the defence's success rate is much lower than in other categories of case, the average discount rate is higher. The success rate of the defence is also much lower in respect of lawyers than other professionals.

The second and third questions are harder to answer. In respect of the third, introducing partial defences has in the past often resulted in courts being less ready to allow total ones such as *volenti non fit injuria*, illegality and (in the restitutionary context) estoppel. But Australian governments have in turn introduced measures which seek to make it easier for defendants to establish *volenti*;[66] and which bar plaintiffs from claiming any compensation at all in cases in which they have tortiously been caused any injury which is an obvious risk of a dangerous recreational activity, even if this is a risk of which they were unaware.[67] To the extent, therefore, that the recognition of comparative negligence represents a cultural shift away from all-or-nothing solutions in the name of ensuring fairness to plaintiffs, Australian governments have sought partially to reverse it. This is not to say that one who places herself at risk by engaging in a dangerous activity should recover in full, but if she did not assent to the risk of a defendant's negligence in that context and was unaware of it, it is hard to see why she should recover *nothing*, when the accident would not have occurred had the defendant properly met his duty of care. The normal logic of partialism, as it applies in contributory negligence cases, seems a fairer and more rational response. It may come as no surprise to learn that the bar on damages in respect of 'obvious' risks of dangerous 'recreational' activities was the product of the lobbying efforts of recreational services providers (including councils). It may also come as no great surprise to learn that courts have allowed the defence on only nine occasions since the legislation was introduced and that on each occasion the plaintiff had failed to prove the breach of any duty of care.[68] There is little appetite for the new absolutism amongst judges.

[65] J Goudkamp and D Nolan, 'Contributory Negligence in the Twenty-First Century: An Empirical Study of First Instance Decisions' (2016) 79 *MLR* 575; J Goudkamp and D Nolan, 'Contributory Negligence in the Court of Appeal: An Empirical Study' (2017) 37 *LS* 437.

[66] See eg Civil Liability Act 2003 (Qld), ss 13, 14. There is little evidence that this change has made any difference.

[67] Civil Liability Act 2003 (Qld), s 19; Civil Liability Act 2002 (NSW), s 5L; Civil Liability Act 2002 (Tas), s 20; Civil Liability Act 2002 (WA), s 5H.

[68] *Jaber v Rockdale City Council* [2008] NSWCA 98; *Vreman and Morris v Albury City Council* [2011] NSWSC 39; *Echin v Southern Tablelands Gliding Club* [2013] NSWSC 516; *Streller v Albury City Council* [2013] NSWCA 348; *Price v Southern Cross Television (TNT9) Pty Ltd* [2014] TASSC 70; *Campbell v Hay* [2014] NSWCA 129; *Sharp v Parramatta City Council* [2015] NSWCA 260; *Goode v Angland* [2017] NSWCA 311; *Samahar Miski v Penrith Whitewater Stadium Ltd* [2018] NSWDC 21.

B. Gain-Based Claims and the Defence of Change of Position

Turning to gain-based claims, the defence of change of position is a classic example of partialism providing a more rational response to questions of allocation between plaintiffs and defendants than former, absolute, 'no liability' rules. Its development is analogous in this regard to the defence of contributory negligence in tort. Like the latter defence, its partialism poses a potential challenge not just to strict 'no-recovery' rules, but also to absolute defences capable of applying on the same facts, such as bona fide purchase and estoppel. Although it was at first suggested that it might entirely supersede the former of these,[69] that prediction has proven incorrect, because, whilst there is some historical overlap in the rationales of the respective defences in equity, the bona fide purchase has always had an additional, instrumental function in securing title to property in order to release it to the market for unencumbered economic exchange. That, distinct function requires an absolute all-or-nothing rule to protect property purchasers outright and to clear the title of the relevant property of all claims.[70] The result is that the two defences now operate side-by-side. The difference in their rationale means that they can co-exist without significant normative tension.

Matters are less clear regarding estoppel and it is still possible that a fully-developed change of position defence will result in it withering away entirely. It does not feature anywhere in the recent *Third Restatement of Restitution and Unjust Enrichment*. There have been very few, if any, cases since the advent of change of position in which estoppel has operated to bar a restitutionary claim *in toto* and it seems to be accepted that its operation as a total bar will be exceptional now that a partial solution exists.[71] The fact that estoppel's own rules of operation can be modified so as to allow it to operate partially in cases in which it would be unconscionable for it to operate totally;[72] and the fact that the change of position defence can itself bar a claim completely if this is necessary to avoid unfairly prejudicing D,[73] have significantly reduced the points of tension between the two defences. In practice, although one protects expectations and the other out-of-pocket loss, both can now operate partially in the right conditions and where they operate totally, this appears to be a product of courts recognising the proper balance of justice between the parties, not an adhesion to all-or-nothing thinking for its own sake.

[69] P Key, 'Bona Fide Purchase as a Defence in the Law of Restitution' (1994) *LMCLQ* 421; The Hon Sir Peter Millett, 'Tracing the Proceeds of Fraud' (1991) 107 *LQR* 71, 82.

[70] K Barker, 'After Change of Position: Good Faith Exchange in the Modern Law of Restitution' in P Birks (ed) *Laundering and Tracing* (Oxford, Clarendon, 1995) ch 7.

[71] *Scottish Equitable plc v Derby* [2001] 3 All ER 818, 828–30.

[72] *Derby* (n 71); *National Westminster Bank v Somer International Ltd* (2002) QB 1286.

[73] *Hills* (n 33).

The defence of change of position only goes so far in apportioning the gains and losses of the parties to a defective or wrongful transaction. Some statutory regimes that effect restitution (such as those that provide for the consequences of contractual frustration) go much further and allow the pooling and subsequent division of the combined losses and gains of *both* P and D.[74] By contrast, change of position only allows for D's detriment to be brought into account in reduction of P's claim for a benefit bestowed by P. This is less sophisticated, but also less complicated and, therefore, less likely to dissolve into an unfathomable discretionary process. To the extent that wider sharing of the losses of both P and D appears to be sanctioned in some frustration regimes, it is probably the result of neither party being responsible for the transactional failure and neither having agreed to accept the risk of the failure, which might provide a case for similar outcomes where neither P nor D are responsible for a mistaken payment.

The defence can also assume at least three different forms, which are progressively more complicated. Under the first, which is current in England, D is completely disqualified from the defence and is left to carry his own losses where he was in bad faith, or a 'wrongdoer'.[75] Under the second, which is the dominant model in the United States ('relative fault'), D is disqualified if he is more at fault than P. Otherwise, his liability is reduced to the full extent of the detriment suffered.[76] Under the third model ('comparative fault'), which prevails in New Zealand, the defence operates in all cases to apportion D's losses to P and D in accordance with their respective fault, whichever of P or D happens to be more to blame.[77] A fourth possible model, sitting between the third and the fourth, would be to disqualify D completely if he is more at fault than P, but in other cases to allow him to set off a proportion of his losses, calculated by reference to his fault relative to P. Each of these positions strikes a different compromise. As in the case of contributory negligence, there are uncertainties about the exact criteria of distribution, which tend to focus on the respective roles of P and D in relation to D's enrichment and their actual or (in some jurisdictions) constructive knowledge of the defect.

If the new defence is to operate coherently, its underlying logic clearly needs to be understood. In chapter eight, Ross Grantham sets out to advance this project, dismissing the view, which was at one time popular, that the defence responds to the diminution of D's enrichment, rather than to detriment he or she has suffered. He seeks to justify the existence and operational features of the defence by reference to the underlying logic of unjust enrichment claims themselves, arguing

[74] See E McKendrick, 'Frustration, Restitution and Loss-Apportionment' in A Burrows (ed), *Essays on the Law of Restitution* (Oxford, Clarendon, 1991) ch 6.

[75] *Dextra* (n 36); *Niru Battery Manufacturing Co v Milestone Trading Ltd* [2003] EWCA Civ 1446, [164]–[165]. Whether fault disqualifies in Australia was not decided in *Hills* (n 33).

[76] *Restatement of Restitution* (n 33) §52(3), §65, comment (a), (g) and illustrations 24–26. Note that some of P's losses associated with the transaction can also be brought into account in the US system: §52(2).

[77] *Waitaki* (n 33).

that such claims are only normatively justified to the extent that they leave D no worse off. Since the normative force of restitutionary claims lies in some defect in P's decision-making or purposiveness, D should, he suggests, have the defence wherever he has innocently integrated the benefit received into his own purposes, such that restitution would detrimentally affect his life choices. There are in this account detectable echoes of Kantian thinking that contrast with the more pragmatic distributive schemes implicit in some of the more complex models identified above.

C. Allocating the Risk of Causal Uncertainty Through Other Rules

Contributory negligence rules are not the only ones to distribute the risk of causal uncertainties between plaintiffs and defendants. In all jurisdictions, there are rules permitting similar risk-allocations in cases in which causal processes are impossible to penetrate, or where facts are causally over- or under-determined. Some of these strategies are 'all-or-nothing' in the sense that they place the risk of the uncertainty fully on either P or D. Examples in this category are rules allowing for reversals in the legal or evidential onus of proof[78] or the drawing by courts of 'robust inferences' of causation in cases where the normal standards of proof simply cannot be met. *Fairchild*[79] is one such example.

Other strategies, however, split the risk of insuperable causal uncertainties between P and D – a tactic generally applauded by Helmut Koziol[80] and by Jenny Steele and Rob Merkin[81] in this book. This can be done by deploying a probabilistic approach to causation rules themselves (the result arguably achieved in England in *Barker v Corus UK Ltd*[82] and used in some civilian jurisdictions[83]), or by reformulating P's damage in terms of a 'loss of chance'. The cases in which this is permitted to occur vary from jurisdiction to jurisdiction. A particularly striking anomaly is that loss of chance analyses and 'part damages' are allowed in Australia and the UK in cases in which P's damage is purely economic, but not where he or she has suffered physical injury; whereas in the US, the

[78] For example, the doctrine of *res ipsa loquitur*.

[79] *Fairchild v Glenhaven Funeral Services Ltd* [2003] 1 AC 32 (HL). Note that the court did not determine the issue whether Ds liabilities were total (solidary), but this has now been affirmed in respect of mesothelioma victims, in reaction to *Barker v Corus UK Ltd* (n 82 below) by the Compensation Act 2002 (UK), s 3. For a different scenario, but similar 'robust' approach to causal rules in Australia, see *Chappel v Hart* (1998) 195 CLR 232 (HCA).

[80] Ch 3.

[81] Ch 12.

[82] [2006] 2 AC 572 (HL). The case is limited to cases involving scientific uncertainty and singular types of risk.

[83] See generally, Gilead, Green and Koch (n 14), 1–67.

position is precisely the reverse.[84] In ethical or public policy terms, one might think that the Americans have it right, given that the body should be more highly valued than the dollar, but the explanations are more complicated than that. The perceived role of tort rules in deterring malpractice is a factor underpinning the American position, whereas in England and Australia, courts are evidently concerned about the financial consequences of loss of chance claims for public health services.

Another set of rules that allocates the risk of uncertainties are the rules governing the quantification of monetary awards – both gain-based and loss-based ones. In chapter nine, Simone Degeling takes these rules to task in the context of awards for breach of fiduciary duty, where speculation is required in calculating the value of an opportunity allegedly lost or gained by P or D (respectively) as a result of a fiduciary's wrong. In respect of both the calculation of loss and gain, she argues that, although probabilistic reasoning is normally permissible to discount awards, the nature of a defendant fiduciary's primary duty to a principal should preclude any discount for the possibility that the plaintiff principal would not have taken up the opportunity that the fiduciary wrongly exploited. Although this approach throws up some tensions with existing rules, it uses the underlying logic of the primary liability rule (here – deterrence) to inform the way in which risks of uncertainty are in split in apportioning monetary relief, which appears to be rationally justified.

VI. Apportionment Between Defendants

This brings us finally to the rules apportioning liabilities between multiple defendants responsible for the same harm. Of all apportionment rules, these are probably the least well understood and most complicated. Their ethics and politics have been discussed above. A full exposition of their detail is not possible here, but the following table provides an overview of some of the current possibilities. It draws on the *Third Restatement of Torts*, but also pinpoints other approaches and reform suggestions in the footnotes. It models a hypothetical in which three defendants (D1, D2, D3) are responsible for P's indivisible harm, with D1 and D2 both being 40 per cent responsible for it and D3 being 20 per cent responsible. D3 is insolvent (or otherwise not susceptible to judgment), so that there is always an 'uncollectible share' of liability. Save where otherwise indicated in the table itself, the assumption is that P is not herself also responsible for the harm. Where she is, the rules in some (American) jurisdictions combine the processes of plaintiff-defendant and defendant-defendant apportionment into a broader, collective 'all parties' allocation system. Such systems probably represent the apogee of system complexity.

[84] Compare *Gregg v Scott* [2005] UKHL 2; *Tabet v Gett* [2010] HCA 12; *Matsuyama v Birnbaum* 452 Mass 1; 890 NE 2d 819 (Mass, 2008).

A. Multiple Defendant Liability Apportionment Models

System	Basic Regime	Variant 1	Variant 2	Variant 3
Solidary Liability ('Joint and Several' Liability) Examples	D1, D2, D3 all individually liable 100% to P. No contribution between Ds.[85] If P sues D1, D1 is liable for 100%. D1 may recover nothing from D2 or D3.	As for basic regime, but contribution available between Ds. No provision for reallocating unrecoverable shares between Ds.[86] If P sues D1, D1 is liable for 100%. D1 may recover only 40% from D2. D3's 20% share is uncollectible and cannot be reallocated, so is born wholly by D1. D1 bears a total of 60% liability.	As for Variant 1, but provision is made for reallocating unrecoverable shares of liability between Ds in proportion to their relative responsibility.[87] If P sues D1, D1 is liable for 100%, but may now recover 50% from D2 (D3's 20% share is split equally between D1 and D2).	As for Variant 2 but, where P is also partly responsible, D3's share can be reallocated to *all* parties (D1, D2 *and P*) in proportion to their relative responsibility.[88] If the responsibility shares are D1: 40%; D2: 40%; D3: 10% and P: 10%, then, if P sues D1, D1 is liable (after deduction for P's 10% share) for 90% in total, but may, on proving D3's insolvency, apply for reallocation of a proportion of that uncollectible share to P.

[85] This model has been superseded in virtually all jurisdictions.

[86] This variant remains dominant in the UK, New Zealand, Canada and almost all European jurisdictions.

[87] This solution is proposed by Cheifetz in ch 10.

[88] This variant was endorsed in the US Uniform Comparative Fault Act (1979) (now replaced by the Uniform Apportionment of Tort Responsibility Act – see n 90 below) and exists in Ireland and some US jurisdictions (*Restatement of Torts* (n 14) §C18, §C21). Certain Ds are precluded from seeking reallocation: intentional tortfeasors, tortfeasors acting in concert; vicariously liable parties and defendants who were primarily responsible for protecting P against other Ds' intentional torts.

System	Basic Regime	Variant 1	Variant 2	Variant 3
Proportionate Liability ('Several' Liability')	D1, D2, D3 liable to P only for only 40%, 40% and 20% respectively. No contribution is possible between Ds.[89]	As for the basic regime, but P can apply for D3's uncollectable share to be reallocated proportionately between remaining defendants D1and D2.	As for Variant 1, but the reallocation of D3's share is made proportionately between D1, D2 *and P* if P is also responsible.[90]	
Hybrid Models	Solidary liability where D's own share of responsibility exceeds a set threshold (eg 20%). Otherwise, proportionate liability only.[91]	Solidary liability where P's harm is of one type; proportionately liability where it is of another.[92]	Solidary Liability where P's loss is below a certain threshold level, proportionate liability where it is above it.[93]	Proportionate liability, with broad discretion to revert to solidary liability where it is 'just and equitable' to do so.[94]

[89] This model applies in some US jurisdictions in cases in which the defendants' liability is several (ie where they have committed independent wrongs), irrespective of the type of harm: *Restatement of Torts* (n 14) §B18 and illustration 3.

[90] This is the basic regime under the US Uniform Apportionment of Tort Responsibility Act, s 5 (as from 2003).

[91] *Restatement of Torts* (n 14) §D18. A model of this sort was suggested as a possibility in cases of economic harm only by the NZ Law Commission, in the form of a limited, minor defendant' exception to solidary liability: NZLC, *Liability of Multiple Defendants* (Rep No 132, 2014), recs 3–5. It has not been implemented.

[92] This approach applies generally in Australia and in some US jurisdictions, with opposite patterns. In Australia, solidary liability hence applies in all cases of personal injury and proportionate liability is confined to cases of property damage and economic loss. By contrast, in the US jurisdictions taking this hybrid approach, solidary liability applies to the economic portion of damages and proportionate liability to the non-economic portion: *Restatement of Torts* (n 14) §E18.

[93] A model limiting proportionate liability to claims of AUD $500,000 or more was originally proposed in Queensland. The final legislation dropped that approach, but incorporated a limited 'consumer plaintiff' exception instead: Civil Liability Act 2003 (Qld), s 28(3)(b). That exception now appears in draft model provisions: Parliamentary Counsel's Committee for the Commonwealth Attorneys-General Standing Council on Law and Justice, *Proportionate Liability Model Provisions* (PCC-386, 26 September 2013), ss 2(3)(b),(c).

[94] This type of approach can be found in the Canada Business Corporations Act RSC 1985 c C-44, s 237.6(1), (2) (which applies in respect of the liability of auditors and others for pure economic loss). A solution of this type is suggested for Australia by McDonald in ch 11 as a possible salve for the ills of the current proportionate liability system.

Each of the solutions identified above allocates the risks of litigation and of defendant insolvency in a slightly different way. In all variants of solidary liability, the 'litigation onus' is on D1, if D1 wishes to avoid total liability for the harm caused, whereas in all systems of proportionate liability, the litigation onus is on P if P is to avoid having to bear the loss of D3's uncollectible share. I confine myself here to a few observations regarding general patterns of distribution and three challenges forming the central focus of the contributions to this book.

B. Patterns of Distribution

A first point to note is the stark contrast in apportionment strategies between Australian and US jurisdictions, on the one hand, and European jurisdictions, Canada and New Zealand, on the other. The former have slipped from the basic solidary liability rule towards proportionate liability, or have endorsed 'hybrid' systems in which proportionate liability plays a significant part, whereas the latter have held more firmly to the original rule. Why proportionate liability lobbyists have been more active and successful in some jurisdictions than others is a fascinating question beyond the scope of this work. The answer most likely lies in contextual factors, such as litigation culture, local economic conditions, insurance markets, and the nature and strength of the connections between business interests and government legislative programmes. It probably also lies in a different social policy outlook. It has hence been observed that 'solidary liability is so deeply embedded in European systems that … its abolition would amount to a legal revolution of a profoundly "anti-claimant" nature.'[95] In New Zealand, the culture of welfare and plaintiff compensation is strong, the impact of global economic crisis has been less pronounced and the virtual absence of accidental personal injury litigation (owing to the national accident compensation scheme) has meant that there are fewer pressures on defendants in that area of risk.

A second observation relates to the startling array of different criteria – across jurisdictions that admit of some choice – that are regarded as being relevant in determining whether solidary or proportionate liability applies to a particular defendant. These include: (a) the type of harm (physical or economic) suffered by P;[96] (b) whether P was a 'consumer,' or suffered damage falling below a particular threshold value;[97] (c) whether or not P was also at fault in respect of the harm;[98] (d) the extent of D's responsibility for the harm, relative to other defendants (whether or not it falls below a magic threshold percentage, or – the terms chosen by the New Zealand Law Commission – whether the defendant is just a

[95] Rogers (n 14) 288.
[96] Hybrid model variant 1 and n 91.
[97] Hybrid model variant 2 and n 93.
[98] Solidary liability model variant 3, Proportionate liability model variant 2 and nn 88, 90.

'minor' defendant);[99] (e) whether the defendant was acting in concert with the other defendants;[100] (f) whether the defendant was vicariously responsible for another defendant;[101] (g) whether a defendant owed P a primary legal duty to protect P against the wrongs of other defendants;[102] and (h) whether or not the defendant's own wrong was intentional.[103] There are many other, more specific variables and limitations.

A particularly intriguing contrast with respect to these criteria between the US and other jurisdictions is that Americans are more ready to make D only proportionately liable for non-economic, than economic harm. Why this is so is unclear, but it may in the end again come down to politics. Damages for non-economic harm are customarily much higher in the US than in other jurisdictions and therefore more likely to have been targeted by defendant lobbying groups. If one were to divide the risks in accordance with moral interests, most people would, I suspect, conclude that if P had to go uncompensated for something, it should be for injury to her pocket, not her person. Another questionable criterion in the above list is whether or not P was herself in some measure responsible for her own harm (as in solidary liability, variant 3, in the table). Since this will already have been taken into account and her damages already reduced accordingly as against all defendants through deductions for her contributory negligence, using her responsibility a second time as a reason to assign to her part of the risk of D3's insolvency is surely double-counting. For this reason, I suggest, there is more merit in the second variant of solidary liability (endorsed by David Cheifetz later in this volume) than in either the third identified variant of solidary liability, or the second variant of proportionate liability, both of which allow for this odd type of double jeopardy effect.

C. Challenges

One problem addressed by both David Cheifetz in chapter ten and Geoff McLay in chapter thirteen relates to the inadequate reach or operation of contribution rules in some jurisdictions in which solidary liability is the basic governing rule. Cheifetz astutely notes that, in cases involving multiple defendants (D1, D2, D3), the current Canadian machinery appears to leave the risk of D3's insolvency to fall on a single contribution claimant (D1), when the fairer solution would be to split the risk proportionately between D1 and D2. That solution, he convincingly suggests, is probably already available if courts interpret the legislation correctly in accordance with equitable contribution principles. In New Zealand, the defects of

[99] Hybrid model, 'Basic Regime' and n 91.
[100] See text to n 50 above.
[101] ibid.
[102] ibid.
[103] ibid.

the relevant legislation are more serious, because it formally still limits contribution claims to cases involving joint tortfeasors, when it clearly needs to be updated to allow claims between all defendants liable in respect of the same harm. That move is mandated by the logic of unjust enrichment underpinning contribution claims. Courts have made good the defects in this instance by bypassing the legislation and using equitable contribution principles instead, which produces just distributions, but as McLay points out, it leaves the relevant law unwritten and therefore uncertain.

A second, associated, problem identified by both McLay and McDonald lies in motivating governments to reform apportionment rules. The fact that they are dragging their feet in fixing the chaos of current proportionate liability legislation in Australia is particularly ironic, considering that it was they that created the mess by rushing in such precipitous fashion to their own, random solutions in the first place. McDonald makes a series of sensible suggestions for resolving some of the uncertainties and inconsistencies, but refers with frustration to the lack of governmental appetite for sorting out the mess. Some of the more self-interested reasons why government might not be keen to peel back the reforms have already been mentioned above, but it is probably also true to say that there are simply too few votes in private law generally to make even more moderate adjustments an interesting project. The upshot is that in both New Zealand and Australia, it is currently being left to courts to sort out the irregularities of apportionment rules as best they can. They are making some worthy contributions in this regard, but their operations can only be limited and in many instances their hands are now tied.

A third and final question posed by McLay is this – are proportionate liability reforms simply answering the wrong question? If what has produced them are real pressures on particular defendant groups that have been created by increased shared liabilities, or wider primary duties in respect of pure economic loss, then would it not be better to tailor the solutions to the actual source of the relevant problems? One possibility he accordingly suggests is to curb the liabilities of public authorities for pure economic loss that have given rise to concern in New Zealand. Another would be to cap the liabilities of particular defendant groups where they can prove that these liabilities are genuinely causing social problems. This is not, of course, to rule out all possibility of 'proportional' liability for multiple defendants, for in some instances this can be a rational and fair response to insuperable difficulties that a plaintiff may face in proving which member of a group of defendants is responsible for causing harm that has undoubtedly been caused by one of them. In chapter twelve, Rob Merkin and Jenny Steele hence convincingly defend the form of partial liability endorsed by English law in *Fairchild* and *Barker* as fair and appropriate in both tort and insurance law. The point about this form of apportionment solution is that it actually works to P's *advantage* by adjusting the way in which normal causal rules operate and assigning the risk of exceptional scientific uncertainties to each defendant in accordance with the extent to which he or she individually exposed P to the risk of the relevant harm. This is morally very different to the type of defendant-oriented 'proportionate' liability solution set out above, which operates to the *detriment* of P, even when P has established that *every* defendant in the group has wrongly caused her damage. It would hence be perfectly rational to scrap existing 'proportionate' liability reforms entirely, whilst retaining the type of partial liability solution found in *Barker* in exceptional instances.

VII. Conclusions

This book is not the final word on apportionment, nor even the final paragraph. The field is vast and the rules complicated, even within non-federal legal systems. The reader will have the sense that fierce debates are still to be had and that the complexities of the field are not simply technical, but moral and political. If there are three lessons to be taken forward from this, starting point, they are nonetheless these:

First, there is clearly no singular logic to the sorts of apportionment in which private law engages and it is often harmful to pretend that there is. It is hoped that the above investigation will encourage greater, more explicit and more careful discrimination between the different types of 'sharing' solution and their various justifications. 'Compromise' may be the right approach both ethically and politically in some instances, but not in others. Everything is fine-grained. The most important distinction to respect in this way is that between, on the one hand, sharing responsibility fairly between plaintiffs and defendants and, on the other hand, sharing liability fairly between defendants. Although that distinction has been deliberately obfuscated in the course of recent proportionate liability reforms, it must now be kept very clearly in mind.

Secondly, different types of apportionment rule engage in very different trade-offs between sensitivity to the distributive criteria that underpin them, on the one hand, and systemic sophistication, or complexity on the other. I have suggested above that where sharing responsibility is ethically justified, bluntness should not be preferred simply for the additional certainties it may bring. On the other hand, systems in which the criteria of distribution are unstated, or in which the choice between all or nothing solutions and sharing ones is left to an open and unarticulated judicial discretion are not easy to accept, especially (but not only) in commercial contexts. The very minimum standard is that the criteria of distribution be clearly articulated and make normative sense. There is space in this regard for making stronger connections in many instances between the reasons for imposing shared liabilities and the ways of then sharing them. Beyond this, any process that weighs and balances a number of different normative criteria in the process of apportionment will necessarily entail a degree of unpredictability. That is an inescapable fact and should not, perhaps, give rise to an undue sense of insecurity.

The third, final, and rather depressing message, is that politics have not helped in recent years to create the morally rational apportionment solutions that we deserve, or indeed to fix up the law's technical problems. They have too often been used as a neo-liberal lever for redistributing risk back to victims and away from commercial interests, for introducing partialism where it is not ethically warranted; and, even worse, perhaps, for reintroducing 'nothing' as the default apportionment solution in some instances in which 'something' is the right moral result. The same deficits in the political process that spawned this development are now responsible for obstructing the adjustments needed to fix it. In the meantime, as always, it is our judges that have been left to hold the can.

2

Allocating Liability Among Multiple Responsible Causes: Principles, Rhetoric and Power

RICHARD W WRIGHT*

I. Introduction

When more than one person, possibly including the plaintiff, wrongfully or negligently contributed to an indivisible injury to the plaintiff, the issue arises as to how liability for the injury should be allocated among the multiple responsible contributors.[1] The standard method preferred by almost all courts allocates liability as follows: the plaintiff's claim for compensation is reduced by her percentage of comparative responsibility if she was contributorily negligent, those who wrongfully contributed to the plaintiff's injury are each held fully liable for the plaintiff's possibly reduced claim (but the plaintiff cannot recover in the aggregate more than the full amount of her possibly reduced claim), and the wrongdoers who pay the plaintiff are able to maintain contribution actions against the other wrongdoers based on their comparative responsibility.[2]

The full liability of each wrongdoer for the plaintiff's possibly reduced claim is variously referred to as 'joint and several liability', 'concurrent liability' or

[1] I focus in this chapter on situations in which it can be proven that the defendant's wrongful conduct was a cause of the plaintiff's indivisible injury. I do not discuss situations in which the defendant may have been a wrongful cause but it is inherently impossible to prove or disprove causation. In those situations, I believe liability should not be full but instead should be proportionate to the probability of causation, unless it is a situation in which the defendant is a possible wrongful cause and has the ability to determine who or what actually caused the injury. See R Wright, 'Proving Causation: Probability versus Belief' in R Goldberg (ed), *Perspectives on Causation* (Oxford, Hart Publishing, 2011) 195, 212–20.

[2] D Dobbs, *The Law of Torts* (St Paul, West Group, 2000) s 201 at 503–04, ss 385–387 at 1077–81; J Fleming, *The Law of Torts*, 8th edn (Sydney, LawBook Co, 1992) 275–76; A Honoré, 'Causation and Remoteness of Damage' in A Tunc (ed), *International Encyclopedia of Comparative Law, XI, Torts, Pt. 1* (Leiden, Brill, 1983) ss 7-141, 7-189(2), 7-193; C von Bar, *The Common European Law of Torts* (Oxford, OUP, 1998) Vol 1, 334–38; T Weir, 'Complex Liabilities' in A Tunc (ed), *International Encyclopedia of Comparative Law, XI, Torts, Pt. 2* (Leiden, Brill, 1983) ss 12-79 to -86, 12-105 to -109, 12-131 to -133.

'solidary liability'.[3] For ease of reference and to avoid issues arising from differing historical interpretations of 'joint', 'several' and 'concurrent' in the United States and other common law countries,[4] I will generally refer to 'solidary' liability. Also for ease of reference, I will employ 'liability' to describe not only a defendant's liability to the plaintiff or to another defendant (in an indemnity or contribution action) but also the assignment of some or all of the plaintiff's damages to the plaintiff, even though plaintiffs are not technically liable to anyone, including themselves.

A substantial majority of states in the United States depart from the standard method by completely barring recovery by a contributorily negligent plaintiff if the plaintiff's comparative responsibility is, depending on the state, either equal to or greater than the defendants' aggregate comparative responsibility. A majority of states in the United States and (for injuries other than injuries to the plaintiff's person) all the Australian states have replaced the solidary liability of wrongful contributors to a plaintiff's injury, in some or almost all situations and in a large variety of ways, with proportionate liability, according to which each wrongdoer is only liable, initially and ultimately, for a portion of the injury that he wrongfully caused equal to his percentage of comparative responsibility. Both of these deviations from the standard method have almost always been made by the state legislatures, at the behest of defence interests.[5]

In Section II below, I evaluate the standard method and various deviations from it from the perspective of the basic principles of justice. I focus first in Section II(A) on situations in which the victim was innocent, before turning in Section II(B) to the more complicated issues that arise when the victim was contributorily negligent. I argue that both the standard method and a modified version of it, which would allow wrongdoers who pay the plaintiff to have a contributorily negligent plaintiff share in bearing the portion of damages that are uncollectible from other wrongdoers, can be justified, with the latter being fairer, but that the proportionate liability rules adopted in the United States and Australia are neither justifiable nor fair.

In Section III, I explain and criticise the rhetorical arguments used by the defence advocates in the United States (and Australia?) to attempt to convince judges (unsuccessfully) and legislators (successfully) that replacing solidary liability with proportionate liability is necessary to be consistent with the common law and allocation of liability consistent with each person's responsibility.

In Section IV, I describe: (i) the primary role played by recurrent cycles of 'soft' and 'hard' liability insurance markets, made possible by lack of proper regulation of the insurance industry, in creating recurrent liability insurance crises, (ii) the successful effort of the insurance industry and other defence interests to portray

[3] Fleming (n 2) 257–58; W Prosser, 'Joint Torts and Several Liability' (1937) 25 *California LR* 413, 414–15, 418–19, 424, 439; K Barker and J Steele, 'Drifting Towards Proportionate Liability: Ethics and Pragmatics' (2015) 74 *Cambridge LJ* 49, 49.

[4] See Section III(A) below.

[5] See *Restatement Third of Torts: Apportionment of Liability* (St Paul, American Law Institute, 2000) s 17 comment a and s B18 comment a, reporters' note at 170–71; Barker and Steele (n 3).

tort liability rather than the flaws in the liability insurance market as the cause of the recurrent liability insurance crises in order to promote 'tort reform' while avoiding needed regulation of the insurance industry, and (iii) the recurrent failure of the enacted 'tort reforms' to provide the promised reduction or moderation in liability insurance premiums.

Although I occasionally refer to legal rules and debates outside the United States, I generally focus on the rules and debates in the United States, for two reasons. First, my limited familiarity with the rules and debates outside the United States. Secondly, because Kit Barker and Jenny Steele have recently comprehensively discussed the rules and debates outside (as well as within) the United States.[6]

II. Principles[7]

A. Substantive Justice

Since at least Aristotle's time, it generally has been assumed that the purpose of law is or should be the implementation of justice:[8] the creation and maintenance of those conditions that are properly specifiable by law for the promotion of each person's equal external freedom as a free and equal rational being seeking to fully develop her humanity.[9] The external exercise of freedom depends on sufficient access to instrumental goods and sufficient security against interferences by others with one's person and whatever instrumental goods one happens to possess. Distributive justice defines the scope of persons' positive freedom – their access to a fair share of the societal stock of instrumental goods (housing, food, clothing, health care, education, political power, etc) needed to go about their lives, and is evaluated and implemented by their respective ranking compared to all others in society under the proper distributive criterion, which is primarily based on need but also takes into account merit and effort.[10] Interactive justice, which is usually

[6] Barker and Steele (n 3).

[7] For discussion of efficiency theorists' inability to identify efficient allocation rules or to justify and explain existing allocation rules, see R Wright, 'Allocating Liability Among Multiple Responsible Causes: A Principled Defense of Joint and Several Liability for Actual Harm and Risk Exposure' (1988) 21 *UC Davis LR* 1141, 1169–79 (hereafter 'Allocating Liability'); R Wright, 'Throwing Out the Baby with the Bathwater: A Reply to Professor Twerski' (1989) *UC Davis LR* 1147, 1151 fn 20, 1152 fn 21 (hereafter 'Reply').

[8] See, eg, Aristotle, *Politics* (B Jowett trans) in J Barnes (ed), *The Complete Works of Aristotle* (Princeton, Princeton University Press, 1984), Vol 2, bk 3 ch 6 at 1279a 17–19 ('governments which have a regard for the common interest are constituted in accordance with strict principles of justice'); I Kant, *The Metaphysics of Morals* (M Gregor trans, Cambridge, Cambridge University Press, 1991) *318 ('By the well-being of a state is understood … that condition in which its constitution conforms most fully to principles of Right [justice]'); J Madison, *The Federalist No 51* (Benjamin Fletcher Wright ed, 1961) 358 ('Justice is the end of government. It is the end of civil society').

[9] See R Wright, 'The Principles of Justice' (2000) 75 *Notre Dame LR* 1859, 1864–65, 1871.

[10] ibid, 1886, 1887, 1888.

misleadingly referred to as 'corrective' justice,[11] defines the scope of persons' negative freedom – the security of their persons and of their existing stocks of resources in interactions with others. It requires that one's conduct that might affect others' person or property be consistent with those others' equal external freedom.[12] A person's practical exercise of her freedom in the external world must be consistent with the equal external freedom of every other person. As Kant put it in his supreme principle of Right: '[S]o act *externally* that the free use of your choice can coexist with the freedom of everyone in accordance with a universal law.'[13]

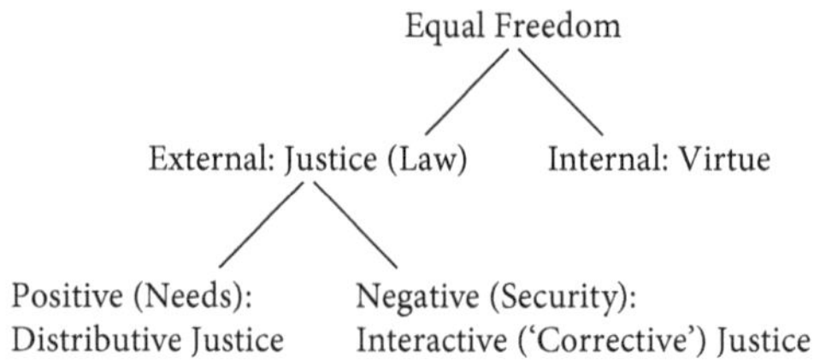

B. Innocent (Non-Negligent) Plaintiff

If a defendant wrongfully (by acting inconsistently with others' right to equal external freedom), actually and 'proximately'[14] caused a legally cognisable injury to an innocent plaintiff's legally protected interests, he is as a matter of interactive justice required to rectify the wrongful injury by fully compensating the plaintiff.[15] If the injury is ongoing or imminent and sufficiently serious and it is practically possible to prevent the injury, the defendant can be enjoined from acting wrongfully.

If more than one person wrongfully and 'proximately' caused an indivisible (theoretically and practically non-separable) injury to the plaintiff, interactive justice requires that she receive full compensation from the wrongdoers. The solidary liability rule assures this by making each wrongdoer fully liable for the injury, while limiting the plaintiff's aggregate recovery to the full amount of her losses.

[11] The usual phrase, 'corrective justice', erroneously implies (and has misled many into assuming) that this type of justice is only concerned with correcting or rectifying wrongs after they have occurred, and not with preventing them beforehand or with defining the nature of the wrong being corrected. See ibid 1883 and fn 113.

[12] ibid, 1887–90.

[13] Kant (n 8) *231 (emphasis added).

[14] So-called 'proximate' causation exists if the defendant was an actual cause of the plaintiff's injury and there are no applicable limitations on the scope of the defendant's legal responsibility. The ambiguous and misleading nature of this phrase has led to its abandonment in the *Restatement Third*. See *Restatement Third of Torts, Liability for Physical and Emotional Harm* (St Paul, American Law Institute, 2010) s 26 comment a, ch 6 'Special Note on Proximate Cause', s 29 comment b.

[15] If the injury would have occurred anyway in the absence of any wrongful conduct by the defendant or others, as a result of non-responsible conditions such as acts of God or the plaintiff's own negligence, the interactive justice claim fails. See R Wright, 'The Grounds and Extent of Legal Responsibility' (2003) 40 *San Diego LR* 1425, 1434–67.

The full liability of each wrongful contributor is clearly justifiable when his wrongful conduct was either necessary or independently sufficient for the occurrence of the injury.[16] If it was necessary for the occurrence of the injury, then the plaintiff would not have suffered the injury at all if not for his wrongful conduct. If it was independently sufficient,[17] then his wrongful conduct was sufficient to produce the plaintiff's injury regardless of any other person's wrongful involvement.

Courts have had more difficulty with those cases, typically pollution cases, in which the defendant's wrongful behaviour was neither necessary nor independently sufficient for the plaintiff's injury, but yet clearly was a cause of the injury. Consider a situation in which three drops of some poison are sufficient to kill a person, each of four persons independently wrongfully put one drop of the poison in the plaintiff's cup, and the plaintiff drank the contents of the cup and died from the poisoning. Each wrongdoer's drop of poison was a cause of the plaintiff's indivisible death.[18] If not, who or what caused the death? If there had been only three wrongdoers, each of them would clearly have been fully responsible as a necessary cause of the injury. There is no apparent reason why this full responsibility should be reduced to responsibility for only a fourth of the injury merely because another drop was wrongfully put in the cup by a fourth wrongdoer. If adding more wrongdoers enables each wrongdoer to reduce his share of damages to successively smaller fractions, there would be a substantial incentive for wrongdoers to engage in perverse 'tortfests' involving as many wrongdoers as possible.

Yet some courts have been reluctant to impose liability for the entire indivisible injury upon each wrongdoer in these circumstances. They have treated the injury as being divisible, even though it was not, to justify a shift to proportionate liability. Other courts, recognising the single, indivisible nature of the injury, have adhered to solidary liability.[19] It has been suggested that the reluctance of some courts to impose full liability on each wrongdoer was due to the then existing rule preventing a wrongdoer who compensated the plaintiff from seeking contribution

[16] See WP Keeton, D Dobbs, R Keeton and D Owen, *Prosser and Keeton on the Law of Torts*, 5th edn (St Paul, West Publishing, 1984) s 52 at 345–46.

[17] No condition by itself is sufficient for any result. The complete cause of any result consists of all the actual conditions that participate in the complete instantiation of a set of abstract conditions that are minimally sufficient, when instantiated, for the occurrence of the result. Each actual condition that participates in that complete instantiation is a cause of (contributed to) the entirety of the indivisible result, rather than, illogically, only some part of the indivisible result. An 'independently sufficient' condition is a condition that is sufficient by itself to instantiate one of the necessary conditions in an otherwise fully instantiated minimally sufficient set. See R Wright and I Puppe, 'Causation: Linguistic, Philosophical, Legal and Economic' (2016) 91 *Chicago-Kent LR* 461, 466–67, 482–84, 486–87.

[18] ibid, 484, 486–87; *Restatement Third: Physical and Emotional Harm* (n 14) s 27 comment f.

[19] See Keeton et al (n 16) s 52 at 345–46, 349, 351, 354–55. Compare *Restatement Second of Torts* (St Paul, American Law Institute, 1965) s 433A illustration 5 (harm caused by multiple discharges of oil into stream: 'divisible' and apportionable) with, ibid, illustrations 14 and 15 (same: not divisible so solidary liability). The *Restatement Third* properly treats injuries as being divisible only if there are separable injuries or losses that can be attributed to different persons based on causation. *Restatement Third: Physical and Emotional Harm* (n 14) s 26.

(reimbursement) from the other wrongdoers.[20] When a defendant was neither a necessary nor an independently sufficient cause of the plaintiff's injury, it may seem unfair to impose full liability when he is not allowed to seek reimbursement for a portion of the damages from the other wrongful contributors to the injury. However, the unfairness exists only among the wrongdoers, rather than there being any unfairness or injustice with respect to the plaintiff's interactive justice claim for full compensation by any person who wrongfully contributed to her indivisible injury. If a person's contribution was neither necessary nor independently sufficient and de minimis when compared with the other wrongful contributions considered separately, rather than in the aggregate, he generally will be absolved from liability due to a lack of 'proximate' causation.[21]

Initially, in both common law and civil law jurisdictions, any defendant who compensated the plaintiff for an injury was not allowed to seek contribution (reimbursement) from any other wrongful contributor to the injury.[22] This rule might be explained by a strict view of justice: while the plaintiff has an interactive justice claim against each person who was a wrongful cause of her injury, no wrongful contributor has a similar claim against any of the other wrongful contributors, each of whom wrongfully invaded the plaintiff's rights but not each other's rights. This is true even if he fully compensates the plaintiff and thus extinguishes the plaintiff's claim against the other wrongful contributors, since the plaintiff is not entitled to more than full compensation. He has not paid any compensation on behalf of them, but merely, as required, discharged his own responsibility to the plaintiff.

Nevertheless, there is a strong equity claim by a defendant who paid the plaintiff for a sharing of the damages that he paid to the plaintiff by all those persons who were wrongful contributors to the plaintiff's injury and thus were also fully responsible for the injury as a matter of interactive justice. This claim should not, as some have argued,[23] be viewed as a 'localised' distributive justice claim, simply because of the rhetorical circumstance that what is being sought is a 'distribution' of ultimate liability among several persons. The claim being made is not, as required for a valid distributive justice claim, that the defendant does not have his

[20] Keeton et al (n 16) s 52 at 349.

[21] See *Restatement Third: Physical and Emotional Harm* (n 14) s 36. A basis for less than full liability of a defendant to each person whom he wronged may also exist when he has similarly wronged many persons, in order to enable a fair allocation of the defendant's available funds among his many victims. See T Keren-Paz and R Wright, 'Liability for Mass Sexual Abuse' (2019) 56(1) *American Criminal LR* (forthcoming) pt III.C.3.

[22] See Keeton et al (n 16) s 50 at 336.

[23] See J Finnis, *Natural Law and Natural Rights* (Oxford, OUP, 1980) 179 (treating 'apportionment of damages where there is contributory negligence or [apportionment] of the costs of litigation', or any other act of adjudication, as a 'matter of/for distributive justice'); Barker and Steele (n 3) 65, 68; J Gardner, 'What is Tort Law For? Part 2. The Place of Distributive Justice', in J Oberdiek (ed), *Philosophical Foundations of Tort Law* (Oxford, OUP, 2014) 335; S Perry, 'The Moral Foundations of Tort Law' (1992) 77 *Iowa LR* 449, 512 (stating that corrective justice is a 'localized distributive justice inquiry, as constrained by outcome responsibility').

fair share of society's instrumental goods and that the other persons who are also responsible for the plaintiff's injury have more than their fair share of society's instrumental goods. Even if both of these conditions were true, it still would not be a valid distributive justice claim. Such one-to-one distributive justice claims are fundamentally flawed, since persons other than the plaintiff usually will have even less of their proper distributive justice share of society's instrumental goods, and persons other than the other responsible causes of the plaintiff's injury will usually have even more of their proper distributive justice share. Valid distributive justice claims can only be made with respect to scarce material resources based on a society-wide comparison of resources and needs.[24]

The contribution claim by a defendant who paid the plaintiff is rather an equity claim based on interactive justice: all those who are responsible for the plaintiff's injury as a matter of interactive justice should equitably share the compensation paid to the plaintiff. As with the similar claim for a sharing of liability between a defendant and a contributorily negligent plaintiff, which is discussed below,[25] courts and legislatures in common law jurisdictions, especially the various states (but not the federal government) in the United States, resisted this claim for a long time.[26] Several reasons have been suggested for their resistance: (1) the 'unclean hands' of the other responsible contributors; (2) an inability to conceive of liability other than in all-or-nothing terms; (3) a desire to avoid the practical complications introduced by sharing of liability; and (4) an inability to formulate a specific method or yardstick for measuring comparative responsibility.[27]

A major impediment to a shift to comparative responsibility rules in both contexts seems to have been the inability to formulate a specific method or yardstick for measuring comparative responsibility. In an 1869 decision discussing the bar against recovery by a contributorily negligent plaintiff, the California Supreme Court stated:

> The law does not justify or excuse the negligence of the defendant. It would, notwithstanding the negligence of the plaintiff, hold the defendant responsible, if it could. It merely allows him to escape judgment because, from the nature of the case, it is unable to ascertain what share of the damages is due to his negligence. He is both legally and

[24] See Wright, 'Principles' (n 9) 1884–87, 1890–91.

[25] See text at nn 36–40 below.

[26] See *Norfolk & Western Railway Co v Ayers* (2003) 538 US 135 (Federal Employers Liability Act); Keeton et al (n 16) s 50 at 337–38 and fn 17, 341 fn 44, s 51 at 344–45 and fns 30–31, s 67 at 476–77; H Drion, 'Contributory Negligence in Europe' (1963) 12 *Cleveland-Marshall LR* 437, 438–39.

[27] See Keeton et al (n 16) s 50 at 336–37, s 65 at 452–53, s 67 at 470–71. Instead of allowing contribution claims, many states adopted indemnity rules, which permit a paying wrongdoer to shift his entire liability to another wrongdoer. Indemnity generally was (and remains) limited to situations in which the indemnitee has a responsibility for the injury that is clearly secondary to the indemnitor's primary responsibility, as with the vicarious liability of employers for the injuries negligently caused by their employees within the scope of employment. Some courts formulated distinctions similar to those used under the contributory negligence allocation rules discussed in Section II(C) below, eg, between 'active' and 'passive' or 'slight' and 'gross' negligence, to permit indemnity in a broader set of circumstances. ibid, s 51 at 341–44 and fns 26 and 31.

> morally to blame, but there is no standard by which the law can measure the consequences of his fault, and therefore, and therefore only, he is allowed to go free of judgment. The impossibility of ascertaining in what degree his negligence contributed to the injury being then the sole ground of his exemption from liability, it follows that such exemption cannot be allowed where such impossibility does not exist; or, in other words, the general rule that a plaintiff who is himself at fault cannot recover, is limited by the reason upon which it is founded.[28]

In both contexts, especially the contribution-among-defendants context, the initial shifts away from the all-or-nothing allocation rules employed per capita rather than comparative responsibility allocation rules: liability was split equally among the responsible parties based on the number of responsible parties. However, these rules often resulted in liabilities that varied substantially from the parties' comparative responsibility and eventually were replaced by comparative responsibility allocation rules as courts became more comfortable with rough evaluations of comparative responsibility.[29]

The wrongdoers' equitable contribution claims against each other based on their comparative responsibility are subordinate to the innocent plaintiff's interactive justice claim against each of them for full compensation of her injury. If a wrongdoer who provides compensation to the plaintiff cannot obtain contribution from one or more of the other wrongdoers, this does not, contrary to the defence advocates' arguments,[30] result in his being held liable for more than he wrongfully caused or for the other wrongdoers' wrongful conduct. Whether or not he can obtain contribution, he is liable to the plaintiff for the full amount of the damages that he wrongly caused. His paying all of the damages fulfills his own responsibility to the plaintiff; it is not a shifting to him of the other wrongdoers' responsibilities. His bearing all of the damages is unfair only in the context of his equitable contribution claim against the other wrongdoers, which is secondary to the plaintiff's interactive justice claim against each person who wrongfully contributed to his injury.

Practical considerations reinforce the arguments as a matter of principle in support of solidary liability. In an ideal world of costless litigation and available, solvent wrongdoers, there would be no practical differences between solidary liability with contribution and proportionate liability, each based on comparative responsibility. Each wrongdoer would ultimately pay its equitable share of the plaintiff's damages. However, in the real world of costly litigation and insolvent or otherwise unavailable wrongdoers, there are major practical differences between the two allocation methods.

Under proportionate liability, the plaintiff can obtain full compensation for her injury only if she is able to successfully locate, sue and collect from every person

[28] *Needham v SF & SJR Co* (1869) 37 Cal 409, 419.

[29] See, eg, *United States v Carroll Towing Co* (2d Cir 1947) 159 F2d 169 (liability split one-third each among two defendants and the contributorily negligent plaintiff); Dobbs (n 2) s 387 at 1080–81; Keeton et al (n 16) s 50 at 340–41, s 51 at 344, s 67 at 471.

[30] See Section III(B) below.

who wrongfully contributed to her injury. The plaintiff therefore bears a substantial risk of receiving less than full compensation if any wrongful contributor is insolvent or otherwise unavailable. In addition, the plaintiff bears the expense and delay of the multiple actions that are required to obtain theoretically full compensation, which will substantially delay and diminish her ultimate net compensation even if she can successfully sue and collect from each wrongful contributor. This delay problem will be compounded by each wrongdoer's reduced incentive to settle the plaintiff's claim, since from the beginning each wrongdoer's liability is limited to his percentage of comparative responsibility. Conversely, under solidary liability with contribution the risk of insolvent or otherwise unavailable wrongdoers and the expense of multiple actions is placed on the solvent wrongdoer(s) from whom the plaintiff initially obtains compensation. The plaintiff can obtain full compensation in the initial suit, and the wrongdoer(s) who pay the plaintiff must seek contribution from the other wrongdoers.

When the plaintiff was not negligent, it should be especially clear that those who wrongfully injured her, rather than she, should bear the expense, risk and delay involved in attempting to recover from the multiple wrongdoers. She bears no responsibility for her injury. As the injured party, she is often urgently in need of compensation and can least afford the expense and delay. Each wrongdoer, on the other hand, was a wrongful, actual and 'proximate' cause of the plaintiff's entire injury and thus bears independent full responsibility for the injury.

C. Negligent Plaintiff

An argument has been made, similar to the argument discussed above for barring contribution claims among defendants who wrongfully contributed to the same injury,[31] that a plaintiff's negligent contribution to her injury should not bar or reduce her claim against any person who wrongfully caused her injury. The plaintiff has an interactive justice claim against each person who wrongfully caused her injury, but none of the wrongdoers has a similar claim against her with respect to her injury. Indeed, if the plaintiff put only herself at risk, it would be improper to describe the plaintiff as having been negligent in the sense of a breach of a legal duty, since the plaintiff owes no legal duty to herself.[32]

Nevertheless, if the plaintiff unreasonably put herself at risk and thus failed to properly respect and promote her humanity, she as well as the defendant is morally

[31] See text following n 22 above.

[32] See, eg, J Fleming, 'Report to the Joint Committee of the California Legislature on Tort Liability on the Problems Associated with *American Motorcycle Association v Superior Court*' (1979) 30 *Hastings LJ* 1464, 1483; R Stevens, 'Should Contributory Negligence Be Analogue of Digital?' in A Dyson, J Goudkamp and F Wilmot-Smith (eds), *Defences in Tort* (Oxford, Hart Publishing, 2015) 253–54; G Schwartz, 'Contributory and Comparative Negligence: A Reappraisal' (1978) 87 *Yale LJ* 697, 701–02 and fns 31 and 33, 722–23 and fns 117 and 118.

responsible for her injury, and her responsibility as well as the defendant's moral and legal responsibility should be taken into account on a comparative responsibility basis when assessing the defendant's liability under her interactive justice claim against him.[33] If her relevant conduct also unreasonably put the defendant or others at risk, that also should be taken into account in an assessment of her comparative responsibility vis-a-vis the defendant.[34]

The traditional common law viewed her negligent contribution to her injury much more seriously. It did not weigh her responsibility in comparison to the defendant's responsibility in order to apportion liability between her and the defendant. Instead, although she, unlike the defendant, committed no legal wrong,[35] while the defendant did, she was completely barred from recovering from the defendant, no matter how slight her negligence was compared to the defendant's.[36]

Several rationales, including those offered to support the bar against contribution among defendants, were offered for this harsh result, most of which do not stand up to even minimal scrutiny.[37] The 'unclean hands', distrust of juries, and industry subsidisation rationales were undermined by: (a) the existence of various formal rules that allowed plaintiffs to recover, on an all-or-nothing basis, if the defendant had the 'last clear chance' or his negligence was active or gross while the plaintiff's was passive or slight; (b) the informal practice according to which the contributory negligence issue rarely was taken away from juries, which sometimes or often allowed negligent plaintiffs to recover some or all of their damages through juries' employment of an unauthorised, hidden and unguided form of de facto comparative responsibility; and (c) the tendency of judges and juries to assess plaintiffs' conduct more leniently while assessing defendants' strictly.[38]

The most plausible explanation for the prolonged failure by many states in the United States to replace the clearly unjust and inequitable complete bar against recovery by a contributorily negligent plaintiff with a comparative responsibility recovery rule is a combination of four factors: (1) the inability to formulate a specific method or yardstick for measuring comparative responsibility;[39]

[33] See Schwartz (n 32) 724–25; R Wright, 'The Standards of Care in Negligence Law' in D Owen (ed), *Philosophical Foundations of Tort Law* (Oxford, Clarendon Press, 1995) 249, 257, 259, 269–71; R Wright, 'Hand, Posner, and the Myth of the "Hand Formula"' (2003) 4 *Theoretical Inquiries in Law* 145, 223–35.

[34] See R Wright, 'Negligence in the Courts: Introduction and Commentary' (2002) 77 *Chicago-Kent LR* 425, 469, 472–73 and fn 187.

[35] If her negligent conduct resulted in harm to another (including the defendant in her lawsuit) in addition to herself, that other person would be the plaintiff in a distinct lawsuit in which she would be the defendant.

[36] Keeton et al (n 16) s 65 at 451–52, 461.

[37] ibid, s 65 at 452–53, s 67 at 470–71.

[38] ibid, s 66 at 462–63, s 67 at 469–70; G Schwartz, 'Tort Law and the Economy in Nineteenth-Century America: A Reinterpretation' (1981) 90 *Yale LJ* 1717, 1759, 1761–63; G Schwartz, 'The Character of Early American Tort Law' (1989) 36 *UCLA LR* 641, 661-66; T Weir, 'All or Nothing' (2004) 78 *Tulane LR* 511, 549.

[39] See text at n 28 above.

(2) strong opposition by defence interests; (3) failures by most legislatures to act given the financial and related political power of the defence interests; and (4) reluctance by state courts to remedy the legislative inaction due to institutional deference and the same political concerns. I believe the second element was the critical one.

Eventually, the state courts gave up on waiting for action by the state legislatures and, despite opposition by the defence interests, exercised their judicial power regarding the common law to replace the complete bar to recovery by a contributorily negligent plaintiff with a recovery regime based on comparative responsibility. The reasons for doing so were stated succinctly by one of the first courts to do so, the California Supreme Court, in *Li v Yellow Cab Co*:[40]

> It is unnecessary for us to catalogue the enormous amount of critical comment that has been directed over the years against the 'all-or-nothing' approach of the doctrine of contributory negligence. The essence of that criticism has been constant and clear: the doctrine is inequitable in its operation because it fails to distribute responsibility in proportion to fault. Against this have been raised several arguments in justification, but none have proved even remotely adequate to the task. The basic objection to the doctrine – grounded in the primal concept that in a system in which liability is based on fault, the extent of fault should govern the extent of liability – remains irresistible to reason and all intelligent notions of fairness.
>
> Furthermore, practical experience with the application by juries of the doctrine of contributory negligence has added its weight to analyses of its inherent shortcomings: 'Every trial lawyer is well aware that juries often do in fact allow recovery in cases of contributory negligence, and that the compromise in the jury room does result in some diminution of the damages because of the plaintiff's fault. But the process is at best a haphazard and most unsatisfactory one.' It is manifest that this state of affairs, viewed from the standpoint of the health and vitality of the legal process, can only detract from public confidence in the ability of law and legal institutions to assign liability on a just and consistent basis.[41]

The state courts' move toward adoption of comparative responsibility rules for allocating liability between negligent defendants and plaintiffs spurred state legislatures to act, both to iron out details and to limit the effect of the shift to comparative responsibility. While state courts generally have preferred the 'pure' form of comparative responsibility that governs in all civil law jurisdictions and (almost all?) common law jurisdictions outside the United States, which allows a plaintiff to recover damages reduced by her percentage of comparative responsibility no matter how high that percentage might be, the state legislatures in the United States, at the behest of the defence interests, have generally adopted a 'modified' form that continues to bar any recovery by the plaintiff if the plaintiff's percentage of comparative responsibility is, depending on the jurisdiction, either equal to or greater than that of the defendants in the aggregate.[42]

[40] *Li v Yellow Cab Co* (1975) 532 P2d 1226.
[41] ibid, 1227–28 (citations omitted).
[42] Dobbs (n 2) s 201 at 505–06; Keeton et al (n 16) s 67 at 470–73.

When the courts adopted comparative responsibility rules to govern the relationship between a negligent defendant and a negligent plaintiff, they did not disturb the previously long established rule applying solidary liability to multiple wrongful contributors to a plaintiff's injury.[43] Defence advocates, quoting statements by the *Li* court and other courts that legal responsibility should be distributed 'in proportion to fault'[44] and treating percentages of comparative responsibility as stating defendants' actual individual responsibility, attempted to convince the courts and legislatures to adopt instead a proportionate liability rule, which limits each wrongdoer's liability, initially and ultimately, for the injury that it wrongfully caused to a portion of the injury equal to its percentage of comparative responsibility.[45] Their argument was correctly rejected as being invalid by almost all the courts that considered it, which instead retained solidary liability.[46] However, a few courts[47] and many state legislatures accepted or at least were confused by this argument, along with other invalid arguments, and adopted

[43] *Rozevink v Faris* (Iowa 1983) 342 NW2d 845, 849 ('of the thirty-eight other states that have adopted comparative negligence … twenty-nine have completely retained joint and several liability, five have retained the doctrine in a modified form, and only three have done away with it (two by statute, one by court decision)'); *Restatement Third: Apportionment* (n 5) s A18 comment a reporters' note at 163 (citation omitted); Keeton et al (n 16) s 67 at 475.

[44] See text at n 41 above.

[45] See Section III(B) below.

[46] See, eg, *Norfolk & Western Railway Co v Ayers* (2003) 538 US 135, 160–64; *Arctic Structures, Inc v Wedmore* (Alaska 1979) 605 P2d 426; *Walton v Tull* (Ark 1962) 356 SW2d 20, 26; *American Motorcycle Ass'n v Superior Court* (Cal 1978) 578 P2d 899; *Tucker v Union Oil Co of California* (Idaho 1979) 603 P2d 156, 163–69; *Coney v JLG Indus* (Ill 1983) 454 NE2d 197; *Best v Taylor Machine Works* (Ill 1997) 689 NE2d 1057, 1084–89; *Rozevink v Faris* (Iowa 1983) 342 NW2d 845; *Maday v Yellow Taxi Co* (Minn 1981) 311 NW2d 849; *Duncan v Cessna Aircraft Co* (Tex 1984) 665 SW2d 414, 429; *Seattle First Nat'l Bank v Shoreline Concrete Co* (Wash 1978) 588 P2d 1308, 1311–14; *Sitzes v Anchor Motor Freight* (W Va 1982) 289 SE2d 679, 684–85; *Wisconsin Natural Gas Co v. Ford, Bacon & Davis Constr Corp* (Wisc 1980) 291 NW2d 825, 833–35; *Kirby Bldg Systems v Mineral Explorations* (Wyo 1985) 704 P2d 1266.

[47] The three state courts that on their own replaced solidary liability with proportionate liability each uncritically accepted the defence advocates' argument that solidary liability results in a defendant's being held liable for more than it caused or for which it was responsible. *See Bartlett v New Mexico Welding Supply* (NM App 1982) 646 P2d 579, 582 (assuming the doctrine 'hold[s] a person liable for an amount greater than the extent that person caused injury'), cert denied, (NM 1982) 648 P2d 784; *Laubach v Morgan* (Okla 1978) 588 P2d 1071, 1074 ('By doing away with joint liability plaintiff will collect his damages from the defendant who is responsible for them.'), limited by *Boyles v Oklahoma Natural Gas Co* (Okla 1980) 619 P2d 613 (retaining solidary liability for innocent plaintiffs); *McIntyre v Balentine* (Tenn 1992) 833 SW2d 52, 58 (assuming that adoption of proportionate liability was necessary to ensure that 'a particular defendant will henceforth be liable only for the percentage of a plaintiff's damages occasioned by that defendant's negligence'). See also *Brown v Keill* (Kansas 1978) 580 P2d 867, 871–74 (construing statute as eliminating joint and several liability and stating that '[t]here is nothing inherently fair about a defendant who is 10% at fault paying 100% of the loss'); *Smith v Department of Ins* (Fla 1987) 507 So 2d 1080, 1091 (upholding against constitutional challenge a legislated shift to proportionate liability in certain types of cases because the right of access to the courts under the state constitution 'does not include the right to recover for injuries beyond those caused by the particular defendant'); *Prudential Life Ins Co v Moody* (Ky 1985) 696 SW2d 503, 505 (Vance J concurring) ('[it is unfair] for a defendant who is only 50% responsible for an injury to be saddled with 100% of the liability'); *Walt Disney World v Wood* (Fla 1987) 515 So 2d 198, 202 (McDonald CJ dissenting) ('the law of joint and several liability should be repudiated and each defendant held accountable for only the percentage of damages found by the trier of fact to have been caused by his conduct').

a wide and inconsistent variety of proportionate liability rules applicable in some or almost all situations.[48]

The defence advocates unashamedly insisted upon employing 'pure' proportionate liability for wrongdoers while at the same time inconsistently insisting upon a 'modified' rather than 'pure' rule for determining a contributorily negligent plaintiff's portion of damages, which under the 'modified' rule results in the negligent plaintiff's bearing all of her damages, rather than a percentage equal to her comparative fault, if her percentage of comparative responsibility is equal to or more than 50 per cent.

The proportionate liability rule results in innocent as well as negligent plaintiffs' bearing a portion of their damages that is much greater than their percentages of comparative responsibility if, as often will be the case, one or more of the wrongdoers is unavailable or insolvent, and it will delay and reduce their ultimate recovery due to litigation expenses even if all of them are available and solvent.[49] Contrary to the defence advocates' constant refrain,[50] it is the proportionate liability rule, rather than traditional solidary liability with contribution allowed, that departs from principled allocation of liability based on the various contributors' distinct individual and comparative responsibilities. As the *Restatement Third* explains:

> [S]everal [proportionate] liability shifts the burden of insolvency from defendants to plaintiffs and creates a symmetrical unfairness to that existing with pure joint and several liability when a plaintiff is also comparatively responsible for damages. Indeed, several liability is especially unfair in universally imposing the risk of insolvency on plaintiffs, even though some [being non-negligent] are not comparatively responsible for their damages.[51]

[48] For lengthy but incomplete listings that nevertheless demonstrate the large variation in approaches in the United States, see *Restatement Third: Apportionment* (n 5) s 17 comment a; Wright, 'Allocating Liability' (n 7) 1165–68 and fns 74 and 76–93; Wright, 'Reply' (n 7) 1147 fn 2.

[49] See the last three paras in Section II(B) above.

[50] See, eg, US Attorney General Tort Policy Working Group, *Report of the Tort Policy Working Group on the Causes, Extent and Policy Implications of the Current Crisis in Insurance Availability and Affordability* (Feb 1986) 31–35, 64–65 (hereafter *Reagan Report*); US Attorney General Tort Policy Working Group, *An Update on the Liability Crisis* (Mar 1987) 54, 76–78 (hereafter *Reagan Report Update*); 'The Need for Legislative Reform of the Tort System: A Report on the Liability Crisis from Affected Organizations' (1987) 10 *Hamline LR* 345, 349, 359–61, 384 (originally published as a monograph in May 1986) (hereafter 'Industry Report'); C Mutter, 'Moving to Comparative Negligence in an Era of Tort Reform: Decisions for Tennessee' (1990) 57 *Tennessee LR* 199, 204, 306–07, 312–13, 318–19; R Pearson, 'Apportionment of Losses Under Comparative Fault Law – An Analysis of the Alternatives' (1980) 40 *Louisiana LR* 343, 361–63. For discussion of the many problems with this argument, see R Wright, 'The Logic and Fairness of Joint and Several Liability' (1992) 23 *Memphis St Univ LR* 45, 71–81 (hereafter 'Logic and Fairness').

[51] *Restatement Third: Apportionment* s 11 comment a at 109; see ibid s C21 comment a, reporters' note at 214–15 (citation omitted): '[E]ven with the plaintiff sharing some fault, each defendant (as well as the plaintiff) is still a legal cause of all of the plaintiff's damages. Shifting the entire risk of insolvency to the plaintiff "merely transform[s]the inequity of imposing that risk entirely on solvent defendants into the equal and opposite inequity of imposing the risk entirely on the plaintiff."' See ibid, s 17 comment a at 149 ('imposing the risk of insolvency on an innocent plaintiff is unwarranted'); ibid s A19 comment e, reporters' note at 167 (same); ibid, s B18 comment a (same); ibid, s B19 comment d (describing effects of proportionate liability on plaintiffs as 'harsh').

As the *Restatement* notes, under the solidary liability rule with allowed contribution the available, solvent wrongdoers will end up having to bear the share of damages that equitably should have been borne by unavailable or insolvent wrongdoers. However, contrary to the defence advocates' repeated arguments, this does not result in their being made liable for injuries and losses for which others, rather than they, are responsible.[52] They have only been made to pay for injuries and losses that they wrongly caused and for which they thus are responsible. Their inability to obtain contribution from the unavailable and insolvent wrongdoers who also were fully responsible results in an unfairness among the wrongdoers, but in no way makes their having to fully rectify their wrong to the plaintiff unfair or unjust.

Nevertheless, would it be fairer to require negligent plaintiffs to share with the available and solvent wrongdoers the portion of the damages that equitably should have been borne by unavailable or insolvent wrongdoers? Those who answer 'no' to this question emphasise the significant differences in the bases for the wrongdoers' and the negligent plaintiff's responsibility for the plaintiff's injury. As was explained above, the plaintiff has an interactive justice claim against each wrongdoer for the entirety of the indivisible injury that was wrongfully caused by each of them, while no wrongdoer has an interactive justice claim against the plaintiff, but rather only a claim that, when assessing liability for his wrongful causation of the plaintiff's injury, the plaintiff's own moral responsibility for the injury should be taken into account. A wrongdoer's equitable claim for contribution by the other wrongdoers is based on the fact that his completely or partially fulfilling his interactive justice responsibility to the plaintiff by fully or partially compensating her extinguished the plaintiff's interactive justice claims against the other wrongdoers by the amount of his payment. His compensation of the plaintiff did not extinguish any liability or responsibility that the plaintiff had to anyone. Indeed, if the plaintiff was contributorily negligent, the wrongdoers have instead already had the benefit of having the plaintiff's interactive justice claims against each of them reduced in accord with the plaintiff's comparative responsibility.[53]

I have previously endorsed this argument,[54] and I still think it has considerable force. It justifies and explains the position that has been adopted by almost all countries around the world and by almost all the courts in the United States that have addressed the issue.[55] However, I now think that, regardless of the significant differences in the bases of the wrongdoers' responsibilities for the plaintiff's injury and her own responsibility if she negligently contributed to the injury, the fact remains that the plaintiff, as well as each wrongdoer, is responsible for the entirety of the injury. The plaintiff has behaved negligently and her negligent conduct,

[52] See Section III(B) below.

[53] See, eg, *American Motorcycle Ass'n v Superior Court* (Cal 1978) 578 P2d 899, 906; *Coney v JLG Indus* (Ill 1983) 454 NE2d 197, 205; Weir (n 2) s 12–86.

[54] Wright, 'Allocating Liability' (n 7) 1191–93.

[55] See sources cited in nn 2 and 46 above.

as well as each wrongdoer's wrongful conduct, was an actual and 'proximate' cause of the entire injury. As such, it seems fair that the negligent plaintiff should share with the available and solvent tortfeasors the portion of the damages that equitably should have been borne by unavailable or insolvent wrongdoers, based on their comparative responsibility. This would avoid situations such as the 1987 Florida case in which a defendant with 1 per cent comparative responsibility was held liable for 86 per cent of the plaintiff's damages after subtraction of her 14 per cent comparative responsibility, with little likelihood of obtaining contribution from the other defendant, plaintiff's husband, who had 85 per cent comparative responsibility.[56]

For reasons discussed above,[57] the negligent plaintiff's sharing with those who wronged her of the share of damages that should have been borne by unavailable or insolvent wrongdoers should occur under a modified solidary liability rule rather than a modified proportionate liability rule. The plaintiff's claim against each wrongdoer for full compensation (reduced by plaintiff's percentage of comparative responsibility if the plaintiff was negligent) has priority over any wrongdoer's equitable claim for sharing of liability. Moreover, the injured plaintiff can least afford the expense and delay involved in locating all the wrongdoers, successfully suing and collecting initial comparative responsibility shares from the available and solvent wrongdoers, and then repeating these steps to obtain from (hopefully still) available and solvent wrongdoers the shares that should have been borne by unavailable or insolvent wrongdoers.[58]

The modified solidary liability rule also has the advantage of being able to be applied across the board, in situations involving innocent as well as contributorily negligent plaintiffs, while the modified proportionate liability rule is clearly unjustified in situations involving innocent plaintiffs. The modified solidary liable rule was adopted in the Uniform Comparative Fault Act[59] and has been endorsed as the fairest approach in the *Restatement Third*[60] and by prominent tort scholars.[61]

[56] *Walt Disney World v Wood* (Fla 1987) 515 So 2d 198.

[57] See last three paras in Section II(B) above.

[58] To eliminate the risk of a wrongdoer's being unable to collect from a negligent plaintiff the plaintiff's proper share of damages that end up not being collectible from unavailable or insolvent wrongdoers, the court could require the plaintiff to provide a financial guarantee or put the appropriate portion of the wrongdoer's payment into an escrow account until ultimate liability shares are resolved.

[59] Uniform Comparative Fault Act s 2, 12 ULA 39 (West Supp 1990). Due to opposition to the 'pure' form of comparative responsibility between plaintiffs and defendants, it was adopted by only a few states and was replaced in 2002 by the Uniform Apportionment of Tort Responsibility Act, which replaced pure comparative responsibility between plaintiffs and defendants with modified comparative responsibility and replaced modified solidary liability for defendants with modified proportionate liability (reallocation of proportionate shares).

[60] *Restatement Third: Apportionment* (n 5) s C21 comment a; see ibid s 17 comment a, 148.

[61] Fleming (n 34) 1483–84, 1491–93; J Wade, 'An Evaluation of the "Insurance Crisis" and Existing Tort Law' (1987) 24 *Houston LR* 81, 87–88.

III. Rhetoric

The defence advocates have repeatedly confused and misused legal terms in attempts to portray solidary liability, as well as other aspects of traditional tort doctrine, as deviations from or obsolete elements of the traditional principles of tort liability. In this part, I will focus on two primary examples.

A. 'Joint' and 'Several' Liability

The defence advocates have repeatedly asserted that 'joint and several' (solidary) liability initially applied only to defendants acting in concert, that application of this rule to other situations is a recent innovation which leads to highly inequitable treatment of defendants, and hence that the rule should be eliminated except for defendants who acted in concert.[62] As the United States Supreme Court stated recently in rejecting this argument, as well as the argument that solidary liability is inconsistent with allocation regimes based on comparative responsibility, the defence advocates failed to heed warnings in the sources that they cited of the need to distinguish the historical uses of the words 'joint' and 'several'.[63]

The terms 'joint tort', 'joint liability' and 'joint tortfeasors' initially were primarily procedural terms that were applied to situations in which defendants could be joined in the same lawsuit, which under the traditional common law was allowed only in situations involving concerted action, in which each tortfeasor could be held liable for the consequences of each other's acts as well as their own acts, or in other situations involving vicarious liability (primarily that of employers for the injuries caused by their employees within the scope of employment). Independently acting tortfeasors who tortiously contributed to the same injury, who in England are still called 'concurrent tortfeasors' rather than 'joint tortfeasors', could not be joined in the same action. However, as the defence advocates have failed to acknowledge, each was 'severally' (separately) fully liable for the injury.[64] As the *Restatement Third* explains:

> [B]efore the advent of comparative responsibility [rather, 'tort reform'], 'several liability' was employed to describe a defendant who was responsible for all of the plaintiff's

[62] Eg, *Reagan Report* (n 50) 33–34 and fns 29–30, 64–65; *Reagan Report Update* (n 50) 76–78; 'Industry Report' (n 50) 360; V Schwartz, *Comparative Negligence*, 2nd edn (Charlottesville, Lexis Law Pub, 1986) s 16.3 at 257, s 16.5 at 261 fn 74; L Pressler and K Schieffer, 'Joint and Several Liability: A Case for Reform' (1988) 64 *Denver Univ LR* 651, 660–62 and fn 49; Illinois 84th Gen Assembly, Reg Sess, Senate Debates, May 21, 1986, 91–92 (Senator Kustra); Petitioner's Brief, *Norfolk & Western Railway Co v Ayers* (2003) 538 US 135, at 12–13, 32 and fn 26, 34–36, 39–40, 49.

[63] *Norfolk & Western Railway Co v Ayers* (2003) 538 US 135, 163–65; see, eg, Prosser (n 3) 413 ('the separate problems of joinder of parties in the same action, as a matter of procedure, and the substantive liability of two or more parties for the same result, require separate consideration, and have very little in common').

[64] C Baker, *Tort*, 4th edn (1986) 142–43; Fleming (n 2) 255, 257–58; Keeton et al (n 16) s 46 at 322–23, s 47 at 324–25 and fn 3, 328–29; Prosser (n 3) at 413–15, 418–19, 424, 430, 439.

damages but who could not be joined in a suit with any other defendant who may also have been responsible.[65]

Procedural joinder of independently acting tortfeasors is now allowed, indeed encouraged, and it therefore is customary in the United States to refer to such independently acting tortfeasors, as well as tortfeasors acting in concert, as 'joint tortfeasors'.[66] Both before and after this procedural change, each tortfeasor, whether acting in concert or independently, was 'severally' (fully) liable for the entirety of any injury that was caused by his tortious conduct, regardless of whether other tortfeasors or natural events also contributed to the same injury.[67] Hence, as the *Restatement Third* explains, 'Many courts, even before the 20th century, [allowed procedural joinder and thus] imposed *joint* and *several* liability on independent tortfeasors when their acts caused truly indivisible harm.'[68] It traces such joint and several liability for independent tortfeasors at least as far back as 1771.[69]

During the recent period of 'tort reform', the term 'several liability' has come to mean fractional or partial liability, rather than full liability, for the harm to which one contributed. As the *Restatement Third* notes, this use of the term 'several liability' is 'imprecise and potentially confusing' and historically inaccurate, for the reasons discussed above.[70] However, deferring to the now prevalent usage, the *Restatement Third* uses the term 'several liability' in its current sense of fractional or partial rather than full liability for a harm to which one wrongfully contributed.[71] A more precise and less confusing term for such fractional or partial liability for injuries and losses, which is used in this chapter, is 'proportionate liability'.[72]

B. Individual Full versus Relative Comparative Responsibility

The most powerful (and hence most frequently asserted) argument against the solidary liability rule is that it unjustly and unfairly holds a defendant who caused or was responsible for only a portion of the plaintiff's injury liable for the entire

[65] *Restatement Third: Apportionment* (n 5) s 11 comment a, reporters' note at 109–110 (citation omitted). Defendants who caused distinct separate injuries to the same plaintiff were similarly held 'severally' (fully) liable 'for the portion of the plaintiff's injury caused by that defendant' (ibid).

[66] Keeton et al (n 16) s 47 at 325–26.

[67] See, eg, *Miller v Union Pacific R Co* (1933) 290 US 227, 236 ('The rule is settled by innumerable authorities that if injury be caused by the concurring negligence of the defendant and a third person, the defendant is liable to the same extent as though it had been caused by his negligence alone') (citing a number of US Supreme Court and Federal Circuit Court cases from the 19th and early 20th centuries); *Restatement Third: Apportionment* (n 5) s 10 comment b, reporters' note at 104; C Baker, *Tort* (n 64) 142–43; Keeton et al (n 16) s 46 at 322, s 47 at 328–29.

[68] *Restatement Third: Apportionment* (n 5) s A18 comment a reporters' note at 163 (emphasis added) (citations omitted).

[69] ibid.

[70] ibid, s 11 comment a, reporters' note at 109–10.

[71] ibid.

[72] See *Best v Taylor Machine Works* 689 NE2d 1057 (Illinois 1997) 1084–89 ('proportionate several liability').

injury or, to the same effect, for injuries for which others but not he was a cause.[73] The arguments made by the defence advocates in Illinois are typical of those made throughout the country.[74] Senator Rupp argued:

> [I] have been adjudged to be … six percent at fault and yet … I could be called on to pay not only what I have been adjudged responsible for but the main one, the highest percentage.[75]

Senator Barkhausen queried:

> [S]hould a defendant have an obligation to pay proportionately more than that defendant is found to be at fault and is … obligated to pay by a judge or jury[?] As a matter of simple justice, the answer to that proposition would seem to be no.[76]

[73] eg 'Industry Report' (n 50) 360 ('courts have expanded the doctrine to require any defendant who is responsible for any portion of the plaintiff's injury to be jointly liable for all of the damages'); ibid 361 ('It is manifestly unfair that [a defendant] who is held to be only five percent liable (if that) for the economic loss may be forced to pay 100% of the damage'); *Reagan Report* (n 50) 64 ('Joint and several liability … is now in many cases applied to all defendants, regardless of their connection to the injury'); *Reagan Report Update* (n 50) 76 ('a 1% finding of liability will guarantee plaintiff a 100% recovery'); ibid 77 ('it is unfair for a defendant to bear the cost of another person's responsibility'); ibid 78 ('A person [should be liable] only for those damages directly attributable to the person's pro-rata share of fault or responsibility for the injury'); D Ball, 'A Reexamination of Joint and Several Liability Under a Comparative Negligence System' (1987) 18 *St Mary's LJ* 891, 891 (joint and several liability 'can result in a defendant, who is minimally at fault in comparison to other parties, paying not only the damage he caused but also the damage caused by others'); Pearson (n 50) 362 (assuming that the only loss 'attributable to' a party's negligence is the fraction of the injury corresponding to the party's percentage of comparative responsibility); ibid 366 (assuming that a person with 13% comparative responsibility is 'only 13 percent negligent' and thus essentially indistinguishable from a totally innocent plaintiff); Petitioner's Brief (n 62) 1–2, 31–33 and fn 26, 40 and fn 35, 43 fn 38, 46–47.

[74] I make this assertion based on its being true for every legislative debate that I have read or read about, including review of materials generously provided to me by Aaron Twerski, as well as its being included in the reports prepared at the national level for the defence interests, which are quoted in n 73 above. See, eg, *Texas House/Senate Joint Committee on Liability Insurance and Tort Law and Procedure, Majority Report* 182 (filed with the 70th Leg, Jan 1987) ('[a] defendant who is found jointly liable for the injuries of a plaintiff is liable for the *entirety* of the damages awarded in favor of the plaintiff even if he is only *partly* responsible for the injuries.') (emphasis in original); *Wisconsin Comm'r of Insurance, Final Report of the Special Task Force on Property and Casualty Insurance* (Aug 1986) 19: '[A]bolishing joint and several liability for [noneconomic] damages would require defendants responsible for causing noneconomic injuries to pay the noneconomic damages. This should alleviate some concerns that wealthy defendants too often get saddled with paying … noneconomic damages when [they] did not cause the noneconomic injuries. The task force felt that joint and several liability should remain for economic damages to assure the victim of full compensation for economic injuries.' See also B Clark, 'Joint and Several Liability: The Battle in California Moves to the Courts' (1986) 16 *Lincoln LR* 121, 121–36, 145–49 (describing the debate in California); J Montford and W Barber, '1987 Texas Tort Reform: The Quest for a Fairer and More Predictable Texas Civil Justice System' (pt. 2, 1988) 25 *Houston LR* 245, 281–91 and fn 180 (describing the debate in Texas); R Wright, 'Understanding Joint and Several Liability' (1991) 2 *Shepards Ill Tort Rep* 278, 279–83 (describing the debate in Illinois); Wright, 'Reply' (n 7) 1150–51 (describing the debate in Maine); Wright, 'Logic and Fairness' (n 50) 52–53 fn 21 (quoting numerous statements by Professor Carol Mutter, who was a consultant to the special committee of the Tennessee Senate that considered the solidary liability issue, in which she referred to the 'glaring' injustice of a defendant only '*X* percent at fault' or '*X* percent responsible' being held liable for more than *X* percent of the damages).

[75] Illinois Senate Debates (n 62) 84.

[76] ibid 90.

Senator Watson noted 'the injustice [that occurs when] someone can be one percent liable and … end up being a hundred percent responsible for the award.'[77] Senator Schuneman objected that the proposed legislation would only protect defendants from joint and several liability who were 'less than 25 percent liable.'[78] Representative Regan argued:

> [T]ort law simply means if you do damage to someone …, you must pay for that and I totally agree with that. … Hey, [but], only if you are at fault. … [Under this provision] [m]edical bills have to be paid 100 percent by the person that's not at fault or that maybe he's five percent at fault. … [W]hy should an innocent party pay for an injury that they didn't have much to do with[?][79]

Unfortunately, as in almost every other state where the issue was debated, the defenders of solidary liability in Illinois for the most part seemed to accept, or at least failed to clearly rebut, the defence advocates' criticisms of solidary liability. For example, Representative Greiman stated:

> [J]oint and several liability … means that if you are one percent negligent, you must pay the entire judgment. … We have changed that. We have heard from … people all across the state that we are concerned that we are minimally liable, five, 10 percent liable, 15 percent liable, and we're stuck for the whole thing. So we have said that there should be a threshold. If you are 25 percent liable, you are so much involved with causing that accident … that you should respond in damages for the entire amount. But if you are less than 25 percent, then you should pay only your share. … The minimally liable are no longer liable for any more than their share. Those people only who have a significant part of the liability will remain [fully] liable.[80]

If solidary liability resulted in a defendant's being held liable for what he did not cause or for the actions of others rather than his own actions, it indeed would be unjust. However, as was noted above,[81] almost all courts in the United States that have considered this argument have correctly held that it is patently false. For example, the United States Court of Appeals for the Ninth Circuit stated in 1941:

> Where the independent tortious acts of two persons combine to produce an injury indivisible in its nature, either tortfeasor may be held liable for the entire damage – not because he is responsible for the act of the other, but because his own act is regarded in law as a cause of the injury.[82]

In its opinion rejecting the defence advocates' arguments, the Supreme Court of Illinois stated:

> We note that the proposition which defendants offer as the primary explanation for abolishing the doctrine of joint and several liability, *i.e.*, the assertion that the

[77] ibid 89.
[78] ibid, June 30, 1986, 84.
[79] Illinois 84th Gen. Assembly, House of Rep Transcription Debate, June 30, 1986, 67.
[80] ibid 8–9; see ibid 59 (similar statement by Representative Homer).
[81] See n 46 above.
[82] *Husky Refining Co v Barnes* (1941) 119 F2d 715, 716 (citations omitted).

> doctrine requires tortfeasors to pay for more damages than they caused, is at odds with this court's explanation of joint and several liability in [*Coney v JLG Indus*, (1983) 454 NE2d 197] … [T]he *Coney* court stated: 'The feasibility of apportioning fault on a comparative basis does not render an indivisible injury "divisible" for purposes of the joint and several liability rule. *A concurrent tortfeasor is liable for the whole of an indivisible injury when his negligence is a proximate cause of that damage.* *** The mere fact that it may be possible to assign some percentage figure to the relative culpability of one negligent defendant as compared to another *does not in any way suggest that each defendant's negligence is not a proximate cause of the entire indivisible injury*.'[83]

As the Court went on to explain,[84] solidary liability applies only to injuries for which the defendant himself is fully responsible. He is responsible for an injury only if the tortious aspect of his behaviour was an actual cause of the injury.[85] He is not liable for injuries, including separable portions of injuries, to which he did not contribute. He is not liable if, for reasons of policy or principle, his connection to the injury is considered too remote or minimal to be 'proximate'.[86]

The Court emphasised the fundamental difference between each tortfeasor's *individual full responsibility* for an injury that he tortiously caused and the *comparative responsibility percentages* that are obtained by comparing the tortfeasors' individual full responsibilities for the injury (and the plaintiff's if the plaintiff was contributorily negligent).[87] For example, if two defendants were each negligent, actual and 'proximate' causes of a plaintiff's injury, neither is merely '50 per cent negligent', a cause of only 50 per cent of the injury, or only '50 per cent responsible'. Such statements make as much sense as saying that someone is 50 per cent pregnant or caused 50 per cent of a death or a broken leg. Rather, each defendant was 100 per cent negligent, and each defendant's negligence was an actual and 'proximate' cause of 100 per cent of the injury. Each defendant therefore is fully responsible for the entire injury. Only when we *compare* their individual full responsibilities, and assume that they were equally negligent, does it make sense to say that each defendant, *when compared to the other*, bears 50 per cent of the total *comparative* responsibility for the injury.

Similar rebuttals were rare in the state legislative debates.[88] Instead, plaintiffs' advocates often played into the hands of the defence advocates by relying solely on

[83] *Best v Taylor Machine Works* (1997) 689 NE2d 1057, 1086 (emphasis added by the court).
[84] ibid.
[85] R Wright, 'Causation in Tort Law' (1985) 73 *California LR* 1735, 1759, 1766–71.
[86] Keeton et al (n 16) s 47 at 328–29, s 52 at 345–46, 347–49; see text at n 21 above.
[87] *Best v Taylor Machine Works* (n 60) 1086–87.
[88] The only strong rebuttal at the state level that I have read was a statement by Mack Kidd on behalf of the Texas Trial Lawyers Association during the legislative debates in Texas. See Wright, 'Logic and Fairness' (n 50) 53 fn 22. A sustained challenge to the defence advocate's argument in a Congressional hearing made the defence advocate quite uncomfortable. *See Product Liability: Hearings on H.R. 2238 Before the Subcomm on Commerce, Consumer Protection, and Competitiveness of the House Comm. on Energy and Commerce*, 100th Cong, 1st Sess (1987) 488–90 (colloquy between Rep Florio and Alfred W Cortese Jr).

an 'innocent plaintiff needs compensation' argument,[89] which is weak even with respect to innocent plaintiffs as a matter of interactive or distributive justice and obviously is of no help to negligent plaintiffs.

For example, Senator Berman, the principal defender of the solidary liability doctrine in the Illinois Senate, stated:

> [I]t has been the social policy decision of the courts … that when a person who has been injured is entitled to compensation that they should go away with all of their compensation, and the people that contributed to some extent to that injury shall bear the cost of that injury. … [I]t is better that the people that were at fault should pay the plaintiff rather than the plaintiff should go home with less than [he is] entitled to. That's the whole theory behind joint and several liability. Now this amendment says that in weighing those types of policy decisions we're going to modify it somewhat. … [T]he person who is liable less than the plaintiff won't have to pay more than what he is responsible for.[90]

Senator Berman at one point argued that, in a hypothetical involving two negligently driven automobiles that collided and caused injury to a pedestrian, the driver who was 'twenty-five percent at fault' should be fully liable because '[i]f that car hadn't been in the intersection … [the pedestrian] would not have been injured.'[91] But he apparently failed to grasp the full import of this argument, since he immediately proceeded to return to an argument based on the plaintiff's need for compensation rather than each wrongdoer's full responsibility for the injury that he wrongfully caused:

> You're only debating here as to whether somebody who is responsible should pay more than their share. … [Should] the person who was hurt and [has] not contributed to his injury … bear the loss or should the person that contributed to the injury pay more than their loss? And there's arguments on both sides. I suggest to you the more socially acceptable policy, the more humane policy, the policy that spreads the risks and saves … the taxpayers an awful lot of money because … if the plaintiff is not made whole, it winds up on public aid and other types of taxpayer funded programs [is that the] person that has contributed to that injury should be the one that pays along with others that have contributed to that injury.[92]

Similarly, Representative McPike at one point argued for solidary liability based on the defendant's being an actual and 'proximate' cause of the plaintiff's injury in an actual/hypothetical case in which the defendant municipality failed to replace a manhole cover,[93] but failed to make the same point for an actual case in which the

[89] See, eg, Nevada Trial Lawyers Association, 1987 Press Packet, *Statement on Joint and Several Liability*, which states: 'The law presently does not lose sight of who the victim is in a case. The company is a "wrongdoer", it has broken the law and caused the damage. Although it may not be fair for the one company to have to pay, it is more just than to let the victims become losers once again.'

[90] Illinois Senate Debates (n 62) 85.

[91] ibid, 109–10.

[92] ibid, 111.

[93] Illinois House Debate (n 79) 76.

defendant municipality allowed foliage to eliminate or seriously obscure viewing of a stop sign:

> The park districts, the cities, they're concerned because they're really not liable. … [They say] 'We're a passive tortfeasor. We were drug into the case by the tip of our tail. We really didn't do anything wrong. And the truth of the matter is, but for us, this accident would have happened anyway, and now we're stuck with the bill.' So we said, 'Well, you're right.' Somehow, the civil justice system has become distorted, so we will correct that. Five percent, six percent, eight percent, 10 percent. No, we said 25 percent. We went overboard. The truth is that many Members on this side said we went too far. And we did that to try to answer this legitimate problem.[94]

In Maine, the Commission to Examine Problems of Tort Litigation and Liability Insurance based its majority recommendation that no change be made in the solidary liability doctrine on the 'innocent plaintiff needs compensation' rationale:

> Maine law, in most instances, permits a liable defendant to bear responsibility for only that portion of the plaintiff's damages attributable to his fault. … [W]hile in a few cases a defendant may pay more than his portion of a plaintiff's damages because another defendant at fault has no assets, this result is the fairest option. A more unfair option is to have an innocent or less blameworthy plaintiff absorb the loss.[95]

The same arguments were reiterated in the debates in the Maine legislature. Supporters of solidary liability explicitly noted their confusion over the doctrine.[96] Those on both sides of the debate erroneously assumed that a defendant held liable for more than her percentage of comparative responsibility was being held liable for damages for which she was not responsible. However, the majority thought that the balance weighed in favour of 'fairness to the innocent plaintiff' based on the plaintiff's need for full compensation, especially given the lack of any evidence that elimination or modification of joint and several liability would improve insurance availability or affordability.[97]

The principal academic spokesperson for the defence advocates, Professor Aaron Twerski, who testified on their behalf before several legislative committees, has argued that legislators were not confused by the defence advocates' arguments. He asserts that legislators were well aware of the best arguments for both sides and weighed them against each other to reach various compromise solutions based on

[94] ibid, 75.

[95] Maine State Legislature, *Draft Report of the Commission to Examine Problems of Tort Litigation and Liability Insurance in Maine* (Oct 1 1987) 95–96.

[96] eg, *Maine Legislative Record* (March 16, 1988) H-288 (remarks of Rep Paradis).

[97] ibid, H-288 (remarks by Representative Paradis defending joint and several liability); ibid, H-290 (remarks of Representative MacBride defending joint and several liability); ibid, H-289 (remarks of Representative Hanley opposing joint and several liability); ibid, S-309–11 (March 17, 1988) (remarks of Senators Brannigan and Black favouring joint and several liability); ibid (remarks of Senators Collins, Whitmore and Dillenback opposing joint and several liability). The attempt to modify the solidary liability rule failed by an overwhelming vote in the House and by a single vote in the Senate. ibid H-291 (101 to 30 vote), S-311 (15 to 14 vote, with two paired votes).

liability concerns not related to the basic justice and fairness of solidary liability, but which are exacerbated by solidary liability.[98]

Contrary to Twerski's assertions, the defence advocates, including Twerski himself,[99] consistently hammered away on the argument that solidary liability unfairly requires a defendant to pay for more damage than he wrongfully caused or for which he was responsible, and thus makes him responsible for others' tortious actions in addition to his own, and that argument was usually accepted and repeated by legislators. As Twerski himself framed the issue regarding insolvent defendants,[100] the 'fairness to plaintiffs' argument was consistently stated as an 'innocent plaintiff needs compensation' argument for making wrongdoers liable for harm for which they allegedly were not responsible, rather than as an individual full responsibility argument based on the each wrongdoer's actual and 'proximate' causation of the plaintiff's indivisible injury.[101] Any 'compromise' allocation rule, such as reallocating the uncollectible shares among the solvent responsible parties or retaining joint and several liability for economic damages only, allegedly would be unjust since a solvent defendant would be made to pay 'more than his portion of damages'[102] and would be based on the plaintiff's need for compensation rather than on any principle of responsibility:

> If we are to achieve a true fault based system of responsibility, pure several [proportionate] liability is essential. The various modified systems are only a partial solution to the injustice inherent in joint and several liability. … The advantage of these methods is that the plaintiff is guaranteed [sic] full recovery. To achieve this, however, defendants must act as insurers for the actions of others, over whom they exercise no control.[103]

IV. Power

The major push in the United States for full or partial replacement of wrongdoers' solidary liability by proportionate liability occurred in the mid-1980s,[104] when

[98] A Twerski, 'The Joint Tortfeasor Legislative Revolt: A Rational Response to the Critics' (1989) *22 UC Davis LR* 1125, 1127, 1129–33, 1144–45.

[99] ibid, 1128 ('industry advocates contend that joint and several liability is unfair because a defendant is held responsible to pay more than the proportional share of harm *which she caused*') (emphasis added); ibid, 1139 ('ten percent liability … effectively means 100%').

[100] ibid, 1127, 1129–30 and fn 19.

[101] See, eg, Wisconsin Commissioner of Insurance, *Final Report of the Special Task Force on Property and Casualty Insurance* (Aug 1986) 19: '[A]bolishing joint and several liability for [noneconomic] damages would require defendants responsible for causing noneconomic injuries to pay the noneconomic damages. This should alleviate some concerns that wealthy defendants too often get saddled with paying … noneconomic damages when [they] did not cause the noneconomic injuries. The task force felt that joint and several liability should remain for economic damages to assure the victim of full compensation for economic injuries.'

[102] Maine Liability Crisis Alliance, *Response to Draft of the Commission to Examine Problems of Tort Litigation and Liability Insurance in Maine, Appendix A: Joint and Several Liability* (Oct 1987) A–5.

[103] ibid, A-6; see ibid, A-4 (same).

[104] See sources cited in n 50 above; J Granelli, 'The Attack on Joint and Several Liability' (1985) 71 *ABAJ* 61.

two critical factors coincided: a 'liability insurance crisis' generated by 'the most infamous hard market in the United States' with resulting 'dramatic increases in commercial liability insurance premiums and reductions in coverage availability'[105] and Ronald Reagan's landslide Presidential election victory, which swept in on his coattails pro-business Republican Party legislators at both the national and state levels across the country.

Due to substantial delays ('float' time) between receipt of premium income and pay out on claims, significant changes in financial markets, difficulties in forecasting future casualty losses, and lack of transparency or regulation, the liability insurance market goes through repeated 'soft' and 'hard' cycles:

> Simply described, the ['soft' and 'hard'] economic cycle occurs because insurers make most of their money from investment income. During years of a strong stock market, high interest rates and/or excellent insurer profits, insurance companies engage in fierce competition for premium dollars to *invest* for maximum return. This results in competitive *underpricing* of policies [based on expected claims], when rates rise less than inflation. This is called the 'soft market'. … However, when investment income decreases because the stock market plummets (or as in past cycles, interest rates drop) and/or cumulative price cuts make profits unbearably low, the industry responds by sharply increasing premiums and reducing coverage, creating a 'hard market.' For policyholders, a 'liability insurance crisis' is the result.[106]

During soft markets, to gain market share insurers take on riskier insureds as well as lowering premiums and sometimes understate expected claims or draw on built-up excess reserves to show profitability to justify the lower premiums to state insurance agencies, which puts pressure on competing firms to also lower premiums. Such behaviour is facilitated by limited liability, risk-insensitive guaranty programs and insurers' ability to use reinsurance to conceal low prices and excessive growth. When investment returns decrease due to declining interest rates or stock market returns or financial crises such as the 2008 real estate financing crisis in the United States and/or a sharp increase in claim costs due to catastrophic natural events or alleged major increases in tort liability costs, reserves and surpluses built up during prior hard markets may be depleted; if so, a new hard market occurs, the severity of which is exacerbated by aberrant (especially risky) behaviour during the soft market. A few insurers may default, but most will adjust by dropping clients and/or coverages as well as raising premiums, often overstating expected claims to justify higher premiums and build up surpluses.[107]

[105] S Harrington, 'Tort Liability, Insurance Rates, and the Insurance Cycle' (2004) *Brookings-Wharton Papers on Financial Services* 1.

[106] JR Hunter and J Doroshow, *Premium Deceit 2016: The Failure of 'Tort Reform' To Cut Insurance Prices* (New York, Americans for Insurance Reform, Nov 2016) 4; see Harrington (n 105) 1, 18; see Federal Insurance Office, *Annual Report on the Insurance Industry* (June 2013) 22–29.

[107] See Harrington (n 105) 1–2, 19 and fns 12 and 13, 23; JR Hunter and J Doroshow, *Repeat Offenders: How the Insurance Industry Manufactures Crises and Harms America* (New York, Americans for Insurance Reform, Dec 2011) 2–6, 10, 18–24.

In the United States, the McCarran-Ferguson Act exempts the insurance industry from antitrust regulation unless boycott, coercion or intimidation is involved and prohibits federal regulation.[108] The industry created and controls a for-profit company, the Insurance Services Office Inc, which insurers use to share data among themselves and state insurance departments for rate-making purposes. Insurers are subject to regulation by state insurance departments, but few state insurance offices have the authority or funding to collect relevant data, validate it, and use it to exercise proper control over insurance rates. Neither the federal government nor states regulate the rates or terms of coverage set by reinsurers, which insurers use to shift and spread some of their claim risks. Some state insurance departments are authorised to collect data from domestic insurers, but rarely do. They are supposed to assure insurers' solvency, but they only have authority to require foreign reinsurers, such as Lloyd's of London, to post security for their reinsurance obligations.[109]

From 1978 to 1984 the liability insurance market in the United States was soft. Premium growth grew dramatically, with indications of aberrant insurer behaviour, while insurer profits and surplus declined. However, interest rates fell sharply between 1984 and 1986. Operating margins were 'substantially negative during 1982–1985 with particularly large losses during 1983–1984'.[110] As interest rates began to fall sharply in 1984, insurers began to discuss among themselves the need to quit competing for premium income and instead collectively institute a significant raise in premiums. Initially, no mention was made of tort liability costs.[111] Indeed, St Paul, then the nation's largest medical malpractice insurer, told the *National Underwriter* magazine in December 1984 that 'there is not a malpractice crisis around the corner' and that any problem in the medical malpractice insurance field 'can be dealt with through rate adequacy, improved risk management, more intensive underwriting practices, and improved claims handling ability and strategy.'[112]

However, plans were already underway to follow the same path that was taken during the earlier 1974–1977 hard market, which primarily affected medical malpractice and product liability insurance.[113] The industry's Insurance Information Institute informed insurers at a meeting in 1984 that it would be launching a massive advertising and public relations effort 'to market the idea that there is something wrong with the civil justice system in the United States.'[114] The industry took advantage of its exemption from antitrust laws or any other significant regulation

[108] 15 USC ss 1011–1015. The US Supreme Court has held that insurance companies may not boycott their insureds by agreeing to deny them coverage entirely. *St Paul Fire & Marine Inc Co v Barry* (1978) 438 US 531 (1978).

[109] *Repeat Offenders* (n 107) 7–8.

[110] Harrington (n 105) 7.

[111] *Repeat Offenders* (n 107) 10–11.

[112] *National Underwriter*, 14 December 1984, 40.

[113] See *Repeat Offenders* (n 107) 8–9.

[114] *National Underwriter*, 21 December 1984, 1, 2, 46; see *Repeat Offenders* 13–14.

and the lack of governmental or public access to relevant information regarding its past and projected expenses and income to collude on eliminating or reducing coverages and sharply raising premiums. Insurers were pressured by other insurers and reinsurers to avoid premium competition and to instead raise premiums well above rates necessary along with investment income to cover expected claims costs in order to restore and enhance reserves and surplus as quickly as possible and to put pressure on legislators and voters to enact 'tort reforms'.[115]

The hard market began in 1985, with sharp premium increases and related increases in reported profits and surpluses.[116] Operating margins following the premium increases were 'large and positive … peaking at about 35 percent in 1987'.[117] The resulting liability insurance crisis affected most lines of coverage. The insurers instituted a nationwide campaign to blame the crisis on alleged sharp increases in tort liability claim costs and to push for 'tort reform'.[118] They had eager allies among business interests and in the pro-business Reagan Administration, which published the first of its two reports on the crisis and the alleged need for tort reform in February 1986.[119] Tremendous pressure was exerted on legislators across the country to enact 'tort reform'.[120] A principal object of this pressure was replacement of the solidary liability rule by proportionate liability.[121] As Senator Berman in Illinois noted in explaining his support of a limited modification of the solidary liability rule, despite his belief that modification of the rule was unjustified, 'I don't like to try to hold the ocean back, this is a compromise amendment'.[122]

When asked for data to back up their claims, the insurance industry could not or would not supply it.[123] After conducting its own independent investigation, the Ad Hoc Insurance Committee of the National Association of Attorneys General concluded:

> The facts do not bear out the allegations of an 'explosion' in litigation or in claim size, nor do they bear out the allegations of a financial disaster suffered by property/casualty insurers today. They finally do not support any correlation between the current crisis in availability and affordability of insurance and such a litigation 'explosion.' Instead, the available data indicate that the causes of, and therefore solutions to, the current crisis lie with the insurance industry itself.[124]

[115] See *Repeat Offenders* (n 107) 15–18.

[116] Harrington (n 105) 4–5, 11, 18.

[117] ibid, 7.

[118] *Repeat Offenders* (n 107) 11–19.

[119] *Reagan Report* (n 50).

[120] See Granelli (n 104); Illinois Senate Debates (n 62) 121 (Senator Rupp).

[121] Illinois Senate Debates (n 62) 89 (Senator Barkhausen); Illinois House Debates (n 79) 59 (Representative Homer).

[122] Illinois Senate Debates (n 62) 86; see ibid 93 (Senator Rock); Illinois House Debates (n 79) 59 (Representative Homer).

[123] See *Repeat Offenders* (n 107) 14.

[124] F Bellotti et al, *Analysis of the Causes of the Current Crisis of Unavailability and Unaffordability of Liability Insurance* (Boston, Ad Hoc Insurance Committee of the National Association of Attorneys General, May 1986). Several state commissions reached similar conclusions. See, eg, New Mexico State Legislature, *Report of the Interim Legislative Workmen's Compensation Committee On Liability*

Business Week magazine similarly reported:

> Even while the industry was blaming its troubles on the tort system, many experts pointed out that its problems were largely self-made. In previous years the industry had slashed prices competitively to the point that it incurred enormous losses. That, rather than excessive jury awards, explained most of the industry's financial difficulties.[125]

Even industry insiders occasionally acknowledged the true source of the recurrent liability insurance crises. Maurice R Greenberg, then President and Chief Executive Officer of American International Group Inc, one of the largest insurers, told an insurance audience in Boston in 1986 that the industry's problems were due to price cuts taken 'to the point of absurdity' in the early 1980s. Had it not been for these cuts, Greenberg said, there would not be 'all this hullabaloo' about the tort system.[126]

Nevertheless, the insurers were successful, as they had been during the 1974–1977 hard market, in using the liability insurance crisis generated by their unregulated market behaviour to convince numerous state legislatures to enact (additional) tort reforms, including replacement of solidary liability for wrongdoers wholly or partly with proportionate liability. They were successful again, using the same strategy, during the subsequent 2002–2006 hard market, which primarily affected property and medical malpractice liability insurance.[127] During each of the three hard markets, legislators, regulators and the public were told that 'tort reform' would ease the liability insurance crisis and result in lower insurance premiums.[128] Not surprisingly, since the variations in premium rates were primarily due to the cyclical soft and hard liability insurance markets rather than tort liability, this did not happen. States with little or no 'tort reforms' experienced approximately the same changes in insurance rates as those states that enacted severe restrictions on tort liability. Indeed, some states that had enacted tort reforms based on promises of rate reductions instead had rates increase substantially after the reforms were enacted or had reductions less than states with no or more limited reforms.[129]

Insurance and Tort Reform (Nov 12, 1986); Michigan House of Representatives, *Study of the Profitability of Commercial Liability Insurance* (Nov 10, 1986); Insurance Committee. Pennsylvania House of Representatives, *Liability Insurance Crisis in Pennsylvania* (29 September 1986).

[125] 'What Insurance Crisis?' *Business Week*, Jan 12, 1987; accord, Stanoch, 'Insurance Crisis or Tort Crisis? Explaining the Myths and Examining the Facts' (1987) 10 *Hamline LR* 443, 460.

[126] M Greenwald, 'Insurers Must Share Blame: AIG Head' *Business Insurance*, 31 March 1986, 3.

[127] *Repeat Offenders* (n 107) 20–24; see T Baker, *The Medical Malpractice Myth* (Chicago, Univ of Chicago Press, 2007). The insurers' attempt to create a hard market after Hurricanes Irene and Sandy in 2011 and 2012 failed. *Repeat Offenders* (n 107) i–ii, 5, 28–36.

[128] *Repeat Offenders* (n 107) 14–15, 18. During soft markets, on the other hand, advocates of 'tort reform' claim that they never said or would say that 'tort reform' would lower insurance premiums. ibid 20.

[129] ibid 19–22, 24, 25; *Premium Deceit* (n 106) 5–6, 11–15, 19–20, 22–23.

V. Conclusion

Contrary to the assertions of the defence advocates, the standard method for allocating liability among the multiple responsible causes of an indivisible injury – which reduces a plaintiff's recovery for her injury by her percentage of comparative responsibility, holds those who wrongly contributed to her injury solidarily liable for the (reduced) damages, and allows contribution among the wrongdoers based on their comparative responsibility – is consistent with the basic principles of justice and proper allocation of liability in accord with each person's legal and/or moral responsibility. Not surprisingly, it is the method favoured by almost all courts and is employed by almost all governments, including the federal government in the United States. The proportional liability method urged by the defence advocates in the United States and Australia clearly is neither just nor consistent with allocation of liability in accord with persons' respective legal and/or moral responsibility.

The defence advocates in the United States have tried to argue otherwise by employing misleading rhetorical arguments that: (i) ignore and confuse the distinct historical meanings of the words 'joint' and 'several', and (ii) treat a person's percentage of *comparative* responsibility for an indivisible injury for which he was a wrongful, actual and 'proximate' cause as stating (illogically) that he caused and therefore is responsible for only that per cent of the indivisible injury. They have taken advantage of liability insurance crises generated by unregulated cycles of soft and hard liability insurance markets, rather than tort liability, to employ their misleading rhetorical arguments for 'tort reform'.

In a recent article, Kit Barker and Jenny Steele make very similar points regarding the recent replacement of solidary liability with various inconsistent versions of proportionate liability in all the Australian states for injuries other than to one's person. They describe the unprincipled nature of proportionate liability, the misleading rhetorical arguments by the defence advocates that confuse the grounds for reducing a plaintiff's recovery by her comparative responsibility with the quite distinct issue of each wrongdoer's full responsibility for the wrongful injury that he caused, and the use by the defence advocates of the shock caused to the financial and insurance markets by the collapse of Enron and a major Australian indemnity insurance company in 2001, both clearly due to internal fraud and mismanagement rather than tort liability issues, as a springboard for 'tort reform'.[130] Hopefully, this chapter will add to their warning to other countries to watch out for these moves and tactics by the defence advocates and maybe even serve, along with their article, as encouragement of and support for restoration of the standard method for allocating liability in the United States and Australia.

[130] Barker and Steele (n 3) 49–54, 59, 61–63, 67–69.

3

Full, No, or Partial Liability? That is the Question – Some Answers from a Civilian Perspective

HELMUT KOZIOL

I. Introduction

In this chapter, I explore the principle of 'partial liability' in civilian systems. I use the term 'partial liability' to refer solely to the liability of a defendant to compensate part of *one and the same harm*, as distinguished from his or her liability for one or more of a number of harms which are separate and distinct. It is often not easy to draw a clear boundary between cases that involve the same harm and distinct, separate harms. By splitting a single harm up into different harms and attributing only some of them to the defendant, one can sometimes achieve the same results as by imposing partial liability for the undivided harm. The preliminary distinction between the 'same' and 'distinct' damage is important and can be decisive, but I do not pursue it further here.[1]

The basic starting point in nearly all continental European countries is the principle of *comprehensive compensation of damage* – meaning that defendants are liable for no less, but also no more[2] than the damage caused. For example, Article 1382 of the French Code Civil provides: 'Any act whatever of man, which causes damage to another, obliges the one by whose fault it occurred, to compensate it'.[3] § 249(1) of the German Civil Code (BGB) stipulates, in more detail, the liable party's obligation to 'restore the position that would exist if the circumstance obliging him to pay damages had not occurred'. Likewise, the 'difference method' of calculating damage, which accords with this provision and is generally accepted, effects full compensation in that it compares the current, actual state of the legal

[1] See further, in particular, K Oliphant (ed), *Aggregation and Divisibility of Damage* (Vienna, Verlag Österreich, 2009).

[2] H Koziol, 'Comparative Conclusions' in H Koziol (ed), *Basic Questions of Tort Law from a Comparative Perspective* (Vienna, Sramek, 2012) no 8/312, with references to the country reports.

[3] Translation by O Moreteau in K Oliphant & BC Steininger (eds), *European Tort Law: Basic Texts* (Vienna, Sramek, 2011) 85.

good with the hypothetical state that would have existed but for the behaviour which caused the damage, and provides for compensation of the balance.[4]

The old Austrian Civil Code (ABGB), dating from 1811, which is still valid, provides a remarkable exception. Like the other European codes, § 1323(1) of the ABGB starts out by requiring a liable party to restore everything to its previous state (or, where appropriate, pay the estimated value of the claimant's loss), but the basic principle is then immediately limited by its following, often-criticised provision, § 1324: only in cases of *serious fault* is full satisfaction – that is, comprehensive compensation including both loss of profit and non-pecuniary loss – awarded. In cases of slight negligence, by contrast, the victim is merely entitled to compensation of his or her 'actual loss' (diminution of his or her existing patrimony), which is assessed according to its market value.[5]

The general rule of full liability is also broken in all continental European legal systems by exceptions which can be sorted into two groups. The first and more general category (considered in Part II below) concerns cases involving solely one victim and one injurer. The second (Part III) comprises cases involving several damaging events, several victims, or both.

II. Lone Injurer

A. The Main Examples

One example of partial liability has already been mentioned: under Austrian law, the tortfeasor who acts with slight negligence has to compensate only 'actual loss,' not loss of profit. This rule achieves an appropriate balance between the gravity of the grounds for imputing legal responsibility and the legal consequences.[6]

More common under continental European legal systems are restrictions on a defendant's liability that flow from the idea of *adequacy*,[7] or which limit recovery to loss falling within the *protective purpose* of a rule.[8] These ideas correspond to rules of legal causation, or remoteness of damage, in the common law tradition.[9]

[4] cf E Deutsch and H-J Ahrens, *Deliktsrecht*, 6th edn (Munich, Vahlen, 2014) no 625.

[5] ABGB, § 1332, § 305.

[6] See H Koziol, 'Damages under Austrian Law' in U Magnus (ed), *Unification of Tort Law: Damages* (The Hague, Kluwer, 2001) 8 ff; *Basic Questions of Tort Law from a Germanic Perspective* (Vienna, Sramek, 2012) no 8/2 with references to W Wilburg, *Die Elemente des Schadensrechts* (Marburg an der Lahn, Elwert, 1941) 249 f; H Koziol, *Österreichisches Haftpflichtrecht I*, 3rd edn (Vienna, Manz, 1997) no 1/16.

[7] According to this theory liability is precluded for atypical damage, which could only have arisen due to a coincidental, objectively unforeseeable combination of circumstances.

[8] See further C van Dam, *European Tort Law*, 2nd edn (Oxford, Oxford University Press, 2013) 1103-2; H Koziol, *Basic Questions of Tort Law* (n 6) no 7/7 ff and 7/15 ff and the references to the country reports in Koziol (n 2) no 8/290.

[9] cf van Dam (n 8) 1102, 1104; H Koziol, 'Natural and Legal Causation' in L Tichý (ed), *Causation in Law* (Prague, Univerzita Karloova, 2007) 53 ff.

Additionally, in Germany and Austria, in the field of strict liability, *caps on liability* are still common. In Switzerland and other legal systems, such limitations are fortunately unknown.[10]

Throughout the European Union product liability law provides for a liability *threshold,*[11] but it remains under discussion whether this is a proper threshold, or rather a deductible.

There may also be partial compensation when the injurer lacks capacity to commit a delict due to his or her age, or mental state. According to both § 829 of the BGB and § 1310 of the ABGB, such persons may be ordered to compensate only part of the damage if this is justified in all the circumstances, in particular considering their financial capacity to bear the loss. No such rule is known to other continental European legal systems, the *Principles of European Tort Law* (PETL), or the *Draft Common Frame of Reference* (DCFR).[12]

A *reduction of damages* is also possible in exceptional cases in which full compensation would be oppressive to the defendant, under rules in Dutch, Norwegian, Polish and Swiss Law, as well as under PETL, Article 10:401 and DCFR, Article VI.-6:202.[13] Under Russian law,[14] courts may, in a rather one-sided manner, decrease compensation in order to take into account the tortfeasor's financial situation, save in cases where the damage was intentional.

According to § 2 of the Austrian Employee's Liability Law (Dienstnehmerhaftpflichtgesetz), a judge can release an employee, who has caused damage to his or her employer, from contractual and tortious liability in whole or in part. In so doing, regard must be had, above all, to the extent of the employee's fault, but also to the extent of his or her responsibility for the activity in question, the risk associated with it, the employee's remuneration and level of education, the conditions under which he or she was employed, and the extent to which experience shows that the damage was a probable, or near-inevitable consequence of the relevant activity. The employee bears no liability at all for *culpa levissima* ('Entschuldbare Fehlleistung' – 'slightest carelessness'). Under German law, legal theory and case law have developed a very similar limitation upon employee liability.[15]

[10] Koziol, *Basic Questions of Tort Law* (n 6) no 7/42 ff. For comparative references, see BA Koch and H Koziol, 'Comparative Conclusions' in BA Koch and H Koziol (eds), *Unification of Tort Law: Strict Liability* (The Hague, Kluwer, 2002) 428 f; Koziol (n 2) no 8/294.

[11] See 85/374/EEC Art 9 b: 'For the purpose of Article 1, 'damage' means: damage to, or destruction of, any item of property other than the defective product itself, with a lower threshold of 500 ECU, provided that the item of property is of a type ordinarily intended for private use or consumption, and was used by the injured person mainly for his own private use or consumption.'

[12] See further the country reports and comparative report in M Martín-Casals (ed), *Children in Tort Law I: Children as Tortfeasors* (Vienna, Verlag Österreich, 2006); N Ferreira, *Fundamental Rights and Private Law in Europe. The Case of Tort and Children* (Oxford, Routledge, 2011) 141 ff.

[13] O Moréteau, in European Group on Tort Law (ed), *Principles of European Tort Law Text and Commentary* (Vienna, Verlag Österreich, 2005) 179 ff; T Finke, *Die Minderung der Schadensersatzpflicht in Europa* (Universitätsdrucke Göttingen, 2006); Koziol, *Basic Questions of Tort Law* (n 6) no 8/24 ff; Koziol (n 2) no 8/317 and 323 with more references.

[14] Civil Code, art 1083(3).

[15] BGH in NJW 1994, 852; NJW 1996, 1532; H Otto, R Schwarze, R Krause, *Die Haftung des Arbeitnehmers*, 3rd edn (Berlin, De Gruyter, 1998) no 25 ff and no 190; B Sandmann, *Die Haftung von Arbeitnehmern, Geschäftsführern und leitenden Angestellten* (Tübingen, Mohr Siebek, 2001) 51 ff.

Last, but not least, is the principle of *contributory responsibility*, which leads to only partial compensation under all European legal systems.[16] One could say that this area lies on the borderline between the 'lone injurer' and 'plurality of injurers' categories: since there are grounds for imputing the damage in such cases to both the victim and the injurer, one could view it as an example of the partial liability of several persons who are responsible for the same harm. It may therefore be of particular importance in solving the problems arising in cases involving a defendant's liability for damage caused by a plurality of events. Regard must nonetheless be had to the specific and distinctive feature that one of the two injurers, the victim, is responsible for causing harm to her- or himself.

B. General Principles

To make coherent sense of all these examples, we must leave aside the damages threshold under product liability law, which seems to derive from the imperfect implementation of a *de minimis* threshold concept[17] and lacks any convincing rationale. The other cases of limited compensation do not really build a coherent, overall system.

Nonetheless, some of the examples demonstrate a basic, general idea: *the weaker the grounds for imputing legal responsibility to the injurer, the less comprehensive the compensation*,[18] although countervailing grounds of responsibility on the side of the victim must also be taken into consideration. The idea that weakness in the grounds for imputation may lead to limited liability was probably also behind the original introduction of caps in the field of strict liability, as this area was, at least formerly, seen as a type of liability based on lesser grounds for imputation.

The basic position is therefore that the injuring party must compensate the victim's entire interest in respect of every degree of fault and every equivalent ground for imputation, subject to the bounds of average adequacy and the protective purpose of the liability rule. On the other hand, weakness in the grounds for imputing responsibility to the injurer may lead to more stringent adequacy (remoteness) and protective purpose requirements and may make it appropriate to require the victim to bear part of the risk of the damage by reducing the injurer's liability in the light of his or her financial, or other, circumstances.

As regards the other examples considered above, the key idea is that, where there are *similar reasons for imputing the harm to both the defendant and the victim*, responsibility must be divided between them. The idea of equal treatment, or

[16] U Magnus and M Martín-Casals (eds), *Unification of Tort Law: Contributory Negligence* (The Hague, Kluwer, 2004); Koziol (n 2) no 8/285 ff. Art 1083(2) of the Russian Civil Code provides that only the victim's gross negligence leads to partial liability.

[17] Koziol, *Basic Questions of Tort Law* (n 6) no 6/20.

[18] Proportionality between liability grounds and the extent of the compensation has been urged several times. See F Bydlinski, *System und Prinzipien des Privatrechts* (Vienna, Verlag Österreich, 1996) 225 ff with additional references, but the legislature has not yet systematically followed up.

mirror image, is influential.[19] This is not only true for the victim's contributory fault or dangerous activity, but also, to some extent, for the rules limiting the liability of employees: the idea being that the special risks of the enterprise fall in the employer's, not the employee's sphere of responsibility.

III. Plurality of Events

A. Preliminary Terminology

Rogers[20] has pointed out that, where damage is caused by the concurrent actions of a number of different tortfeasors, the common law traditionally refers to their 'joint and several liability', but that this terminology has often been criticised as not conveying a very clear message. The language may be misleading, first, because it could wrongly be taken to suggest that all the tortfeasors must be sued together; secondly, because of the possible association with 'joint tortfeasors', who are only a sub-group of those exposed to 'joint and several liability'; and thirdly, because the terminology is wholly alien to most continental European legal systems. He has therefore suggested using the 'civilian' term 'solidary liability' instead. I adopt this suggestion and use that term in contrast to the concept of partial liability, to refer to cases in which each tortfeasor is in principle liable for the full amount of the damage done.

It is also useful – as is usual under German and Austrian law – to distinguish between, on the one hand, several tortfeasors acting *independently* so as to cause the same damage (Nebentäter), and, on the other hand, several tortfeasors who have come to a common decision to perform a wrong and thus have acted *jointly* (Mittäter).[21]

B. Several, Independent Tortfeasors

If several persons, independently of each other, are responsible for a *conditio sine qua non* in respect of the *same damage*, it would not seem far-fetched[22] to assume that liability for specific shares in the damage would be an option – a proposition now

[19] See further Koziol, *Basic Questions of Tort Law* (n 6) no 6/204 ff.

[20] WVH Rogers, 'Comparative Report on Multiple Tortfeasors' in WVH Rogers (ed), *Unification of Tort Law: Multiple Tortfeasors* (The Hague, Kluwer, 2004) 272; cf also B Winiger, 'Comparative Report on Damage Caused by Multiple Tortfeasors' in B Winiger, H Koziol, BA Koch and R Zimmermann (eds), *Digest of European Tort Law I: Essential Cases on Natural Causation* (Vienna, Verlag Österreich, 2007) no 5/29/1.

[21] See Winiger in Winiger et al (n 20) 5/27 ff.

[22] See G Viney, P Jourdain, S Carval, *Les Conditions de la Responsabilité*, 4th edn (Paris, LGDJ, 2013) 359.

accepted under Australian law.[23] The counterargument is that the entire damage is imputable to each of them, as each defendant is the author of a condition necessary for the emergence of the loss, and that it would therefore be wrong to say that one of four defendants is only '25 per cent negligent', or caused only 25 per cent of the loss.[24] Despite this, there are general rules expressly providing that each of several debtors is liable only for a part of the whole debt. In the Netherlands, Article 6:102 of the Burgerlijk Wetbetboek (BW, Dutch Civil Code) hence reads:

> If two or more debtors are obliged to perform, they are obliged in equal shares unless it follows from a statutory provision, common practice, or juridical act, that they are obliged either in unequal shares or jointly and severally.

Further, § 889 of the Austrian Civil Code provides, although only for contractual obligations, that if the debt owed to the creditor can be divided (in particular when it is monetary debt), the debtor is only partly liable.

Nevertheless, there is a widespread view in tort law,[25] even under Dutch law,[26] that solidary and not partial liability applies when several persons are independently responsible for a *conditio sine qua non* in respect of the same damage. Such a departure from the partial liability rule applying in contract law can be convincingly justified in tort law. First of all, if each injuring party is responsible for the entire damage, solidary liability does not result in a disproportionate extra burden for any one of them, but simply means that they do not enjoy the advantage of partial liability. Secondly, partial liability is disadvantageous for the victim if one of the tortfeasors is insolvent – and it is more appropriate that the risk of one tortfeasor's insolvency is borne by other responsible tortfeasors, than by the innocent victim. Thirdly, partial liability would impose an excessive burden on the claimant to identify and pursue each and every author of the harm – this is a particularly heavy burden, when the internal shares of liability are unknown. For these reasons, the European Group on Tort Law was convinced that solidary liability is a more reasonable solution than partial liability in cases involving independent tortfeasors.[27] Article 9:101(1)b of the PETL thus provides that liability is solidary where one person's independent behaviour causes damage to the victim and the same damage is also attributable to another person. In the same way, Article 6:105 of the DCFR provides: 'Where several persons are liable for the same legally relevant damage they are liable solidarily.'[28]

[23] See further ch 11 in this volume: B McDonald, 'Reforming a Reform: Why Has it Been so Hard to Reform Proportionate Liability Reforms?'.

[24] cf Rogers (ed), *Multiple Tortfeasors* (n 20) 274.

[25] See Rogers (ed), *Multiple Tortfeasors* (n 20) 273; Moréteau, 'France' in Koziol (n 2) no 1/119 f and 124; K Ludwichowska-Redo, 'Poland' in Koziol (n 2) no 3/80. See further PETL, Art 9:101(1)(b); DCFR, Art VI.–6:105; G Brüggemeier, *Haftungsrecht: Struktur, Prinzipien, Schutzbereich* (Berlin, Springer, 2006) 187; Winiger, *Multiple Tortfeasors*, in Tichý (n 9) 79.

[26] See W van Boom and I Giesen, 'Netherlands', in Winiger et al (n 20) no 5/9/12.

[27] Rogers (ed), *Multiple Tortfeasors* (n 20) 274 ff; Rogers, 'Multiple Tortfeasors', in European Group on Tort Law (ed), *Principles* (n 13) 143 f.

[28] For policy consideration see C von Bar, *Non-Contractual Liability Arising out of Damage Caused to Another* (Munich, Sellier, 2009) 952.

C. Joint Tortfeasors

The real difficulties – and therefore the disagreements – appear in all legal systems in the context of multiple perpetrators acting in concert.[29] In such instances,[30] the problem is that it is often nearly impossible to prove the extent of each individual's contribution to the harm – it being entirely possible that the other defendants would have carried out the act in any event, without the individual's involvement. As psychological states can seldom be established accurately in retrospect, these cases almost always involve little more than a suspicion of causal contribution.

According to the general rule, solidary liability can only apply if the (often purely psychological) causal contribution of each individual perpetrator can be proven. For this reason, joint perpetrators are subject to only partial liability in French law.[31]

In Hungarian law, however, solidary liability is assumed and claims by a joint perpetrator that the other perpetrators would have carried out the act without his involvement are ignored.[32] The same seems true under the PETL, since Article 9:101 provides (without exception) that liability is solidary where: '(a) a person knowingly participates in, or instigates, or encourages wrongdoing by others which causes damage to the victim'. Article 4:102 of the DCFR likewise rules that 'a person who participates with, instigates or materially assists another in causing legally relevant damage is to be regarded as causing that damage'. There is no mention that proving the contrary is allowed. Thus, potential causation – together with other elements of liability – is sufficient to establish liability.

German and Austrian law also proceed on the basic premise of solidary liability, without requiring proof of causation by each individual.[33] This is based on the notion that the joint nature of the actions allows the assumption that each of those involved – psychologically or otherwise – caused the damage. Further, it has been pointed out that the attenuation of the causation requirement under such systems is compensated for by the fact that an especially serious degree of fault, specifically intention, must be shown.[34] Finally, there is an apparently convincing argument that each of the co-perpetrators acted – in a highly dangerous manner for which he or she may be held responsible – to create a situation in which victim is unable to resolve the casual issue. For these reasons, liability for merely *potential causation* is affirmed. Nonetheless – unlike under Hungarian law – it remains open to each individual involved to prove that his or her contribution was not a *conditio sine qua non* for the occurrence of the damage.

[29] See the country reports in Winiger et al (n 20) ch 5.

[30] See Rogers (ed), *Multiple Tortfeasors* (n 20) 276 ff and the country reports and the comparative report therein. See further the comparative report by Winiger in Winiger et al (n 20) 5/29.

[31] Moréteau, 'France' in Koziol (n 2) no 1/129.

[32] cf A Menyhárd, 'Hungary' in Koziol (n 2) no 4/94.

[33] Koziol, *Basic Questions of Tort Law* (n 6) no 5/73 f.

[34] See F Bydlinski, 'Mittäterschaft im Schadensrecht', *Archiv für die civilistische Praxis* (AcP) 158 (1959/60) 411 f.

In Polish law, this problematic issue has not given rise to any special rule so that, even in the case of joint actions, causation still has to be proven.[35]

D. Alternative Causation

i. Alternative Tortfeasors

A very important category in practice is formed by cases of *alternative causation*. The German Supreme Court[36] describes the problem in such cases clearly:

> Two (or more) persons must have created, in a way that is legally attributable to them, a risk which might have caused the loss. The loss must have been caused by either the one or the other person; or while it is certain that the actions of each of the two persons alone could have caused the loss, the extent to which it was caused by each of them can no longer be established. And finally, it has to be impossible to determine which person actually caused the loss. Each of the potential tortfeasors would then be in a position to exonerate himself by referring to the other potential tortfeasor.

The court underlines the point that the injured person in such cases faces a specific difficulty of proof, and that it would be obviously inequitable to leave him without compensation when he undoubtedly has a valid claim against one or other of the two 'contributors'. Therefore, the court stresses, solidary liability has to be accepted according to § 830(1) of the BGB.

However, this view is not taken in all countries.[37] According to English,[38] Norwegian[39] and Swiss[40] law, liability cannot be established in respect of the two events, because causation can be proven for neither of them, although, even in the common law, as the reader will know, diverging opinions are put forward. In France,[41] it seems that *solidary liability* applies only if the events were caused by perpetrators acting as a group. The Netherlands,[42] Lithuania,[43] Poland,[44]

[35] See Ludwichowska-Redo, 'Poland' in Koziol (n 2) II no 3/80.

[36] Decision from 23 June 1976, BGHZ 67, 14; described and commented on by Zimmermann and Kleinschmidt, 'Germany' in Winiger et al (n 20) no 6a/2/1 ff.

[37] See in more detail the country reports and the comparative report on 'Damage Caused by Less Than All Possible Harmful Events Outside the Victim's Sphere' in Winiger et al (n 20), no 6a. See further the country reports in I Gilead, M Green and BA Koch (eds), *Proportional Liability: Analytical and Comparative Perspectives* (Berlin, de Gruyter, 2013).

[38] K Oliphant, 'England and the Commonwealth' in Koziol (n 2) no 5/106 ff; 'Causal Uncertainty and Proportional Liability in England and Wales' in Gilead et al (n 37) 123.

[39] B Askeland, 'Norway' in Koziol (n 2) no 2/59; 'Causal Uncertainty and Proportional Liability in Norway' in Gilead et al (n 37) 249 ff.

[40] Koziol, *Basic Questions of Tort Law* (n 6) no 5/83; P Widmer and B Winiger, 'Causal Uncertainty and Proportional Liability in Switzerland' in Gilead et al (n 37) 323 ff.

[41] Moréteau, 'France', in Koziol (n 2) no 1/124.

[42] See the cases described and commented on by van Boom and Giesen, 'Netherlands' in Winiger et al (n 20) no 6a/8/1 ff; van Dam (n 8) 1108-2.

[43] S Drukteiniene and L Saltinyte in E Karner and BC Steininger (eds), *European Tort Law. Yearbook 2015* (2016) 359 ff.

[44] Ludwichowska-Redo, 'Poland' in Koziol (n 2) no 3/81 ff; cf further E Bagińska, 'Causal Uncertainty and Proportional Liability in Poland', in' Gilead et al (n 37) 253 ff.

Hungary[45] and Japan,[46] on the other hand, go further, presuming each of the perpetrators to have caused the damage. This means that all the perpetrators are solidarily liable unless one proves that he himself was not causal. The German[47] and Austrian[48] codes, as well as the Chinese Tort Liability Law of the People's Republic of China,[49] provide for solidary liability without exception. Partial liability is rejected by all legal systems. The DCFR also supports the solidary liability solution in respect of all of the alternative perpetrators (Article VI –4:103).

Very interesting for our purposes is the fact that the European Group on Tort Law[50] has proposed a different and – at least in the opinion of the group – more modern rule in Article 3:103(1) of the PETL:

> In case of multiple activities, where each of them alone would have been sufficient to cause the damage, but it remains uncertain which one in fact caused it, each activity is regarded as a cause to the extent corresponding to the likelihood that it may have caused the victim's damage.

This complex problem provides an excellent opportunity to review the different methods of thinking, different ways of arguing and the ways different legal instruments are used under different legal systems.

Let us start with an example which is of no great, practical significance but which is suitable for variation: claimant C, a mountain-climber, is hit and injured by a falling stone. At the same time, another stone flies past, just missing his head. One of these stones fell because of the carelessness of mountain climber A1 and the other because of the carelessness of mountain climber A2; however, it cannot be ascertained which stone was dislodged by which mountain-climber, and which of these hit C.

In 1909, the following case came before the Austrian Supreme Court, the OGH,[51] and it has parallels in other legal systems:[52] hunters A1 and A2 were standing close to each other, both wanted to shoot a partridge and both fired a shot at the same time. They overlooked the fact that their line of fire crossed a pathway. A person walking on this pathway was hit by a pellet. It could not be ascertained whether this came from A1's gun, or A2's gun.

There is a related Hungarian case,[53] in which the claimant and the defendant were classmates in a grammar school. During a break, some of the children began

[45] A Menyhárd, 'Hungary' in Koziol (n 2) no 4/88 and 94.
[46] K Yamamoto, 'Japan' in Koziol (n 2) no 7/351.
[47] German Civil Code, § 830(1) line 2.
[48] Austrian Civil Code, § 1302.
[49] Art 10.
[50] J Spier, 'Causation' in European Group on Tort Law (ed), *Principles* (n 13) 47 ff. See further, based on the principles, Gilead, Green, and Koch, 'General Report. Causal Uncertainty and Proportional Liability: Analytical and Comparative Report' in Gilead et al (n 37) 58 ff and the references to the country reports.
[51] *Juristische Blätter* 1909, 81. A short English description of this and one more such case is given by Koch 'Austria' in Winiger at al (n 20) 6a/3 no 1 ff.
[52] See M Graziadei and D Migliasso, 'Italy' in Winiger et al (n 20) 6a/9 no 12; O Moréteau and C Pellerin-Rugliano, 'France' in Winiger at al (n 20) 6a/6 no 1 ff.
[53] A short English version is published in Winiger et al (n 20) 6a/25 no 1 ff.

to throw screws. One of the screws caused serious injury to the claimant's eye. Two pupils admitted that they had taken part in the throwing and the defendant could not exclude the possibility that the screw which he had thrown was the one that had hurt the claimant.

There are undoubtedly cases in the medical and environmental fields that are of even greater practical significance. In a case decided by the Dutch Hoge Raad in 1997,[54] C's water had been contaminated by either A1, or A2. The Hoge Raad ruled that, whenever a tortfeasor is liable for an act that may have caused the entire damage, he is liable in full, even if other persons have in fact caused (part of) the damage and the injured party cannot prove that the (entire) damage was in fact caused by the tortfeasor.

As already mentioned, A1 and A2 would also always be solidarily liable in these examples under Austrian and German law, provided that both A1 and A2 satisfy all the other prerequisites for liability, aside from causation. On such facts, this would clearly be the case.

Bydlinski[55] sees the foundation for liability under German and Austrian law in such cases as lying in the fact that the victim's entitlement to compensation has been established in principle and it merely cannot be ascertained whose conduct gives rise to his claim. This, he suggests, justifies recognising as sufficient grounds for liability an unlawful, culpable action which is highly dangerous and *potentially causal*. Canaris[56] puts it in following way:

> Since the conduct of the party involved was possibly causal and moreover in fact likely to cause damage, it would constitute undeserved good fortune for him should he be spared liability simply because someone else may have caused the damage.

A further aspect worthy of mention is that both parties' unlawful, culpable conduct has contributed to creating a situation which cannot be clarified.

In accepting that liability attaches to merely *potential causation* on the part of the two alternative perpetrators, a serious exception is accepted to the fundamental rule that the defendant must compensate only such damage as he or she is proven to have caused. This solution can nonetheless be backed up by Wilburg's[57] flexible system. When it comes to establishing liability, Wilburg argues, it is not only the actual factors speaking for liability that are important, but also the degree to which they are present and their total, combined weight. Liability can, therefore, be affirmed even if one factor is absent (or only present to a minor degree), if the

[54] See the case described and commented on by van Boom and Giesen, 'Netherlands' in Winiger et al (n 20) no 6a/8/4. I have simplified the facts of the case by reducing the number of potential tortfeasors from three to two.

[55] F Bydlinski, 'Aktuelle Streitfragen um die alternative Kausalität' in O Sandrock (ed), *Festschrift G Beitzke* (Berlin, de Gruyter, 1979) 3.

[56] K Larenz and C-W Canaris, *Lehrbuch des Schuldrecht II/2: Besonderer Teil*, 13th edn (Munich, Beck, 1994) § 82 II 3b.

[57] Wilburg (n 6); *Die Entwicklung eines beweglichen Systems im bürgerlichen Recht* (Graz, Kienreich, 1950), translated into English by Hausmaninger: Wilburg, *The Development of a Flexible System in the Area of Private Law* (Wien, Manz, 2000). See further Koziol, *Basic Questions of Tort Law* (n 6) no 4/24 ff.

total weight of the other factors is greater than is normally required. In order to determine the extent to which it is necessary to have more, or less, of a particular factor on the facts of any given case, it is essential to have a standard of comparison which serves as a base-line for measuring the extent of the acceptable deviation. This base-line is drawn by the 'basic values' of the legal system.[58] Liability will only exist if the combined weight of all the grounds for liability corresponds to the weight required by the basic values of the law. Basically, the law requires the presence of each of the grounds for liability only in the least degree respectively possible, that is, causation, slight negligence and adequacy to a slight degree.

Since, in cases of alternative causation, only the weak form of potential causation is present,[59] in order for liability to be justified, the other grounds for liability must be present to a greater degree, so that the total weight required according to the basic values is attained. Hence, Bydlinski emphasises that alternative tortfeasors are only liable if the conduct of each of them posed an *acute, concrete risk* in the given situation. In other words, adequacy must be present not only in the usual, very weak, form, but instead to the greatest possible degree. The requirement of acute, concrete risk posed means that events with a low degree of probability for causing damage are ignored.[60] Further, it is preferable that the causal uncertainty be borne by the possible tortfeasors, rather than by the victim: first, because both tortfeasors have acted unlawfully and culpably and, secondly, because they have also caused the uncertainty regarding causation by their specifically dangerous conduct.

It must also be pointed out that a perpetrator who has compensated the victim has a right of recourse against any jointly liable perpetrator, so that – presuming both tortfeasors to be solvent – each of them bears half of the damage. If one of the tortfeasors is insolvent, then the other tortfeasor, and not the victim, must bear this risk in full.

In Switzerland, the solidary liability of alternative tortfeasors is predominantly rejected. A look at the Swiss standpoint is informative in order to demonstrate core questions and misunderstandings.

In demonstrating the imaginary, terrible consequences of affirming liability in the case of alternative causation, the following example is cited:[61] C invited a large number of people to a reception in his house. Something was stolen from a room which was open during the reception. It is established that only guests A1, A2 and A3 entered this room. Swiss lawyers assert that, if liability in the case of alternative causation is accepted, then these three persons will be obliged to pay compensation; and this result is unacceptable. However, this view totally overlooks the fact that, of course, no advocate of liability for alternative causation would

[58] B Schilcher, *Theorie der sozialen Schadensverteilung* (Berlin, DuckerHumblot, 1977) 204.

[59] This is emphasised by Bydlinski, 'Causation as a Legal Phenomenon' in Tichý (n 9) 19.

[60] From this point of view, the question raised by Gilead, Green and Koch in Gilead et al (n 37) 4 f, 12 as to whether regard has to be had to each and every uncertainty must be answered in the negative.

[61] A von Tuhr and H Peter, *Allgemeiner Teil des Schweizerischen Obligationenrechts* I/1, 3rd edn (Zurich, Schulthess Polygraph, 1979) 94.

actually grant the victim compensation in this case. For liability to be justified, it would be necessary for each of the possible perpetrators first to have acted in a manner justifying imputation, that is, unlawfully and *culpably;* and for his or her conduct to have posed a *concrete danger*, in other words, to have been highly adequate for the occurrence of the damage.[62] If these principles are applied to the Swiss horror spectacle, liability is already precluded: it has not been proven that any of guests A1, A2 or A3 was guilty of unlawful and culpable conduct. Nor can it be proven that their respective conduct posed an acute, concrete danger. For instance, if one of the guests entered the room after the item in question had already been stolen by another guest, then his or her conduct simply cannot have posed a danger in relation to the theft.

The opinions presented up to now, which suggest either solidary liability or no liability, are different from the partial liability solution put forward in the PETL. Whether the tortfeasors are solidary liable, or only partially liable, is not usually of great significance, it is true, because a party who is solidarily liable has recourse against other joint tortfeasors, so that each, in end effect, has only to compensate in part. In fact, therefore, the only important, practical question is who is to bear the risk of insolvency: should this be the victim, or the potential tortfeasors?

The European Group on Tort Law opts, in Article 3:103(1) of the PETL, for a liability in proportion to the degree of likelihood, so as to distribute the insolvency risk between the solvent tortfeasors and the claimant. The well-known Swiss scholar Emil Stark[63] has also advocated partial liability. He emphasises that, in cases of alternative causation, liability is without proven causation, so that milder liability consequences are appropriate. A further, weighty argument is that the victim might have had to bear the insolvency risk alone in the event that it had been possible to prove that the insolvent wrongdoer caused the damage: if both A1 and A2 are possible perpetrators and A1 is insolvent, then the victim would not be able to enforce his compensation claim at all, if it turned out that A1 was the tortfeasor. The claimant should not be entirely relieved of this risk where there is uncertainty as to whether it was A1 or A2 who caused the damage, that is, where both are being held liable only on the basis of potential causation.

ii. A Tortious Event and a Non-Tortious 'Coincidence' as Competing Causes

The PETL also proposes a rule for the even more difficult case in which the alternative causes are one tortious event and one non-tortious, chance event: in logical extension of Article 3:103(1), Article 3:106 provides a rule that the potential injuring party must bear only part of the damage.

A variation of the mountain-climber case illustrates the problem. The claimant C, a mountain-climber, is hit and injured by a falling stone. At the same time,

[62] See Koziol, *Haftpflichtrecht* (n 6) no 3/31.
[63] K Oftinger and E Stark, *Schweizerisches Haftpflichtrecht I*, 5th edn (Zurich, Schulthess, 1995) 148.

another stone flies past, just missing his head. One of the stones was caused to fall by the carelessness of mountain-climber A, and the other by a mountain-goat, but it cannot be ascertained which of the two stones struck C and the animal cannot, of course, be held liable.

There are other, more practical examples in the field of medical malpractice. After being discharged from hospital, C falls ill. It cannot be established whether this illness is the result of a proven medical error, or of his equally-demonstrable medical predisposition. Alternatively, consider a case in which it cannot be established whether delay in the treatment of a cancer patient has caused his or her death, but where it is known that the patient's chances of recovery would have been substantially higher, had the treatment been administered without delay.

Where one of two alternative events is non-tortious and thus, in this sense, a 'coincidence,' Bydlinski[64] combines the general approach to solving cases of alternative causation with the basic notion behind § 1304 of the ABGB (§ 254 of the BGB; Article 44(1) of the Swiss OR), according to which damages are apportioned for a victim's contributory responsibility. Here, the fact that the victim must normally bear the risk of coincidental events in his or her own sphere is seen as a form of the victim's own contributory responsibility. This leads Bydlinski to the conclusion that the victim in such cases must be compensated for part of the damage.

A possible objection to Bydlinski's solution is that it places cases involving two, alternative tortious causes and cases involving one possible tortious cause and one coincidence on an equal footing. It may be protested that it is only in the former case that the victim would definitely have an enforceable claim if causation were ascertained, such that he would not be required to bear the loss himself. By contrast, in the latter case, the victim would not be entitled to relief, if it were established that the coincidence was the cause. It is therefore sometimes concluded that the victim in the latter case ought not to be granted a partial claim. This understanding is widespread in many legal systems,[65] which continue to require decisive proof, for example, that a patient's deterioration in health (or death) was caused by a doctor's mistake, before the patient will be entitled to any compensation.

However, there are weighty grounds to favour Bydlinski's partial liability solution. If the solidary liability of alternative tortious perpetrators is justified merely on the basis of their potential causal role, then the same must be true in cases involving one tortious perpetrator and one, coincidental event in respect of which the victim normally bears the risk. If the potential tortfeasor and the victim must jointly bear the consequences of the damage in this instance, then this means – as in cases of contributory responsibility (§ 1304 of the ABGB, § 254 of the BGB, Article 44(1) of the OR) – that the potential tortfeasor should compensate in part.

[64] Bydlinski (n 55) 30 ff; 'Haftungsgrund und Zufall als alternativ mögliche Schadensursachen' in M Enzinger et al (eds), *Festschrift G Frotz* (Vienna, Manz, 1993) 3.

[65] See M Faure, 'Comparative Analysis' in M Faure and H Koziol (eds), *Cases on Medical Malpractice in a Comparative Perspective* (Vienna, Verlag Österreich, 2001) 276 ff.

In 1995, the Austrian Supreme Court (OGH) followed Bydlinski's line of thought and reasoned it out in detail.[66] The case in question dealt with an injury caused at the claimant's birth either by a medical mistake, or by an illness of the mother. It was impossible to establish which of the two circumstances was the real cause. The OGH emphasised that only Bydlinski's doctrine provided a fair solution to the problem:

> One would otherwise be forced either to the view that the victim must lose any entitlement to compensation because of the impossibility of proving which of the two events were in fact causal, or that the tortfeasor must compensate the victim in full regardless of the fact that it has not been established at all that his action caused the injury. Either solution would contravene the fundamental principles of Austrian tort law.

In 2011, the OGH decided a skiing case[67] in the same manner. The claimant fell without third party fault on a skiing slope operated by the defendant. In the course of his fall, he crashed into the pillar of an orientation sign, which was not padded. It could not be ascertained whether the injuries were caused by his fall, or his subsequent crash into the pillar. The court underlined that both events involved a high-risk, concrete danger of causing such injuries and were, if considered separately, highly likely to have caused them. The OGH outlined that, in such cases of alternative causation between an event in the claimant's own sphere and an event triggering liability (the crash into the unpadded pillar), damage should be divided between the claimant and the defendant, analogously to the rule on contributory negligence. It is noteworthy that the OGH stressed that the part to be borne by the claimant would be higher if he acted with contributory negligence than if mere chance weighs in to the detriment of the defendant.

The partial liability solution has met with increasing international approval[68] and – as already mentioned – has been incorporated into the PETL (Article 3:106). The Austrian Draft for a new law of damages[69] also provides for partial liability of the potential tortfeasor; imputing the coincidence to the victim and requiring him or her to bear the corresponding proportion of damage (§ 1294 of the Draft). This solution is also supported by the economic analysis of law.[70] On the other

[66] OGH in *Juristische Blätter* 1996, 181.

[67] 1 Ob 63/11p in K Oliphant and BC Steininger (eds), *European Tort Law Yearbook 2011* (Berlin, de Gruyter, 2012) 51 ff.

[68] AJ Akkermans, *Proportionel aansprakelijkheid bij onzeker causal verband* (Tilburg, Tjeenk Willink, 1997) 70 ff; 'Theorie en praktijk van proportionele aanspraklijkheid' in A Akkermans, M Faure and T Hartlief (eds), *Proportionele aanspraklijkheid*, 2nd edn (Den Haag, Boom Juridische uitgevers, 2000) 85 ff; Th Kadner Graziano, 'The "Loss of a Chance" in European Private Law. "All or nothing" or Partial Compensation in Cases of Uncertainty of Causation' in: Tichý (n 9) 143 ff; Larenz and Canaris, *Schuldrecht II/2* 13th edn § 82 II 3c; Oftinger and Stark (n 63) 152; G Wagner, 'Proportionalhaftung für ärztliche Behandlungsfehler de lege lata' in G Müller, E Osterloh, T Stein, *Festschrift für Günter Hirsch* (Munich, Verlag CH Beck, 2008) 453.

[69] Draft proposal submitted by the working group set up by the Federal Ministry of Justice for a new Austrian law of damages, Preliminary Final Version of June 2007.

[70] M Faure and V Bruggeman, 'Causal Uncertainty and Proportional Liability' in Tichý (n 9) *Causation* 108 ff.

hand, the partial liability solution continues to be rejected vigorously in many countries.[71]

E. The Doctrine of Loss of Chance

Above, I mentioned the case in which it could not be established whether delay in the treatment of a cancer patient had in fact caused his or her death, but where the chances of recovery would have been substantially higher, had the treatment been administered without delay. We discussed this as a problem of alternative causation. However, under French law,[72] such cases are seen from a very different perspective. The doctor can be held liable even though he or she cannot be proven to have caused the illness or death, provided he or she demonstrably caused the loss of a chance of recovery. The claim is thus based not on the *bodily injury* but on the destruction or diminution of the *chance of recovery*.

Similar arguments are made in cases involving lawyers: a lawyer misses the deadline for submitting an appeal; as a consequence the judgment becomes final. It cannot be established whether the appeal would have been successful, had it been filed on time, but there was a substantial chance of success. In a slightly different context, the Belgium Cour de Cassation had to deal with the question whether one can recover for the loss of a chance of a successful job application.[73] The claimant, a member of the police force, was the subject of a disciplinary procedure that was repeatedly delayed by the State. Due to this slowness, he was not in a position to apply for a job as head of the police force. According to him, he would have been able to apply for the job, absent the culpable delay. The Cour de Cassation decided that his loss must be assessed as a function of the lost chance.

Importantly, claimants may also claim for the loss of a chance of profit. In one case, the Austrian OGH[74] had to decide on the compensation payable to a claimant who had wrongfully been denied a licence to trade in foreign currency by the Austrian Central Bank. Assessing the resulting loss of future profit in this case presented substantial difficulties, making an assessment of the chance of profit thus frustrated at the time of the damaging action an attractive approach.

The loss of a chance ('perte d'une chance') doctrine comes from France, but has spread to other countries[75] and has been endorsed in the International Institute for

[71] See Koziol, 'Comparative Report' in Winiger et al (n 20) 6b/29 no 3. Also, parts of the Austrian doctrine oppose the partial liability solution: R Welser, 'Zur solidarischen Schadenshaftung bei ungeklärter Verursachung im deutschen Recht,' *Zeitschrift für Rechtsvergleichung* 1968, 42 ff; R Welser and B Zöchling-Jud, *Bürgerliches Recht II*, 14th edn (Vienna, Manz, 2015) no 1375 ff; M Lukas, 'Anmerkungen zu OGH 1 Ob 2139/96g' *Juristische Blätter* 1997, 395 f.

[72] van Dam (n 8) 1110–1.

[73] 23 October 2015, C. 14.0589.F. = E Karner/BC Steininger (eds), *European Tort Law Yearbook 2015* (Berlin, de Gruyter, 2016) 41 f.

[74] OGH (Supreme Court) in *Österreichisches Bank Archiv* (ÖBA) 1996, 213.

[75] cf Koziol, 'Schadenersatz für verlorene Chancen?' *Zeitschrift des Bernischen Juristenvereins* (ZBJV) 2001, 889; T Kadner Graziano, 'Ersatz für Entgangene Chancen im europäischen und im schweizerischen Recht,' *Haftung und Versicherung* (HAVE) 2008, 63 f; van Dam (n 8)1110. See further the country reports and the comparative report in Winiger et al (n 20) ch 10.

the Unification of Private Law (UNIDROIT) *Principles of International Commercial Contracts*, Art 7.4.3(2) of which provides: 'Compensation may be due for the loss of a chance in proportion to the probability of its occurrence.'

The starting points of the theory of alternative causation and the doctrine of loss of chance are quite different. In contrast to the alternative causation theory, the loss of chance doctrine redefines damage,[76] which leaves the *conditio sine qua non* test fully workable.[77] In cases of personal injury, for example, it is no longer the injury to the victim's health that is at stake, but the loss of a chance to get healed, which has been caused by improper treatment. This is therefore no longer a problem of causation, but a problem of damage. Nonetheless, both theories aim at the same goal, namely avoiding the contrary and arbitrary results that can otherwise flow from 'all-or-nothing' solutions as a result of small factual differences: if claimants can prove causation, they receive full compensation, if they fail to do so, they get nothing at all.

Undoubtedly, the 'perte d'une chance' theory is capable of producing satisfactory outcomes by providing proportionate compensation and avoiding extreme results which turn on very slight differences in the assessment of probability.[78] It is doubtful, however, that it offers an appropriate, systemic solution. The reasons for scepticism can be clearly demonstrated using a sub-problem concerned with the loss of a chance of physical recovery.

A first point is that there are some cases in which the defendant has not destroyed any chance of recovery by his wrongful conduct, and the question is simply whether the defendant brought about the illness, or the claimant was already ill. For example, in the Austrian case mentioned above, the OGH[79] had to decide whether a child's handicap was caused either by a medical error at the time of birth, or by the mother's incurable, pre-existing illness at the time of conception. If the child was already deformed from the time of conception, then there was simply no chance of recovery at the time of birth and the medical error did not in fact destroy any such chance. If, however, the child was healthy up until birth, then the medical error did not just destroy any chance of recovery, it actually caused the injury to the child's health. A similar case has been decided by the French Cour de Cassation,[80] but the court in that instance awarded proportionate damages using the loss of chance analysis, without realising that no chance had been lost because it never, in fact, existed.

In such cases, one is not confronted with the destruction of a chance, but only with the impossibility of clarifying what caused the illness itself. The logic behind the doctrine of 'perte d'une chance' cannot help and the doctrine must admit its

[76] See the country reports in Winiger et al (n 20): Austria (10/3 no 6); Belgium (10/7 no 5); Ireland (10/14 no 5); Scotland (10/13 no 4); Slovenia (10/26 no 3); Italy (10/9 no 4); cf also van Dam (n 8) 1110-4.

[77] Some countries use the loss of chance theory to overcome the problems with establishing a causal link. See England (10/12 no 2) and Ireland (10/14 no 5) in Winiger et al (n 20).

[78] cf Gilead, Green and Koch in Gilead et al (n 37) 39 ff.

[79] OGH in JBl 1996, 181.

[80] 28 January 2010, no 08-21692, Bull I no 19; H Koziol and BC Steininger (eds), *European Tort Law. Yearbook 2010* (Berlin, de Gruyter, 2011) 182 ff.

limitations. Both the above case involving an injury existing at the time of birth and cases in which the doctrine of 'perte d'une chance' is genuinely applicable involve the same, core problem: it is impossible to establish whether the doctor caused the injury, or not. No evaluative criteria are discernible that can persuasively explain why the victim's compensation claim should depend on whether or not the injured party still had a chance of recovery at the time of the doctor's malpractice. In both cases, the real issue is that it is not possible to know how the damage was caused.

A further, decisive problem identified by the German scholar Hans Stoll[81] is that the chance of recovery is not an independent, legally-protected interest that can trigger duties to compensate, when that interest is harmed. Only bodily integrity is comprehensively protected. Thus, interfering with a chance is by no means always unlawful.

The point is that chances of recovery have not, in principle, been seen as independent, legally protected interests. Currently, only bodily integrity, health and life are viewed in this way, not (or not to the same extent) the chance to become healthy, which must be categorised as a purely pecuniary interest attracting lesser protection. The unlawfulness of a perpetrator's conduct can only arise in the field of delicts from the endangerment of the victim's bodily integrity and it must therefore also be the detrimental change of health – and not the loss of a chance – which is decisive in establishing the duty to compensate.[82]

This is not the right moment to discuss in detail all the deficiencies of the loss of chance doctrine.[83] Nevertheless, I would like to mention some reasons why I am not one of its admirers. Basing the claim on the idea of chance of recovery as a compensable interest would, as Stoll[84] has pointed out, lead to a most unfortunate consequence: as such claims do not depend on causing bodily injury, patients would logically be entitled to damages for loss of a chance of recovery even if, in the end, they never suffer any damage to their health. The Israeli Supreme Court has tried to avoid this result, by ruling that liability cannot be imposed unless the medical risk ultimately materialises and physical injury ensues.[85] But this is inconsistent, if the court at the same time insists that it is the lost chance, and not the injury itself, that forms the actionable harm.

The opposite problem is also unsolved, namely, how to prevent a victim seeking compensation for the loss of a chance as well as for the impairment of health which actually occurs. If these really were two, independent legal interests, then a claim for double compensation seems to be unavoidable.

[81] H Stoll, 'Schadensersatz für verlorene Heilungschancen vor englischen Gerichten in rechtsvergleichender Sicht' in E Deutsch et al (eds), *Festschrift Steffen* (Berlin, de Gruyter, 1995) 475 f.

[82] G Mäsch, *Chance und Schaden* (Tübingen, Mohr Siebeck, 2004) 237 ff, 294 ff, takes this into consideration in that he basically only recognises a duty to compensate for destruction of a chance in the field of contractual liability, where he takes the existence of contractual duties to preserve chances as a starting point.

[83] cf Koziol, *Basic Questions of Tort Law* (n 6) no 5/93 ff.

[84] Stoll (n 81) 475 f.

[85] See R Perry, 'Israel' in E Karner and BC Steininger (eds), *European Tort Law Yearbook 2015* (Berlin, de Gruyter, 2016) 687.

In my opinion, these two difficulties very clearly reveal the problem inherent in the loss of chance theory. The value of any pecuniary good depends on the degree of probability with which such a good can be used. The value of a claim, for instance, depends on the probability of its realisation; the value of a thing depends on its prospective useful life. If the chance of the enforceability of the claim, or the long-term use of a thing, is reduced, then the market value of the good itself is diminished. The diminution or destruction of a chance is thus reflected in the objectively calculable reduction in the value of the pecuniary good itself. Hence, the chance of using the pecuniary good cannot be considered an independent asset to be evaluated separately and in addition to it, in the sense that the chance's destruction can be included as a separate loss of value in the pecuniary balance. This would mean the same interest was counted twice, thus leading to a doubling of the damage and the risk of double compensation.[86]

All this speaks very clearly against adopting the loss of chance doctrine. This is all the more so, because there is another, coherent, systemic solution already available to deal with the problem, namely the doctrine of alternative causation, as it applies in cases involving one tortious event and a competing, coincidental, event falling within the victim's sphere of responsibility. The European Group on Tort Law has therefore wisely rejected the doctrine of 'perte d'une chance', and instead aims to solve the problem according to the general rules on liability that apply in the case of potential causation.

F. Alternative Tortfeasors and Alternative Victims[87]

This type of problem can be illustrated via another variation of the alpine example. As in the original case, mountain climbers A1 and A2 each culpably cause a stone to fall. Now assume that one stone injures claimant C1 and the other stone claimant C2, but that it cannot be ascertained which stone hit which claimant.

Cases of great practical relevance can be found here too. A worldwide example is that of the diethylstilboestrol cases ('DES cases'). Several pharmaceutical enterprises produced very similar medicines containing DES. The pills caused an illness that presented only after an incubation period of several years, by which time individual claimants were no longer in a position to identify the manufacturers of the particular medication they had taken. In Europe, a Dutch case decided by the Hoge Raad in 1992[88] has become particularly famous. In the

[86] T Schobel, *Der Ersatz frustrierter Aufwendungen* (Vienna, Verlag Österreich, 2003) 107 ff.

[87] See further T Bodewig, 'Probleme alternativer Kausalität bei Masseschäden,' *Archiv für die civilistische Praxis* (AcP) 185 (1985) 505; J Koch, *Haftungsprobleme bei Produktspätschäden* (Berlin, Centaurus-Verlagsgesellschaft, 1987) 97 ff; T Müller, *Wahrscheinlichkeitshaftung von Alternativtätern* (Peter Lang, 2001); K Otte, *Marktanteilshaftung: Rechtsvergleich und Alternativen im US-amerikanischen und deutschen Recht* (Berlin, Dunker & Humblot, 1990); also the country reports and the comparative report in ch 6d in Winiger et al (n 20) 448 ff.

[88] Described and commented on by van Boom and Giesen, 'Netherlands' in Winiger et al (n 20) no 6a/8/1 ff.

1950s and 60s, a pregnancy-enhancing drug was marketed by a number of pharmaceutical companies, which was later discovered to cause physical harm to both mothers and their daughters. A number of injured daughters claimed compensation from several different manufacturers, without presenting evidence of the precise origin of the tablets that their mothers had taken. The Hoge Raad decided that each manufacturer that had distributed unreasonably unsafe drugs was liable in full, unless it could prove that its act certainly did not cause the damage.

At first glance, the problems here might appear similar to those discussed above under the title of 'alternative tortfeasors'[89] – A1 and A2 are alternative causes of the damage suffered by C1; and the same applies to the damage suffered by C2.

There is indeed a similarity, but this group of cases nonetheless has important, specific features. Each of the two perpetrators has *definitely* caused damage, namely either the injury to C1, or that to C2.[90] For the sake of simplicity, let us assume that the damage to both is equally great, then we know that A1 and A2 have both caused damage and the amount of the damage caused is also known. The uncertainty present in the case of simple, alternative causation – whether A1 or A2 has caused *any* damage – does not arise, as each of the two perpetrators has definitely caused damage to a measurable extent and neither is being made liable when he is not responsible for any damage at all. The only thing that needs to be decided is which damage is to be reckoned against which tortfeasor – that is, who must compensate whom. This is why the additional prerequisites of liability that apply in cases involving potential, alternative perpetrators are unnecessary in this case: it is not necessary for any particular perpetrator concretely to endanger any particular victim in order for the causal relationship between them to be assumed. The fact that the perpetrator can be proven to have caused damage thus mitigates the problem that otherwise exists in alternative causation cases.

On the other hand, one must also take into account the fact that each defendant has injured only one of the claimants, and so definitely cannot be liable for *both* injuries. Making both perpetrators *solidarily* liable for the injuries to *both* victims is hence precluded on all accepted precepts,[91] because it would make them liable for damage which they clearly *did not cause*. Nonetheless, one must take account of the fact that neither perpetrator can be ordered to compensate either specific victim. The case is one of alternative perpetration. The risk of a particular tortfeasor defaulting cannot be imposed on one individual victim alone and the best solution is therefore for both perpetrators to be proportionately liable (in the mountain climbers case both being half liable) to both victims.

The solution described here undoubtedly involves substantial, practical problems when a large number of parties is involved, as in the case of so-called

[89] Section III(D)(i).

[90] For the sake of simplicity, I have assumed that the damage to both is known and equal.

[91] This is emphasised also now by Müller (n 87) 80 f. Nevertheless, like the Dutch Hoge Raad, the French Cour de Cassation has ruled that each of the defendants has to prove that its product did not cause the damage. On the basis of this idea, the defendants are solidarily liable as long as the presumption cannot be rebutted; see van Dam (n 8) 1108-2.

'mass torts'. The best known example is provided by the aforementioned DES cases, where similar, equally damaging medications were offered by several manufacturers to large numbers of consumers. Because victims in such cases are rarely able to prove precisely which manufacturer's medication they took, it is usually impossible to show that any particular manufacturer put any particular victim at a concrete risk, with the consequence that not even the requirements of liability for alternative causation are satisfied. Nonetheless, such cases are special, because, while it cannot be proven that any particular perpetrator has harmed any individual victim, it can collectively be assumed that, in all likelihood, each of the manufacturers has in fact caused damage.[92] In the case of equally dangerous products, it can be assumed that they have all led to equal damage. The proportion of the entire damage caused will, therefore, correspond to the market share of each medication. Uncertainty remains only in relation to which individuals were injured by which individual manufacturers, which it is almost impossible to tell.

In support of the liability of each manufacturer, it can be argued that each one has certainly caused a proportion of the entire damage corresponding to its market share. Liability cannot go beyond this share because it would impose responsibility for damage which the manufacturer certainly did not cause. For the same reason, manufacturers cannot be liable on a solidary basis towards all victims: this would result in each manufacturer being liable for far more damage than it caused. The only viable solution – recognised in Austrian law and under the PETL (Article 3:103(2))[93] – is proportionate liability of the manufacturers towards each victim.

Under this system, each victim is obviously confronted with considerable enforcement difficulties: he or she must sue all potential manufacturers for their respective shares of the damage. That is not only laborious; it is also costly. However, the existing law provides no alternative. It is impossible for each victim to be allotted his full claim against a particular tortfeasor, because this would mean that the risk of non-payment would affect victims unequally: some victims might be left with an insolvent defendant, others with a solvent one. Practical help is at hand, however, when victims organise themselves, or assign their claims to a trustee, who is then able to enforce the collected claims against the individual tortfeasors.

Defining the individual manufacturers' shares is also difficult. If some victims can prove they were damaged by a particular medication, then these victims can seek full compensation from the corresponding manufacturer(s). But this must then be taken into account when defining the manufacturer's share of liability to the other victims. Further, it may be that, in some regions, the products of only certain manufacturers (and not others) were used. This too must be taken into account, as the other manufacturers are clearly not even potentially causally responsible for the damage in these regions. The calculation of the relevant shares is thus very difficult and complex. Finally, one must consider that the calculation of the shares can change over time, for instance if it is proven that the injuries caused by a defendant differ from its market share.

[92] cf Koziol, 'Comparative Report' in Winiger et al (n 20) 6d/29 no 3.

[93] See Spier in European Group on Tort Law, *Principles* (n 13) 49 f; K Graziano, 'Principles of European Tort Law' in Winiger et al (n 20) 6d/28 no 3 ff.

Even if no special procedural measures are made available to assist with such cases, it is certainly still better for the law to take this difficult path than to deprive victims of all compensation. Moreover, some alleviation of the practical difficulties is available in the present day when all the sub-claims are collected together by means of assignment to a single claimant.[94]

G. Cumulative Causation

Cumulative causation comes into play when two real events take effect simultaneously and each of them would have brought about the same damage on its own; that is, each event was a sufficient condition for the damage that occurred and for establishing liability. A well-known example involves A1 and A2 simultaneously inflicting fatal shooting injuries upon C. A more practical illustration involves the simultaneous introduction into a river of toxic wastewater by two companies, killing fish, when either discharge would have been sufficient to kill them on its own.

Although in such cases neither of the two events is a *conditio sine qua non* for the occurrence of the damage[95] (because in each instance the other event would have brought about the same harm anyway[96]) it would be wrong to refuse compensation to the victim just because several events – each of which is sufficient for liability on its own – have happened to coincide.

It is almost universally accepted that cumulatively causal perpetrators are solidarily liable.[97] At first glance, it is perhaps surprising that no one has advocated partial liability instead, as in the case of alternative causation. However, regard must be had to the fact that, in this constellation, *each* of the perpetrators undoubtedly would have caused the entire damage in a manner for which he is accountable. His liability is thus established when the other cause is imagined away. By contrast, in the case of alternative causation, it is clearly not the case that each of the two alternative causes would have caused the damage on its own – it is known that only one of them did, but it is uncertain which.

From this perspective, partial liability is of little to no interest in cases of cumulative causation. However, for those who favour partial liability in cases involving alternative tortious and coincidental (non-tortious) events, partial liability also seems to offer a reasonable solution in cases in which those events are cumulative.[98]

[94] See further J Hager, 'Die Kausalität bei Massenschäden' in A Heldrich (ed), *Festschrift Canaris I* (Munich, Beck, 2007) 413 ff.

[95] See, eg, P Apathy and A Riedler, *Bürgerliches Recht III: Schuldrecht Besonderer Teil*, 5th edn (Vienna, Verlag Österreich, 2015) no 13/61; Koziol, *Haftpflichtrecht* (n 6) no 3/52 ff with additional references. See further J Neethling, 'Element of Causation in South African Law of Delict' and H Koziol, 'Causation under Austrian Law, both in J Spier (ed), *Unification of Tort Law: Causation* (The Hague, Kluwer, 2000) 102 and 20.

[96] Therefore, it does not make much sense to say that each of the actors was 'fully causal.' See E Deutsch and H-J Ahrens (n 4) no 60.

[97] cf Koziol, 'Comparative Report' in Winiger et al (n 20) no 7/29/1 ff.

[98] cf Koziol, *Haftpflichtrecht* (n 6) no 3/57.

H. Superseding Causation

Superseding causation involves two, successive events that bring about the same damage. The first event, Event1, causes real damage, but the same damage would have been brought about anyway by a later event, Event2. For example, claimant C is injured by A1 and loses his capacity to work. Subsequently, he is injured anew by A2 in an accident that would also have caused him to lose his capacity to work. Alternatively, A1 damages C's car and A2 then writes it off shortly afterwards in an unrelated accident.

The problem in such cases is that A1 did not cause the damage according to the necessary condition formula. Both the loss of his earning capacity and the damage to his car after Event2 are losses that would have been sustained later anyway, although in the injury case, A1 is a necessary cause of C's initial injury and of the loss of earning capacity in the period prior to Event2.

In contrast to cases of cumulative causation, the proper solution in cases of superseding causation is hotly disputed.[99] The predominant view is that A1 *in reality caused* the damage in an unlawful manner and should not be exempted from liability just because A2 would subsequently also have brought about same damage; A2's liability is denied as he or she has not caused the damage.[100] The opposite view supports solidary liability.

However, the situation is different in cases involving two successive events, where one is tortious and the other a non-tortious, coincidental event lying in the victim's sphere of risk.[101] Those who advocate partial liability in the corresponding cases of alternative and cumulative causation, also support – for the sake of consistency – partial liability in such cases of superseding causation.[102]

IV. Concluding Remarks

All of the deviations from the all-or-nothing-rule that we looked at in Part III above are connected with uncertainty in respect of causation. The difficult, overarching question seems to be whether partial compensation should be more generally accepted than it currently is, as an alternative to full, or no, compensation. In Part II of the chapter, we saw that, while the principle of full compensation is generally recognised, it is subject to boundaries drawn by the principle of adequacy and the protective purpose of the liability rule, as well as exceptions that take account of a victim's contributory responsibility and make other reductions. There is therefore little doubt that the law already deviates very substantially from

[99] See Koch, 'Comparative Report' in Winiger et al (n 20) no 8a/29/3 ff.
[100] See also PETL, Art 3:104(1).
[101] See Koch, 'Comparative Report' in Winiger et al (n 20) no 8b/29/1 ff.
[102] See F Bydlinski, *Probleme der Schadensverursachung* (Stuttgart, Enke Verlag, 1964) 78 ff, 95 ff; Koziol, *Basic Questions of Tort Law* (n 6) no 5/118. cf also PETL, Art 3:106.

the all-or-nothing principle. The key question is whether partial liability should be extended to further cases of uncertainty, beyond these exceptions and the cases of potential causation mentioned above.

As a matter of general principle, the arguments are about legal certainty, on the one hand, and the need to do justice in the specific case, on the other. Certainty suffers if the extent of recoverable compensation is unforeseeable because it is made to depend on too many, imprecise, discretionary prerequisites. On the other hand, justice in the particular case is compromised when boundaries are drawn so rigidly that minor factual differences result in a claimant obtaining either full compensation of the damage suffered, or no compensation at all. It must be stressed that in such instances, legal certainty is also impaired on account of the difficulty of predicting whether a particular, given fact will lead a court to place a case on one side of the line, or the other. This uncertainty is generally increased by the common law rule on proof,[103] which requires a case to be proven on the balance of probabilities. This makes the outcome of the case depend on whether the inexactly ascertainable probability is found to be 49 per cent or 51 per cent.

Therefore, for those who support partial liability in cases of alternative causation it is an interesting question whether partial liability solutions could reasonably be expanded to cover a much broader area.

Discussion can begin with a question connected with the measure of proof,[104] namely whether it is really reasonable for the common law to make the predominant probability rule govern the decision on liability. The argument that doing away with the rule would cause difficulties in understanding how courts arrive at their decisions is dubious because the rule itself is very much open to manipulation. Apart from that, where the case involves nearly equal probabilities, is a judge's claim to be able to make a clear decision between distinct causes anything more than an insincere pretence? Would it not be more honest and more reasonable to admit the impossibility of deciding clearly between them?

Under Continental European legal systems, the situation is more favourable, as cases turn not on the balance of probabilities rule, but on a judge being convinced. However, the accuracy of the court's level of conviction cannot always be confirmed, as it too is surrounded by a grey zone of uncertainty. Would it not be fairer to stick to partial solutions if the conviction is on a knife-edge?

Despite the various concerns, I think one has to be cautious in concluding that partial solutions have to be acceptable *across the board* if they are accepted in the specific area of uncertain *causation*. In cases of alternative causation, the probability of two events causing damage is on the same (or nearly the same) level and differential treatment of the two events is therefore not possible. There are also other arguments that speak against releasing both, alternative tortfeasors from liability just because causation is uncertain. The claimant needs protection and should receive compensation. A decisive point is that, causation aside, all other

[103] cf van Dam (n 8) 1104; RW Wright, 'Proving Facts: Belief Versus Probability' in H Koziol and BC Steininger (eds), *European Tort Law 2008* (Vienna, Verlag Österreich, 2009) 79 ff.

[104] See Gilead, Green and Koch in Gilead et al (n 37) 20 ff and the country reports.

prerequisites of liability are satisfied in respect of both tortfeasors. Returning to the hunters illustration, if the causal uncertainty is caused by both tortfeasors' faulty and highly dangerous conduct, both should reckon with their responsibility for the damage and would surely consider it a stroke of luck if their liability were negated. Furthermore, the weakness of one liability requirement (causation) is balanced out by the fact that another factor is present to a higher degree. Liability is only imposed when the conduct of each defendant posed a very acute, concrete risk in the given situation; adequacy has to exist to the greatest possible degree. According to the PETL, designed by the European Group on Tort Law, both alternative tortfeasors are partially liable.[105]

A similar argument seems possible where the uncertainty relates to the amount of *damage* a claimant has been caused to suffer. This idea has already been realised in some legal systems insofar as they provide that a court is permitted to estimate a claimant's damage, if it cannot be proven. In calculating the damage, the court can take account of the probability of certain losses eventuating. It would be worth considering providing judges with a discretion to choose a figure midway between the highest and lowest possible amounts of damage that the defendant may have caused (ie, the average).

It is a very different matter, I think, when the uncertainty relates to whether or not a defendant has *violated a duty of care, or is subjectively at fault.* These questions must be resolved by the court one way or the other and the answer can only be 'yes,' or 'no'. To my knowledge, no legal system accepts partial liability corresponding to the probability that the factors for establishing wrongfulness or fault exist. The fact that partial compensation solutions are almost exclusively advocated in the field of causal uncertainty, not in cases involving uncertainty about wrongfulness or fault, is presumably due to the fact that the perpetrators in causation cases at any rate provably carried out a highly dangerous, concrete act and are thus accountable for the lack of clarity as regards causation. However, when it comes to determining breach of duty of care or fault, it is not even clear whether the persons in question are blameworthy at all. For this reason, they cannot be deemed accountable for the lack of clarity in the same way.

On the other hand, different levels of fault and the legal consequences that follow from it have been accepted for centuries. These are graduated, to some extent, corresponding to the gravity of fault and thus to the weight of the argument for attributing liability.

As to *wrongfulness* itself, there is widespread opinion that it cannot be graded. Some nonetheless suggest that even wrongfulness can have different weights.[106] I think this is true, as the violation of a duty of care in respect of the highest ranking interests – the life and health of persons – can be weightier than misbehaviour in respect of a flower in a neighbour's garden. Therefore, there is no reason in principle why legal consequences cannot differ according to the gravity of a defendant's wrongful act.

[105] cf Koziol, *Basic Questions of Tort Law* (n 6) no 5/85.
[106] See Koziol (n 2) no 8/222.

PART II

Originating Doctrines

4

Vicarious Liability: A Pailful of Slops and Other Hazards

WARREN SWAIN

> You'll be thought most improvident,
> A catastrophe-happy fool, if you don't make your will before
> Venturing out to dinner. Each open upper casement
> Along your route at night may prove a death-trap:
> So pray and hope (poor you!) that the local housewives
> Drop nothing worse on your head than a pailful of slops.[1]

In Rome and the other major cities of the Empire much of the population lived in apartment buildings, or *insulae*. The wealthier residents lived close to ground level, with the poor living higher up.[2] Passers-by ran the risk of injury from domestic waste thrown from widows. There was no difficulty in bringing a claim where the thrower could be identified.[3] But the building might be large, and the night might be dark, making it hard for a victim to identify who had done the throwing. The Praetor came up with a solution.[4] The occupier of the premises, whether they were the owner, hirer or a gratuitous resident, became liable for anything thrown or poured from the building. Justinian's *Institutes* elaborates, '[he] is said to be bound *quasi ex maleficio*, for he is not exactly bound *ex maleficio*, as it is generally by the fault of another, a slave, for instance, or a child, that he is bound'.[5]

In common with other ancient legal systems, the Romans regarded delict, which overlapped with much of what modern lawyers call tort, as resting on personal responsibility.[6] Imposing liability on occupiers for things thrown or poured by others is one obvious exception. The fact it was an exception may explain why

[1] P Green (trans), Juvenal, *The Sixteen Satires* (London, Penguin, 1974) 96–97.

[2] G Aldrete, *Daily Life in the Roman City: Rome, Pompeii and Ostia* (London, Greenwood Press, 2004) 78–80.

[3] The proper remedy was an *actio utilis* for personal injury: A Watson et al (trans), *The Digest of Justinian* (Pennsylvania, University of Pennsylvania Press, 1998) D 9.2.13pr.

[4] T Sandars (trans), *The Institutes of Justinian* (London, Longmans, 1948) Inst 4.5.1.

[5] ibid.

[6] D Ibbetson, 'Wrongs and Responsibility in Pre-Roman Law' (2004) 25 *Journal of Legal History* 99.

liability was categorised as a type of quasi-delict, rather than a delict.[7] There are other examples within quasi-delict involving liability for the actions of another. Building occupiers were liable when anything was suspended from the building in a way that it was dangerous and might fall.[8] Closer to what we would now think of as vicarious liability, ship's masters, innkeepers and stable owners were liable for items damaged or stolen by an employee.[9] The final quasi-delict involved a judge who 'makes a case his own'[10] and does not involve liability for another.[11]

Tony Thomas has described other occasions in Roman law where one person is made liable for another as 'the truest instance of vicarious liability'.[12] A *paterfamilias* was liable for family members. An owner was liable for damage caused by his slave or animals. Unlike the quasi-delicts, the focus lay on the causal agent (the family member, slave or animal) who caused the injury, but was not legally responsible. This was reflected by the rule that, if a slave was sold, liability was transferred to the new owner.[13] Liability was noxal, meaning the child, slave or animal could be surrendered to the victim in satisfaction of the claim. Noxal liability for children was described as 'ancient' in the *Institutes* and was apparently obsolete, 'For who could bear to deliver as noxa a son and still more a daughter?'[14]

The imposition of liability for something dangerous suspended over a street resembles a Roman version of health and safety legislation and is in a category by itself. The other situations share common features. They all occur when damage is caused and there is otherwise a high likelihood, or in the case of noxal liability, a certainty, that the victim will go uncompensated. Public policy was also a relevant consideration. Ulpian observes that, 'it is in the public interest that everyone should move about and gather together without fear or danger'.[15] What was lacking was a general principle of vicarious liability. Roman law consisted of a series of single instances, in which one party was liable for another. A convincing or sophisticated justification for this form of liability was missing.

Distinguishing true vicarious liability from primary liability could be troublesome. In the context of a *locatio conductio rei* (a lease):

> If a tenant farmer's stoker-slave drops asleep at the furnace and the house is burned down, Neratius says that the tenant must nevertheless make good the damage in

[7] The precise rationale for the quasi-delicts is still debated: PBH Birks, 'The Problem of Quasi-Delict' (1969) 22 *Current Legal Problems* 164.

[8] Sandars (n 4) Inst 4.5.1.

[9] ibid, Inst 4.5.3; DS Bogen, 'Ignoring History: The Liability of Shipmasters, Innkeepers and Stablekeepers under Roman Law' (1992) 36 *American Journal of Legal History* 326.

[10] Sandars (n 4) Inst 4.5pr.

[11] For a contrary argument that this *is* a form of vicarious liability see: FH Lawson (ed), WW Buckland and A McNair, *Roman Law and Common Law*, 2nd edn (Cambridge, Cambridge University Press, 1952) 396.

[12] JAC Thomas, *Textbook of Roman Law* (Amsterdam, North-Holland Publishing Company, 1976) 381.

[13] Sandars (n 4) Inst 4.9.5.

[14] ibid, Inst 4.8.7.

[15] Watson (n 3) D 9.3.1.1.

> accordance with the agreement in the contract of letting, if he was negligent in choosing his workers.[16]

The farmer was liable because he was at fault in using a somnolent slave. Likewise, but perhaps in an even more half-hearted fashion, there was an attempt to identify fault on the part of an innkeeper or ship-owner in employing someone dishonest who then steals from a guest or passenger.[17] There are parallels here with English law, where tensions about the proper scope of responsibility are a constant theme from the Middle Ages.

I. English Law: Customs of the Realm

English law before the nineteenth century was structured around the forms of action. The actions were named after the writs by which medieval plaintiffs instigated litigation. In tort law, there were two forms of action: trespass, which was the oldest, and trespass on the case.[18] A number of actions of trespass on the case were based on customs of the realm.[19] At a time when buildings were made of timber, fire was an ever-present danger. An action on the case based on a custom of the realm for allowing the escape of a domestic fire was found in the early fifteenth century.[20] In *Beaulieu v Finglam* in 1401, Markham J, explained that:

> A man is bound to answer for his servant's act, as for his lodger's act, in such a case. For if my servant or lodger puts a candle on the wall and the candle falls into the straw and burns the whole house, and also my neighbour's house, in this case I shall answer to my neighbour for the damage which he has suffered.[21]

The house owner was liable for a servant and, perhaps more surprisingly, for a lodger, because of custom. The custom of the realm came to apply to outdoor fires as well.[22] A further custom of the realm ensured that carriers and innkeepers were liable for loss or damage to goods entrusted to their care, even when they were

[16] ibid, D 9.2.27.9; R Zimmerman, *The Law of Obligations* (Oxford, Oxford University Press, 1996) 376–77.

[17] Sandars (n 4) Inst 4.5.3.

[18] For an overview of the actions see, JH Baker, *An Introduction to English Legal History,* 4th edn (London, Butterworths, 2002) 60–64.

[19] There were earlier precedents in some of these situations in trespass writs, see M Arnold (ed), *Select Cases of Trespass from the King's Courts 1307–1399 (vol I),* Vol 100 (London, Selden Society, 1984) lxiv–lxx.

[20] JH Baker, 'Trespass, Case, and the Common Law of Negligence 1500–1700' in E Schrage (ed), *Negligence: The Comparative Legal History of the Law of Torts* (Berlin, Duncker & Humblot, 2001) 47, 60–62.

[21] (1401) YB Pas 2 Hen IV pl. 6, fo. 18 (KB) reproduced in JH Baker, *Baker and Milsom Sources of English Legal History*, 2nd edn (Oxford, Oxford University Press, 2010) 610–11.

[22] See the discussion of *Tuberville v Stamp* (n 51) below.

damaged or stolen by a third party.[23] With the passage of time, this liability came to be subject to exclusion, limitation or straightforward allocation of risk between the parties.[24]

II. Masters and Servants: Commands

Beyond situations falling within customs of the realm, the law was slow to recognise liability for the acts of another.[25] Masters were, however, liable for an act of a servant if they commanded them to act in a way that caused harm. The servant's act was seen as the master's act. The master was liable, but these are not instances of vicarious liability in the way that it is used in the modern law. The servant was merely an extension of the master. This approach was closer to an agency idea. A statute on legal process of 1354 suggests that, within these parameters, the general principle was quite broad. The legislation states that a master would forfeit his goods where the servant's trespass occurred at the command of the master, or in the course of an office given to them by the master.[26] Command was a somewhat ambiguous concept for lawyers. A command can be quite specific and refer to a particular act. It can also be used more broadly, as approval for a more general course of conduct. The term was used by lawyers in both senses.

In *Caunt's Case*,[27] an action on the case for deceit was bought against both a master and his servant for warranting a butt of rumney wine sound, when it was 'unwholesome and unsuitable'.[28] It emerged in the pleading that it was the servant who had sold the wine. Martin J explained that:

> But if your servant, with your collusion and by your command, sells some unwholesome wine, the buyer shall have an action against you; for it is your own sale. If the case is that you did not command your servant to sell the wine to this plaintiff, then you may say that you did not sell it to the plaintiff.

Martin J adopted a narrow definition of command, by suggesting that the servant has to be commanded to sell the wine to the particular plaintiff for the

[23] *The Innkeeper's Case* (1368) in G Sayles (ed), *Select Cases in the Court of King's Bench (vol VI) Edward III*, Vol 82 (London, Selden Society, 1965) 152, 42 Edw III, Lib Ass p 17 (KB) reproduced in Baker (n 21) 603–04.

[24] See, eg, in the context of an innkeeper: *Richard Basse v Anon* (1444) 22 Hen VI pl. 8 fo. 38b-39a (KB).

[25] For broad overviews of the history of the subject see J Wigmore, 'Responsibility for Tortious Acts: Its History. II.' (1894) 7 *Harvard Law Review* 51; D Ibbetson, *A Historical Introduction to the Law of Obligations* (Oxford, Oxford University Press, 1999) 69–70, 181–84.

[26] (1354) 27 Edw III, stat 2 c 19.

[27] (1430) YB Mich 9 Hen VI pl. 37, fo. 53 (KB) reproduced in Baker (n 21) 561–62.

[28] Rumney wine is a Greek sweet wine which was popular in England in the Middle Ages. See E Power, *Medieval People*, 8th edn (London, Methuen, 1946) 123.

master to be liable. Other judges saw command differently. In *Anon*,[29] an action for deceit was brought against a servant for warranting cloth was a certain length, when it was shorter. Choke J said that 'the sale is the master's sale, and the warranty is the servant's act, and so upon this warranty I shall not have an action against the servant'. Bryan CJ agreed. Littleton J, in contrast, accepted that the sale was the master's, but thought that, because it was made by the servant who gave the warranty, the servant should be liable. On the majority view, command was a broad concept. It consisted of the servant selling cloth. Whatever the accepted scope of a command, it might not have been too difficult to find that the master had ratified the servant's act, which, in practice, was just as good as commanding it.[30]

Anon provides one illustration of the difficulties of ensuring the plaintiff brought a claim against the appropriate defendant. An argument of Serjeant Yelverton in 1443 shows that it was safest to declare against both master and servant:

> … if one by my fraud and command take the goods of another person, or beat him by my command, the writ is maintainable against he who did the deed and (against) me, and if he who did the deed die, yet the writ is maintainable against me, because I was party to the trespass.[31]

This reasoning is based on the assumption that both are liable on the particular facts. Often this would not be the case. Judges throughout this period began to work out the scope of the responsibility of masters and servants.

In 1468 Choke J stated that 'in every case where the master does not have power to do a thing, he who does this by his (the master's) command is a trespasser, as well as the master'.[32] It was not entirely clear if the servant could escape their own liability if they acted on a master's command. In *More v Halyngworth*,[33] a servant acting as a bailiff for a sheriff arrested a man under the capias process.[34] A majority held that the bailiff was guilty of false imprisonment when the arrest was illegal because the sheriff had failed to return the writ. Rede CJ, who thought that the bailiff was not at fault, disagreed.[35] When the case came on again after an adjournment, Rede CJ repeated that it was unreasonable to punish the servant. It was, however, different when: 'I command him to do a thing lawfully, and he acts contrary to [my] command, he commits a wrong, to which I did not agree, it is reason to punish him, and to excuse me.'[36]

[29] (1471) YB Trin Edw IV fo. 6, pl. 10 (KB) reproduced in Baker (n 21) 563–65.

[30] *Lampen v Ford* (1320) (KB) in M Arnold (ed), *Select Cases of Trespass from the King's Courts 1307–1399 (vol II)*, Vol 103 (London, Selden Society, 1987) 416.

[31] (1443) YB Pasch 21 Hen VI pl. 6, fo. 39b (KB).

[32] (1468) YB 8 Mich Ed IV pl. 24, fo. 17b–18a (KB).

[33] JH Baker (ed), *Reports of Cases by John Caryll, Part II. 1501–1522*, Vol 116 (London, Selden Society, 1999) 532–33. The same case is slightly differently reported in a year book: (1505) YB 20 Mich Hen VII pl. 23, fo. 13a–13b (KB).

[34] Capias was a form of legal process in which the body of the defendant was seized. See Baker (n 18) 64.

[35] Rede CJ's judgment only appears in the year book report.

[36] (1506) 21 Hen VII pl. 14 fo. 22a–23b (KB). A shorter report appears in Baker (n 33) 548.

Some of the difficulties of applying the traditional command test to more complex transactions can be illustrated by *Southern v How*.[37] The plaintiff was asked by the defendant's factor to sell some jewels to the King of Barbary. These turned out, quite unknown to the plaintiff, to be counterfeits. One of a number of issues was whether the defendant was liable for the factor. During the first hearing, it was argued that,

> … the deceit done to the plaintiff is charged to be done by his servant; and the jury find that the master did not command the servant to conceal them to be counterfeit; and then by his general power to sell, the master shall not be charged if the servant exceed his power.

At a second hearing, the plaintiff argued that, in addition to a command in the form of the defendant's 'direction for the sale', the defendant received the money from the sale and this 'assent subsequent' made him liable. The court found for the defendant. It is difficult to know what to make of this. The decision may turn on the fact that a factor is a type of agent, rather than a straightforward servant. Ultimately, liability was a question for the jury. If the jury had found that the defendant master had commanded the servant to pretend that the jewels were real then he would be liable. A factor was likely to be operating on commission, and therefore more inclined to mislead a buyer about the quality of the jewels, hoping for a greater profit.

One issue has echoes in the modern problem of criminal wrongdoing by an employee. It was said that, if a servant was sent to market to buy or sell, a master would not be liable if the servant beats or kills someone at the market.[38] This reflected a more general principle of absolving the master where the servant did something that wasn't commanded, or went beyond the scope of a master's command.[39] Equally, if a claim was brought against the servant, then they could seek to absolve themselves by pleading that they were acting on the command of the master.[40]

There was friction in the application of the command test as long ago as *Anon* in 1471. It is impossible to know how widespread these difficulties were because liability was ultimately a matter for a jury. Getting a true picture of what had actually happened must have been difficult at a time when the parties were excluded from giving evidence themselves. At the same time, it would be surprising if jury deliberations on this question were not informed by contemporary notions of employment. The relationship between masters and servants was highly regulated,

[37] (1618) 2 Roll Rep 5, Cro Jac 468, Poph 143, Bridgman 125, 81 ER 621, 79 ER 400, 79 ER 1243, 123 ER 1248 (KB).

[38] *Waltham v Mulgar* (1606) Moore 776, 72 ER 899 (KB).

[39] (1498) *Anon* YB Hil 13 Hen VII pl. 10 fo. 15 (KB); *Kingston v Booth* (1685) Skin 228, 90 ER 105 (KB).

[40] (1481) 21 Pasch Edw 4 pl. 10 fo. 5a (KB); (1506) 21 Hen VII pl. 14 fo. 22a-23b (KB); *Miles v Solebay* (1678) 2 Mod 242, 244, 86 ER 1050 (KB).

with duties and obligations on both sides. The body of law, which developed out of the Statute of Labourers[41] and subsequent legislation, reached a level of some complexity by the seventeenth century.[42] The dynamics of the relationship between masters and servants was quite different from the modern one we now associate with an employer and employee. One, very obvious difference is the way that domestic servants were often seen as members of the family unit.[43] In the late seventeenth century the way in which liability was rationalised began to change. The principle of authority emerged alongside command.

III. Masters and Servants: Authority

Once a master's liability for a servant started to be based on authority, rather than command, the law almost imperceptibly moved closer to vicarious liability in the modern sense. It is much more difficult to conceptualise a servant acting within the master's authority as standing in the master's shoes in the same way as one who is commanded to do a thing. Whilst command can be used in a broad or narrow, and more specific sense, authority more naturally refers to a course of conduct. Authority sits on a continuum between command and course of employment which would become popular in the nineteenth century.

Wigmore has suggested that, as a result of the growing complexity of commercial and employment relationships, the established command test was no longer viable.[44] The seventeenth century did witness significant economic expansion and change.[45] There are examples in the period in which commercial need shaped legal development.[46] Proving a link between legal developments and the economy is difficult, and more prosaic explanations may be equally relevant. In common with the Romans, there was an element of practical convenience in the idea that a plaintiff should not be left without a remedy because the loss was caused by a servant. In *Lane v Cotton*,[47] a majority of the King's Bench refused to find the Post-Master General liable on an action in a case when some exchequer bills were

[41] Statute of Labourers (1349) 23 Edw III c 1-8, on which, see WS Holdsworth, *A History of English Law*, vol II, 3rd edn (London, Methuen, 1923) 459–64.

[42] D Hay, 'England, 1562–1875' in D Hay and P Craven (eds), *Masters, Servants and Magistrates in Britain and the Empire, 1562–1955* (Chapel Hill, The University of North Carolina Press, 2004) 59, 62–82.

[43] K Wrightson, *Earthly Necessities* (New Haven, Yale University Press, 2000) 33.

[44] Wigmore (n 25) 392–93.

[45] J Appleby, *Economic Thought and Ideology in Seventeenth-Century England* (Princeton, Princeton University Press, 1978).

[46] W Swain, 'Lawyers, Merchants and the Law of Contract in the Long Eighteenth Century' in D Ibbetson and M Dyson (eds), *Law and Legal Process* (Cambridge, Cambridge University Press, 2013) 186–216.

[47] (1700–1701) 1 Salk 17, 1 Ld Raym 646, Holt 582, Carth 487, 12 Mod 472, 91 ER 17, 91 ER 1332, 90 ER 1222, 90 ER 880, 88 ER 1458 (KB).

lost in the post. Holt CJ's dissent was more revealing. He drew an analogy with cases of carriers and innkeepers:

> And this case is within the same reason with those cases that make men responsible for negligent keeping, viz. that they could not be charged without assigning a particular neglect, they might cheat any man living, and it would not be in his power to prove it … It would be hard in this case to put the plaintiff to prove a particular neglect amongst such a multitude of under-officers; ergo the postmaster is charged with it.[48]

Holt CJ was in a minority, but his judgment shows that some judges were more inclined to impose liability on a master for the acts of a servant than previously. The same judge expressed himself with equal terseness in *Boson v Sandford*,[49] when he remarked, 'whoever employs another is answerable for him, and undertakes for his care to all that make use of him'.[50]

Liability was broadened at this time by asking if the servant acted with the master's authority. *Tuberville v Stamp*[51] concerned the spread of an outdoor fire which was intended to clear stubble. The plaintiff counted against the owner of the land, but it was clear from the evidence that it was his servant who had started the fire, which had then spread. One of the arguments raised by the defendants was that they did not command the servant to light the fire.[52] A majority accepted that there was liability for the spread of an outdoor, as well as indoor, fire. Holt CJ explained why the master was responsible:

> [I]f the defendant's servant kindled the fire in the way of husbandry, and proper for his employment, though he had no express command of his master, yet his master shall be liable to an action for damage done to another by the fire; for it shall be intended that the servant had authority from his master, it being for his master's benefit.[53]

As the same judge explained a couple of years later, 'no master is chargeable with the acts of his servant, but when he acts in the execution of the authority given by his master, and then the act of the servant is the act of the master'.[54] The same formula was used elsewhere.[55] During this period, the terms 'authority' and 'command' are sometimes used interchangeably.[56] Blackstone discussed the nature of the relationship between master and servant in some detail in the mid-eighteenth century. He used the command test in such a way that it had become closer to the idea of authority: 'whatever a servant is permitted to do in the usual course of his business, is equivalent to a general command'.[57] Authority, or what

[48] (1700–1701) 1 Salk 17, 18 (KB).
[49] (1691) 2 Salk 440, 91 ER 382 (KB).
[50] ibid.
[51] (1697) 1 Ld Raym 264, 12 Mod 152, Carth 425, Comb 459, Comyns 32, Holt 9, Skin 681, 91 ER 1072, 88 ER 1228, 90 ER 846, 90 ER 590, 92 ER 944, 90 ER 963, 90 ER 303 (KB).
[52] As reported in (1697) Skin 681.
[53] (1697) 1 Ld Raym 264, 264–65.
[54] *Middleton v Fowler* (1699) 1 Salk 282, 91 ER 247 (KB).
[55] *Jones v Hart* (1699) 2 Salk 441, 91 ER 382 (KB).
[56] *Boucher v Lawson* (1734) Cas T Hard 85, 88 (by counsel for the defendant), 95 ER 53 (KB).
[57] W Blackstone, *Commentaries on the Laws of England, vol I* (Oxford, Clarendon Press, 1765) 418.

Blackstone calls 'general' or 'implied' command, does not express a narrow idea. It goes beyond a simple employment relationship: 'A wife, a friend, a relation, that use to transact business for a man, are quoad hoc his servants; and the principal must answer for their conduct: for the law implies that they act under a general command.'[58]

Blackstone justified the notion of general command on the basis that, otherwise, 'no mutual intercourse between man and man could subsist with any tolerable convenience'. His explanation owes more to contract law than tort law. He argued that a tradesman who deals with a servant needs to be able to trust that the servant is coming with the authority of the master. Similar ideas come through in the case law. At its core was the notion that it is better that a master be liable, than that a victim go without a remedy. This approach was used to justify a different outcome in a case which bears some similarity to *Southern v How*. Once again, a factor had deceitfully represented the quality of some goods. Yet in *Hern v Nichols*,[59] Holt CJ held that the merchant was liable in deceit for his factor: 'for seeing somebody must be a loser by the deceit, it is more reasonable that he that employs and puts confidence in the deceiver should be a loser than a stranger'.

IV. Vicarious Liability, Pleading and the Boundary Between Trespass and Case

From the time that the action of trespass on the case emerged out of trespass, the boundary with the parent action was problematic.[60] Joinder in the same action was prohibited, which made it necessary to determine whether the correct action had been used. Case enjoyed procedural advantages, including the fact that it was cheaper to plead.[61] Another reason is highly relevant. Vicarious claims were not traditionally allowed in trespass.[62] The relaxation of the narrow version of the command test made it easier to bring vicarious claims, which in turn made the proper form of action a more prominent issue in this context.

In *Mitchell v Allestry and Scrivener*[63] in 1676, it was alleged that the plaintiff's wife had been seriously injured by 'two wild untamed mares'. The horses were being broken in to pull a coach in Little Lincolns Inn Fields – a public place. The owner of the coach, Allestry, and the coachman, Scrivener, are both named as defendants. Judgment was given for the plaintiff. The reports are unclear over whether the owner authorised the activity. The report in Keble suggests that the owner is

[58] ibid.

[59] (undated) 1 Salk 289, 91 ER 256 (KB).

[60] *Berden v Burton* (1382) YB 6 Ric II pl. 9 fo. 19 (KB); *Anon* (1390) (KB) in T Plucknett (ed), *Year Books of Richard II. 13 Richard II. 1389–1390* (London, Spottiswoode, Ballantyne Co, 1929) 103.

[61] This was because the pleadings were shorter.

[62] Baker (n 20) 69.

[63] Baker (n 21) 630–33. For a discussion see, Baker (n 20) 68–69.

liable if 'he gave order for it'.[64] Levinz states that it would be presumed that he did order it.[65] On the facts this seems not to matter, because of the allegation that Allestry was present. Yet, the reports show that his presence was a fiction. This pleaders device allows a successful claim in case if either the master or the servant can be shown to have caused the injury, at least assuming that the behaviour of the servant is commanded or authorised. Pleaders were much wiser to bring an action in case. An action of trespass against a master would fail if it turned out that, on the evidence, the injury was caused by a servant.

The development of vicarious liability cannot be divorced from the wider question about the scope of tortious liability. In the eighteenth century the broader debate centred on the correct form of action. Various formulas were used to determine if trespass or case was the right action.[66] By the middle of the century, the dominant test was whether the injury was caused directly or indirectly by the defendant. Where the injury was directly caused, then the proper action was trespass. An injury caused indirectly was properly an action on the case. This seems to have made it problematic to bring a claim against a servant as well as a master. It was certainly not internally consistent in the same action. In *Ogle v Barnes*,[67] two ships collided. The plaintiff brought two counts. The first was against Barnes personally. The second was against Barnes in his capacity as owner alongside the other owners vicariously. It was difficult to argue on the personal count that the injury was not direct: Barnes steered his ship into another vessel. Lord Kenyon avoided the issue; focusing on the fact that the plaintiff alleged negligence. Negligence was equated with non-feasance. The accident occurred because of the failure of Barnes to act, and therefore was treated as indirect. This solution preserved a convenient method of pleading, so long as negligence was alleged, but this tactic was blocked by Lord Ellenborough in 1803.[68] A resolution was finally found in *Williams v Holland*,[69] which meant that, provided the injury was negligently caused, irrespective of whether the injury was direct or indirect, trespass on the case could be used.

By the late eighteenth century vicarious liability was looking increasingly unstable. As long as the servant stood in the place of the master, as the older theory would suggest, it was not difficult to see the master as the person responsible. This attribution of responsibility became problematic. Blackstone's justification for liability has echoes in the idea that an employer is liable for losses that occur through the operation of his enterprise. Judicial perceptions of the boundaries of

[64] (1676) 3 Keb 650, 84 ER 932 (KB).

[65] (1676) 2 Lev 172, 83 ER 504 (KB).

[66] This story is too complex to tell here but for some discussion see: M Prichard, *Scot v Shepherd (1773) and the Emergence of the Tort of Negligence* (London, Selden Society, 1976).

[67] (1799) 8 TR 188, 101 ER 1338 (KB).

[68] *Leame v Bray* (1803) 3 East 593, 102 ER 724 (KB).

[69] (1833) 2 LJ CP (NS) 190 (CP). See, M Prichard, 'Trespass and Case and the Rule in Williams v Holland' [1964] *CLJ* 234.

liability were exposed in some rather unusual authorities. In *Stone and Another v Cartwright*,[70] the plaintiff was a landowner. There was a mine under his land which was run by a steward, who was appointed by Chancery to manage the property for an infant. Workers employed by the steward were negligent and the mine shaft collapsed, and with it the plaintiff's land and buildings. Kenyon CJ explained that the appropriate defendants were either the mine owner, or the workers. The steward 'has no interest in the colliery, nor was it worked for his benefit'.[71]

Taken to its logical conclusion, enterprise liability was potentially very broad as far as an employer was concerned. In *Bush v Steinman*,[72] Rooke J stated that '[h]e who has work going on for his benefit, and on his own premises, must be civilly answerable for the acts of those whom he employs'.[73] A successful claim was brought against the owner of a house when he contracted with a builder, who sub-contracted the work. The sub-contractor purchased some lime, this was left in the road by a servant of the seller and caused the plaintiff's carriage to overturn. The relationship between the house owner and the servant of the lime-seller was extremely tenuous, and yet they found themselves liable. Eyre CJ agreed with his colleagues but he was clearly uneasy about the outcome. As he pointed out, the owner 'appeared to be so far removed from the immediate author of the nuisance, and so far removed even from the person connected with the immediate author'.[74]

V. The Uncertain Scope of Vicarious Liability

The growing body of case law in the decades either side of 1800 did little to introduce much clarity. Several different tests were used, and it is not even clear if these were consistently applied. The law was very fact dependent. As in previous centuries, little thought was given to justifying vicarious liability. Those justifications that did exist were not particularly sophisticated; as Ibbetson has observed, 'vicarious liability became an exceptional situation to be justified (if at all) by unprincipled, and relatively feeble, explanations in terms of the maxims *Respondeat Superior* and *Qui facit per alium facit per se*'.[75]

Savignac v Roome[76] was decided on a narrow point of pleading, but illustrates a number of key themes around the turn of the nineteenth century. An action of case was brought against a master for a servant wilfully driving a coach against

[70] (1795) 6 TR 411, 101 ER 622 (KB).
[71] ibid, 412–13.
[72] (1799) 1 B & P 404, 126 ER 978 (CP).
[73] ibid, 409.
[74] (1799) 1 B & P 404, 406.
[75] Ibbetson (n 25) 182. In addition to the authority cited by Ibbetson, see *Ellis v Turner* (1800) 8 TR 531, 101 ER 1529 (KB).
[76] (1795) 6 TR 125, 101 ER 470 (KB).

the plaintiff's chaise. Espinnase, for the defendant, argued that a master was not liable for the wilful act of a servant unless he commanded it. Bayley, for the plaintiff, submitted that the master was liable if the injury was done during the course of employment. The decision turned on the proper action. It was said that case could not be used. The proper action was trespass. It is not clear why trespass was the correct action. The servant was certainly guilty of trespass, yet earlier actions against a master vicariously were in the action of trespass on the case. It would seem to suggest that the proper action against the master was determined by the proper action against the servant. If so, then we are back to a world when the servant stands in the place of the master. Other contemporary authority stands closer to enterprise liability than agency.

On one level, a decision like this is about the proper form of declaration. On another, it touches on something more fundamental: where the responsibility of a master ends. Despite *Savignac v Roome*, some judges were uneasy about making a master liable for the trespass of a servant.[77] In *McManus v Crickett*,[78] Lord Kenyon confirmed that a master was not liable for a wilful trespass of a servant, unless it was committed at the express command of the master. By the 1820s this had become a rule that an action of trespass, whether wilful or not, could not be brought against a master unless he commanded it.[79] Authorities in the 1840s made clear that a master was not liable in trespass unless he ordered the servant to commit a trespass, irrespective of whether or not the servant was acting in the course of his employment.[80] Following the Common Law Procedure Act 1852, the pleading rules were relaxed and joinder of trespass and case in the same action became possible. This must have ameliorated many of the difficulties of pleading.[81]

The law remained uncertain in its application. Despite the survival of the idea of command in the context of a master's liability in trespass, judges increasingly referred to the servant having authority. There was no ambiguity in the statement of Lord Kenyon in *Laugher v Pointer* that: 'I admit of the principle, that a man is answerable for the conduct of his servants in matters done by them in the exercise of the authority that he has given them.'[82] By the mid-nineteenth century, the authority test was superseded in turn by a scope of employment test.[83] 'Command', 'authority' and 'scope of employment' can be viewed as concepts on a continuum. Command is the narrowest idea, but once it goes beyond an express command for a particular act it is closer to authority. Authority is broader than command.

[77] *Morley v Gaisford* (1795) 2 H Bla 442, 126 ER 639 (CP).

[78] (1800) 1 East 106, 102 ER 43 (KB).

[79] *Gregory v Piper* (1829) 9 B & C 591, 109 ER 220 (KB).

[80] *Gordon v Rolt* (1849) 4 Exch 365, 154 ER 1253 (EXCH); *Sharrod v London and North Western Railway Co* (1849) 4 Exch 581, 154 ER 1345 (EXCH).

[81] J Willes and H Keating (eds), JW Smith, *A Selection of Leading Case on Various Branches of the Law, vol I*, 4th edn (London, William Maxwell, 1856) 351.

[82] (1826) 5 B & C 547, 577, 108 ER 204 (KB).

[83] For an early example see: *Nicholson v Mouncey* (1812) 15 East 384, 392, 104 ER 890 (KB).

Authority can be given without being commanded, but also overlaps with acting in the scope of employment. The final formula, which in modern times is termed 'course of employment', sits a little more easily with the idea of enterprise liability, than acting within authority.

The absence of a principled and coherent doctrine of vicarious liability was not an accident. It reflects the way in which the scope of responsibility was attuned to contemporary perceptions of the employment relationship. In earlier times, issues of social class and public policy were largely hidden behind the decisions of juries. These issues were now closer to the surface because of the way that litigation structured. By the middle of the nineteenth century, the boundary between law and fact was firming up. This was an aspect of the long decline of the civil jury.[84] Questions of law were for judges. Questions of fact were for juries. Vicarious liability sits within this wider change in contract and tort litigation.[85] Terms like 'master', 'servant' and 'scope of employment' were legally defined. The application of the definitions was still a jury question.[86] The same process happened elsewhere within tort. It was seen in the way that judges, who developed the tort of negligence using duties of care, started to determine whether the defendant's behaviour fell within the definition of breach.[87]

More insight can be gained by looking at the application of the doctrine, than by attempts to articulate its purpose. In a discussion of agency, the American writer Joseph Story wrote that *respondeat superior* was founded on 'public policy and convenience'.[88] The English writer Charles Smith expressed himself with some brevity:

> A master is ordinarily liable to answer in a civil suit for the tortious or wrongful acts of his servant, if those acts are done in the course of his employment in his master's service: the maxims applicable to such cases being, *Respondeat superior*, and … *Qui facit per alium facit per se*.[89]

Smith notes that a master is responsible for his servants acting in the course of employment, even when they are neither commanded, nor acting with the authority of the master.[90] The application of the law was less straightforward. As Smith himself freely admitted: 'Upon this subject nice questions often arise as to how far the servant was acting in his master's service at the time the injury was

[84] M Lobban, 'The Strange Life of the English Civil Jury, 1837–1914' in J Cairns and G McLeod (eds), *The Dearest Birth Right of the People of England* (Oxford, Hart Publishing, 2002) 173–209.

[85] D Ibbetson, 'The Tort of Negligence of the Common Law in the Nineteenth and Twentieth Centuries' in Schrage (ed) (n 20) 229, 240–41; W Swain, *The Law of Contract 1670–1870* (Cambridge, Cambridge University Press, 2015) 23–29.

[86] Though if there was insufficient evidence a judge could withdraw the question: *Whatman v Pearson* (1868) LR 3 CP 422 (CP).

[87] *Bridges v North London Railway Co* (1871) LR 6 QB 377 (EXCH); *Metropolitan Railway Co v Jackson* (1877) 3 App Cas 193 (HL).

[88] J Story, *Commentaries on the Law of Agency* (Boston, Little and Brown, 1839) 465 §452.

[89] C Smith, *A Treatise on the Law of Master and Servant* (London, S Sweet, 1852) 151.

[90] ibid, 152.

done: though the law is clear, it is sometimes difficult of application to particular cases.'[91]

Vicarious liability formed part of a much larger work, of just over 600 pages, in which Smith discusses all aspects of the master and servant relationship. This gives some indication of the complexity of the master/servant relationship by the mid-nineteenth century. The way the law responded to the employment relationship was constantly evolving.[92] By the 1830s, judges had become less inclined towards protecting the position of servants at the expense of the master.[93] Vicarious liability was a quite discrete body of law, but it would be surprising if the law developed in isolation. Attempts to define the scope of vicarious liability had never been easy. This didn't change. Difficulties in the application of the course of employment test reflected a broader unease about the proper scope of vicarious liability.

VI. Servants Acting in the Course of Employment

A general statement on the scope of vicarious liability in the mid-nineteenth century was provided by Willes J in *Barwick v English Joint Stock Bank*:[94]

> The master is answerable for every such wrong of the servant or agent as is committed in the course of the service and for the master's benefit, though no express command or privity of the master be proved.

Whether or not the person committing a wrong was a servant of the defendant was a more difficult question. The outcome would turn on whether or not the employer exercised control. The distinction is neatly illustrated by an example given by Baron Bramwell, speaking extra-judicially, and quoted by Sir Frederick Pollock in his leading treatise, in the context of a contract to build a wall, in which the builder has a right to say to the employer, 'I will agree to do it, but I shall do it after my own fashion; I shall begin the wall at this end, and not at the other'; there the relation of master and servant does not exist, and the employer is not liable.[95]

The reality was messier. Ibbetson has suggested that this was because the definition of servant 'owed more to notions of social class than hard legal analysis'.[96] He contrasts the case of a common labourer, paid five shillings to clear a drain,

[91] Smith (n 89) 157.

[92] For a study over centuries see S Deakin, 'The Contract of Employment: A Study in Legal Evolution' available at: https://www.cbr.cam.ac.uk/fileadmin/user_upload/centre-for-business-research/downloads/working-papers/wp203.pdf.

[93] Hay (n 42) 115.

[94] (1867) LR 2 Ex 259, 265 (EXCH).

[95] F Pollock, *The Law of Torts: a Treatise on the Principles of Obligations arising from Civil Wrongs in the Common Law* (London, Stevens and Son, 1887) 69.

[96] Ibbetson (n 25)182.

who fell within the definition of a servant, with a surveyor, paid a salary of £250 a year, who did not.[97]

The control test was sometimes difficult to reconcile on its own terms. Pollock gave the example of hiring a coach and coachman, where the hirer is not liable if someone is injured by the coachman's negligent driving.[98] It is otherwise, he suggests, where the hirer authorises the specific act of careless driving.[99] Pollock was clearly uneasy about this outcome. He notes that 'rather slight evidence of personal interference' by the hirer was sufficient to render him vicariously liable.[100] It is difficult to see how the coachman is under the control of a hirer. Were he asked to drive recklessly by his passenger, he was at liberty to refuse. Liability here can only rest on some vaguer idea that the hirer is responsible for failing to stop a coachman from driving recklessly, or alternatively it reflects some broad notion of enterprise liability.

The sort of scenario described by Pollock caused judges some difficulties as well. In *Laugher v Pointer*,[101] the defendant owned a carriage and hired a pair of horses for the day to draw it along with a coachman from a stable-keeper. The carriage was driven negligently and injured the plaintiff. Abbott CJ and Littledale J held that the defendant wasn't liable. Holroyd and Bayley JJs disagreed. Littledale J pointed out that the relationship between the defendant and the driver was not one like that between master and servant. Crucially, the defendant could not dismiss the coachman.[102] Were the defendant to be liable, Littledale J observes that every time someone was hired for 'benefit or pleasure,' the hirer would be liable.[103] This is a clear rejection of a broad notion of enterprise liability. Bayley J, who reached the opposite conclusion, stressed that, '[t]he service is performed for me. It is my work that the driver does'.[104] Borrowed servants continue to cause the law problems[105] but it is usually not too difficult to sever the link between a hired employee and his usual employer. For example, a sailor who works for a stevedore under his orders and who is paid by him is more obviously a servant of the stevedore than of the ship owner for whom he habitually works.[106]

By the middle of the nineteenth century a line had been drawn around independent contractors. In *Reedie v The London and North Western Railway Company; Hobbit v The London and North Western Railway Company*,[107] the plaintiffs

[97] *Sadler v Henlock* (1855) 4 El & Bl 570 (labourer), 119 ER 209 (QB); *Knight v Fox* (1850) 5 Ex 721 (surveyor), 155 ER 316 (EXCH).
[98] Pollock (n 95) 70–71.
[99] ibid.
[100] Pollock (n 95) 71.
[101] (1826) 5 B& C 547, 108 ER 204 (KB).
[102] ibid, 555.
[103] ibid, 555.
[104] ibid, 570.
[105] *Mersey Docks and Harbour Board v Coggins and Griffith (Liverpool) Ltd* [1947] AC 1 (HL).
[106] *Murray v Currie* (1870) LR 6 CP 24 (CP).
[107] (1849) 4 Ex 244, 154 ER 1201 (EXCH).

were killed after a bridge that was negligently constructed by the servants of the defendant's contractor collapsed on them. Despite a term in the contract giving the defendant's power to dismiss employees of the contractor, it was held that they were not vicariously liable. *Bush v Steinman* was expressly doubted.[108] The same conclusion could be reached in cases of hired coachmen. As Baron Parke explained, 'the servant is the servant of another, and his act the act of another'.[109]

Whilst independent contractors were squeezed out of vicarious liability, they could be accommodated elsewhere.[110] It was sometimes possible to treat the employer as jointly liable with the independent contractor;[111] some duties were non-delegable and, '[i]f such a duty was cast upon the defendant he could not get rid of responsibility by delegating the performance of it to a third person'.[112] *Rylands v Fletcher*[113] was the most striking example of using an alternative legal doctrine to ensure that an employer was liable for an independent contractor. The decision is usually seen as inventing a rule that there was strict liability for the escape of a dangerous thing brought onto land. Another aspect of the reasoning is usually overlooked.[114] It was negligence by independent contractors that caused the neighbouring mine to be flooded by the reservoir. In finding the defendant liable, this was the imposition of vicarious liability under a different name.[115]

The law relating to employees, rather than independent contractors, was less troublesome, but still caused some vexation when an employee went beyond their permitted role. Nineteenth century judges began to describe a servant acting outside the course of his employment as on 'a frolic of his own'.[116] Whether or not the servant was on a frolic was determined by a jury as a question of fact against the backdrop of a legal definition of course of employment. There was a series of authorities on this question. As Pollock observed, '[d]istinctions are suggested by some of the reported cases which are almost too fine to be acceptable'.[117] *Limpus v The London General Omnibus Company*[118] arose out of a dispute between two rival bus companies. It was alleged at trial that the driver of one of the company's buses ran into the other company's bus. The incident was a result of a 'system

[108] (1849) 4 Ex 244, 256.

[109] *Quarman v Burnett* (1840) 6 M & W 499, 509, 151 ER 509 (EXCH).

[110] For further details see Ibbetson (n 25) 183.

[111] *Ellis v Sheffield Gas Consumers Co* (1853) 2 El & Bl 767, 118 ER 955 (QB).

[112] *Hughes v Percival* (1883) 8 App Cas 443, 446 (Lord Blackburn) (HL).

[113] (1865) 3 H & C 774, (1866) LR 1 Exch 265 (EXCH), (1868) LR 3 HL 330, 159 ER 737 (HL). For a discussion of the decision in context, see AW Brian Simpson, *Leading Cases in the Common Law* (Oxford, Oxford University Press, 1995) 195–226.

[114] The cases even began as one in straight forward negligence see Simpson, ibid, 212–16.

[115] J Salmond, *The Law of Torts: a Treatise on the English Law of Liability for Civil Injuries*, 2nd edn (London, Stevens and Haynes, 1910) 206.

[116] *Croft v Alison* (1821) 4 B & Ald 590, 106 ER 1052 (KB); *Huzzey v Field* (1835) 4 C M & R 432, 150 ER 186 (EXCH); *Joel v Morison* (1834) 6 C & P 501, 172 ER 1338 (NP); *Mitchell v Crassweller* (1853) 13 CB 237, 138 ER 1189 (CP).

[117] Pollock (n 95) 74.

[118] (1861) 2 F & F 640,175 ER 1221 (NP); (1862) 1 H & C 526, 158 ER 993 (EXCH).

of unfair opposition' by means of 'unfair following, dodging, crossing and the like'.[119] Baron Martin directed the jury that, if the act of the driver was wilful, then they should find for the defendants. If it was merely reckless, then the defendants were vicariously liable. The case went on error to the Exchequer Chamber, which was divided. The question before them was whether the direction to the jury was correct, but, in the process of defining the scope of 'course of employment', the court was forced to contemplate the nature of vicarious liability. A majority, who thought that the employer should be liable, stressed that the employee was 'acting for the master's' benefit, and not for any purpose of his own'.[120] It was also said that it was important to ensure that those injured by a negligent bus driver did not go uncompensated.[121] Blackburn J had no difficulty in accepting that wilful behaviour did not absolve the employer of liability, if the employee was acting in the course of employment.[122] Wrightman J, who disagreed, adopted quite a different approach. He looked instead to the employee's core task, which made it relatively easy to conclude that, '[t]he defendants' coachman was not employed to obstruct or hinder the plaintiff's omnibus, nor was it in the course of his service, in the proper sense, to do so'.[123]

Limpus v The London General Omnibus Company, and other decisions during this period, do not suggest that judges were particularly anxious to allow employers to escape liability on the grounds that their employees were on 'a frolic of their own'.[124] When, in *Seymour v Greenwood*,[125] a bus conductor used unwarranted force and violence to remove a passenger who was seriously injured, the employer was liable for those injuries. In the hearing before the Exchequer there was still reference to command in the judgment of Pollock CB.[126] Martin B preferred to utilise course of employment, whilst conceding that not everything done in the course of employment rendered an employer liable.[127] At the beginning of the twentieth century, the case law was reduced to an influential formula by John Salmond:

> A master is not responsible for a wrongful act done by a servant unless it is done in the course of his employment. It is deemed to be so done if it is either (a) a wrongful act authorised by the master, or (b) a wrongful and unauthorised mode of doing some act authorised by the master.[128]

Unfortunately, the reality was less neat, and vicarious liability continued to defy easy rationalisation.

[119] (1861) 2 F & F 640, 641.
[120] (1862) 1 H & C 526, 537 (Williams J) 541 (Byles J).
[121] ibid, 539 (Willes J).
[122] ibid, 541.
[123] ibid, 537–38.
[124] *Whatman v Pearson* (1868) LR 3 CP 422 (CP); *Story v Ashton* (1869) LR 4 QB 476 (QB); *Bayley v Manchester, Sheffield and Lincolnshire Railway Company* (1872) LR 7 CP 415 (CP); (1873) LR 8 CP 148 (EXCH).
[125] (1861) 7 H & N 355, 158 ER 511 (EXCHCH).
[126] (1861) 6 H & N 359, 364, 158 ER 148 (EXCH).
[127] ibid, 365.
[128] Salmond (n 115) 85.

VII. Vicarious Liability in a Welfare State

A basic definition of vicarious liability could be given with some degree of confidence by the end of the nineteenth century. In his work aimed at a general readership, Edward Spike wrote that, 'it may now be taken as a general rule that a master is liable for an act of misfeasance by a servant of his in the ordinary course of employment'.[129] To this general rule there was one major limitation. Often but incorrectly attributed to *Priestley v Fowler*,[130] the doctrine of 'common employment' prevented an employee bringing a claim against an employer for an injury caused to him by another employee.[131] One reason for limiting employer liability was the changing nature of the employment relationship.[132] Whilst the implications of this rule were serious for those involved, they were not quite as far reaching after 1880, with the rise of statutory liability for workplace injury.[133] The doctrine of 'common employment' lingered on, but exceptions were created. An employer might be liable to an employee for the tort of breach of statutory duty,[134] or because it had failed to provide a safe system of work.[135] The actual 'common employment' doctrine remained in place until 1948.[136]

The 'common employment' doctrine was not the only survivor of an earlier time. The case law in the twentieth century continued to reflect ideas of social class. Doctors were particularly problematic. It is quite difficult to argue that a hospital exercised control over those who are expected to exercise professional skill. In *Hillyer v St Bartholomew's Hospital*,[137] Farwell LJ made the point that:

> They are all professional men, employed by the defendants to exercise their profession to the best of their abilities according to their own discretion; but in exercising it they are in no way under orders or bound to obey the directions of the defendants.[138]

[129] C Bromby (ed), E Spike, *The Law of Master and Servant*, 3rd edn (London, Shaw and Sons, 1872) 31.

[130] (1837) 3 M & W 1, 150 ER 1030 (EXCH). See Simpson (n 113) 100–34.

[131] *Hutchinson v York, Newcastle and Berwick Railway* (1850) 5 Ex 343, 155 ER 150 (EXCH).

[132] E Atkinson, 'Out of the Household: Master and Servant Relations and Employer Liability law' (2013) 25 *Yale Journal of Law & the Humanities* 205.

[133] In the Employers' Liability Act 1880 see: P Bartrip and S Burman, *The Wounded Soldiers of Industry* (Oxford, Oxford University Press, 1983) 126–57; S Deakin, 'Tort Law and Workmen's Compensation Legislation: Complementary or Competing Models?' in TT Arvind and J Steele (eds), *Tort Law and the Legislature* (Oxford, Hart Publishing, 2013) 253–67.

[134] For a discussion of the rule and exceptions see, P Mitchell, *A History of Tort Law 1900–1950* (Cambridge, Cambridge University Press, 2015) 209–40.

[135] This was a form of non-delegable duty: *Wilson & Clyde Coal Co v English* [1938] AC 57 (HL).

[136] Law Reform (Personal Injuries) Act 1948, s 1.

[137] [1909] 2 KB 802 (CA). This decision was followed in *Strangways-Lesmere v Clayton* [1936] 2 KB 11 (KB); *Marshall v Lindsey County Council* [1935] 1 KB 516 (CA). Scottish law was similar: *Lavelle v Glasgow Royal Infirmary* (1932) SLT 179 (CS).

[138] ibid, 824.

By the early 1940s, judges had begun to express a growing dissatisfaction with *Hillyer*, and hospitals were held vicariously liable for a radiographer[139] and a junior house surgeon.[140] Two Court of Appeal decisions, *Cassidy v Ministry of Health*[141] and *Roe v Ministry of Health*,[142] confirmed that *Hillyer* should be distinguished on the narrow ground that, on the facts in that case, the patient employed the surgeon. Denning LJ went further:

> when hospital authorities undertake to treat a patient, and themselves select and appoint and employ the professional men and women who are to give the treatment, then they are responsible for the negligence of those persons in failing to give proper treatment, no matter whether they are doctors, surgeons, nurses, or anyone else.[143]

This was a particularly bold attempt to impose primary, rather than vicarious, liability on the hospital. In this, Denning LJ was in a minority, but his view reflected a larger shift in the way that liability came to be perceived. The term servant was antiquated by the 1950s and fell out of use. The control test was also out of step with modern employment practices.[144]

The control test wasn't the only way in which the older law fitted awkwardly with modern realities. Post 1945, English tort law was dominated by a compensation model. This was reflected in the expansionist approach towards new types of duty, but also more generally. Vicarious liability was no exception,[145] despite the fact that compensation as a rationale for tort law is highly simplistic.[146] The effect of these changes was leavened to a degree by the acceptance that an employer which finds itself vicariously liable might claim an indemnity from an employee.[147]

In the last decade or so the debate about vicarious liability has come to be dominated by a series of decisions in which an employer has been held liable for sexual abuse carried out by an employee. These cases are not easy. The obvious sympathy felt for the victims in these instances meets the reality that the perpetrator will not be in a position to pay compensation. In *Lister v Hesley Hall*,[148] a warden of a boys' school employed by the defendants had abused boys in his care. The wrong was intentional. The established course of employment test was

[139] *Gold v Essex County Council* [1942] 2 KB 293 (CA).
[140] *Collins v Hertfordshire County Council* [1947] 1 KB 598 (KB).
[141] [1951] 2 KB 343 (CA).
[142] [1954] 2 QB 66 (CA).
[143] [1951] 2 KB 343, 362.
[144] O Kahn-Freund, 'Servants and Independent Contractors' (1951) 14 *MLR* 504, 505–6; P Giliker, *Vicarious Liability in Tort: A Comparative Perspective* (Cambridge, Cambridge University Press, 2010) 69–73; P Morgan, 'Recasting Vicarious Liability' [2012] 71 *CLJ* 615.
[145] PS Atiyah, *The Damages Lottery* (Oxford, Hart Publishing, 2000) 74–78.
[146] J Murphy, 'Juridical Foundations of Common Law Non-Delegable Duties' in J Neyers, E Chamberlain and S Pitel (eds), *Emerging Issues in Tort law* (Oxford, Hart Publishing, 2007) 369, 371–72.
[147] *Lister v Romford Ice and Cold Storage Co Ltd* [1957] AC 555 (HL). There are much earlier traces of this rule, see JA Jolowizc, 'The Right to Indemnity between Master and Servant' [1956] 14 *CLJ* 101, 103.
[148] [2002] 1 AC 215 (HL).

described as 'simplistic' by Lord Steyn'.[149] Sexual abuse could not be described as a wrongful and unauthorised way of undertaking an authorised act. Instead, the House of Lords held that a court needed to ask whether the wrong was 'so closely connected with his employment that it would be fair and just to hold the employers vicariously liable'.[150] On the facts, the sexual abuse was 'inextricably interwoven' with the duties of the warden.[151] This conclusion was made possible by characterising the duty of the employer as caring for the boys – a task that they entrusted to their employee.[152]

Lord Millett suggested that there was a time when there was no vicarious liability for deliberate wrongdoing by an employee.[153] Certainly the law has always struggled with wilful acts. The debate about the availability of trespass in the nineteenth century is just one example. In the Second Dialogue of St German's *Doctor and Student* in 1530, it was said that a master was not liable for a felony or murder committed by a servant, unless it was done at his command.[154] As late as 1905 an employer was held to not be vicarious liable for a theft of bailed goods committed by a servant.[155] Irrespective of whether the act was criminal, it was sometimes suggested that a wilful act by a servant precludes vicarious liability.[156] There are contrary examples from medieval innkeepers, who were liable for thefts by employees to the defendant in *Savignac v Roome*.[157] Any doubts that an employee could be liable for a wilful act, even a criminal one, had evaporated by the early twentieth century.[158]

VIII. Vicarious Liability: A Return to Enterprise Liability?

There are examples across the Commonwealth of factual situations very like the one in *Lister v Hesley Hall*. These are highly atypical examples of vicarious liability involving criminal acts by an employee.[159] It may be even doubted whether liability is best characterised as vicarious at all. As Stevens points out, there are passages in the speeches which are more consistent with liability founded on a

[149] ibid, 227.
[150] ibid, 230 (Lord Steyn).
[151] ibid.
[152] ibid, 229–30 (Lord Steyn) 237 (Lord Clyde), 241–42 (Lord Hobhouse), 250 (Lord Millett).
[153] ibid, 245.
[154] T Plucknett and JL Barton (eds), *St German's Doctor and Student* (London, Selden Society, 1974) 269.
[155] *Cheshire v Bailey* [1905] 1 KB 237 (CA).
[156] *Croft v Alison* (1821) 4 B & Ald 590, 592, 106 ER 1052 (KB).
[157] (1795) 6 TR 125.
[158] *Lloyd v Grace, Smith & Co* [1912] AC 716 (HL); *Morris v CW Martin & Sons Ltd* [1966] 1 QB 716 (CA).
[159] *Bazley v Curry* [1999] 2 SCR 534 (SCC); *Jacobi v Griffiths* [1999] 2 SCR 570 (SCC); *EDG v Hammer* [2003] 2 SCR 459 (SCC); *New South Wales v Lepore* (2003) 212 CLR 511 (HCA).

non-delegable duty.[160] This is a form of primary liability. The defendant had assumed responsibility to look after the pupils, and, having done so, could not discharge itself of responsibility by delegating the care of the children to an employee. Liability is based on assumption of responsibility and, once assumed, it cannot be given away. Non-delegable duties were traditionally a residual category with an important role in filling in gaps in the law. The category was, for example, used to impose liability on an employer for injuries caused by an independent contractor carrying out particularly hazardous activities.[161] The utilisation of a non-delegable duty is still open to the objection that it merely frames the same problem in different terms.[162] It remains necessary to determine when a duty will be deemed to be non-delegable, and the scope of the duty.[163] The use of a non-delegable duty recently proved attractive to the Supreme Court in *Woodland v Swimming Teachers Association and others*.[164] On the facts, it provided a solution to the problem of independent contractors, albeit at the expense of the traditional ideas of risk allocation and understanding of the relationship between contract and tort.[165] Whether, in cases like *Lister v Hesley Hall*, judges will actually go beyond the rhetoric of non-delegable duty and fully embrace the concept remains to be seen. Lord Sumption did add a note of caution when he said that: '[t]he main problem about this area of the law is to prevent the exception from eating up the rule. Non-delegable duties of care are inconsistent with the fault-based principle on which the law of negligence is based, and are therefore exceptional'.[166] In *Prince Alfred College Incorporated v ADC*,[167] the High Court of Australia rejected an attempt to deploy non-delegable duties in this sort of situation. Because the objections were framed in formal terms relating to the way the claim was pleaded, firm conclusions cannot be drawn on the substantive merits of actions of this sort.[168]

Another explanation for cases like *Lister v Hesley Hall* does not depend on a non-delegable duty. There is a long history of justifying vicarious liability using the notion of enterprise liability. There are slightly different versions of this theory which do not fit easily with every factual situation.[169] A workable version is found in Lord Millett's speech in *Lister v Hesley Hall*:

> If the employer's objectives cannot be achieved without a serious risk of the employee committing the kind of wrong which he has in fact committed, the employer ought to

[160] R Stevens, *Torts and Rights* (Oxford, Oxford University Press, 2007) 272–73. The same point was made by Gummow and Hayne JJ in *New South Wales v Lepore* (2003) 212 CLR 511, 584.

[161] *Honeywill & Stein Ltd v Larkin Brothers (London's Commercial Photographers) Ltd* [1934] 1 KB 191 (CA).

[162] For a discussion of the rationale for non-delegable duties, see Murphy (n 146).

[163] For an example of these issues see, *Armes v Nottinghamshire County Council* [2016] QB 739 (QB).

[164] [2014] AC 537 (SC).

[165] J Morgan, 'Liability for Independent Contractors in Contract and Tort: Duties to Ensure that Care is Taken' [2015] 74 *CLJ* 109.

[166] [2014] AC 537, 582–83.

[167] [2016] HCA 37.

[168] ibid [36].

[169] For a discussion of some of the weaknesses of this explanation of vicarious liability see: J Neyers, 'A Theory of Vicarious Liability' (2005) 43 *Alberta Law Review* 287, 297–300.

> be liable. The fact that his employment gave the employee the opportunity to commit the kind of wrong is not enough to make the employer liable.[170]

The idea of enterprise liability has waxed and waned over the centuries. It fell out of favour in the nineteenth century, but it may be fashionable once more. *Lister v Hesley Hall* can certainly be explained in this way.[171] In *Various Claimants v Catholic Child Welfare Society and others*,[172] Lord Phillips, with whom the rest of the Supreme Court agreed, was quite explicit in the way that he drew on the idea of enterprise liability:

> Starting with the Canadian authorities a common theme can be traced through most of the cases to which I have referred. Vicarious liability is imposed where a defendant, whose relationship with the abuser put it in a position to use the abuser to carry on its business or to further its own interests, has done so in a manner which has created or significantly enhanced the risk that the victim or victims would suffer the relevant abuse.[173]

The same sort of analysis was used in *Cox v Ministry of Justice*[174] in order to justify imposing vicarious liability on the prison service when an employee was injured by a prisoner. It made no difference, according to Lord Reed, that the defendant did not seek to make a profit.[175] It was enough that '[t]heir (the prisoners') activities form part of the operation of the prison, and are of direct and immediate benefit to the prison service itself'.[176]

In *Mohamud v WM Morrison Supermarkets plc*,[177] Lord Dyson observed that '[t]o search for certainty and precision in vicarious liability is to undertake a quest for a chimaera'.[178] Lord Toulson referred extensively to a series of decisions of Holt CJ already mentioned. The seventeenth century was described as a period in which vicarious liability 'began to be broadened'.[179] Vicarious liability seems to be going through a similar phase at the moment. History shows that this has all happened before. As on earlier occasions, it is to be hoped that a period of retrenchment, or at least fuller elucidation, will follow.

[170] [2002] 1 AC 215, 244.
[171] D Brodie, 'Enterprise Liability: Justifying Vicarious Liability' (2007) 27 *Oxford Journal of Legal Studies* 493.
[172] [2013] 2 AC 1 (SC).
[173] ibid, 26.
[174] [2016] AC 660 (SC).
[175] ibid, 674.
[176] ibid.
[177] [2016] AC 677 (SC).
[178] ibid, 695.
[179] ibid, 684.

5

Accessories, Joint or Independent Liability and Apportionment

JOACHIM DIETRICH*

I. Introduction

Accessory liability arises where a party is involved in another's wrongdoing – the primary wrong – while possessing a sufficient mental state to be held legally culpable. That culpability justifies the accessory (A) being held liable to the claimant (C), alongside the primary wrongdoer (PW), to remedy the consequences of the primary wrong. There does not exist, however, a single unified cause of action, or even approach to, accessory liability in private law. Accessory liability is given effect by multiple doctrines and through different tests and elements of liability. It is often described by different nomenclature.

These observations notwithstanding, it is possible to discern an organising principle or analytical framework that provides guidance in understanding and applying the specific rules of accessorial liability. In *Accessories in Private Law*,[1] Pauline Ridge and I advocate an analytical framework that can be applied to all accessory liability problems; but the specific content of the accessory liability rules themselves currently do, and in some cases, *should*, differ as between different areas of law. The specific rules of accessory liability therefore continue to operate in their specific contexts.[2] The absence of a uniform law of accessories, however, means that there is uncertainty and inconsistency as to what, precisely, the consequences are of

* I thank Pauline Ridge and Iain Field for their helpful comments on earlier drafts of this chapter; any remaining errors are my own.

[1] J Dietrich and P Ridge, *Accessories in Private Law* (Cambridge, Cambridge University Press, 2015).

[2] We therefore concluded that accessory liability is not a single, liability-determining principle or cause of action and ought not to operate as such. Paul S Davies, *Accessory Liability*, (Oxford, Hart, 2015), by way of contrast, advocates an approach whereby the elements of accessory liability are uniformly interpreted and applied to all private law wrongs. Davies therefore supports the call that there should be 'one law on the civil liability of accessories': ibid, 9, citing PBH Birks, 'Civil Wrongs: A New World' in *Butterworth Lectures 1990–91* (London, Butterworths, 1992) 100. For scepticism about such an assimilation of the different rules, see, eg, S Baughen, 'Accessory liability at common law and in equity – "The redundancy of knowing assistance" revisited' [2007] *Lloyd's Maritime and Commercial Law Quarterly* 545; and Lee Pey Woan, 'Accessory liability in tort and equity' (2015) 27 *Singapore Academy of Law Journal* 853.

finding a party liable as an accessory. After briefly considering how accessory liability arises in private law, this chapter focuses on three aspects going to the nature of that liability. First, how do we characterise the respective obligations of the primary wrongdoer, and accessory, to remedy the wrong committed and the relationship between the two? Related to this is the further issue of what remedies are available against the accessory and against the primary wrongdoer, and whether these may differ. Lastly, how is liability for those remedies apportioned as between accessory and primary wrongdoer in the different areas?[3]

I consider these issues by reference to three accessory liability doctrines: joint tortfeasance arising from accessorial involvement in another's tort; the tort of inducing breach of contract, which is the law's mechanism for imposing accessory liability for breaches of contract; and equitable accessory liability for breaches of trust or fiduciary duty. The focus is on Australian and English law, which I will assume to be similar, unless specific differences are spelt out.

Many cases are concerned with claimants who seek compensation for their loss. Where this loss alone is at issue, the liability of A and PW is generally solidary ('joint and several'), both parties being liable for the full loss. This is so, perhaps self-evidently, where A and PW are liable as joint tortfeasors for PW's primary wrong, but it is also the case in respect of (independently wrongful) equitable accessory liability. Matters are not always so straightforward, however. This chapter discusses and explains the following complexities. First, in the context of parties who are 'joint tortfeasors', where A and PW are culpable to different degrees, damages may be assessed differently as between the different tortfeasors: one party's conduct may attract exemplary or aggravated damages. Secondly, it is not certain whether liability in *tort* for inducing breach of contract to compensate for losses is solidary with that of the primary *contract* breaker. Some courts and commentators assume that this is so, but the correctness of this assumption has not been analysed. To the extent that the parties are liable for the same damages, however, contribution ought to be available as between the inducing party and the contract-breaker. Thirdly, where parties' *gains* are at issue (in equity), liability is not generally joint and several. Instead, the liability to account for profits is generally measured by the individual's respective gains, although legitimate exceptions arise in the context of parties acting through corporate alter egos, or where merged conduct or identities are at stake.

Where several parties are liable for the same loss, it is necessary to consider how apportionment operates in differing accessorial contexts. For the sake of clarity, I use the term contribution to refer to the *right* of a defendant (D1) to seek to hold another defendant (D2) responsible for the liabilities of D1. In contrast, I use 'apportionment' to refer to the process by which a court then determines the

[3] We do not consider the effect of releases and covenants not to sue on the rights of parties to seek contribution. On these, see Dietrich and Ridge (n 1) [5.6.2] (tort) and [8.6.2] (equity); and the extensive discussion of the issue in the context of equitable liability in A Gurr, 'Accessory Liability and Contribution, Release and Apportionment' (2010) 34 *Melbourne University Law Review* 481, 502–11.

respective share of each defendant's responsibility, should such right to contribution exist. In other words, D1 may seek contribution from D2 and, if contribution is available, the court will *apportion* responsibility as between D1 and D2.

Where contribution is available, this chapter briefly considers how a 'just and equitable' apportionment might be determined as between accessory and primary wrongdoer. Finally, I consider briefly whether proportionate liability under statutory schemes can ever apply in the context of accessory liability.

First, however, it is necessary briefly to outline how accessory liability comes about.

II. The Framework of Accessory Liability

An accessory is wrongfully involved in another's wrong. In *Accessories in Private Law*, Pauline and I argue that there are three key elements of accessory liability as it manifests in private law, namely:

(1) a primary wrong committed by a person other than the accessory;
(2) involvement, through conduct, by the accessory in that wrong; and,
(3) a requisite mental state, generally established by reference to the accessory's knowledge of the primary wrongdoer's wrong.

These three elements form the analytical framework of accessory liability in private law. Although our construction of the framework is largely (and designedly) a descriptive exercise, in some areas of private law, where the elements of our framework are not necessarily adverted to by the courts, those elements are nonetheless relevant. As such, our framework has a further, explicitly normative function in that it may assist in explaining and understanding the law in a conceptually coherent way.

One of the challenges to identifying accessory liability is that the law takes two, seemingly distinct, approaches in formulating or characterising an accessory's liability. In its first form, an accessory is considered jointly liable for PW's *primary* wrong, *as if* A is also a primary wrongdoer for that same wrong.[4] Accessory liability as a joint tortfeasor for PW's tort is an example (probably the only example). But although A is liable in this context for the same wrong as has been committed by PW, such liability is still based on A's distinct conduct. Importantly, whereas PW's liability depends on proof of the elements of the primary wrong, A's liability is determined by proof of very different facts and a different set of (accessorial) elements – namely, in general terms, knowing involvement in PW's wrong. As will be seen, however, the fact that A is liable for PW's primary wrong does not mean that the *measure* of the remedy awarded against A need be identical to that awarded against PW and this is further evidence that A and PW may be differently implicated (morally) in the effects of PW's wrong.

[4] This has also been described as 'direct' liability': see Baughen (n 2).

In other cases, accessory liability takes the form of an independent and distinct wrong.[5] Examples include equitable accessory liability and the tort of inducing breach of contract.[6] Despite being described as independent wrongs – the accessory is not treated as a contract breaker or fiduciary, for example – these causes of action are forms of accessory liability. Liability is parasitic, or derivative, upon a primary wrong being committed by another party. Further, the conduct that renders A liable must be accessorial in nature: that is, A must be knowingly involved in the commission of PW's primary wrong to create a participation link to that primary wrong. It follows that different remedies to those available against PW are, logically, potentially available against A.[7]

Irrespective of the 'form' that accessory liability takes, however, our analytical framework is equally applicable and relevant.[8] Importantly, irrespective of the form of liability, that liability is not duplicative. In other words, A's liability and PW's liability need not be identical and the remedy awarded against A need not mirror precisely the remedy awarded against PW. The remedies awarded against either party ought separately to reflect each wrongdoer's respective culpability, or the respective consequences of their wrongdoing (such as, for example, whether one party alone has made a gain). As will be discussed below, the law, in general, accepts that position, even where A is liable for the same wrong as PW.

III. Accessory Liability in Tort Law

A. The Basis of Liability

There are two main grounds for accessory liability in tort law: (1) common design, and (2) procurement.[9] The elements that are needed in order to establish a common design were restated by the United Kingdom Supreme Court in *Sea Shepherd*

[5] This has been described as 'indirect' or 'secondary' liability by, eg, Baughen (n 2). The label 'secondary' liability is best avoided, however, because it has multiple meanings and is not used consistently in different contexts.

[6] On inducing breach, see *OBG v Allen* [2007] UKHL 21; [2008] 1 AC 1 and *Zhu v Treasurer (NSW)* [2004] HCA 56; (2004) 218 CLR 530 [121]–[122]. On equitable accessory liability, see *Michael Wilson & Partners Ltd v Nicholls* [2011] HCA 48; (2011) 244 CLR 427 [106].

[7] See, eg, *Michael Wilson* (n 6) [106]. Indeed, a converse process of reasoning may be at work: because different remedies may or do apply, A's liability is described as distinct.

[8] Although the form of liability does not determine liability or dictate remedy in any principled way, there may be practically different consequences depending on the form of liability. One consequence is that where accessory liability takes the form of an independent wrong, then a party may be held to be an accessory to that independent wrong; in effect, an accessory to the accessory. See, eg, *Multinail Australia Pty Ltd v Pryda (Aust) Pty Ltd* [2002] QSC 105 (director liable for company's tort of inducing breach of contract). Where liability is not independent, however, an accessory would only be liable for her own involvement in the primary wrong, and not for her involvement in another accessory's conduct.

[9] There is also at least one other basis for accessory liability, namely authorisation. Little attempt has been made in tort law, however, to explain 'authorisation', although that concept has been the subject

UK v Fish & Fish Ltd.[10] For liability on that basis to arise, a party must, first, 'have assisted the commission of an act by the primary tortfeasor'; secondly, that party must have done so 'pursuant to a common design [with that person] that the act be committed; and, thirdly, the act must constitute a tort as against the claimant'.[11] To satisfy the first, conduct, element, a party must have taken some more-than-*de-minimis* or minimal steps[12] in furtherance of the commission of the tort;[13] agreement alone does not suffice.[14] There must also be a mental element (agreeing to a 'common end'). This is in part established by what A knew, that is, liability generally requires some knowledge by A of PW's acts, or intended acts, that constitute a tort.[15] Importantly, English courts have accepted that the common design need not be express and can arise even in the absence of a prior agreement.[16]

The appellant in *Sea Shepherd* had given financial and other support to the primary wrongdoer, an activist environmental organisation. Problematically, the Supreme Court agreed with the Court of Appeal that the appellant was party to a common design and that it had sufficient knowledge of the intention of the primary wrongdoer to commit the specific types of torts in the circumstances that arose. It is not clear, however, on what basis the Supreme Court inferred that a common design existed. Although this was not the focus of the judgments, as the claim failed for other reasons, Lord Toulson considered that 'the acts were done in pursuit of a campaign of which the appellant approved with knowledge that the campaign involved a preparedness … to use violent intervention.'[17]

By identifying a requirement of both a conduct and mental element, *Sea Shepherd* goes some way – consistently with our framework – to giving content to the notion of a common design. However, the case (like earlier authorities), did not identify more precisely what further element(s) – whether knowledge or conduct – must be satisfied to establish the 'common design' itself, in the absence of an

of definition and more judicial analysis in the context of the statutory tort of authorising intellectual property infringement. See further, Dietrich and Ridge (n 1) [9.2].

[10] [2015] UKSC 10; [2015] AC 1229 ('*Sea Shepherd*'). I am assuming that these principles also reflect Australian law, but there are few Australian cases on point.

[11] ibid [55] Lord Neuberger; [37] Lord Sumption; compare the two elements of Lord Toulson [21], merging the second and third elements. See also *The Koursk* [1924] P 140 (CA), 156 and 155 (Scrutton LJ) and 159 (Sargent LJ).

[12] See *Sea Shepherd* (n 10) [57] Lord Neuberger ('substantial' assistance); [49] Lord Sumption ('material' assistance), but both define these negatively as more than minimal or trivial.

[13] *Unilever Plc v Gillette (UK) Ltd* [1989] RPC 583, 609. The accessory need not have 'joined in doing the very act constituting the tort': *Sea Shepherd* (n 10) [38] Lord Sumption (dissenting on the facts).

[14] *Unilever Plc v Chefaro Proprietaries Ltd* [1995] 1 All ER 587; [1994] FSR 135.

[15] *Sea Shepherd* (n 10) [65]–[66], Lord Neuberger suggesting that knowledge of PW's intention to commit, or the inevitably of PW committing, the tortious acts, as necessary for a common design.

[16] Potentially, therefore, even quite minor acts of assistance by A that further PW's wrong, may be used to infer 'tacit' 'common designs'. See Mustill LJ in *Unilever* (n 13) 609. *Sea Shepherd* (n 10) is itself an example. See, eg, *Shah v Gale* [2005] EWHC 1087 (QB), where the finding that A was implicated in a 'common design' has been described as perhaps based on very 'thin' evidence (*Sea Shepherd* ibid [38] Lord Sumption).

[17] *Sea Shepherd* (n 10) [27]. See also *Fish & Fish Ltd v Sea Shepherd UK* [2013] EWCA Civ 544; [2013] 1 WLR 3700 [59]–[69]. In short, apart from 'approval', nothing further than the appellant's *knowing* assistance is identified as sustaining the common design.

express agreement.[18] Our framework does not dictate those further element(s), but it does require that they be explicitly identified (or else discarded).[19]

The second basis for imposing accessorial liability is that of procurement or inducement of an act that is a wrong. Outside the law on inducing breach of contract, there has been little attempt in the cases to define procuring (or inducing), or to explain what, precisely, needs to be proved: whether there has been procurement is essentially a question of fact. The language of 'procurement' identifies conduct that clearly constitutes a sufficient involvement in PW's tort, namely some positive acts aimed at bringing about PW's wrongful acts. It also implicitly suggests a sufficient mental state, as the accessory will have actual knowledge of the intended consequences of that conduct.[20] Few cases of procuring liability have been successfully established in tort.[21]

B. The Remedial Consequences of Liability

In *Dougherty v Chandler*, Jordan CJ stated:

> If a number of persons jointly participate in the commission of a tort, each is responsible, jointly with each and all of the others, and also severally, for the whole amount of the damage caused by the tort irrespective of the extent of his participation.[22]

As a general rule, the plaintiff can sue all or some of the joint tortfeasors: each is liable for the full damage caused.[23] (This assumes that proportionate liability does not apply, as to which see further below). This means the defendant may be liable for all damage done by a group, even where he is only one of many tortfeasors.[24] The reasons for this appear to be twofold. First, since the liability has historically been described as joint, the parties are liable for the *one* wrong; that must, of necessity, mean that each is liable for all the consequences of that wrong.[25] Secondly, and

[18] One suggestion is that an *intention* that PW commit the wrong is what is required by 'common design': see, eg, *Sea Shepherd* (n 10) [41], [44] (Lord Sumption). This is not overly helpful. It may well be an accurate conclusion in many cases that A 'intended' that PW commit the wrong. But this is not always so – A may be indifferent as to how a desired outcome is achieved, whether by PW committing a wrong or not – and even where accurate, can generally only be inferred by judging A's conduct considering what A knew. Compare also Lee (n 2) 863.

[19] The requirement of a common design may in fact be superfluous.

[20] Compare the statement that A 'intends and procures and shares a common design that infringement shall take place' in *CBS Songs Ltd v Amstrad Consumer Electronics plc* [1988] 1 AC 1013, 1058, though this statement does conflate procuring with common design.

[21] See, however, *Twentieth Century Fox Film Corporation v Newzbin Ltd* [2010] EWHC 608; [2010] ECC 13, in which an internet search engine provider was held liable as a joint tortfeasor, both as a procurer and based on common design, for multiple infringements from which it profited considerably.

[22] (1946) 46 SR (NSW) 370, 375.

[23] See, eg, *Mitchell v Tarbutt and Others* (1794) 5 TR 649; 101 ER 362.

[24] See, eg, *Hume v Oldacre* (1816) 1 Starke 351; 171 ER 494.

[25] Joint and several liability is not limited, however, to parties who are liable for the same wrong; it extends to several concurrent tortfeasors who are merely responsible for the same damage, albeit this is the result of statutory rules.

perhaps more importantly, one or other item of damage that flows from the wrong (or forms part of the wrong) will in most cases be indivisible (such as a broken arm); it is simply not possible to separate out different consequences of specific acts or contributions to the wrong.[26]

In any case, since A's conduct need only be a contributing cause to PW's decision or capacity to commit the wrong, there does not need to exist any direct causal link to the damage suffered by the claimant. This does not mean, of course, that once joint liability arises, a court is not required to apportion *as between the* parties; it merely means that the court must allocate responsibility, not that the damage is divisible.[27] Nor does it mean that the remedial response as against each wrongdoer needs to be the same: that response may include consideration of the conduct of each party.

Liability for the full damage arises even where different parties committed *distinct* torts as part of the common endeavour.[28] However, even where distinct damage is linked to distinct acts, there are good reasons to give the claimant the benefit of full compensation[29] and to throw the risk of an inability to spread the liability on to all the wrongdoers.

This might suggest that A's and PW's liabilities duplicate or mirror each other – that is, each is always fully liable for the identical consequences and, therefore, damages – and earlier cases did not distinguish between parties' liabilities for 'aggregate' injury suffered from the conduct of the combined parties,[30] even where one party did 'greater wrong' than the other.[31] This remains the case where strictly compensation is at issue. However, more recent Australian decisions have held otherwise in relation to aggravated and exemplary damages.

In *XL Petroleum (NSW) Pty Ltd v Caltex Oil (Australia) Pty Ltd*,[32] the High Court of Australia had to consider the availability of exemplary damages against one of two joint tortfeasors. The claimant (the appellant, XL) intended to commence business as a discount petrol station and had acquired the right to occupy land that

[26] Even where it is possible to attribute to one party a particular interference, tort law treats all parties as responsible for each of those individual (indivisible) interferences. And see also below n 28.

[27] I would therefore reject any argument that each party should only be responsible for so much of the damage as he or she 'caused', since that question would in any case be impossible to answer in most cases. Contrast Davies (n 2) 257, arguing for such a position in the context of equitable accessory liability. The point is discussed further below, Part VI.

[28] Even in an example such as the case of *Smithson v Garth* (1691) 3 Lev 323, 324; 83 ER 711, 712, where each party does distinct acts that constitute distinct torts (one committed battery, another imprisoned the plaintiff and the third 'took the [silver] buttons'), such that each party could be said to be responsible for a distinct wrong, the individual consequences of each wrong are still indivisible. Therefore, once the law holds, say, all three responsible for the battery, no further divisibility is therefore possible.

[29] The same conclusion need not apply to damages, such as punitive or aggravated damages, as discussed immediately below.

[30] See, eg, *Clark v Newsam and Edwards* (1847) 1 Ex 130; 154 ER 55, a case of false imprisonment, though compare the headnote with some of the equivocal and cryptic statements of Pollock CB and Alderson B, at 140, about aggravated damages based on the differing motive of the tortfeasors.

[31] *Heydon's Case* (1612) 11 Co Rep 5a, 5b; 77 ER 1150, 1151.

[32] (1985) 155 CLR 448 (HCA).

the respondent, Caltex, had formerly used. Caltex employed an industrial plumber to spike the underground petrol tanks on the premises. The damage to the tanks and loss of profits resulting from the damage was assessed at $5,527, which was awarded against both Caltex and the plumber; however, a sum of $150,000 exemplary damages was also awarded against Caltex. The High Court held that such a separate award was justifiable in the circumstances.[33] Gibbs CJ considered that 'it does not seem … in the least impracticable to give separate judgments against two defendants'.[34] It has similarly been concluded that separate judgment sums can be awarded against different joint defendants to reflect 'differing amounts attributable to aggravated damages'.[35] In short, the award of damages need not always be the same against each party.

There might appear to be some inconsistency here, in so far as there is solidary liability for the same damage, while at the same time different awards in damages are made as between the various defendants. Certainly, some commentators assume that joint tortfeasor liability is parasitic and duplicative rather than merely derivative; that is, the same remedies must apply to A as to PW.[36] As the Australian authorities demonstrate, this does not follow, nor is it desirable. There is no reason why the remedy against each joint tortfeasor should not be considered separately to reflect each tortfeasor's *culpability*, such as a malicious state of mind, or exacerbating conduct. The damage is indivisible, and the damages necessary to compensate for the ordinary consequences of that damage are to be borne equally by all defendants, but once remedies are sought that reflect the culpability and motives of the respective wrongdoers, then drawing individual distinctions is warranted.

The position under English law is different; only one judgment is possible for a single sum against defendants all joined in the same action and therefore exemplary damages cannot be awarded against one joint tortfeasor only.[37] Such an inflexible approach may cause potential injustice to claimants[38] and is undesirable, especially since it appears that applicable legislation (the Law Reform (Married Women and Tortfeasors) Act 1935 (UK) and derivatives) intended to abolish the single judgment rule in its entirety.[39]

[33] The conclusion followed from legislative changes – originally contained in s 6 of the Law Reform (Married Women and Tortfeasors) Act 1935 (UK) – abolishing the common law rule that the cause of action against joint tortfeasors is one and indivisible. See *Thompson v Australian Capital Television Pty Ltd* (1996) 186 CLR 574 (HCA); *Wah Tat Bank Ltd v Chan* [1975] AC 507 (PC), *Bryanston Finance Ltd v de Vries* [1975] 1 QB 703. See now, eg, s 3 of the Civil Liability (Contribution) Act 1978 (UK).

[34] (1985) 155 CLR 448 (HCA), 460.

[35] *McFadzean v CFMEU* [2004] VSC 289 [142] and [116], [141]. See also obiter in *Myer Stores Ltd v Soo* [1991] 2 VR 597 (CA) and *De Reus v Gray* [2003] VCA 84; (2003) 9 VR 432 [24]–[32] (Winneke P).

[36] See, eg, R Stevens, *Torts and Rights* (Oxford, University Press, 2007) 277. Indeed, Stevens goes further and denies that the liability is accessorial at all.

[37] See *Broome v Cassell and Co* [1972] AC 1027. The same rule may apply in relation to aggravated damages; see 1063 (Lord Hailsham LC).

[38] *Broome*, ibid, held that exemplary damages must not be awarded if any of the defendants do not deserve a punitive award against them.

[39] See Gibbs CJ in *XL Petroleum* (n 32) and *Thompson* (n 33).

IV. Accessories to Breach of Contract: Inducing Breach of Contract

A. The Basis of Liability

Courts and commentators have formulated the elements of the tort of inducing breach of contract in slightly different ways; however, the formulations generally all include, in some form, the need for: (1) a breach of contract by PW, (2) as a result of an act of inducement or procurement by A, (3) done with the *intent* to induce or procure such a breach (that is, with *knowledge* of the existence of the contract and that the course of conduct will lead to a breach of it by PW), (4) that results in damage to C.[40] In this part, I briefly consider what is encompassed by the second and third of these elements: that is, the conduct and mental elements. This leads us to consider how the assessment of damages for the tort may differ from that in contract.

For the conduct element, there must be words or 'affirmative or positive' acts[41] of procurement by A, directed at PW, that seek to achieve or bring about an outcome, by means of 'inducement, incitement or persuasion',[42] money payments,[43] threats,[44] fraud, or the like.[45] The acts used to incite, persuade, etc, may themselves be lawful.[46] Inducing a breach envisages success;[47] invitations or exhortations that do not achieve their aim are not actionable.

Since, in order to induce, one must seek a certain outcome, the inducer is generally the instigating force behind the breach by PW. This is reflected in the requirement that there must be a sufficiently strong causal link between the inducer's actions and the breach of contract. It is probably necessary to show a 'but for' causal connection between PW's decision to breach and A's intentional inducement; that is, that A's acts successfully have procured PW's actions.[48]

[40] Compare Diplock LJ in *Emerald Construction Co Ltd v Lowthian* [1966] 1 WLR 691, 703: three essential elements, 'the act, the intent and the resulting damage'.

[41] These terms are used in the statutory context in *ACCC v SIP Australia Pty Ltd* [2002] FCA 824; (2002) ATPR 41-877 [112] (Goldberg J).

[42] *CBS Songs* (n 20) 1058 (Lord Templeman).

[43] *Smithies v National Association* [1909] 1 KB 310, 335 (strike pay).

[44] *Emerald* (n 40).

[45] See also the dictionary definition used in *National Foods Milk Ltd v McMahon Milk Pty Ltd* [2008] VSC 208 [277] (Hargrave J).

[46] *Independent Oil Industries Ltd v Shell Co of Australia Ltd* (1937) 37 SR (NSW) 394, 418–19 (Jordon CJ).

[47] Compare *Trade Practices Commission v Parkfield Operations Pty Ltd* (1985) 5 FCR 140; 59 ALR 489 (Fox J) in the context of restrictive trade practices.

[48] Compare Lord Hoffmann in *OBG* (n 6) [36]: Did the defendant's [A's] acts of encouragement, threat, persuasion and so forth have a sufficient causal connection with the breach by the contracting party to attract accessory liability? See also *Fightvision Pty Ltd v Onisforou* (1999) 47 NSWLR 473, 534 (Scheller, Stein & Giles JJA): 'A finding of inducing breach of contract carries with it a finding that the defendant's actions caused the breach of contract and the loss which flowed.'

There is some debate about the relationship between the concepts of knowledge and intention, although it is safe to say that they are closely intertwined. Although some courts and commentators have focussed on 'intention' as the central requirement of the tort,[49] other formulations place more emphasis on knowledge.[50] Alternatively, they consider knowledge and intention to be dual requirements,[51] or as a connected, 'twofold' requirement,[52] or even as alternative means of establishing liability.[53] Even where intention is emphasised, however, it can only ever be inferred (unless it is admitted). If there is evidence that A knew PW's acts are likely to be in breach of the contract, and A then proceeds deliberately to pursue that outcome, then the court may conclude that A intended the breach. This is nonetheless inferred from what A knew and did.[54] It follows that knowledge – both of current facts and of the high probability that PW will breach her contract (if A's inducements work) – is really the essence of the tort.

B. The Remedial Consequences of Liability

For the tort of inducing breach of contract, the relevant rules for assessing the tort and contract remedies (against A and PW respectively) necessarily differ, given that each party is liable for an independent wrong and therefore via different sources of liability. Damage is the gist of the action for the tort claim and must both be proved by the claimant and be more than nominal.[55] As Brooking J stated in *Ansett Transport Industries (Operation) Pty Ltd v Australian Federation of Air Pilots (No 2)*:[56]

[49] See, eg, *Allstate Life Insurance Company v Australia and New Zealand Banking Group Ltd* (1995) 58 FCR 26, 43; 130 ALR 469, 484, (Lindgren J, Lockhart and Tamberlin JJ agreeing).

[50] See, eg, seemingly R Bagshaw, 'Inducing Breach of Contract' in J Horder (ed), *Oxford Essays in Jurisprudence*, Fourth Series (Oxford, Oxford University Press, 2000), 142, ('knowledge of the likelihood that conduct will bring about a breach' and persisting with that conduct despite such knowledge); *Short v City Bank of Sydney* (1912) 15 CLR 148 (HCA), 160 (Isaacs J).

[51] Compare S Deakin and J Randall, 'Rethinking the Economic Torts' (2009) 72(4) *MLR* 519, 538–40.

[52] See *Merkur Island Shipping Corp v Laughton* [1983] 2 AC 570 (HL), 608 (Lord Diplock) (knowledge of the contract and an intention to induce breach).

[53] A Simester and W Chan, 'Inducing Breach of Contract: One Tort or Two?' [2004] 63 *CLJ* 132, 159–60, appear to consider the requirements of knowledge and intention as distinct ways of satisfying the mental element of persuasion (that is, of procuring the outcome) for the tort.

[54] *Northern Territory v Mengel* (1995) 185 CLR 307, 342. See also in the context of the tort of misfeasance in public office *Bourgoin SA v Ministry of Agriculture, Fisheries and Food* [1986] QB 716, 777 (Oliver LJ); *Three Rivers DC v Bank of England (No 3)* [2001] UKHL 16; [2003] 2 AC 1, 223 (Lord Hutton).

[55] *Ansett Transport Industries (Operations) Pty Ltd v Australian Federation of Air Pilots (No 2)* [1991] 2 VR 636, 645 (Brooking J); *Goldsoll v Goldman* [1914] 2 Ch 603, 615, (breach 'must in the ordinary course of business inflict damage'), referred to with approval in *Palmer Bruyn & Parker Pty Ltd v Parsons* [2001] HCA 69; (2001) 208 CLR 388, 412 [76] (Gummow J).

[56] *Ansett* (n 55) 644, where Brooking J also states at 646 that 'it is wrong to assert that the measure of damages in all cases of wrongful interference with contractual relations is the amount which the plaintiff might have recovered for damages for breach of contract.' See also *Lumley v Gye* (1853) 2 E and B 216; 118 ER 749, 229–30 (Crompton J), and 233–34 (Erle J).

> Both principle and authority make it clear that the measure of damages for [inducing breach of contract] is not the same as the measure of damages in an action against the contract breaker himself.

To be sure, as Brooking J also stated:

> In many cases where the defendant has tortiously induced a breach of contract the plaintiff can be properly compensated by awarding him the amount he might have recovered from the contract-breaker.[57]

However, this factual conclusion does not determine the nature of A's liability. A's liability is for a different wrong and therefore potentially for different damages than those payable by PW. Those damages are determined by the rules of tort law and not contract law.[58]

A claimant need not prove special damage;[59] instead, damage may be inferred from the circumstances.[60] The claimant must show that A's conduct caused the breach of contract and quantify the loss that flowed therefrom. In some circumstances, the unavailability of a contract claim against PW means that the claimant will not be able to prove that any loss has flowed from the tort; for example, inducing a person to rescind a voidable contract probably does not suffice.[61] In other circumstances, however, the unavailability of a contract claim does not preclude a tort claim. It seems that an inducement to breach an unenforceable contract may give rise to a claim for damages,[62] as might an inducement to breach a contract that is not actionable, such as where PW has contractually excluded the obligation to pay damages.[63]

Further, the tort claim can give rise to an award of damages that is higher than would be awarded against PW for breach of contract.[64] A practical example of this is where a party wrongfully terminates a contract, but could have done so lawfully with an appropriate notice. In such a case, the claim against the contract breaker is

[57] *Ansett* (n 55) 646.

[58] This contrasts with the position in equity (as to which, see below), where the accessory is liable for a different wrong, but compensation is determined by reference to equitable principles. There are no conceptual barriers to such an approach, it should be noted.

[59] *Ansett* (n 55) 645, Brooking J citing *Quinn v Leathem* [1901] UKHL 2; [1901] AC 495, 498 and McCardie J in *Pratt v British Medical Association* [1919] 1 KB 244, 281. All that is necessary is that it is possible to infer some damage, 'from the tendency of the defendant's act in all the circumstances'.

[60] See, eg, *Exchange Telegraph Co v Gregory & Co* [1896] 1 QB 147 (CA) 153, 155–6, 158. Query whether purely non-pecuniary losses would suffice: see *Boase v Seven Network (Operations) Ltd* [2005] WASC 269.

[61] *Proform Sports Management Ltd v Proactive Sports Management Ltd* [2006] EWHC 2903; [2007] 1 All ER 542.

[62] *Ansett* (n 55) 649 (Brooking J), citing *Unident Ltd v DeLong* (1981) 131 DLR (3d) 225.

[63] Stevens (n 36) 277, citing *Merkur Island Shipping* (n 52). Note, however, that Baughen (n 2) 552, considers that this possibility is limited to circumstances of frustration and is therefore no longer a realistic prospect since the inducing tort no longer extends to mere *interference* in contract, and cites Lord Nicholls in *OBG* (n 6) [190]: 'An exceptions clause can scarcely apply to a contracting party who chooses to default.'

[64] See the examples given by Erle J in *Lumley* (n 56) 233–34; 756.

determined by reference to the loss suffered when compared to the situation where proper notice had been given. The tort claim is not so limited, however: allowance may be made for the fact that the contract may have continued but for the inducement.[65] It is also clear that exemplary damages may be awarded in an appropriate tort case, even though such an award is not available for breach of contract against the contract breaker.[66]

Conversely, in some cases, there may be loss with respect to the contract claim, but not the tort claim. For example, if the contract breaker may have abandoned a contract in any case, had she not been induced to do so, then the inducer's breach may not have caused any loss.[67] Further, if the claimant has recovered full damages against PW, then a tort claim against A must fail, as no damage can be shown.[68]

There is support in some commentary and cases for the view that the liability to compensate for losses in the tort of inducing breach of contract is 'joint and several' (that is, solidary) with that of liability for the breach of contract itself. Baughen assumes this to be so even though the tort liability is independent or 'indirect' and therefore for a different wrong.[69] Where PW and A are both liable for damages in the same amount, it has been held that judgment can be ordered against both parties, although obviously there can be no double recovery.[70] As to the question of contribution, which is considered further below, it should be stressed for now that, irrespective of whether the label 'joint and several' is applied, or not, contribution should be available as between the primary wrongdoer and accessory.

[65] *Ansett* (n 55) 647. See also *Vale v International Longshoremen's and Warehousemen's Union, Local 508* (1979) 12 BCLR 249 (CA), and *Morgan v Fry* [1968] 1 QB 521, 548–49 (tort damages may take into account the possibility that employment could have continued for an extended period, in the context of the tort of intimidation).

[66] *Multinail* (n 8) [153]–[164]; *Hospitality Group Pty Ltd v Australian Rugby Union Ltd* [2001] FCA 1040 (FC). Exemplary damages have also been awarded in Canadian cases; see, eg, *HL Weiss Forwarding Ltd v Omnus* (1975) 63 DLR (3d) 654; [1975] SCJ 55 (SCC); *57134 Manitoba Ltd v Palmer* [1985] BCJ 3069 (1985) 8 CCEL 282 (BCSC). And see *Pratt v British Medical Association* [1919] 1 KB 244, 281–82 (McCardie J).

[67] In other words, the inducing party can prove that loss would have been suffered in any event: *Fightvision* (n 48) 534–35. See also *Jones Bros (Hunstanton) Ltd v Stevens* [1954] 1 QB 275, 283, albeit not a case of inducing, and *Multinail* (n 8) [106].

[68] *Fightvision* (n 48) 534, citing *Bird v Randall* (1762) 3 Burr 1345, 1353–54; 97 ER 866, 870–71.

[69] See Baughen (n 2) 546, 552, 557, 558–59. Contrast, however, G Virgo, *The Principles of Equity & Trusts*, 2nd edn (Oxford, Oxford University Press, 2016) 736, fn 220, who states that liability for inducing breach of contract is not 'joint and several' with that of the primary wrongdoer. However, Virgo cites *OBG* (n 6) [39] (Lord Hoffmann), which case does not consider joint and several liability. The paragraph cited does not support the proposition, nor does Virgo's other, cited source, H Carty, 'Joint Tortfeasance and Assistance Liability' (1999) 19 *Legal Studies* 489, 506–7 support his point; indeed, if anything, it supports the opposite conclusion.

[70] *Fightvision* (n 48) 534. The court did not use the label 'joint and several', but the conclusion that liability was solidary follows from the fact that both parties were ordered to pay the entire damages. No order was made as to the parties' respective share of liability.

V. Equitable Accessory Liability

A. The Basis of Liability

Equitable accessory liability is often considered under the broader concept of equitable third party participatory liability.[71] The law on participatory liability differs across jurisdictions and is, in parts, confused. It is necessary to outline the relevant principles of liability only briefly, since the topic has been the subject of voluminous writing.[72]

Broadly speaking, there are currently two frameworks used to determine third party participatory liability for breach of trust and fiduciary duty. The traditional framework differentiates between three, overlapping sources of third party liability that arises with respect to a breach of trust or fiduciary duty: (1) procurement, and (2) knowing assistance in a dishonest or fraudulent design – both forms of accessory liability –; and (3) knowing receipt of trust property.[73] The precise elements of each of these differ but in all of them, culpability is determined according to the third party's knowledge of the primary wrong, albeit that the knowledge requirement for procurement has not been given any real judicial attention. The traditional framework holds sway in Australia.[74]

An alternative, 'reformed' framework has been adopted by the English courts and jurisdictions that follow those courts.[75] It combines liability for procurement and assistance (dishonest assistance). 'Dishonesty' is the culpability test. The reformed framework was initiated by the Privy Council in the landmark case of *Royal Brunei Airlines Sdn Bhd v Tan (Royal Brunei Airlines)*.[76] Dishonest assistance liability is dependent on A dishonestly procuring or assisting in a breach of trust or fiduciary duty. The breach by PW need not itself be dishonest or fraudulent. This is to be contrasted with knowing assistance under the traditional framework.

A recurring question in all jurisdictions concerns the requisite culpability of the accessory to the primary wrong. On this matter, courts have struggled to articulate criteria that provide certainty as well as justice for litigants. Both procurement and knowing assistance require a conduct element, or participation link, as well as a mental element and the extent of A's knowledge about PW's intended wrongdoing is central to the latter, whether the liability is formulated in terms of 'knowing' assistance or in terms of dishonesty.[77]

[71] This concept incorporates the related liability for receipt of trust property (recipient liability).

[72] See Dietrich and Ridge, (n 1) chs 7 and 8.

[73] See *Farah Constructions Pty Ltd v Say-Dee Pty Ltd* [2007] HCA 22; (2007) 230 CLR 89 and *Consul Development Pty Ltd v DPC Estates Pty Ltd* (1975) 132 CLR 373 (HCA). Recipient liability extends to the receipt of property that is subject to a fiduciary duty.

[74] See generally, Dietrich and Ridge (n 1) [8.1.4.1].

[75] ibid [8.1.4.2] and [8.3.4.4].

[76] [1995] 2 AC 378 (PC).

[77] The exact role of knowledge in determining dishonesty remains uncertain, however. See Dietrich and Ridge (n 1) [8.3.5] and [8.3.4.4] and the criticism of 'dishonesty' by Lord Millett (dissenting) in *Twinsectra Ltd v Yardley* [2002] UKHL 12; [2002] 2 AC 164 [134].

B. The Remedial Consequences of Liability[78]

An accessory's liability is in respect of his or her own wrongdoing[79] and the respective remedies against the accessory and the primary wrongdoer 'will be moulded to the particular facts'.[80] A culpable accessory to the breach of an equitable duty is exposed, potentially, to the full range of equitable remedies available against an express trustee.[81] More extensive remedies than those that are available at common law, including gain-based remedies, are available where necessary to meet the different objectives of the equitable liability. In Australia, at least, these equitable remedies are awarded at the court's discretion.[82] Relevant factors in determining relief include the rationale for A's liability, the nature of the primary wrong and the egregiousness of A's conduct. In most instances, however, it is the consequences of PW and A's wrongdoing for C and A respectively, that will determine the remedy or remedies available against A.[83]

As far as losses are concerned, the liability of an accessory who assists in the primary wrong is solidary with that of PW.[84] A's liability is determined on the same basis as that of PW once a connection between A's conduct and PW's primary wrong, rather than between A's conduct and C's loss, is established.[85] This can lead to concerns that the accessory's liability might be disproportionate to the extent of A's culpable involvement, particularly where A has merely assisted PW (for example, through the provision of professional services). Paul Davies has therefore argued that an accessory 'should only be liable for losses suffered as a result of the accessory's participation in the breach'.[86] This appears to require an enquiry as to what losses flowed specifically from A's own wrongful conduct.

[78] These issues are more fully explored in Dietrich and Ridge (n 1) ch 8, and in P Ridge, 'Monetary Remedies for Equitable Participatory Liability' in S Degeling and J Varuhas (eds), *Equitable Compensation and the Disgorgement of Profit* (Oxford, Hart Publishing, 2017) ch 10. I acknowledge that Pauline's scholarship is the source of many of the ideas that follow.

[79] *Michael Wilson* (n 6) [106].

[80] See generally, Ridge (n 78) and particularly, 204–5.

[81] *Grimaldi v Chameleon Mining Ltd (No 2)* [2012] FCAFC 6; (2012) 200 FCR 296 [667] ('*Grimaldi*'); *Novoship (UK) Ltd v Nikitin* [2014] EWCA Civ 908 [82]. A is said to be accountable as a constructive trustee or, more simply, 'accountable in equity'.

[82] *Grimaldi* (n 81) (constructive trust refused); *Novoship* (n 81) [119] (account of profits refused if 'disproportionate in relation to the particular form and extent of wrongdoing'). In English law, there are more doubts as to the extent of a court's discretion, particularly when awarding constructive trusts.

[83] 'It is the case that, in many instances and for many types of equitable wrong, the remedy that is most appropriate will self-select absent unusual circumstances.' *Grimaldi* (n 81) [503].

[84] See *Blyth v Fladgate* [1891] 1 Ch 337; *Cowper v Stoneham* (1893) 68 LT 18; *Trustor AB v Smallbone (No 3)* unreported, May 9 2000, CA [97] (Scott VC); *Ultraframe (UK) Ltd v Fielding* [2005] EWHC 1638; [2006] FSR 17 [600] (Lewison J). In Australia, see *Grimaldi* (n 81) [558].

[85] Further, it is not even necessary to prove that the primary wrong would not have happened but for the accessory's conduct. See, eg, *Balfron Trustees Ltd v Peterson* [2002] Lloyd's Rep PN 1 [21] (Laddie J): it is no answer to an accessory's liability in equity, 'either to say that he only participated in part of a chain of events, all of which led to the breach of trust, or to assert that the breach of trust would probably have occurred without his assistance'.

[86] Davies (n 2) 257 and compare the cryptic statement in *Target Holdings Ltd v Redferns* [1996] 1 AC 421 (HL) 432 (Lord Browne-Wilkinson). See also Virgo (n 69) 736, who argues that a dishonest accessory

There are at least three broad difficulties with Davies' argument. First, to hold that A should only be responsible for that 'part' of the loss caused by his or her accessorial conduct, would be to impose a regime of proportionate liability in circumstances where such regimes – of statutory origin – do not currently apply.[87] Secondly, this approach is not adopted in other areas of the law. As noted above, liability in tort law is solidary and, in any case, losses will rarely be divisible into components that can be causally linked to distinct conduct of A and PW (aggravating and contumelious conduct aside).[88] Similarly, as Ridge points out, this approach is not accepted with respect to loss-based remedies in equity, for knowing or dishonest assistance.[89] A third difficulty is that solidary liability for C's losses is supported by the principled rationales for liability.[90] Crucially, it is only in relation to C that questions of relative responsibility are ignored; as between A and PW such issues are relevant to the questions of apportionment (considered further below). In this way, the risks associated with potentially difficult evidential inquiries into relative responsibility are shifted from C to the two wrongdoers, A and PW.[91]

Given that liability for losses is solidary, it could be argued that once a link is established between A's conduct and the primary wrong through A's participation, A *becomes* PW for remedial purposes.[92] If remedy is considered purely in terms of losses, the 'duplicative liability' thesis might be persuasive,[93] although there are other equally credible explanations for this. The thesis becomes problematic, however, when the focus shifts to the benefits obtained from a breach,[94] as is often the case where equitable wrongs are concerned.

and PW should not be jointly and severally liable for C's losses and that the accessory should 'be liable only to compensate the claimant for loss suffered as a result of the accessory's' conduct. However, Virgo does not see the approach as making a significant difference in the law, as contribution to the whole loss 'will usually be readily established' (737).

[87] See Part VII below.

[88] Ridge (n 78) 213: 'it may be extremely difficult to determine the relative responsibility of [A] and PW where [A] has assisted … the primary wrong.' The example Davies gives ((n 2) 257) of supposedly distinct losses flowing from each party's distinct conduct, with respect, is highly unrealistic. But see also the example given by Virgo (n 69) 737.

[89] As Ridge (n 78) 211–12 points out, the cases cited by Davies do not support his proposition.

[90] ibid, 212–13. These include deterrence, regulating trustee and fiduciary behaviour and vindication of such relationships.

[91] And as already noted, it is not necessary for C to establish a causal connection between A's conduct and C's loss at all. Nevertheless, the potentially onerous and disproportionate consequences of solidary liability for losses for assistance are a reason for setting a high threshold for liability in the first place.

[92] As such, the remedies against A *duplicate* those against PW. See S Elliott and C Mitchell, 'Remedies for Dishonest Assistance' (2004) 67 *MLR* 16, cited with approval in *Ultraframe (UK) Ltd v Fielding* [2005] EWHC 1638 (Ch); [2006] FSR 16 [1600]. The argument was subsequently revised in C Mitchell and S Watterson, 'Remedies for Knowing Receipt' in C Mitchell (ed), *Constructive and Resulting Trusts* (Oxford, Hart Publishing, 2009) 115, 150–53. Elliott and Mitchell drew upon P Sales, 'The Tort of Conspiracy and Civil Secondary Liability' [1990] 49 *CLJ* 491.

[93] See also Virgo (n 69) 723–25, 736, who considers liability to be a mix or hybrid of derivative, secondary liability, and primary liability for A's own wrong.

[94] This was acknowledged by Elliott and Mitchell (n 92) 40. Nor would one expect that in general, A should be liable for PW's gains. See further, S Gardner, 'Knowing Assistance and Knowing Receipt: Taking Stock' (1996) 112 *LQR* 56, 72–73.

Turning then to benefits, liability as a general rule is limited to the actual gains obtained by the accessory, and fiduciary or trustee, respectively.[95] It is often said that A and PW should not be liable for each other's gains resulting from the primary wrong.[96] This is sometimes explained on the basis that equity's jurisdiction is not penal.[97] It also follows from the fact that A's liability is grounded in A's own, independently wrongful, conduct: the remedies available against A should be directed to the consequences of A's wrongdoing.[98] That approach is reflected in a number of cases.[99]

Nonetheless, the merits of such a general position should not preclude alternative approaches where the facts and justice of the case demand it. For example, if the facts suggest that the gains made by one party will in fact benefit both parties, a principled case may be made for solidary liability. Thus, if PW is simply the vehicle for A's enrichment and A is the instigator of the primary wrong, joint and several liability for PW's gains is appropriate. This scenario will often arise where corporate vehicles are used to achieve the wrongful ends.[100]

A further scenario in which solidary liability for gains is justified is where A and PW have jointly participated in the primary wrong, particularly where their separate identities and conduct are obscured. The Court in *Grimaldi* suggested, without needing to decide the question, that:

> If [PW] and the third party assistant or recipient *act in concert* to secure a mutual benefit… they are jointly and severally liable to [C] to restore the trust or to account for the profits made … One can readily understand why, when wrongdoers so entangle their affairs, that the law as a matter of legal policy might wish to make it their responsibility – and not [C's] – to untangle them for accountability purposes.[101]

VI. Contribution and Apportionment

There are two relevant sources of a right to contribution: statute and equity.[102] In some Australian jurisdictions, statutory contribution rights are limited to claims

[95] See generally Ridge (n 78).

[96] See, eg, *Ultraframe* (n 84) [600] (Lewison J). See also, in Australia, *Glandon Pty Ltd v Tilmunda Pastoral Company Pty Ltd* [2008] NSWSC 218; [2008] ASAL 55–186 [108] (Gzell J).

[97] ibid.

[98] *Michael Wilson* (n 6) [106].

[99] See, eg, the cases considered by Davies (n 2) 264–67.

[100] *Grimaldi* (n 81) [556] citing *Green & Clara Pty Ltd v Bestobell Industries Pty Ltd (No 2)* [1984] WAR 32, 40; *Gencor ACP Ltd v Dalby* [2000] 2 BCLC 734 (Ch). There may sometimes be other ways to deal with such scenarios. For example, in a corporate setting, where A has a substantial interest in PW Co, removing the gains of PW Co may have the indirect consequence of withholding or removing gains from A. Similarly, see *Warman International Ltd v Dwyer* (1995) 182 CLR 544 (HCA) 563–64.

[101] *Grimaldi* (n 81) [558] citing inter alia *CMS Dolphin Ltd v Simonet* [2001] 2 BCLC 704 and *Green & Clara* (n 100). See also, eg, *Ultraframe* (n 84) [595]–[600] and C Mitchell, *The Law of Contribution and Reimbursement* (Oxford, Oxford University Press, 2003) [8.28].

[102] Common law rights of contribution are no longer of significance, since 'equitable principles now cover the field': *Burke v LFOT Pty Ltd* [2002] HCA 17; (2002) 209 CLR 282 [38] (McHugh J, citing *Armstrong v Commissioner of Stamp Duties* (1967) 69 SR (NSW) 38, 48).

between tortfeasors liable for the same damage, or parties to contracts whose liabilities are 'concurrent and co-extensive with a duty of care in tort'.[103] In those jurisdictions, a statutory right to contribution applies to all tortfeasors whose conduct led to the same damage. Interestingly, that broad right to contribution overrode the position at common law (and equity followed the law in this regard) that wrongdoers were not entitled to contribution.[104] In other words, despite liability being joint (or, for that matter, several and concurrent), no right to contribution arose.

For claims not involving tortfeasors (such as those against a contract breaker, who in most circumstances is unlikely to have breached a duty of care), contribution rights in the Australian jurisdictions in question will be limited to those that arise in equity. This makes it necessary to consider the equitable principles of contribution, particularly in those jurisdictions.

The United Kingdom and Victoria, however, have a broader statutory regime, based on the United Kingdom's Civil Liability (Contributions) Act 1978. These allow for contribution as between parties who are liable for the 'same damage' irrespective of the cause of action on which liability is grounded (s 1(1)).[105] Those broader statutory schemes also need to be considered, although I would suggest that the questions of principle ought to be resolved in the same way, irrespective of the basis for contribution.

I will outline the two bases for contribution – equitable and statutory – and the relevant principles of apportionment, before applying those principles to the three specific contexts under consideration.

A. Contribution in Equity

Equitable contribution applies both to common law and equitable causes of action.[106] Contribution is available where two (or more) parties share a 'co-ordinate' liability to 'make good the one loss'.[107] The basis for contribution is the parties'

[103] See, eg, Wrongs Act 1954 (Tas) s 2 ('wrongful act'); Law Reform (Miscellaneous Provisions) Act 1946 (NSW) Pt 3; Law Reform Act 1995 (Qld) Pt 3 Div 2.

[104] This was known as the rule in *Merryweather v Nixan* (1799) 101 ER 1337, which was abolished by the Law Reform (Married Women and Tortfeasors) Act 1935 (UK) and derivative legislation. The consequence of this is that rights to contribution as between tortfeasors that exist today 'rests upon statute': J Heydon, M Leeming, P Turner, *Meagher, Gummow and Lehane's Equity Doctrines and Remedies*, 5th edn (Australia, LexisNexis Butterworths, 2015) 396 [10.015]. As to whether equitable rights of contribution can now arise, see *Belan v Casey* [2003] NSWSC 159; (2003) 57 NSWLR 670 [135]–[137].

[105] In Australia, see Wrongs Act 1958 (Vic) s 23A; 23B.

[106] See *Albion Insurance Co Ltd v Government Insurance Office (NSW)* (1969) 121 CLR 342 (HCA), 349–50 (Kitto J).

[107] *Burke* (n 102) [14]–[16] (Gaudron ACJ and Hayne J) citing *Dering v Earl of Winchelsea* (1787) 1 Cox 318; 29 ER 1184; and see also McHugh J [38]–[50]. In *Burke*, reference was also made to parties' 'common obligations', but more recently, the Court in *Friend v Brooker* (2009) 239 CLR 129 (HCA)[41] stated that 'co-ordinate' was the preferable term.

common interest and common burden,[108] where the parties' obligations are 'of the same nature and to the same extent'.[109] Contribution adjusts the rights of the co-obligors when only one of them discharges their co-ordinate liabilities.[110] The High Court of Australia has in a number of cases affirmed the broad basis of, and the flexible application of, the equitable principles.[111]

Nonetheless, these principles are not easy to apply: 'the difficulty in defining which liabilities meet that description [of co-ordinate liabilities] is noted almost as often as the term is used'.[112] The mere fact that obligations are owed to the same party, or are 'otherwise connected in time or circumstances', or that payment of a party has financially benefited another, are not sufficient to ground a right to contribution.[113] For example, in *Burke v Lfot Pty Ltd*, the High Court held that a vendor of property who was liable under statute for misleading conduct to compensate the purchaser, could not seek contribution from the purchaser's solicitor, who had negligently failed to take care in ensuring that reasonable checks were made.[114] Certainly, the types of circumstances in which contribution has traditionally been allowed – such as co-sureties and co-insurers – are very different to the circumstances considered in *Burke*.

B. Statutory Contribution

In the UK[115] and some other jurisdictions, such as Victoria, statutes allow a broad basis for contribution and have lessened the need to rely on the equitable rules.[116] The UK Civil Liability (Contributions) Act 1978 allows for contribution between multiple parties, provided that each is liable with respect to the 'same damage' (s 1(1)) and the claim is one for recovery of 'compensation … in respect of that damage (whatever the legal basis of his liability, whether tort, breach of contract, breach of trust or otherwise') (s 6(1)). Importantly, the requirement is not that

[108] *Dering* (n 107) 322; 1186; and see *Burke* (n102) [41] (McHugh J); and *Ellesmere Brewery Co v Cooper* [1896] 1 QB 75, 79.

[109] *BP Petroleum Development Ltd v Esso Petroleum Co Ltd* [1987] SLT 345, 348 (Lord Ross).

[110] *Burke* (n 102) [42] (McHugh J).

[111] ibid; *Friend* (n 107); *HIH Claims Support Ltd v Insurance Aust Ltd* [2011] HCA 31; (2011) 244 CLR 72.

[112] *Burke* (n 102) [43] (McHugh J, citing Fitzgerald JA in *Stratti v Stratti* [2000] NSWCA 358; (2000) 50 NSWLR 324, 330 [18]).

[113] ibid, [44] McHugh J.

[114] *Burke* (n 102). See, however, seemingly reaching a contrary conclusion on similar facts in a claim for statutory contribution, *Eastgate Group Ltd v Lindsey Morden Group Inc* [2002] EWCA Civ 1446; 1 WLR 643, which was distinguished in *Marlborough District Council v Altimarloch Joint Venture Ltd* [2012] NZSC 11; [2012] 2 NZLR 726, but which decision is itself now open to doubt in New Zealand after *Hotchin v New Zealand Guardian Trust Co Ltd* [2016] NZSC 24; [2016] 1 NZLR 906.

[115] This does not include Scotland, however.

[116] These still apply, however, for example, where contractual obligations to pay money sums are the source of liability, as with contribution between co-sureties, since these do not involve 'compensation' in respect of damage.

damages be the same, but that defendants have caused the same 'damage'. This does not mean substantially 'similar' damage.[117] Where the Act applies, section 2(1) provides that '... the amount of the contribution recoverable from any person shall be such as may be found by the court to be just and equitable having regard to the extent of that person's responsibility for the damage in question'.

C. Apportionment

When it comes to apportionment, two important factors that are relevant to determining the primary wrongdoer's and accessory's respective share of liability are their culpability or moral blameworthiness, and the causal (or causative) potency or impact of their respective wrongful conduct.[118] Relevant to both factors is the fact that A's involvement, or role, in PW's wrong can vary considerably. The role of A can range from A being the 'puppeteer' that 'pulls the strings', so to speak,[119] and *instigates* the wrong committed by PW, through A being an equal player in the scheme, to A being a reluctant lackey, or an obtuse professional agent who is only a minor player in a wrongful enterprise.

The role taken by the accessory is obviously relevant to establishing A's culpability, vis-à-vis PW. An accessory who puts pressure on a person to commit a wrong is clearly more morally blameworthy than the wrongdoer who reluctantly accedes. The reverse would be true where the wrongdoer pressures a reluctant accessory to assist.

The role that the accessory performs is also relevant as a matter of causal potency.[120] Where other factors are equal, it can increase or reduce a party's share of liability. It can also neutralise differences in the parties' respective culpability. 'A more serious fault having less causative impact on the plaintiff's damage may represent an equivalent responsibility to a less serious fault which had a greater causative impact.'[121] Causal potency considers the 'relative importance of [the wrongdoer's] acts in causing the damage'[122] and as such, seems to assume that

[117] See Lord Steyn in *Royal Brompton Hospital NHS Trust v Hammond* [2002] UKHL 14; [2002] 1 WLR 1397 (HL) [27]. This conclusion followed, even though Lord Steyn accepted that 'the Act ought to given a broad interpretation' [26].

[118] See *Downs v Chappell* [1997] 1 WLR 426, 445 (Hobhouse LJ). Causal relevance is another term used to describe the second factor. Other factors may also be relevant to determining apportionment. See generally Mitchell (n 101) ch 10. As Mitchell points out, at 192–93, although the ideas of causal potency and moral blameworthiness are 'closely linked' (and see also, eg, *Corr v IBC Vehicles Ltd* [2008] UKHL 13; [2008] 1 AC 884 [44] on contributory negligence (Lord Walker)), nonetheless the courts have differentiated between the two.

[119] *Allen v Flood* [1898] AC 1 (HL) 152 (Lord McNaughton).

[120] Although some commentators argue that the concept of 'causal potency' is of questionable utility and has not been defined (at least in the context of contributory negligence). See J Goudkamp and L Klar, 'Apportionment of Damages for Contributory Negligence: The Causal Potency Criterion' (2016) 53 *Alberta Law Review* 1. Nonetheless the courts continue to refer to it as relevant in determining parties' respective share of liability.

[121] *Downs* (n 118) 445 (Hobhouse LJ).

[122] *Stapley v Gypsum Mines Ltd* [1953] AC 663 (HL) 682 (Lord Reid).

there are degrees of causation. At the apportionment stage, therefore, the law seeks to unpack the relative causal contribution of the parties, despite the difficulty of making such assessments at the liability stage.[123]

It is necessary to consider how these principles have been applied in the three areas of accessory liability that this chapter discusses.

D. Torts

Given that accessories, as joint tortfeasors, are solidarily liable with the primary wrongdoers for the harm caused by PW's wrong, a right to contribution clearly arises as between the parties and will be determined on the same principles as apply generally to joint (and concurrent) tortfeasors. Of course, where the damages awarded against each party differ, such as where exemplary or aggravated damages are awarded only against one, then no contribution would be available with respect to those damages.

In tort law, Goudkamp and Klar have argued that 'degrees' of causation and causal potency may well be concepts of questionable meaning in cases of contributorily negligent claimants and negligent defendants,[124] where *both* parties' wrongful conduct is a 'but-for' cause of a claimant's loss, unusual exceptions aside.[125] For accessory liability, however, it is clear that A's conduct need not be a 'but for' cause of the wrong;[126] in other words, PW may well have still committed the wrong even in the absence of A's input.[127] In that context, causal potency is potentially a more meaningful concept, as there may well be degrees of causation. This is plausible given that A's conduct need not necessarily even be a 'but for' cause of a claimant's loss, for example, if PW would have proceeded with the wrong even in the absence of A's assistance. Of course, where both A's and PW's actions are 'but for' causes of C's loss (such as where A has procured PW's wrong), then distinguishing between the causal potency of each action becomes more problematic.

How, then, might we apportion each party's respective share of liability where A's conduct need only have had some impact on PW's decision to, or capacity to, commit the wrong? For example, if liability in *Sea Shepherd* had been found to arise (as the dissent did find) and if damages had been sought, how would contribution as between the primary tortfeasor, who rammed the claimant's ship, and the accessory, who provided minor financial support for a general environmental campaign against illegal fishing, be assessed? One would expect that the minimal causal potency of A's actions would be significant, even if the moral blameworthiness of each party's conduct were equal. In the absence of any authorities on point, however, such questions are difficult to answer.

[123] See above text at n 26.

[124] See Goudkamp and Klar (n 120). Although they do not address the issue, their criticisms might equally extend to the use of that concept where contribution between tortfeasors is at issue.

[125] Causal potency applies in this context, nonetheless: see Mitchell (n 101) 184, 192–96.

[126] See, eg, *Shah* (n 16) and the discussion above that assistance need only be non-trivial.

[127] The same applies in equity. See above n 85.

E. Inducing Breach of Contract

If the liabilities of the tortfeasor and contract breaker are appropriately described as joint and several, then one might presume that a right of contribution follows.[128] But the substantive question of whether a right of contribution arises as between contract breaker and tortfeasor does not yet appear to have been answered by the courts and turns on whether the accessory tortfeasor is liable (under statute) for the 'same damage' as the contract breaker or whether (in equity) the parties' liabilities are co-ordinate. Given that the respective sources of A and PW's liability are very different, and that damages are determined by different incidental rules and may differ in quantification, answering these questions is not easy.

Before we consider either statutory or equitable sources of contribution rights, it is worth noting that much of what follows is speculative, since I am not aware of any cases that have considered the availability of contribution sought either by an inducing tortfeasor against a party in breach of contract, or vice versa. There are a number of practical reasons why this might be so:

(1) Many claims for inducing breach of contract are unsuccessful.
(2) Where claimants are successful in establishing tort liability, the claimants often seek only injunctions against the inducers to prevent future infringements.
(3) Many earlier cases arose in the industrial dispute context, and the inducer was a representative entity, such as a union. Such a defendant will not have any interest in pursuing contribution from individual infringing parties, who are likely to be union members. Today, claims often arise in the context of commercial and employment competition. Again, however, inducing parties are unlikely to pursue contribution against the contract breakers, who may (now) be employees or customers of the inducing parties. In short, it is unlikely that an inducing party would seek contribution from the party they have successfully induced.
(4) If a claimant were to proceed with legal action against the party in breach of contract, the inducing party may have agreed to indemnify that party for any damages successfully claimed by the claimant.[129]

i. Contribution in Equity

Do mutual rights to contribution in equity arise as between the contract breaker on the one hand, and the inducing tortfeasor on the other? In the absence of any direct authority on point, any attempted answer is to some extent speculative.

In determining whether equitable contribution is available – whether the liabilities of the tortfeasor accessory and the contract breaker are co-ordinate – two factors

[128] This would be so at least under the current contribution rules, one would assume, even if, historically, the label 'joint liability' did not necessarily equate to rights of contribution. See above n 104.

[129] For an example where a contract breaker sought a partial indemnity before acting in breach of its contract, see *Multinail* (n 8) [101], [105].

may be relevant: the respective culpability of the parties, and the causal significance of each party's respective acts. These must generally be 'equal or comparable'.[130] Whether that is indeed the case is debatable. Some of the competing arguments are considered below after discussion of the broader statutory regimes, since the questions of principle are similar, irrespective of the source of the contribution right.

ii. Statutory Contribution

The critical requirement for contribution to be available under statute is that the parties are liable for the 'same damage'.[131] Although the term 'same damage' has been interpreted widely,[132] can it be satisfied where one party's liability is in tort and requires fault, whereas the other party's liability is in contract and is strict? Certainly, there is no reason in principle why a claim for contribution might not be available in such cases.[133] It has been stated, for example, that the fact that one party's liability is contractual while another's is tortious does not mean, for that reason alone, that those liabilities are not for the same damage.[134] However, some cases have disallowed contribution with respect to contract and tort claims. In *Royal Brompton Hospital NHS Trust v Hammond*, it was held that a claim against an architect for negligent advice and certification was not for the same damage as a claim against a building contractor for breach for delay in completing the work.[135] It was held that the architect's negligence had not led to the delay in the performance of the contract.[136] Similarly, in *Marlborough District Council v Altimarloch Joint Venture Ltd*, a claim for contribution on equitable principles, the party who had made contractual misrepresentations in breach of contract was not entitled to contribution from the council that had, negligently, made the same misrepresentations in a memorandum.[137] These cases suggest that 'damage' is in part defined by the nature of the 'wrong' and the defendant's conduct.

These cases are not necessarily analogous, however, to claims for inducing breach of contract and for breach of that contract because of the inducement.

[130] See *Burke* (102) [16]–[22] (Gaudron ACJ and Hayne J). This means that apportionment in equity is generally equal, although where parties, such as co-sureties, have undertaken more limited obligations vis à vis the other, then equality in equity means proportionate equality determined by their respective financial obligations. See Heydon, Leeming, and Turner (n 104) 407–08 [10-125]. See also Kirby J in *Burke* [119]–[123], arguing for greater flexibility in apportionment.

[131] The requirement that the claims are for 'compensation' is clearly satisfied in this context.

[132] See, eg, *Charter plc v City Index Ltd* [2007] EWCA Civ 1382; [2008] Ch 313.

[133] See also *Heaton v AXA Equity and Law Life Assurance Soc plc* [2002] UKHL 15; [2002] 2 AC 329, 335.

[134] See, eg, *The Carnival* [1994] 2 Lloyds Rep 14 (contribution ordered between the owners of a colliding ship and the contractually liable charterers of the damaged ship who had ordered the ship to an unsafe berth); and see *Eastgate* (n 114).

[135] *Royal Brompton* (n 117) [7] Lord Bingham.

[136] ibid.

[137] *Marlborough* (n 114).

In particular, *Royal Brompton* can be distinguished, since the architect's negligence had not caused the specific breach that occurred; in contrast, an inducer by definition has caused the breach of contract that has occurred. The *Marlborough DC* case can also be distinguished, since the party who had made the misrepresentations in breach of contract had benefited from its wrong, whereas the negligent council had not.[138]

There are certainly arguments both for and against contribution in the context of accessory liability for breach of contract. On the one hand, as noted above, there are statements in the courts to the effect that that measure of damages between the causes of action can differ and that tort damages may be available even when none are available against the contract breaker. Further, each claim protects different interests. The breach of contract claim protects the claimant against loss of the benefits of the performance of the contract – a narrow and specific interest. The tort claim more broadly protects the general economic well-being of the claimant against interference and can focus on the wider consequences of the tortfeasor's infringing conduct. Finally, the liability for breach of contract is strict, whereas the tort liability is fault-based.

On the other hand, the measure of damages for the tort claim will often be the same as that available against the contract breaker. Perhaps most importantly, the breach of contract is the pre-requisite for the tort claim and that breach is actionable per se, so that there is no need to prove an intention to cause damage. That breach of contract will have been caused by the accessory's inducing conduct: in short, absent a breach of contract, no liability can arise in tort.

In my view, contribution ought to be available between the contract-breaker and the inducing accessory irrespective of whether contribution is sought under statute or in equity. The respective claims are either for the same damage (as required by statute), or the liabilities are co-ordinate (on equitable principles). This should be so at least to the extent that damages are quantified as the same (that is, leaving aside any further damages for which the accessory tortfeasor is liable, such as exemplary damages). I take this view because of the clear accessorial nature of the liability. Both parties have contributed to the primary wrong and their respective culpability can vary considerably.

If contribution is available, the same principles as discussed above would, presumably apply to determine the parties' relative apportionment.[139]

F. Equity

In equity, in so far as losses are concerned, there is only limited guidance in the case law as to the rules that govern apportionment as between accessorial and

[138] ibid. See also Heydon, Leeming and Turner (n 104) 403–04 [10-085].

[139] Both culpability and causal potency are also relevant under the statutory schemes in the UK and Victoria. See, eg, *Keller v Metropolitan Ambulance Service of Victoria* [2002] VSC 222 [9]–[10] (Mandle J).

primary wrongdoers. Because PW and A bear joint and several liability for C's losses resulting from the primary wrong,[140] C may sue either wrongdoer for the full sum. As between PW and A, however, the party who discharged the liability may seek contribution from the other. There is still considerable uncertainty as to how the equitable (and statutory) contribution rules operate in relation to accessory liability and the authorities are somewhat confused; however, the following general points can be noted.

One difficulty to overcome is that equity has developed specific rules – trustee contribution and indemnity rules – that apply as between co-trustees and which generally either dictate equal apportionment, or preclude contribution and allow for a trustee to be indemnified.[141] It is sometimes assumed that the co-trustees contribution rules apply to accessories,[142] at least where equity's contribution rules continue to apply (the same is not the case where broader statutory regimes apply).[143] This is not desirable, however. As Alison Gurr has concluded:

> Under the trustee contribution rules there is 'no intermediate position between these two extremes' of equal contribution or full indemnity. The extension of these rules to accessories may lead to artificial and unjust outcomes, as it would be rare for co-trustees, let alone trustees or fiduciaries and accessories, to be equally responsible for the breach.[144]

Instead, the general rules for equitable contribution should apply. The weight of the (limited) authorities favours such application,[145] and supports the view that proportionate apportionment is permissible.[146]

These uncertainties do not apply to English law, since the broader statutory contribution regime, allowing for just and equitable apportionment, would apply in the context of accessories.

Where contribution is available as between A and PW, the same factors relevant to apportionment between the parties, noted above,[147] should apply. The relative

[140] See the authorities cited above, n 84.

[141] See the comprehensive analysis in the context of Australian law by Gurr (n 3) and see also at 493–97, as to the applicability of the joint fraud rule to parties other than co-trustees.

[142] See, eg, *MacDonald v Hauer* (1977) 72 DLR (3d) 110 (Saskatchewan CA) 134–35 (Bayda JA); *Westpac v Savin* [1985] 2 NZLR 41 (NZCA) 54 (Richardson J); *Equiticorp Industries Group Ltd v Hawkins [No 4]* (1992) 5 PRNZ 484, 491; *McNally v Harris* [2008] NSWSC 659 [150]–[154] (White J). See further, Gurr (n 3) 491–93.

[143] The broader statutory contribution schemes also apply to some equitable claims; see Part VI(B).

[144] See Gurr (n 3) 492. The quoted excerpts are from *Bialkower v Acohs Pty Ltd & RA Bashford Consulting Pty Ltd* (1998) 83 FCR 1, 13 (Beaumont, Hill and Sundberg JJ).

[145] See *George v Webb* [2011] NSWSC 1608 [339]–[354] (Ward J), and Gurr (n 3).

[146] See Gurr (n 3) 497–99; *George v Webb* (n 145) [339]–[354] (Ward J) (concluding in obiter that the 'loss should be apportioned pro rata': [354]); *Bialkower* (n 144) 13 (Beaumont, Hill and Sundberg JJ) (contribution founded on proportionate equality); and Kirby J (dissenting) in *Burke* (n 102). See also Mitchell (n 101) [4.21] n 89. Contrast, eg, an earlier decision of Ward J in *The Owners Strata Plan 62930 v Kell & Rigby Holdings Pty Ltd* [2010] NSWSC 612 (29 June 2010) [433]–[435] (without detailed consideration of the point). The strongest case for other-than-equal apportionment is where A procured PW's breach: here, PW may have a right of indemnity under the equitable rules. See *George v Webb* [353] (citing *Burke* (n 102) [19] (Gaudron ACJ and Hayne J).

[147] See above text to n 118ff.

blameworthiness of the parties is perhaps the most significant of these factors, but also relevant is the causal impact of each party's respective wrongful conduct. Thus, where a procurer is the driving force behind PW's wrongdoing, disproportionate apportionment may be appropriate even where the parties' culpability is the same. Another factor of relevance in the context of claims for accessory liability in equity is whether the parties that are sought to be made liable for C's losses have made a profit from their wrongdoing.[148] As a general principle, a party who has gained ought to bear a greater proportion of C's losses than one who has not.

Where each party, A and PW, is only liable for his or her own gain received from the wrong, questions of contribution do not arise. Where, however, each party is fully liable for all gains received, then questions of contribution and apportionment may, in theory, arise.[149]

VII. Proportionate Liability in Australia

The solidary principle that all joint wrongdoers are liable for the full extent of damage caused, such that the risk of non-payment of damages by one defendant rests with the other defendants, has been abolished by legislation in all Australian jurisdictions for economic loss and property damages for some categories of claims. Claimants are therefore only entitled to a proportion of 'apportionable claims' against individual defendants. The proportionate liability legislation has 'dramatically' changed the law.[150] It is also complex and is riddled with uncertainties and difficulties of interpretation. The relevant issue for our purposes is whether proportionate liability can ever apply either to a claim against an accessory, or to a claim against a primary wrongdoer, when each can point to the other as being partly responsible for the loss incurred (that is, as a 'concurrent wrongdoer'). The question of whether proportionate liability can apply to *accessories* is a question that can be answered uniformly with respect to the primary wrongs considered in this chapter. I will address that question first, before turning to the application of proportionate liability to primary wrongdoers.

The proportionate liability regimes are limited in their application to two types of claim: for statutory misleading conduct (which is not of relevance here), or for 'a failure to take reasonable care'.[151] Another limitation on proportionate liability is that if a concurrent wrongdoer intended to cause, or fraudulently caused, the loss,

[148] See Mitchell (n 101) [10.34]–[10.39], albeit discussing cases mostly decided under the broad statutory contribution schemes. See also *Burke* (n 102).

[149] Lady Arden LJ has suggested that equitable contribution should also be available in relation to an account of profits: *Charter v City Index* (n 132) [71].

[150] *Yates v Mobile Marine Repairs Pty Ltd* [2007] NSWSC 1463 (14 December 2007) [93], Palmer J.

[151] State and Territory: Civil Law (Wrongs) Act 2002 (ACT), s 107B; Civil Liability Act 2002 (NSW), Part 4; Proportionate Liability Act 2005 (NT), s 4; Law Reform (Contributory Negligence and Apportionment of Liability Act 2001 (SA), s 3; Civil Liability Act 2002 (Tas), s 43A; Wrongs Act 1958 (Vic), s 24AF; Civil Liability Act 2002 (WA), s 5AI. Compare the wording in the Civil Liability Act 2003 (Qld), s 28.

that wrongdoer is liable for the full damage.[152] Collectively, those limitations will probably preclude *accessories* from relying on proportionate liability as a defence. The first reason for this is that the fraud limitation probably extends to equitable fraud, though there are some doubts about this.[153] But even if it does not so extend, the accessory is unlikely to be able to rely on proportionate liability. Since liability requires that A be actively involved in bringing about PW's wrong, it seems doubtful that A's wrong could ever be characterised as negligence or a failure to take reasonable care,[154] such as to fall within the pre-requisites for proportionate liability. Further, since accessorial liability is based on a certain kind of wrongdoing – culpable involvement with knowledge of the primary wrongdoer's wrong – that conduct is likely to be viewed as *intentional*.[155]

Whether *primary wrongdoers* can rely on proportionate liability depends on whether their wrong amounts to a failure to take reasonable care. This means that the different sources of primary wrong discussed in this chapter need to be considered separately.

The primary wrongs of breach of contract and tort can be dealt with quickly. Although it is possible to conceive of circumstances in which a party in primary breach of contract is in breach of a term to take reasonable care where that breach has been *induced* by the accessory, such circumstances are likely to be rare.[156] Similarly, where the primary wrongdoer is a joint tortfeasor who has committed a tort, it is unlikely that the wrong committed, being planned, is one that merely involves a failure to take care. Even though some cases have suggested the contrary, the better view is that '[t]here can be no accessory liability for tortious negligence'.[157]

This leaves us with the more difficult issue of whether a party in breach of an equitable wrong can rely on proportionate liability. Although the possibility that

[152] Civil Law (Wrongs) Act 2002 (ACT), s 107E; Civil Liability Act 2002 (NSW), s 34A; Proportionate Liability Act 2005 (NT), s 7; Civil Liability Act 2003 (Qld), ss 32D and 32F; Law Reform (Contributory Negligence and Apportionment of Liability Act 2001 (SA), s 4; Civil Liability Act 2002 (Tas), s 43A; Wrongs Act 1958 (Vic), s 24AM; Civil Liability Act 2002 (WA), s 5AJA.

[153] See the discussion in Gurr (n 3) 511 onwards. Gurr rightly argues that the legislation ought not to apply to accessories and it is unlikely that it will directly limit accessories' liability.

[154] This is so even where a mental element of reckless indifference or moral obtuseness suffices for liability, as under the traditional framework in equity: see Dietrich and Ridge (n 1) [8.3.4.4]. That mental element needs to be satisfied alongside the conduct element.

[155] Contrast Gurr (n 3) 515–16, who notes the possibility that an accessory might be liable for a factual failure to take care; but since knowledge-based liability (in the sense of constructive knowledge based on a failure to make reasonable enquiries) does not extend to negligence, this does not seem to be a realistic possibility. Gurr also seems to assume that an accessory who procures a trustee's breach of a duty of care could rely on proportionate liability, but this is not correct: it is the claim against A that must be an apportionable one for A to be able to rely on the defence.

[156] Even if it could be so characterised, importantly, if a claimant claims for other contraventions of strict obligations (even alongside an apportionable claim), those claims, if made out, will not be apportioned. See *Selig v Wealthsure Pty Ltd* [2015] HCA 18; (2015) 255 CLR 661. In other words, a claimant can be tactical and plead multiple claims.

[157] P Cane, '*Mens Rea* in Tort Law' (2000) *OJLS* 533, 546, fn 44. See the extensive discussion of the issue in Dietrich and Ridge (n 1) [5.5.5]. Davies disagrees: (n 2) 187. See also W Gummow, 'The Equitable Duties of Company Directors' (2013) 87 *Australian Law Journal* 753, arguing against equitable accessory liability arising in relation to equitable duties of care. I accept that the preclusion against accessory liability probably applies to careless conduct, such that accessory liability might well apply

the proportionate liability regime might apply to equitable claims was raised when the legislative schemes were first introduced,[158] that possibility has not yet eventuated in the case law and would at most apply to only a limited range of claims. One context in which it might apply, as Alison Gurr has pointed out, is where trustees of an express trust breach trust duties to take reasonable care when administering the trust.[159] In that case, the trustee is liable for a failure to take care and will have, one assumes, not acted fraudulently or with intent to cause loss. Such a trustee could seek to rely on the proportionate liability regime to limit her liability. I am not aware of any cases on point, however, and even if the legislation is interpreted to cover such a scenario, its impact is likely to be very limited.

Overall it is safe to conclude that the proportionate liability regime will probably have no application to accessories and perhaps only very limited application to primary wrongdoers who can identify an accessory as a concurrent wrongdoer.

VIII. Conclusion

The principles that determine accessory liability are becoming more settled as judicial decisions clarify ongoing issues. However, the law's approach to the apportionment of liability for losses, as between accessories and primary wrongdoers, is largely embryonic. In part, this may be because claimants generally only seek to pursue accessories where there are significant impediments to successful claims against the primary wrongdoers. Those impediments – such as insolvency – would equally reduce the likelihood of any contribution claims being brought by the accessories. As a matter of principle, however, contribution giving rise to just and equitable apportionment for damages paid by an accessory should be available in all cases, irrespective of the nature of the primary wrong committed. Statutory rules imposing proportionate liability are unlikely to impinge on that position.

As far as gains are concerned, defendants should generally be liable for the specific gains that they have made, and should not be liable for gains made by other defendants, as accessory or primary wrongdoer. But this is only a general starting position; the law must be sensitive to the facts of the cases and look beyond the form of transactions. There are many circumstance in which it may well be appropriate to find an accessory liable for gains made by the primary wrongdoer, or vice versa.

if a party brings a claim in the tort of negligence for deliberate acts of the primary wrongdoer. Even if such a claim is possible, however, proportionate liability would still not apply because of the intentional conduct.

[158] See VJ Vann, 'Equity and Proportionate Liability' (2007) 1 *Journal of Equity* 199, suggesting a number of circumstances in which equitable liability might be caught by the legislation, although since that article, it does not appear that there have been any successful attempts to circumvent joint and several liability. See, eg, *George v Webb* (n 145).

[159] See Gurr (n 3) 514–15. However, as she notes, although a non-trustee fiduciary may also owe equitable duties to take care, these are not fiduciary duties and accessory liability is unlikely to apply. If the proportionate liability provisions extend to wrongs that are not infringements of express duties of care, but involve merely factual failures to take care, as to which there is uncertainty, then a claim involving such factual failure could, conceivably, be an apportionable one.

PART III

Plaintiff-Defendant Apportionment

6

Contributory Negligence and Apportionment in Canadian Tort Law

LEWIS KLAR*

I. Introduction

All Canadian common law provinces, in line with other common law jurisdictions, have long since abandoned the common law tort principles regarding contributory negligence and the contribution obligations of concurrent wrongdoers.[1] The common law bars, which prevented contributorily negligent plaintiffs from recovering damages from negligent defendants except in certain circumstances and which prevented negligent wrongdoers from recovering contribution from concurrent wrongdoers, were replaced by apportionment and contribution provisions. In many respects, the provisions and issues to which they give rise across the various jurisdictions are similar and well understood.[2] What I propose to do in this

* I would like to thank John Kleefeld, David Cheifetz and James Goudkamp for their helpful comments in my preparation of this chapter.

[1] See Contributory Negligence Act RSA 2000 c C-27; Negligence Act RSBC 1996 c 333; Contributory Negligence Act RSNL 1990 c C-33; Contributory Negligence Act RSPEI 1988 c C-21; Contributory Negligence Act RSS 1978 c C-31; Negligence Act RSO 1990 c N1; Tortfeasors and Contributory Negligence Act RSM 1987 c T90; Contributory Negligence Act RSNS 1989 c 95; Contributory Negligence Act RSNB 2011 c 23. There is also legislation in the territories: see the Contributory Negligence Act RSNWT 1988 c 18; Contributory Negligence Act, RSR 2002 c 42. Three of the provinces have separate statutes dealing with contribution between wrongdoers; namely, Tort-Feasors Act RSA 2000 c T-5; Tortfeasors Act RSNB 19 c T-8; Tortfeasors Act RSNS 1989 c 471. In the Province of Quebec, which is a Civil Law jurisdiction, apportionment of liability is provided for in the Civil Code, Articles 1478 to 1481. This chapter deals with the law in the common law provinces. A very detailed account of the history of the introduction, development, and current state of the legislation and law reform efforts to improve it in Canadian provinces, and specifically in Saskatchewan and Ontario has been written by Professor Kleefeld in 'Concurrent Fault at 90: A History of Ontario's Negligence Act and Canada's Uniform Contributory Fault Act' in E Quill and R Friel (eds), *Damages and Compensation Culture: Comparative Perspectives* (Oxford, Hart Publishing, 2016) and 'The Contributory Negligence Act at Seventy' (2015) 78 *Saskatchewan Law Review* 31. Professor Kleefeld discusses the reform efforts which have occurred in Canada over the decades with particular attention paid to the 1984 Uniform Contributory Fault Act and its recommendations for reform. The leading Canadian text on contributory negligence and contribution between wrongdoers is D Cheifetz, *Apportionment of Fault in Tort* (Aurora Ontario, Canada Law Book Co, 1981).

[2] Glanville Williams' landmark text *Joint Torts and Contributory Negligence* (London, Stevens, 1951) laid out the various issues and has guided common law reforms of this area for over a half century.

chapter is to highlight some of my particular concerns with this area and to identify some uniquely Canadian approaches. I will restrict my comments to contributory negligence issues, leaving for others the much more complex questions which arise with respect to contribution between wrongdoers.[3]

II. Why Apportion at All?

When a plaintiff's own negligent conduct contributes to its injuries, the plaintiff's recovery of damages will be reduced to some extent.[4] It has been explained, and generally accepted by the courts, that a plaintiff can be contributorily negligent in one of three ways.[5] The plaintiff's negligence may have actually contributed to the cause of the accident itself,[6] have consisted in the plaintiff's self-exposure to a risk of involvement in an accident,[7] or it may have consisted in the plaintiff's failure to take precautions to prevent or minimise possible injuries, should an accident occur.[8] If a plaintiff is found to have been contributorily negligent in any of these three ways, a defendant, and, as happens frequently, its liability insurer, will not be fully liable for the injuries which the defendant caused. The plaintiff will not be fully compensated for its injuries and frequently will not have its own insurance to make up for the shortfall. This simple explanation of how contributory negligence works glosses over some interesting questions. The first, and most basic one, is why should a plaintiff's own negligent conduct prevent the full recovery of its damages? The second is, when is conduct sufficiently negligent to justify this result?

Reducing a plaintiff's recovery of damages clearly works against the compensation and deterrence goals of negligence liability, since it results in inadequate plaintiff compensation and less effective deterrence of negligent defendants. Thus, one would expect that there ought to be a good reason to allow this to happen.

The one commonly offered is that it is only fair that all those individuals whose negligent conduct was a factual and legal cause of an injury should bear

[3] See Cheifetz (ch 10, below), which deals with contribution between wrongdoers.

[4] How this is done in the Canadian common law provinces will be discussed shortly, although apportionment in Quebec seems to be dealt with in the same way. Most cases of contributory negligence involve plaintiffs who have themselves been negligent. There are, however, cases of 'imputed fault', whereby the fault of another person is imputed to an innocent plaintiff for the purposes of the contributory negligence provisions. This issue will not be examined in this chapter.

[5] See N Gravells, 'Three Heads of Contributory Negligence' (1977) 93 *LQR* 581. This approach was accepted by the Ontario Court of Appeal in *Zsoldos v Canadian Pacific Railway* 2009 ONCA 55, 93 OR (3d) 321.

[6] For example, not watching where one is going and falling into an unguarded excavation.

[7] For example, getting into a car driven by an intoxicated person.

[8] Failing to wear a seat belt, for example. Failing to take reasonable steps to minimise an injury after it has occurred is treated as a failure to mitigate damages for the purposes of assessment of damages. In Quebec, Art 1479 of the Civil Code specifically provides that defendants are not liable 'for any aggravation of the injury that the victim could have avoided'.

legal responsibility for it, even if one of those persons is the injured person.[9] This 'symmetry of treatment' argument is defensible when applied to the first type of contributory negligence; that is, being part of the causal sequence of events which led to the accident and resulted in the plaintiff's injuries. It seems fair that all of those whose negligent conduct contributed to the accident should bear legal responsibility for it. However, when considering contributory negligence as a defence in situations where the plaintiffs' negligence consisted only in failing to take reasonable steps to prevent, or minimise their injuries, which were caused by someone else's negligent acts, the defence can be questioned.[10]

Whereas the defendant's obligation arises from the defendant's duty not to unreasonably interfere with the plaintiff's right to the security of its person or property, the plaintiff owes no legal duty to the defendant and obviously cannot be said to owe a legal duty to itself. In fact, the opposite is generally true. Canadian common law does not normally require people to act reasonably to protect themselves from harm.[11] Canadian tort law in fact values the personal autonomy of unreasonable people to engage in risky activities, if they so choose. This was made clear by the Canadian Supreme Court in the social host liability case of *Childs v Desormeaux*.[12] One of the reasons offered by Chief Justice McLachlin in her decision to exonerate a social host of liability for injuries arising out of a motor vehicle accident caused by an inebriated guest was that the law 'accepts that competent people have the right to engage in risky activities'. As explained by the Chief Justice, 'the autonomy of risk takers or putative rescuers is not absolutely protected, but, at common law, *it is always respected*'.[13] This is not so when persons are required to take reasonable care to protect themselves from the negligent conduct of others. If, as the Chief Justice asserts, a competent person has the *right* to engage in risky

[9] As discussed by Professor R Stevens in 'Should Contributory Fault be Analogue or Digital' in M Dyson, J Goudkamp and F Wilmot-Smith (eds), *Defences in Tort* (Oxford, Hart Publishing, 2015) ch 13, 254, this is the 'symmetry of treatment' argument advanced by many scholars. For example, Ernie Weinrib in *The Idea of Private Law* (Oxford Scholarship On Line, 2013) 169, n 53 rationalises contributory negligence as follows: 'The defense expresses an idea of transactional equality: the plaintiff cannot demand that the defendant should observe a greater care than the plaintiff with respect to the plaintiff's safety. See Francis H Bohlen, 'Contributory Negligence' (1908) 21 *Harvard Law Review* 233, 255. This idea of equality underlies both the traditional common law rule, which denied all recovery, and the comparative negligence rule, pioneered in Ontario but now widely adopted, which apportions damages based on the degrees of fault.'

[10] As it has been, especially in the failure to wear seat belt cases. In *Philip v Hironka* [1998] 3 WWR 703 (Alta QB), Girgulis J argued that, since failing to wear a seat belt does not cause or contribute to an injury, but may only fail to prevent an injury, it does not fall within the wording of the legislation, although it falls within its 'spirit and intention'. Jurianz JA in *Snushall v Fulsang* (2005) 258 DLR (4th) (Ont CA) was even more direct: '[t]he failure to wear a seat belt "causes" injuries in the sense that the failure to use a prophylactic "causes" pregnancy'. See Klar & Jefferies, *Tort Law*, 6th edn (Toronto, Thompson Reuters, 2017) 636, n 93.

[11] Statute law might do so; for example, seat belt laws. These laws, however, are passed by legislatures for public policy reasons. They are not common law duties.

[12] [2006] 1 SCR 643.

[13] ibid, [39] (emphasis added). Thus, both the autonomy of the bystander to stand by and do nothing, and that of the risk taker to be unreasonable without being interfered with by strangers are respected.

activities, that right is certainly significantly undermined if exercising it may result in a loss of entitlement to be fully compensated for injuries caused by others.[14]

It is also clear that the positions of the two parties are quite different. The defendant's negligent conduct endangers others, which is clearly more egregious and worthy of sanction than conduct which only fails to protect oneself, but endangers no-one else. In addition, plaintiffs whose negligent conduct has failed to prevent or minimise their injuries already bear a heavy price – they must suffer these injuries. The consequences to a defendant of causing injuries to others are solely financial, if that. Whether a plaintiff requires an additional, and often significant deterrent, is questionable.

The argument that not requiring negligent plaintiffs to financially contribute to the costs of their injuries would be to hold defendants responsible for losses which were not fully their responsibility is also misconceived.[15] Those whose negligence contributed to the causing of an indivisible injury are taken as having caused it and therefore as being responsible for the full injury, notwithstanding the fact that there may be others whose negligence also contributed to it. They are therefore responsible for repairing all of its consequences. Each wrongdoer is legally responsible for the entire, indivisible injury and each can be required to compensate the plaintiff in full for that entire loss.[16] The fact that other wrongdoers, including the plaintiff, might not be called upon to pitch in does not mean that the wrongdoer who pays is being held responsible for losses which he or she did not cause. The law does not require all wrongdoers to be sued, and one should not conclude that a wrongdoer overcompensates the victim if part of the loss cannot be shifted to the victim. It would indeed be unfair if wrongdoers were being held liable for losses which were not their responsibility, but that is not happening in contributory negligence cases, even if the plaintiffs' damages are not reduced due to their own negligence.

The second issue is to determine when a plaintiff's conduct is sufficiently negligent to justify an application of the defence. Although the same standard of care principles as are used to determine a defendant's negligence are used in determining contributory negligence, it is clear that the positions of the parties are different. The plaintiff's contributory negligence in cases involving failures to

[14] It has been suggested to me that it is incorrect to state that contributory negligence requires plaintiffs to be reasonable. Negligent plaintiffs have a right to be as unreasonable as they please, but if they act unreasonably they lose their entitlement to full compensation. Although I agree with that terminology, the end result of losing compensation is the same for the contributorily negligent plaintiff, who might have been under the mistaken impression that its autonomy to be unreasonable would 'always' be respected.

[15] This is posited by Stevens (n 9) as an argument offered to justify contributory negligence. It is, however, not his view. Again, one might want distinguish between cases where the contributorily negligent plaintiff actually contributed to the sequence of events leading to the accident and where the negligence only consisted in failing to take self-protective measures, in evaluating this argument.

[16] As will be discussed below, in all Canadian common law provinces other than two, once having been found liable, each defendant is responsible to compensate the plaintiff in full. Joint (solidary), and not several liability, is the approach followed. In British Columbia and Nova Scotia, once a plaintiff has been found contributorily negligent, the defendant's liability is several.

protect oneself endangers no-one else. As noted above, the common law asserts that a person's' autonomy rights to be unreasonable are always respected. The consequences of a finding of contributory negligence for an injured person are severe. All of these considerations probably influence a court before allowing the defence to succeed. How far should the courts go in requiring reasonable 'self-protecting' behaviour on the part of accident victims? We all act unreasonably on occasion, particularly when the foreseeable risk endangers no-one else but ourselves. A recent Canadian case illustrates this concern. In *Wormald v Chiarot*,[17] a 15-year-old teen was injured in a single-vehicle roll-over accident. The vehicle was being driven by the plaintiff's 17-year-old friend. The driver had limited driving experience with only a novice driver's licence, to the plaintiff's knowledge. The driver had been drinking moderately, as had several of the other occupants of the vehicle, including the plaintiff. There were ten teens in the mid-size Honda CR-V, although the vehicle only had five seat belts. The plaintiff was seated in the back hatch area of the vehicle where there were no seat belts. The vehicle had made several stops that evening prior to the accident, during which the plaintiff could have left the vehicle and made her way home by walking, or by bus. One of the stops was for the purpose of buying eggs, some of which the occupants threw at people. Some of the occupants of the vehicle encouraged the driver to speed up to 150 km/h. The driver was speeding and lost control of the vehicle. It left the highway, and rolled over, ending up in a ditch. The plaintiff was injured, but apparently at the time, not seriously.

Was the plaintiff contributorily negligent in participating in this adventure, without objection? The trial judge thought so and reduced her damages by 40 per cent. The Court of Appeal disagreed, and exonerated the plaintiff entirely.[18] As will be discussed below, even if the plaintiff's conduct were negligent, this negligence must have been both the factual and proximate cause of her injuries, before her damages could be reduced on account of it. Therefore, in the case of the plaintiff's decision to sit in an area of the vehicle without available seat belts, it would have had to be shown that, if the plaintiff had worn a seat belt, her injuries would have been less serious. The trial judge held that this had not been proved, and thus, for this reason, correctly held that this was not relevant contributory negligence.[19] How about, however, the plaintiff's other decisions; for example, the decision to be driven in a vehicle which had 10 teens in it, in circumstances where the parties, including the driver, had been drinking, where the driver was speeding, was inexperienced, and in breach of her novice driver's licence? Were these decisions

[17] (2015) BCJ No 323, varied (2016) 33 CCLT (4th) 237, 404 DLR (4th) 186 (BCCA).

[18] Note that in Canada, as in other jurisdictions, 'absent exceptional circumstances', apportionment is a question of fact for the trial judge and should not be varied by an appellate court. See Klar & Jefferies (n 10) 630.

[19] It is not clear from the judgment, the extent to which the causal connection between the failure to wear her seat belt and her injuries was in issue, or argued. Common sense would lead me to believe that being thrown around the interior of a vehicle during a high speed roll-over would cause the passenger greater injury than if she had been securely strapped into her seat.

unreasonable? Were they the factual and proximate causes of the injuries? Relying on an earlier British Columbia trial decision, *Thon v Podollan*,[20] the defendants argued that, even if it could not be shown that the drinking,[21] the overcrowding, the egg-throwing and the lack of seat belt caused the injuries to be more serious than they otherwise would have been, the plaintiff was negligent in initially entering and then staying in the car without objecting to the clearly unreasonable behaviour in which both by the driver and her passengers were engaged. Had the plaintiff avoided this situation, which clearly was fraught with risk, she would not have been injured.[22]

An interesting aspect of the Court of Appeal's decision was the suggestion that the plaintiff's decisions were actually not all that unreasonable. As stated by Donald JA:

> I infer from his reasons that the judge thought that the circumstances were fraught with risk that there might be an accident of some kind. I find that too vague a basis on which to find Ms Wormald contributorily negligent. Life is full of risks, more so perhaps for young people, which society accepts by granting driver's licenses to 16-year-old persons. Accepting a ride with friends in high spirits out on a lark is not an inherently and unacceptably dangerous activity.[23]

Whether the plaintiff acted reasonably or not is a question of fact about which judges can disagree. The trial judge in this case thought that the plaintiff had acted unreasonably, so much so that he apportioned 40 per cent of the responsibility to her. I would venture to say that most persons would agree with the trial judge that the plaintiff's decisions were not reasonable ones and that she willingly participated in an adventure fraught with foreseeable risks. Her decision to participate was certainly the factual cause of her injuries and, I would argue, the proximate one as well. This still leaves open the question, however, as to why the common law should penalise the plaintiff, even if she had been unreasonable by endangering only herself and why it should disentitle her to full compensation for the injuries fully caused by the negligent defendant. This is what the legislation requires, however, and it is to this legislation that I will now turn.

III. The Basis of Apportionment in Canadian Law

Canadian contributory negligence law is unique in the common law world, in that it apportions liability between plaintiff and defendant solely on the basis of comparative blameworthiness, disregarding any issue of 'causal potency'.

[20] 2001 BCSC 194.

[21] The Court of Appeal noted that the drinking was very minimal and the driver was not inebriated.

[22] The speeding did cause the accident, but the Court of Appeal reasoned that, up to that point in time, the defendant's driving was fine and thus the plaintiff was not unreasonable in remaining in the car on that account.

[23] *Wormald* (n 17) [20].

As explained by Professor Goudkamp and myself in a recent article, this approach to apportionment has been made clear in a number of Canadian cases.[24] The Canadian approach is, to a large part, dictated by the very words used in the various provincial statutes, which refer specifically to determining apportionment based upon the degree to which the parties were at 'fault,' or were 'negligent'.[25] None of the provisions speaks in terms of causal potency, or degree. In considering the degrees of fault of the parties, the courts consider a number of factors, which go only to blameworthiness. As outlined by Fruman JA in *Heller v Martens*,[26] these might include the nature of the duty owed by the defendant, the number of acts of fault committed by each party, the sequence (timing) of the negligent acts, the nature of the misconduct, and the extent to which statutory breach was involved. The notion that causal potency is a relevant factor has been explicitly rejected by Canadian courts.[27]

As we suggested in our article, even in those jurisdictions which consider the issue of causal potency or significance as a factor in apportioning liability,[28] the courts have never really explained what the criterion involves and the concept has largely been ignored. We also doubted whether there can be 'degrees of causation'. We agreed with Professor Wright's statement that causation is not 'a matter of degree'. 'Some condition either was or was not a cause' and thus 'true "causal apportionment" is conceptually meaningless'.[29]

IV. The Effect of a Finding of Contributory Negligence

In all Canadian common law provinces, once a plaintiff has been found contributorily negligent and the apportionment decision has been made, a plaintiff's damages will be reduced by reference to its degree of fault. This can, of course, result in a significant financial hit to an injured plaintiff. If one considers, for example, contributory negligence due to a plaintiff's failure to wear a seat belt,

[24] See J Goudkamp and L Klar, 'Apportionment of Damages for Contributory Negligence: The Causal Potency Criterion' (2016) 53 *Alta L R* 849. For a more complete discussion of the Canadian jurisprudence on this matter, see Klar & Jefferies (n 10) 629–32.

[25] The provisions vary somewhat. See Goudkamp and Klar, ibid 858. In the Province of Quebec, apportionment is based on 'the seriousness of the fault' of each person, which includes the fault of the victim. See Art 1478.

[26] [2002] AJ No 638, (2002) 213 DLR (4th) 129 (Alta CA). This was a 'failure to wear a seat-belt' case.

[27] See, eg, *Clyke v Blenkhorn* (1958) 13 DLR (2d) 293, 304 (MacDonald J). Despite this established Canadian position, the Manitoba Law Reform Commission, in Report No 128 *Contributory Fault: The Tortfeasors and Contributory Negligence Act* (2013) recommended that apportionment be based on both blameworthiness and causation, which it believed would better promote fairness and justice between the parties. This recommendation has not been taken up by the legislature.

[28] We considered the law in the United States, Australia and Great Britain.

[29] See Goudkamp and Klar (n 24) 862, citing R Wright, 'Allocating Liability Among Multiple Responsible Causes: A Principled Defense of Joint and Several Liability for Actual Harm and Risk Exposure' (1988) 21 *UC Davis L Rev* 1141, 1146.

reductions of 25–35 per cent are not uncommon in Canada. In some provinces, there is a legislated 25 per cent mandatory reduction.[30] Considering that a failure to wear a seat belt will only result in a modest fine in the region of $200 in most Canadian provinces, the 25 per cent reduction in damages for injuries exacerbated by the failure to have worn a seat belt is, by comparison, very severe. Thus, while the legislatures penalise a plaintiff minimally for this breach, court decisions can result in a 'penalty' of thousands of dollars in lost compensation for injured car accident passengers or drivers who were not wearing their seat belts.

In all but two common law provinces, once the plaintiff's damages have been reduced in proportion to its fault, the liability of 'several, concurrent wrongdoer' defendants is joint and several (or, as is sometimes said in other jurisdictions, 'solidary').[31] This means that the plaintiff is entitled to its full (reduced) recovery from any of the liable defendants. The defendants who are found liable and pay more than their 'fair' share of the damages to the plaintiff can recover contribution from the other wrongdoers.[32] This raises the issue of what happens if some of these other wrongdoers cannot, due to insolvency for example, pay up. Provinces have different ways of handling this. Saskatchewan, for example, provides that the uncollectable shares will be divided by all the parties who are found at fault.[33] Other provinces do not have provisions which allow for the uncollectable share to be redistributed to other wrongdoers.[34] The interesting question which I would like to raise is whether the contributorily negligent plaintiff should participate in this redistribution. The rationale for not involving the plaintiff in redistributing the shortfall is that the wrongdoing defendant, which has paid more than its fair share but which cannot receive contribution from an insolvent co-defendant, is responsible for the full loss and is therefore not overcompensating the plaintiff, even if the plaintiff is not required to participate. One can see, however, that this rationale is inconsistent with the reason given for reducing the plaintiff's damages by its degree of fault in the first place. If what is 'sauce for the goose' should be 'sauce for the gander' on the basis of 'symmetry of treatment' rationale, one would have to conclude that the wrongdoing plaintiff should also be forced to contribute to the shortfall.

In two provinces, British Columbia and Nova Scotia, courts have interpreted their provisions in such a way as to convert the joint liability of wrongdoers into

[30] In Newfoundland and Labrador, see Automobile Insurance Act RSNL 1990 c A-22 s 28; and in New Brunswick see Insurance Act RSNB 173 c I.12 s 265.2(1), as applied in *Jones v Chabot* [2015] NBJ No 168.

[31] Several concurrent wrongdoers are persons whose independent acts of negligence contributed to the causing of an indivisible injury.

[32] See Cheifetz (ch 10, below) for discussion.

[33] Contributory Negligence Act RSS 1978 c C-31 s 3.1 (2). The plaintiff is included in this reallocation only if the plaintiff was contributorily negligent.

[34] See the Manitoba Law Reform Commission Report No 128 (n 27) 20–23, where this issue is discussed.

several liability, when a plaintiff is found contributorily negligent.[35] Although these decisions were based on the construction of the provisions, and not on any point of principle, they do result in all wrongdoers, including the plaintiff, being treated in the same way, consistent with the 'symmetry of treatment' rationale. Unfortunately for the plaintiff, however, any uncollectable amount from one of the other wrongdoers will fall on its shoulders, unless a way is provided to redistribute it to the others.

V. Proximate Cause and 'Last Clear Chance'

At common law, the courts were able to avoid the contributory negligence bar by finding that, despite the plaintiff's negligence, the defendant had the 'last clear chance' to avoid the injury-causing event.[36] In this case, the plaintiff would be entitled to a full recovery. The 'last clear chance' rule could have been justified on the basis that the defendant's last, clear chance to avoid the accident might be treated as having severed the chain of causation between the plaintiff's negligence and the injury-causing event, making the plaintiff's negligence too remote to be considered contributory. Thus, looked at in this way, it was an application of the principle that a negligent act must have been both the factual and the proximate cause of the injury, in order to hold the actor liable for it.[37] If, on the other hand, the rule was applied only as a device, or ruse, to avoid the contributory negligence bar, it was a policy decision made in order to provide compensation to the plaintiff injured by a defendant's negligence. But, in this case, the plaintiff would receive full compensation and its own negligence would have to be ignored, since the common law did not provide for apportionment.

With the introduction of the apportionment legislation, the courts no longer had to worry about disentitling a plaintiff from any compensation if found negligent and therefore did not need the 'last clear chance' rule to deal with this concern. The legislatures had to decide, however, how the 'last clear chance' rule should be accommodated, if at all, in their statutes.

Three approaches are followed in Canada. Some provinces make no mention of the fate of 'last clear chance', leaving it to the courts to decide whether it survived apportionment.[38] Some provinces have expressly abolished it. For example, the

[35] See, among other decisions, *Leischner v West Kootenay Power & Light Co* [1986] 3 WWR 97 (BCCA) and *Inglis Ltd v South Shore Sales & Service Ltd* (1979) 104 DLR (3d) 502 (NSSC AD).

[36] See Klar & Jefferies (n 10) 625, where this issue is discussed more fully.

[37] The same principle would apply if the plaintiff's negligence severed the chain of causation between the defendant's act and the plaintiff's injury. However, it was unnecessary to rationalise the dismissal of the plaintiff's action on this basis, since the contributory negligence bar was a sufficient reason to dismiss the plaintiff's action in any event.

[38] The legislation of Nova Scotia, New Brunswick, Manitoba, and Ontario contains no reference to 'last clear chance'.

British Columbia Negligence Act states that '[t]his Act applies to all cases where damage is caused or contributed to by the act of a person even if another person had the opportunity of avoiding the consequences of that act and negligently or carelessly failed to do so'.[39] Two provinces and the legislation of the Northwest Territories and Yukon have included an express provision of the rule. For example, the Saskatchewan provision states:

> Where the trial is before a judge with a jury the judge shall not submit to the jury any question as to whether, notwithstanding the fault of one party, the other could have avoided the consequences thereof unless in his opinion there is evidence upon which the jury could find that the act or omission of the latter was clearly subsequent to and severable from the act or omission of the former so as not to be substantially contemporaneous with it.[40]

It is my view that the rule of 'last clear chance' was implicitly abolished by the apportionment legislation and no mention need have been made of it in the legislative provisions. In order for a defendant to be found liable to the plaintiff, its negligence must have been both a factual and proximate cause of the plaintiff's injury. Thus, the intervening act of the plaintiff, or a third party, might be treated as having severed the chain of causation between the defendant's negligence and the plaintiff's injury so as to make the defendant's negligence no longer causally connected to it and therefore too remote, as a matter of law. The same can be said of a defendant's negligence. It may have severed the chain of causation between the plaintiff's negligence and the plaintiff's injury, making the plaintiff's injury too remote and therefore not legally contributory.[41] The fact that one party's negligence was the first, or last, in the sequence of events leading to the injury should be of no consequence, once it is determined that the injuries which resulted were within the foreseeable risks of that negligence. Including a provision which either expressly abolishes the rule, or adopts it in modified language, can only lead to confusion in the minds of a judge or jury.

Cases involving vehicles which run into other vehicles negligently parked, or stopped, alongside a road or highway demonstrate the problem. In *Wickberg v Patterson*,[42] for example, a motorcyclist ran into the side of a truck which was backing up alongside a highway, with the truck partly on the shoulder and partly in the driving lane. The truck driver had stopped to assist another driver whose car

[39] RSBC 1996 c 333, s 8. See also the Prince Edward Island and Alberta statutes. The Federal Maritime Liability Act SC 2001 c 6, s 21 also expressly abolishes the rule.

[40] Contributory Negligence Act RSS 1978 c C-31, s 5. There is a similarly worded provision directing judges in trials without a jury to proceed in the same way. The Newfoundland and Labrador Contributory Negligence Act RSNL 1990 C c-33, ss 5 and 6 contains the same provisions.

[41] Some legislative provisions hint at this need for factual and proximate cause, but without going too deeply into it. The Contributory Negligence Act of Alberta, for example, states in s 1(2) that: 'Nothing in this section operates to render a person liable for damage or loss to which the person's fault has not contributed'. What is meant by the word 'contributed' is not explained, but it presumably should be taken to refer to both factual and proximate cause.

[42] 2000 ABCA 251, (1997) 33 CCLT (2d) 231 (Alta CA).

had rolled into a ditch. It was estimated that the motorcyclist had between twelve and eighteen seconds after seeing the truck, in which to avoid hitting it. The trial judge found the plaintiff motorcyclist fully responsible for his injuries, as he held that his negligence was the 'effective and dominant cause' of the accident.[43] This would be so even if the defendant truck driver was partly negligent.[44] At the time of this decision, Alberta's legislation had a provision similar to the one described above for provinces which maintain a 'last clear chance' provision in their Acts; namely, one providing that the ability of one party to avoid the accident is not to be taken into account unless that act 'was so clearly subsequent to and severable from the act or omission of the former as not to be substantially contemporaneous therewith'.[45] Justice Picard, in the Alberta Court of Appeal, reversed the trial judge, noting how the inclusion of the 'last clear chance' provision in the Alberta Act, even in its modified form, was unnecessary and could be a potential 'trap'. As explained by Justice Picard, the provision added nothing to the law of negligence which we did not already know. A party's negligence must be both the factual and proximate cause of an injury before it can be contributory. It is clear that subsequent and several acts can cause a party's prior negligence to be too remote. This is rarely found, however, since, with the introduction of apportionment legislation, judges generally prefer to apportion, as in fact Justice Picard did in *Wickberg*.[46]

The persistence of 'last clear chance' is evident even in provinces which have expressly abolished it. In *Lawrence v Prince Rupert (City)*,[47] the plaintiff tripped over a pole that had been left unattended on the sidewalk by the defendant. The trial judge found that, even though the defendant had been negligent and the rule of 'last clear chance' had been expressly abolished in the British Columbia Act, the defendant's negligence was no longer an effective cause of the accident, since the plaintiff 'had the opportunity and ability to easily avoid tripping over it [ie, the pole].'[48] On appeal, the majority of the Court did not agree that the defendant had even been negligent in leaving the pole unattended. Since, however, the defendant did not dispute the trial judge's finding of negligence, the Court turned to the 'last clear chance'/causation issue. Without delving into this matter in too much depth, Finch CJ for the majority stated that causation is a matter of fact. Finch CJ held that the trial judge's decision that the defendant's negligence in leaving the pole on the sidewalk was not a proximate cause of the plaintiff's injuries, was a reasonable one, which should not be disturbed. The plaintiff should have

[43] This quote is referred to in the Court of Appeal judgment (1997) 33 CCLT (2d) 231 [11].

[44] As noted by Picard JA in the Court of Appeal judgment, ibid, the trial judge 'had said, on a number of occasions, that the respondent (truck driver) was negligent'.

[45] This was found in s 7 of the Act, since repealed.

[46] Justice Picard held the parties to be equally liable. Note that following the Alberta Court of Appeal's judgment in *Wickberg*, the 'last clear chance' provisions of the Alberta Act were repealed; see Justice Statutes Amendment Act SA 2000 c 20, s 72.

[47] [2005] BCJ No 2522 (BCCA).

[48] 2003 BCSC 465 [40].

avoided the pole. The dissenting Justice Esson JA, however, noted that the trial judge found the defendant to have been negligent, in that 'as a reasonable person' it 'would have known that placing and leaving the pole on the sidewalk as it was, without any protective barrier, would create a risk that pedestrians might trip over it and be injured'. Therefore, the trial judge's subsequent holding that, because the plaintiff had the opportunity to avoid tripping over it, the defendant's negligence was no longer causative, could not stand. There were two acts of negligence – the plaintiff's failure to avoid the pole and the defendant's leaving of the pole unattended and unprotected. To ignore the defendant's negligence because the plaintiff could have avoided the risk of injury to which it gave rise, was, in my view, effectively to apply 'last clear chance'. This is wrong, especially when the legislation had expressly abolished the rule. Subsequent British Columbia Court of Appeal judgments have agreed with this argument and have reversed trial judgments which did not apportion liability where both parties were found to have been negligent.[49]

VI. Scope of the Statutory Contributory Negligence Defence

One of the issues which Canadian courts have had to consider is the scope of the contributory negligence statutory defence. The defence is generally utilised in negligence actions. Can it be applied, however, to other causes of action – such as the intentional torts, nuisance, trespass, conversion, or strict liability actions?[50] Is it applicable in negligent statement cases?

Let me first consider liability for negligent statements. In Canada, the 'special relationship' between the representor and representee, which forms the basis of the defendant representor's duty of care owed to the plaintiff representee, is generally agreed to be 'foreseeable and reasonable' reliance. The presumptive duty is owed when it is reasonably foreseeable by the defendant that the plaintiff would rely on the statement and where that reliance would be reasonable.[51] Although the

[49] See, eg, *Skinner v Guo* (2010) 321 DLR (4th) 272 (BCCA) reversing 2009 BCSC 1828, a case involving a collision between the plaintiff's car and the defendant's car, which was unlawfully parked on the highway without using any warning lights. The Court of Appeal held that the trial judge, having found that the defendant created an unreasonable risk of harm, was in error in concluding that this was not a cause of the collision.

[50] The issue of the scope of the defence also arises with respect to the legislative provisions dealing with contribution between wrongdoers. Can there be contribution between defendants who are liable for torts other than negligence? As with contributory negligence, the provincial statutes are not uniform in their wording and judicial decisions vary depending on the jurisdiction. Although this chapter focuses on contributory negligence and not contribution between wrongdoers, judgments defining 'fault' or 'negligence' with respect to the latter issue are informative in dealing with the scope of the contributory negligence defence.

[51] Another interesting feature of Canadian negligent statement law is that the 'special relationship' only creates a presumptive duty. The duty, once found, can be limited or negated by 'policy' considerations at

'voluntary assumption of responsibility' test is seen as the basis of the duty by courts and commentators in other jurisdictions, and has some support in Canada,[52] the foreseeable and reasonable reliance approach is the generally accepted one in Canada.[53]

This then raises an interesting question. Can a duty of care be owed to a plaintiff whose reliance on the advice was unreasonable, subject to the defence of contributory negligence, or is there no duty owed at all? Canadian courts are divided on this issue. Some have held that a duty is owed to a plaintiff who unreasonably relied on advice, but that the damages can be reduced by the plaintiff's contributory negligence,[54] while others have held that the defence of contributory negligence is inconsistent with the recognition of a duty of care.[55] Although I tend to agree with the latter view, I concede that there may be cases where, despite the fact that it was reasonable for the plaintiff to have relied on the advice, other independent actions taken by the plaintiff prior to acting upon the advice might have been unreasonable and contributed to the losses. In that case, apportionment would be appropriate.[56]

stage two of the duty test. This innovation arises from La Forest J's judgment in *Hercules Managements Ltd v Ernst & Young* [1997] 2 SCR 165. La Forest J felt that the negligent statement cases should be fitted into the mould of the *Anns* 'two-stage' duty test, with a *prima facie* duty being established at stage one, and policy considerations brought in at stage two. Prior to *Hercules Managements*, the 'special relationship' contained all the duty elements. Applying this new formula to the facts of *Hercules Managements*, La Forest J decided that, although there was a special relationship and hence a duty owed by auditors to investors, it was negated by policy considerations of indeterminate liability. The investors had used the auditor's report for investment decisions, a purpose for which it had not been prepared. In its later judgment in *R v Imperial Tobacco* 2011 SCC 42, [2011] 3 SCR 45, the Supreme Court further refined its approach to negligent statement cases by utilising its *Cooper v Hobart* 2001 SCC 79, [2001] 3 SCR 537 duty formula. The test is now foreseeability and proximity, which creates the presumptive duty at stage one and residual policy concerns at the second stage of the test.

[52] Both Professor Feldthusen and Justice Russell Brown, in their respective academic writings, support the voluntary assumption of responsibility approach. See B Feldthusen, *Economic Negligence*, 6th edn (Toronto, Carswell, 2012) and R Brown, *Pure Economic Loss in Canadian Negligence Law* (Markham Ontario, LexisNexis, 2011).

[53] For references to a number of Canadian cases, see Klar & Jefferies (n 10) 279.

[54] A leading case which adopted this position is *Grand Restaurants of Canada Ltd v Toronto* (1981) 123 DLR (3d) 349 (Ont HC), affd (1982) 140 DLR (3d) 191 (Ont CA). In *S Maclise Enterprises Inc v Union Securities* 2009 ABCA 424 (Can LII) the Alberta Court of Appeal, while conceding that 'it obviously appears to be inconsistent for the trial judge to find reliance was reasonable and to also find contributory negligence in relying on that representation', held that, where the representee acted negligently in failing to exercise due diligence with respect to matters outside of that representation, a finding of contributory negligence is appropriate.

[55] See, eg, *Betker v Williams* [1992] 2 WWR 534 (BCCA) and *Kripps v Touche Ross & Co* [1999] 3 WWR 629 (BCSC). In the latter case, Lowry J stated at 633: 'It cannot be said that a person relied reasonably on the statement yet acted unreasonably in relying on it.'

[56] This was the approach followed by Cullity J in *Transamerica Life Insurance Co v Hutton* (2000) 33 RPR (3d) 1 (Ont SCJ) additional reasons at (2001) Carswell Ont 6 (SCJ), and by the Alberta Court of Appeal in *Maclise Enterprises* (n 54). However, I would suggest that this should be the rare case. Courts which agree that a plaintiff's reliance on advice was both foreseeable and reasonable should not penalise a plaintiff who fails to take steps to verify the accuracy of the advice, by a finding of contributory negligence.

Whether the defence of contributory negligence should be available in other tort actions, such as the intentional torts, nuisance, trespass, conversion and strict liability torts is a more pressing issue. Since contributory negligence is a statutory defence, one should look first to the statutory provisions for an answer to this question. In defining the scope of the defence, the provincial provisions vary in their language. Some statutes use both words 'fault or negligence'.[57] Others use only the word 'fault'.[58] One statute uses only the word 'negligence'.[59] It is arguable that the term 'fault' is broader than the word 'negligence' and thus that statutes which refer to 'fault', and certainly 'fault or negligence', implicitly include all tort actions based on any type of wrongdoing. This argument however cannot be made in reference to the Manitoba act, where only the word 'negligence' is used.[60]

Putting the issue of language aside, as a matter of principle, should the defence be restricted to negligence actions? I would argue it should not be. It should be available and has been applied in Canada in the intentional torts. In *Berntt v Vancouver (City)*,[61] for example, the defendant police officer was found liable at trial for intentionally firing an anti-riot weapon at the plaintiff during a riot following a hockey game. The plaintiff, however, was held 75 per cent contributorily negligent for having incited the crowd.[62] In Canadian tort law, moreover, provocation by a plaintiff has long been used as a defence to intentional torts and has resulted in the reduction of the plaintiff's damages.[63] Provocation can be viewed as a type of contributory negligence, and there is no reason why other types of unreasonable conduct on the plaintiff's part should be excluded from the

[57] See, eg, the Ontario provision – 'in any action for damages that is founded upon the fault or negligence …'.

[58] See, eg, the Alberta provision – 'where by fault of two or more persons damage is caused …'.

[59] The Manitoba provision – 'in any action for damages that is founded upon the negligence of the defendant …'. It is interesting to note that the Manitoba Law Reform Commission's recent report No 128 (n 27) recommended that the Act use the word 'fault,' rather than 'negligence'. It went even further, recommending that 'fault' be defined as a tort, breach of statutory duty that creates liability for damages, breach of contractual duty of care that creates liability for damages, and a failure of a person to take reasonable care of his own person, property or economic interest, whether or not it is intentional. In a recent Saskatchewan case, *Stoney v Sound Stage Performance* [2017] SJ No 131, the court, dealing with the issue of contribution between wrongdoers, denied an application by a defendant sued for negligence to add as a third party defendant a person liable for an intentional tort. This, despite the fact that the Saskatchewan legislation refers to 'fault'. The court relied on a holding in an earlier Saskatchewan Court of Appeal judgment dealing with defamation, that there could not be contribution between wrongdoers outside of negligence actions. See *Cherneskey v Armadale Publishers* [1974] 6 WWR 162 (Sask CA).

[60] In *Caners v Eli Lilly Canada Inc* [1996] 5 WWR 381 (Man CA) this argument was used by the Manitoba Court of Appeal to refuse to apply the contributory negligence defence to a breach of contract action.

[61] [1997] 4 WWR 505 (BCSC).

[62] The plaintiff's action was subsequently dismissed based on the police officer's successful defence under the Criminal Code. See [2001] BCJ No 2658.

[63] There is a debate in Canadian tort law as to whether provocation reduces all of the plaintiff's damages or only punitive damages, if any are awarded. The weight of the authority is that it reduces all of the damages. This is a sensible approach, as it is unlikely that punitive damages would even be awarded in cases where the plaintiff's behaviour was provocative.

defence of contributory negligence. If, of course, the defendant's conduct is egregious and committed with the intent to injure, it is unlikely that a court will reduce the plaintiff's compensation on account of its own unreasonable conduct.[64]

The defence has also been applied in a nuisance action[65] and in trespass actions where negligence formed the basis of the defendant's wrongdoing.[66]

The application of the defence of contributory negligence to strict liability torts where there was no fault or wrongdoing on the defendant's part is more difficult. How does one compare degrees of fault when the person sued was not at fault?

This question was considered recently in a wild animal injury case, *Cowles v Balac*.[67] The plaintiffs suffered serious injuries when they were attacked by a tiger in a wild game park while sitting in their car. The tiger was able to enter the car through the car's open windows. Although the reason why these windows were open was in dispute, the trial judge concluded that the most reasonable explanation was that the driver's arm inadvertently came into contact with the window switches. The trial judge held that the game park operator was strictly liable as a keeper of a wild animal. With respect to the defence of contributory negligence, the trial judge questioned the applicability of contributory negligence to strict liability cases, but ultimately held that the plaintiffs had not been contributorily negligent.

The issue of the applicability of the defence of contributory negligence to strict liability torts was considered by Justice Borins dissenting in the Court of Appeal's judgment.[68] As with our earlier discussion of 'last clear chance', it appears that

[64] Most cases of intentional torts, such as assault or battery, involve the intention to harm. This, however, is not necessarily true in all cases. In *Brushett v Cowan* (1990) 69 DLR (4th) 743 (Nfld CA), for example, the trial judge found a doctor liable for a medical battery. The doctor performed a medical procedure allegedly without consent. The trial judge stated that contributory negligence could apply to a battery where there was no intent to cause harm. The Court of Appeal held that the plaintiff had consented and dismissed the battery action.

[65] See *Koch Indust Ltd v City of Vancouver* [1982] 4 WWR 92 (BCSC). See also *Funnell v CPR and Bowden* [1964] 2 OR 325 (HCJ). It is interesting to note that, in both of these cases, the defendants who were liable in nuisance had been negligent. Thus, whether the defence of contributory negligence can apply in a nuisance action where there was no negligence on the defendant's part was not in issue.

[66] In *Bell Canada v COPE (Sarnia) Ltd* (1980) 11 CCLT 170 [180] (Ont HC) Justice Allen Linden applied the defence to a case of negligent trespass stating: 'Fault and negligence, as these words are used in the statute, are not the same thing. Fault certainly includes negligence, but it is much broader than that. Fault incorporates all intentional wrongdoing, as well as other types of substandard conduct.' Other Canadian judgments have supported this approach. Canadian tort law is somewhat unique, in that it acknowledges that trespasses can be committed either intentionally, or negligently. This approach is not without controversy. In an earlier Ontario judgment, *Hollebone v Barnard* [1954] OJ No 532, [1954] OR 236, this matter was considered by the Court and it was determined by Wells J that, in an action based on trespass, contributory negligence does not apply. It is important to note, however, that Wells J stated at [9] that, while the negligence of the defendant was 'averred as an alternative plea, it was not relied on and the case was presented as one of trespass'. For a discussion, see Klar & Jefferies (n 10) 64–67.

[67] [2005] OJ No 229 (Ont SCJ), 29 CCLT (3d) 284, affd [2006] 83 OR (3d) 660 (Ont CA).

[68] The dissent related to the decision of the trial judge to strike out the jury before the beginning of the trial. The majority of the Court of Appeal affirmed that decision; Borins JA disagreed.

considerations of 'causation' (ie, was it the defendant's keeping of a wild animal, or the plaintiff's own behaviour that caused the injury?), become intertwined with the issue of apportionment of liability. If the court decides that it was the plaintiff's conduct which caused the injury, and not the defendant's keeping of the animal, then, of course, there can be no apportionment – the defendant is not liable. If, on the other hand, the court decides that the plaintiff's conduct, negligent or not, was not a cause of the injury, but rather it was defendant's keeping and failure to control a wild animal, then, again there is no apportionment – liability falls squarely on the shoulders of the defendant. But, as with the confusion surrounding the 'last clear chance' doctrine, if the court decides that there were two concurrent causes cumulatively necessary for the injury – both the defendant's failure to control a wild animal and the plaintiff's unreasonable actions with respect to it – what then?

Justice Borins, adopting a causation approach to this issue, argued that, if it can be shown by the defendant that the plaintiff's own lack of reasonable care contributed to the cause of his or her damages, the plaintiff's damages must be reduced 'to that extent'. He conceded that while 'it may be doctrinally counter-intuitive to apply comparative negligence principles where a defendant's liability is strict and not dependent on negligence', in his view 'functional and fairness considerations strongly suggest that comparative negligence principles are appropriate where a plaintiff's misconduct or want of care is a contributing factor to his or her damages'.[69]

There are several objections to Justice Borins' approach. The first is that applying the statutory defence of contributory negligence to strict liability actions is clearly outside the express provisions of any of the provincial statutes. As noted above, depending on the province, the defence applies in actions based on 'fault', 'negligence', or 'fault or negligence'. Actions based on 'strict liability' do not fall under any of these characterisations. Secondly, and more to the point, how, under comparative 'fault' principles, can one compare the fault of the plaintiff with the strict liability of the defendant? It cannot be done, unless one is prepared to attribute 100 per cent of the liability to the negligent plaintiff.[70] As discussed above, under Canadian law and as a matter of logic, to apportion liability based upon 'degrees of causation' is wrong.

Depending on the nature of the strict liability claim, there is a solution to this dilemma. In strict liability claims based on *Rylands v Fletcher*,[71] the common law approach articulated by Blackburn J (that, if an escape was caused by the plaintiff's

[69] *Cowles* (n 67) [218]. Justice Borins' judgment on this point was *obiter*. He did not explain how the liability can be apportioned on causal contribution grounds.

[70] It appears that, in some jurisdictions, a plaintiff can be found 100% at fault; see for example Civil Liability Act 2002 (NSW), s 5S. This, to my knowledge, has never been held, or proposed, in Canada. If the plaintiff was 100% at fault relative to the defendant, it is unclear to me why the defendant could even be held liable, unless its liability was strict, or based on some other non-negligent cause of action.

[71] (1868) LR 3 HL 330 affirming (1866) LR 1 Ex 265.

own fault, the strict liability of the defendant does not apply), ought to prevail as current law.[72] This does not, however, mean that the defendant should not be held liable for its negligence in contributing to the escape. And, in that event, claiming that the plaintiff was contributorily negligent and that there should be apportionment is entirely legitimate. In other words, although the fault of the plaintiff may extinguish the defendant's strict liability, it does not extinguish the latter's liability for negligence.

As far as strict liability for wild or dangerous animals is concerned, the animal must have escaped from the control of its keeper for there to be strict liability.[73] If it was the fault of the plaintiff that caused the altercation between the plaintiff and the animal by, for example, the plaintiff provoking the animal, or putting his hands into the animal's cage while the animal was in the control of its keeper, that should be a defence to the strict liability claim. There would have been no escape from the keeper's control of the animal. This does not, however, negate a possible negligence action against the defendant keeper, and, as with *Rylands v Fletcher*, would allow for the defence of contributory negligence and apportionment of liability in appropriate cases. Thus, applying this reasoning to the facts of *Cowles v Balac*, if it is held that the tiger did not escape from the defendant's control, but was allowed into the plaintiff's vehicle due to the plaintiff's negligence, the strict liability action ought to fail. This would not necessarily mean that the defendant could not be found negligent for not having foreseen and prevented this type of occurrence, allowing for apportionment between the parties. If, on the other hand, it is held that the tiger, although being confined in a wild game park, was not in its keeper's control when it entered the plaintiff's vehicle, the act of the plaintiff in opening the car's window ought not to be a defence to the strict liability claim. The escape of the animal from the keeper's control could not, in this scenario, be considered to have been due to the plaintiff's fault, since the animal was not in the keeper's control when the plaintiff opened the window.[74]

Although not a contributory negligence case, but one dealing with contribution and apportionment between concurrent wrongdoers, *Blackwater v Plint* is an important judgment dealing with the applicability of apportionment in strict liability actions.[75] The plaintiff was the victim of sexual assaults perpetrated against him by a dormitory supervisor while in a residential school. He sued both the Government of Canada, which was statutorily responsible for establishing and regulating

[72] (1866) LR 1 Ex 265, 279 (Blackburn J).

[73] There are numerous judgments which affirm this requirement. See, eg, *Rands v McNeil* [1955] 1 QB 253 (CA); *Knott v London County Council* [1934] 1 KB 126; *Maynes v Galicz* (1975) 62 DLR (3d) 385 (BCSC) and *Lewis v Oeming* (1983) 24 CCLT 81 (Alta QB).

[74] I concede there might be scenarios where the wild animal is not in the keeper's control when it injures the plaintiff, but, despite this, the plaintiff acts unreasonably, contributing to the injuries. I would argue that in this case, contributory negligence ought not to be a defence. Keeping a wild animal and not having control of it should eliminate any argument that the plaintiff ought to have acted more reasonably.

[75] [2005] 3 SCR 3, 258 DLR (4th) 275.

boarding schools for Aboriginal children, and the Church which ran the school under an agreement with the Government. The employee who had committed the assaults had been hired by a Principal employed by the Church. Neither the Government, nor the Church, were held to have been negligent with respect to the torts committed by the employee. Nor were they held liable for breach of a fiduciary duty, or breach of non-delegable duties.[76] Were they, however, vicariously liable for the sexual assaults committed by their employee?

The Supreme Court of Canada held that the two parties were 'joint employers' of the employee under a type of partnership arrangement between the Government and the Church and were therefore jointly vicariously liable for the torts committed by the employee. The Supreme Court relied on the 'significant connection' test which it had articulated in its prior vicarious liability judgments.[77] Having found the parties jointly liable, the issue of whether liability could be apportioned between them arose for the purposes of contribution. The trial judge had apportioned liability 75 per cent to the Government of Canada and 25 per cent to the Church for the purposes of contribution between the two defendants.[78] The Supreme Court had to decide whether apportionment of liability was appropriate in a case where two defendants are vicariously liable as joint employers.

The British Columbia provision which applied to this case was the Negligence Act, which provides for contribution between wrongdoers who are at fault and apportionment determined by degrees of fault. Where, however, it is not possible to establish different degrees of fault, liability must be apportioned equally.[79] The argument of the Government of Canada was that, since vicarious liability is not predicated on fault, the apportionment must be equal. While conceding that there is a dispute under Canadian law concerning the applicability of apportionment to intentional torts and torts other than negligence,[80] McLachlin CJ reasoned that vicarious liability is a type of 'fault'. While not based on negligence, vicarious liability is based on the level of 'control' the employer was able to exercise over the employee. Where there are two employers, one might be in a senior position, able to exercise more control, and hence be more at fault. Thus, apportioning liability based on these different degrees of control was acceptable to the Court. With respect, this argument is unconvincing. Being more in control does not, in my opinion, suggest that one was more at fault. There was no fault on the part of either defendant. If being liable vicariously is considered to be a fault for the purposes of either contributory negligence, or contribution between

[76] The trial judge had held that the Government of Canada was in breach of a non-delegable duty. The Supreme Court of Canada rejected that holding.

[77] In particular *Bazley v Curry* [1999] 2 SCR 534 and *Jacobi v Griffiths* [1999] 2 SCR 570.

[78] 2001 BCSC 997, (2001) 93 BCLR (3d) 228.

[79] RSBC 1996 c 333 s 1(2) and s 4(2) (b).

[80] The Chief Justice referred to cases dealing with both contributory negligence and contribution between wrongdoers.

wrongdoers, it is impossible not to consider all tort actions as being encompassed by the legislation.[81]

The Supreme Court of Canada had the occasion to consider the applicability of the defence of contributory negligence in an action for conversion in *Boma Manufacturing Ltd v Canadian Imperial Bank of Commerce.*[82] The case involved the conversion of the plaintiffs' funds from its bank accounts, brought about by forgeries committed by the plaintiffs' bookkeeper. Describing the tort of conversion as a strict liability tort, Iacobucci J stated that 'the notion of strict liability involved in an action for conversion is prima facie antithetical to the concept of contributory negligence'.[83] Iacobucci J stated that, as a matter of principle, contributory negligence is not available in strict liability torts and, if it is to be introduced into this area of the law, this should be done by the legislature.

I would not agree that conversion is a strict liability tort. It is an intentional tort. Although it is true that mistake or innocence is no defence to a tort of conversion, the act of conversion must have been done intentionally. That is, the actor must have intended or known with substantial certainty that his or her act – in this case honouring the cheques – would have the effect of transferring the owner's possessory rights.[84] Thus, whether the defence of contributory negligence should be available in conversion should be considered within the context of other intentional torts, as discussed above.

Whether the defence of contributory negligence ought to be available in a breach of contract action, either by application of the statutes, or at common law, has been the subject of extensive academic commentary and judicial consideration.[85] With the acceptance of concurrent liability in contract and tort, where the tort and contractual duty of care overlap, the issue has become less contentious.[86] Canadian tort law generally allows for the defence of contributory

[81] The Chief Justice referenced the views expressed by DN Husak in 'Varieties of Strict Liability' (1995) 8 *Can JL & Jur* 189, 215, that those found vicariously liable are not selected 'randomly', 'the principles used to identify this defendant are not arbitrary' and thus there must have been some fault committed. Of course, the same argument can be made with respect to anyone liable in tort, whether the action be one of negligence, intention, or strict liability. No defendant in a tort claim is selected 'randomly'. Thus the legislation would apply to all tortfeasors.

[82] [1996] SCJ No 111, [1996] 3 SCR 727.

[83] ibid, [32]. See also, more recently, *Teva Canada Ltd v TD Canada Trust* 2017 SCC 51, another bank conversion case. Abella J writing for the majority, again describes conversion as a 'strict liability' tort rendering any notion of 'fault' on the part of either plaintiff or defendant 'irrelevant'.

[84] See Klar & Jefferies (n 10) 117–18 for a discussion of this point. It is similar to trespass to land. Trespass to land is an intentional (or negligent) tort, even if the defendant was unaware that it was doing anything wrong, or unlawful. This does not make it a 'strict liability' tort as that phrase is generally understood, eg, as in *Rylands v Fletcher* (n 71).

[85] The Manitoba Law Reform Commission Report No 128 (n 27) 45–55 extensively considered this issue. There are a large number of judicial decisions and academic contributions discussing it. See Klar & Jefferies (n 10) 623, n 38 for a reference to some of this material.

[86] As a result of the Supreme Court of Canada's judgments in *Central Trust Co v Rafuse* [1986] SCJ No 52, [1986] 2 SCR 147, and *BG Checo International v BC Hydro & Power Authority* [1993] SCJ No 1, [1993] 1 SCR 12, when a duty of care in tort is co-extensive with a duty of care in contract, the plaintiff has the option of suing in either. Although these cases dealt with pre-contractual representations, the concurrent liability approach is not limited to this area.

negligence in breach of contract actions where the duty of care in tort is co-extensive with the contractual duty of care. Nevertheless, difficult questions remain. Should the extension of contributory negligence to breach of contract actions be based on the statutes, or the common law?[87] Should the defence only be available where there is concurrent liability in tort and contract and the duty is one of due care? Where the defendant's contractual liability is strict, should the possibility of apportionment exist? The Manitoba Law Reform Commission carefully canvassed the case law, recommendations offered by other law reform commissions, and statutory approaches existing elsewhere, before concluding that Manitoba law should provide for apportionment for contributory fault in respect of any breach of contract that creates a liability for damages.[88]

VII. Conclusion

The issues raised in Canadian common law stemming from its apportionment legislation are similar to the issues raised in other jurisdictions and, for the most part, the solutions adopted have been the same. This chapter has attempted to discuss the more important of these issues and to highlight some of the unique features of the Canadian approaches.

[87] Recall that some of the provisions refer specifically to 'torts' and 'tortfeasors', thus seemingly excluding non-tort claims.

[88] Manitoba Law Reform Commission Report No 128 (n 27) Rec 12.

7

Contributory Negligence and Professional Negligence: An Empirical Perspective

JAMES GOUDKAMP AND DONAL NOLAN*

I. Introduction

The doctrine of contributory negligence reduces the compensation which the victim of a wrong receives where the victim was partly to blame for his or her own damage. Paradigmatic examples of conduct that is likely to constitute contributory negligence include failing to wear a seatbelt while a passenger in a motor vehicle, failing to check the depth of a swimming pool before diving into it, and crossing a road without looking for oncoming traffic. The contributory negligence doctrine is one of the most important doctrines in private law. It is frequently relied on by defendants both in litigation and in negotiating settlements, and damages are regularly discounted for contributory negligence by substantial amounts. With regard to settlements, it has been said that 'much of the negotiation' may involve trying to agree a discount to reflect the possibility of a finding of contributory negligence were the case to go to court.[1] However, despite the importance of the contributory negligence doctrine, remarkably little is known about how it works 'on the ground'. Furthermore, although contributory negligence is usually associated with accident cases, it is frequently pleaded by defendants who have been sued for negligence in the performance of their professional duties, and yet even less is known about the

* We are immensely grateful to Charles Austin, Eleni Katsampouka and Mengfei Ying for collecting, coding and checking the data on which this chapter is based, and to Lindsay Lee and Mercy Akoth, who carried out the statistical analysis. Earlier versions of this chapter were presented at symposia at Hong Kong University, the University of Queensland and the Professional Negligence Bar Association and we are indebted to the participants for their comments and suggestions. This research was funded by the John Fell Oxford University Press (OUP) Research Fund and the Travers Smith Oxford Law Faculty Fund. This chapter forms part of a much larger empirical study of the law of contributory negligence, which is forthcoming as J Goudkamp and D Nolan, *Contributory Negligence in the Twenty-First Century* (Oxford, Oxford University Press, 2019).

[1] P Cane and J Goudkamp, *Atiyah's Accidents, Compensation and the Law*, 9th edn (Cambridge, Cambridge University Press, 2018) 255.

impact of the doctrine in professional negligence litigation.[2] In this chapter, we seek to fill this gap, by means of both empirical and qualitative analysis of recent contributory negligence case law in the UK. This analysis suggests that there are certain distinctive features of the operation of the contributory negligence doctrine in the professional negligence context.

Our chapter draws upon a large-scale empirical study of the operation of the contributory negligence doctrine in the UK courts since the year 2000. This study comprises two related enquiries, one concerned with first instance decisions, and the other concerned with appellate decisions. For the first enquiry, we looked at 572 first instance decisions from across the UK decided between 2000 and 2016. The sample for this part of the study comprised every first instance decision in which a formal determination was made on contributory negligence that was handed down during the study period and which we were able to access electronically. For the second enquiry, we looked at 129 appellate decisions using similar inclusion criteria. The two central questions at which our study was directed were: how often a defendant's plea of contributory negligence was successful; and the quantum by which a claimant's damages were reduced when a finding of contributory negligence was made. We considered the extent to which the answers to these questions depended on a number of variables, including the claimant's age, the claimant's gender, the type of damage suffered by the claimant (personal injury, property damage or pure economic loss) and the contextual setting of the claim.

The structure of our chapter is as follows. In Part II, we provide a summary of the central features of the law governing contributory negligence in the UK. In Part III, we briefly outline the methodology of our empirical study. In Part IV, we report the results of our empirical study in so far as they pertain to decisions in professional negligence cases. And finally, in Part V, we discuss these results in the light of qualitative analysis of the professional negligence case law in our study and the existing literature on the operation of contributory negligence in this context.

Although our focus is on the UK, our analysis may also be suggestive of the state of play as regards the contributory negligence doctrine in the professional

[2] For helpful general treatment of the topic, see DW Marks, 'Professional Negligence: Contribution and Contributory Negligence' (1988–1989) 15 *University of Queensland Law Journal* 209; and AM Dugdale and KM Stanton, *Professional Negligence*, 3rd edn (London, Butterworths, 1998) 523–32. There is a more extensive body of literature on contributory negligence in the medical negligence context: see especially RB Harper, 'The Application of Contributory Negligence Principles to the Doctor/Patient Relationship' (2001) 9 *TLJ* 1; YSH Ventresca, PW Kryworuk and SD Chambers, 'With Patient Rights Come Patient Responsibilities: Contributory Negligence in Medical Negligence Actions' (2007) 33 *Advocates' Quarterly* 207; J Herring and C Foster, 'Blaming the Patient: Contributory Negligence in Medical Malpractice Litigation' (2009) 25 *Professional Negligence* 76; EI Picard and GB Robertson, *Legal Liability of Doctors and Hospitals in Canada*, 4th edn (Toronto, Carswell, 2007) 368–74; and JM Yule, 'Defences in Medical Negligence: To What Extent Has Tort Law Reform in Australia Limited the Liability of Health Professionals?' (2011) 4 *Journal of Australasian Law Teachers Association* 53, 54–56.

negligence setting in Australia. The apportionment statutes in Australia are couched, for the most part, in very similar terms to the corresponding legislation in the UK.[3] Furthermore, several of the leading cases on the application of the UK's apportionment statutes have been followed in Australia. This is not to deny the possibility, of course, that there might well be important variations between Australia and the UK as regards the application of the law of contributory negligence, both in professional negligence cases and more generally. Our point is simply that the two legal systems are sufficiently closely aligned with each other in relevant respects that this chapter may prove useful for the purposes of understanding the material Australian law and practice, although it does not, of course, obviate the need for a similar study to be carried out specifically in relation to Australia.

II. The Law of Contributory Negligence in Outline

The brief discussion of the law on contributory negligence that follows is intended to serve simply as a reminder of the key features of the law in the UK. A full exposition of the relevant law should be sought elsewhere.[4]

The first point that should be made is that contributory negligence must be pleaded by the defendant before the doctrine will be considered by the judge. The court cannot raise it on its own motion.[5] Where contributory negligence has been pleaded, the judge engages in a two-stage analysis. At the first stage, the judge determines whether the claimant is guilty of contributory negligence. A claimant will be guilty of contributory negligence if he or she failed to take reasonable care of his or her own interests and this failure contributed to the damage he or she suffered. The standard of care is objective,[6] although sometimes personal characteristics of the claimant are attributed to the reasonable person, such as his or her age.[7]

The second stage of the analysis is relevant only if the claimant is found guilty of contributory negligence. It centres on the statutory apportionment provision.

[3] Legislative interventions in certain Australian states have created some disparities with the UK position, but these are unlikely to be relevant in the professional negligence context. For a summary of the current law of contributory negligence in Australia, see K Barker et al, *The Law of Torts in Australia*, 5th edn (Oxford, Oxford University Press, 2012) 599–610.

[4] See, eg, J Goudkamp and D Nolan, *Contributory Negligence: Principles and Practice* (Oxford, Oxford University Press, 2018); and WE Peel and J Goudkamp, *Winfield & Jolowicz on Tort*, 19th edn (London, Sweet & Maxwell, 2014) para 23-036ff. The classic English study of contributory negligence is GL Williams, *Joint Torts and Contributory Negligence* (London, Stevens & Sons, 1951).

[5] *Fookes v Slaytor* [1978] 1 WLR 1293.

[6] 'In determining [the issue of contributory negligence], the law eliminates the personal equation': *Froom v Butcher* [1976] QB 286, 294 (Lord Denning MR).

[7] *Gough v Thorne* [1966] 1 WLR 1387 (holding child claimants to the standard of a reasonable child of the same age).

This provision is found in section 1(1) of the Law Reform (Contributory Negligence) Act 1945 (UK),[8] which stipulates that:

> Where any person suffers damage as a result partly of his own fault and partly of the fault of any other person or persons, a claim in respect of that damage shall not be defeated by reason of the fault of the person suffering the damage, but the damages recoverable in respect thereof shall be reduced to such extent as the court thinks just and equitable having regard to the claimant's share in the responsibility for the damage.

By convention, a judge who has made a finding of contributory negligence must assess the parties' respective shares of responsibility for the damage as two percentages that add up to 100 per cent.[9] The respective shares of responsibility are determined by reference to the parties' comparative blameworthiness and the relative causative potency of their faulty conduct.[10] The court then reduces the claimant's damages by the percentage of responsibility that has been assigned to him or her.[11] Judges are not supposed to treat the apportionment exercise as a scientific exercise but to approach it 'in a broad, jury-like and commonsense way'.[12]

As regards the legal rules governing the application of the contributory negligence doctrine in professional negligence claims in particular, it is important to remember that most such claims are pleaded in both tort and contract, with the professional's conduct being alleged to be in breach of concurrent duties of reasonable care.[13] There are, however, cases where only an action in tort is available to the claimant, as where the claimant was not in a direct contractual relationship with the defendant, but was linked to the defendant by a chain of contracts,[14] or where the defendant provided their professional services gratuitously.[15]

[8] The corresponding statute in Northern Ireland is the Law Reform (Miscellaneous Provisions) Act (NI) 1948 (see s 2(1)). It is couched (in relevant part) in identical terms.

[9] Cases involving multiple defendants are subject to special rules: see *Fitzgerald v Lane* [1989] 1 AC 328. As to the Australian position, see *Barisic v Devenport* [1978] 2 NSWLR 111 and, as regards the different approaches, see JG Fleming, 'Contributory Negligence and Multiple Tortfeasors' (1988) 104 *LQR* 6.

[10] *Stapley v Gypsum Mines Ltd* [1953] AC 663, 682 (Lord Reid).

[11] Different percentages may be assigned to the parties in respect of different periods of time: *Barings Plc (in liq) v Coopers & Lybrand (a firm)* [2003] EWHC 1319 (Ch) [1060], [1069] (Evans-Lombe J).

[12] *Badger v Ministry of Defence* [2005] EWHC 2941 (QB), [2006] 3 All ER 173 [16] (Stanley Burnton J).

[13] This has become the norm since the decision of the House of Lords in *Henderson v Merrett Syndicates Ltd* [1995] 2 AC 145. Since *Henderson*, 'the orthodox analysis [has been] that a professional person in a contractual relationship with a client will ordinarily owe that client a concurrent duty of care': J Powell et al, *Jackson & Powell on Professional Liability*, 8th edn, (London, Sweet & Maxwell, 2017) para 2.117 (footnote omitted).

[14] See, eg, *Smith v Eric S Bush (a firm)* [1990] 1 AC 831 and the actions by the 'indirect Names' in *Henderson v Merrett Syndicates Ltd* [1995] 2 AC 145.

[15] As a practical matter, this is most relevant where medical treatment is provided under the National Health Service: see *Jackson & Powell on Professional Liability* (n 13) para 13.002.

For a time, it was uncertain how the contributory negligence doctrine functioned in cases of concurrent liability. However, at least since the decision of the Court of Appeal of England and Wales in *Forsikringsaktieselskapet Vesta v Butcher*,[16] it has been clear that the doctrine may apply where a defendant who owed concurrent duties in tort and contract is alleged to have caused damage by failing to exercise reasonable care,[17] although the position will be otherwise where the complaint is that the professional breached, whether or not through negligence, a strict contractual duty.[18] Furthermore, in such cases the doctrine is potentially applicable irrespective of the precise way in which the claim is framed, so that a claimant cannot avoid the contributory negligence rule by suing only for breach of contract.[19]

III. Methodology

In this section we briefly outline the methodology of our empirical study, so that readers of the chapter can evaluate the methods that we used and draw their own conclusions regarding the results. A more detailed account of our methodology can be found in two articles relating to an earlier version of our study that was limited to the operation of the contributory negligence doctrine in the courts of England and Wales.[20]

A. First Instance Decisions

We located the first instance decisions directly and indirectly. We were able to obtain decisions directly where the full text of the judgment was electronically available. We also gleaned the salient facts of many other cases indirectly either from a reported summary of the decision or, where there had been an appeal, from the judgment of the appellate court.

The fact that we proceeded in this way introduced two selection biases into our study. The first selection bias arose because the first instance decisions that

[16] [1989] AC 852 (CA).

[17] The approach in *Vesta* was rejected by the High Court of Australia in *Astley v Austrust Ltd* [1999] HCA 6, (1999) 197 CLR 1, with the High Court holding that the contributory negligence doctrine has no application to proceedings for breach of contract, whether or not the plaintiff asserts a right to redress in tort in parallel with the contractual claim. However, the effect of *Astley* was swiftly overturned by all Australian legislatures (see, eg, the Law Reform (Miscellaneous Provisions) Amendment Act 2000 (NSW), amending the Law Reform (Miscellaneous Provisions) Act 1965) (NSW)) and Australian law on this point is now the same as that in the UK.

[18] For a clear statement of the rules in this regard, see *Secretary of State for the Environment, Transport and Regions v Unicorn Consultancy Services Ltd* [2000] NPC 108 [123] (Rimer J).

[19] Clearly stated at first instance in [1986] 2 Lloyd's Rep 179, 197 (Hobhouse J).

[20] J Goudkamp and D Nolan, 'Contributory Negligence in the Twenty-First Century: An Empirical Study of First Instance Decisions' (2016) 79 *MLR* 575, 580–88; J Goudkamp and D Nolan, 'Contributory Negligence in the Court of Appeal: An Empirical Study' (2017) 37 *LS* 437, 440–46.

were directly accessible to us were more likely to involve larger and more complex claims than cases in the general population of claims. And the second selection bias arose because most of the first instance decisions that were only indirectly accessible to us had either been the subject of an appeal, or a summary of the decision had been compiled by a law reporter. It may well be that such cases are unrepresentative.

Two possible consequences of these selection biases should be highlighted.[21] One is that the figures in this chapter on the success rate of pleas of contributory negligence may be a little higher than one would find if one looked at the general population of cases. The other is that it seems quite likely that the figures relating to the average discount in this chapter may, again, be a little higher than one would find if one looked at the general population of first instance decisions. However, despite these caveats, we feel confident that the cases in our sample are *reasonably* representative of the general population of relevant cases. We say this partly because the two selection biases offset each other to a degree, since including indirectly accessed cases considerably increased the number of decisions of county courts or their institutional equivalents in the sample, while the vast majority of the cases that we accessed directly were not the subject of an appeal.

Our study was limited to cases that were decided between 1 January 2000 and 31 December 2016. Cases in which contributory negligence was pleaded in response to a counter-claim[22] or cross-claim[23] were included. Where a deduction for contributory negligence had been agreed by the parties, the case was included only if the agreement had been formally approved by the judge because the claimant was a protected party. Where a case involved multiple claimants, or multiple defendants,[24] we generally created separate entries for each individual claim in which contributory negligence was an issue.[25] This reflected the fact that, in such cases, claims that are technically distinct from each other are joined together in the same set of proceedings merely for reasons of procedural convenience. Accordingly, from this point onwards we use the language of 'claims' rather than 'cases'.

We excluded several categories of claim from the study, most significantly: (1) claims where the first instance decision on contributory negligence was

[21] See further Goudkamp and Nolan (2016) (n 20) 581–82.

[22] See, eg, *Logical Computer Supplies Ltd v Euro Car Parks Ltd* 2001 WL 825094; *Wellesley Partnership LLP v Withers LLP* [2014] EWHC 556 (Ch), [2014] PNLR 22.

[23] See, eg, *Dunlop Haywards Ltd v Barbon Insurance Group* [2009] EWHC 2900 (Comm), [2010] Lloyd's Rep IR 149.

[24] We did not treat actions brought against an employee and his or her employer as involving multiple defendants since, in reality, the employer is the only defendant in such cases.

[25] We say that we generally proceeded in this way because in one case, *Adams v Atlas International Property Services Ltd* [2016] EWHC 3120 (QB), there were 16 separate, but similarly situated claimants, and in this instance we treated their actions as one claim to avoid distorting the data by giving undue prominence to a single case.

a contingent finding that did not affect the outcome of the claim at that stage; (2) professional negligence claims against lawyers concerning earlier litigation or an earlier settlement in which contributory negligence had potentially been an issue; and (3) claims in which the *only* determination pertaining to contributory negligence was whether the doctrine applied to the cause of action for which the claimant was suing.[26]

The total number of first instance claims in our study was 572. Of these, 402 were from England and Wales, 42 were from Northern Ireland, and 128 were from Scotland. Our research assistants scrutinised all of these decisions in order to ascertain whether the plea of contributory negligence succeeded and, if so, the discount that the judge had applied to the damages award as a result. They also coded the claims for several other variables. One of these variables was the type of damage suffered by the claimant. The types of damage were: (1) personal injury (including fatal accident and psychiatric injury claims); (2) property damage; and (3) pure economic loss. Where a single action was brought in respect of more than one type of damage, we treated this as two separate claims. Another of these variables was the contextual setting of the claim. For this purpose, the categories of claim were: (1) road accident; (2) employers' liability;[27] (3) occupiers' liability;[28] (4) public liability;[29] (5) professional negligence; (6) sports injury; and (7) 'other'. We took a fairly broad view of what amounted to a professional negligence claim, and included within this category claims against (among others) lawyers, medical practitioners, valuers/surveyors, bankers, architects, engineers, accountants and insurance brokers.

Once the coding was complete the data in the spreadsheets were analysed by trained statisticians. The statisticians used a statistical programme known as 'R' to run the tests and to produce the graphs. They ran Pearson's chi-square tests to test independence between categorical variables (such as the frequency with which claimants were found guilty of contributory negligence) and t-tests or analysis of variance (ANOVA), as appropriate, to measure the significance of observed disparities in the values of continuous variables (such as the size of discounts for contributory negligence) across different categories of data (such as male claimants and female claimants). Wilcoxon rank sum tests with continuity correction were run as a cross-check on the results produced by the t-tests. Linear and logistic regression analyses were conducted to control for confounding variables.

[26] For fuller explanations of these categories of claim, see Goudkamp and Nolan (2016) (n 20) 584–85.

[27] Defined as claims in which the defendant was sued in their capacity as the claimant's employer.

[28] Defined as claims in which the defendant was sued in their capacity as the occupier of premises.

[29] Defined as claims in which the defendant was sued in their capacity as a public authority.

B. Appellate Decisions

Our study of appellate decisions was also limited to cases decided between 1 January 2000 and 31 December 2016. We similarly included in this study only cases in which the appellate court made a formal determination as to whether or not the claimant was guilty of contributory negligence, or as to the appropriate discount for contributory negligence. Where an appeal involved multiple claimants, or multiple defendants, we again created separate entries for each individual claim in which contributory negligence was an issue. And as with our first instance study, we excluded several categories of claim from the appellate study, most significantly: (1) claims where the appellate court discussed the issue of contributory negligence but did not make a formal determination in relation to it; and (2) claims in which the *only* determination pertaining to contributory negligence was whether the doctrine applied to the cause of action for which the claimant was suing. 129 appellate claims were included in our study. Of these, 111 were from England and Wales, three were from Northern Ireland, and 15 were from Scotland.

IV. Results

In this section, we present the results of our empirical study pertaining to professional negligence. We begin by setting out some general information about the claims in the two samples and then proceed to the findings. We divide our discussion of the findings into three parts: the success rate of the plea of contributory negligence; the discount applied when contributory negligence is found; and some additional observations about the professional negligence claims in the two samples. Our primary aim in this section is simply to present the findings of the study, although we do also make some observations about their importance. Fuller discussion of key findings in the light of the case law and academic literature is postponed until the following section.

A. General Information

Our first instance spreadsheet contained entries for 572 claims in which the defendant had pleaded contributory negligence. As seen in Figure 1, the vast majority of these claims (87 per cent) were for personal injury, with the remaining claims being in respect of pure economic loss (10 per cent) or property damage (3 per cent).

Figure 1 Number of first instance claims by damage type

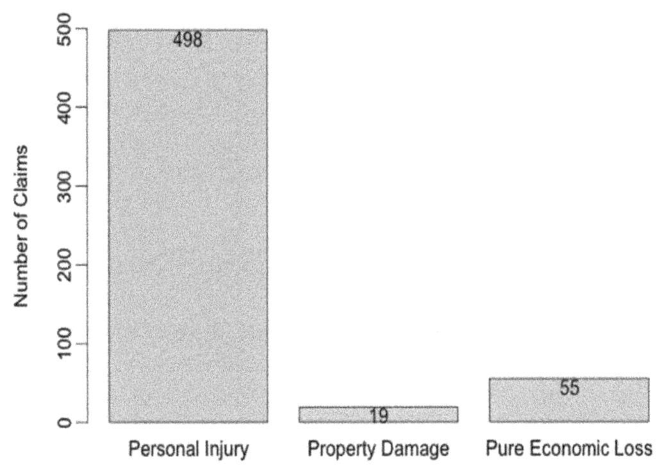

There was a more even spread of the claims across our seven categories of claim type (or contextual setting), as seen in Figure 2. Professional negligence claims made up just under 10 per cent of the total number of first instance claims. An appendix setting out the essential details of the 57 professional negligence claims in the first instance sample can be found at the end of the chapter.

Figure 2 Number of first instance claims by claim type

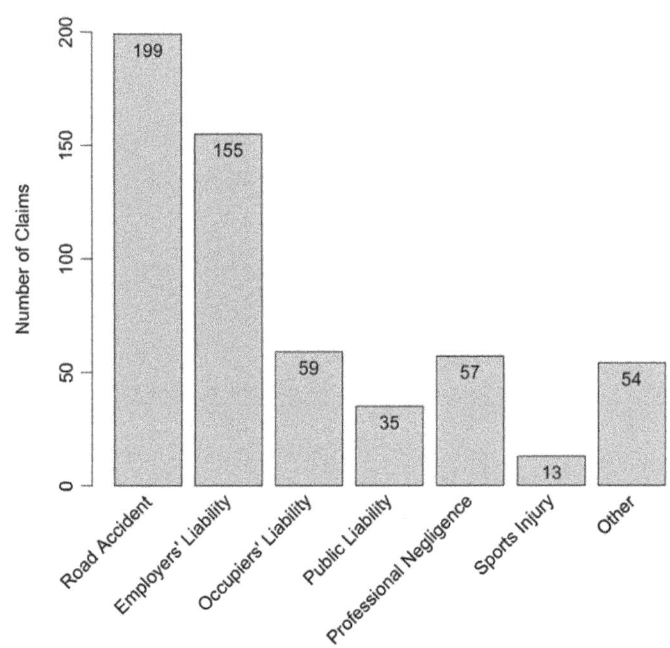

In the appellate spreadsheet, there were only four professional negligence claims. Of these, three were property damage claims and the fourth was a pure economic loss claim. The number of professional negligence claims in the appellate sample is so low that no meaningful empirical conclusions can be drawn therefrom. Nevertheless, we will occasionally draw upon the judgments in the four appellate decisions on contributory negligence in the professional negligence context in our qualitative analysis in the next section of the chapter.

B. Success Rate of the Plea of Contributory Negligence

Out of the 572 claims in our first instance sample, the plea of contributory negligence succeeded in 331 claims (58 per cent) and failed in 241 claims (42 per cent). As shown in Figure 3, the success rate of the plea of contributory negligence is very similar for personal injury claims and property damage claims (62 and 58 per cent respectively), but markedly lower in pure economic loss claims (24 per cent). Statistical analysis suggests that this disparity is very unlikely to be attributable to chance.[30]

Figure 3 Success rate of plea by damage type

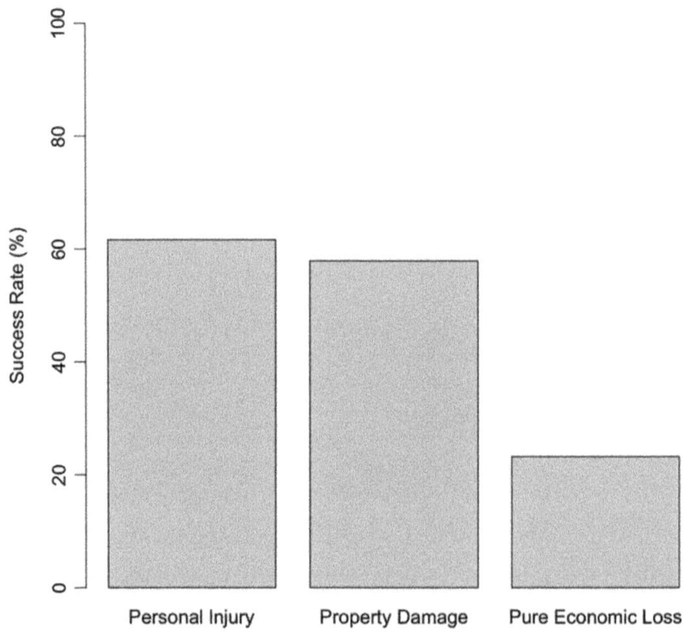

[30] A Pearson's chi-square test on the null hypothesis that the success rate of the plea of contributory negligence is the same across all types of damage gave a p-value of < 0.001. A p-value is the probability of obtaining an effect at least as extreme as the one in the sample data, assuming the truth of

Figure 4 Success rate of plea by claim type

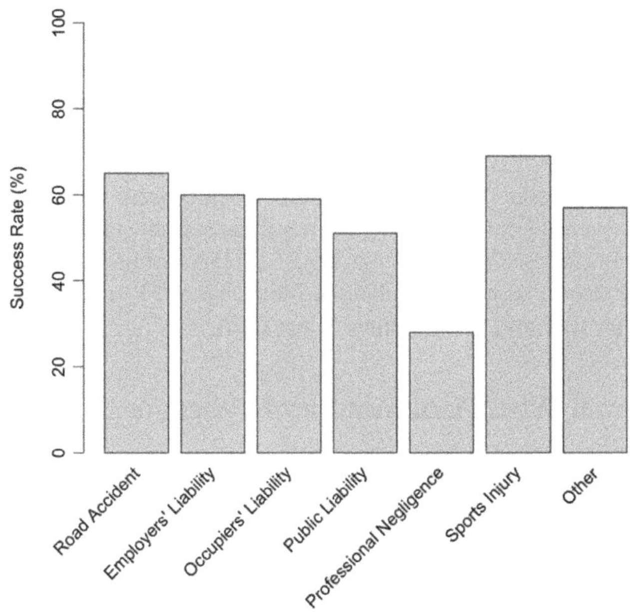

The explanation for the difference in the success rate of the plea of contributory negligence between personal injury and property damage claims on the one hand, and pure economic loss claims on the other hand, emerges when we break down the success rate of the plea by type of claim (Figure 4). This reveals that the plea of contributory negligence has a very low success rate in professional negligence claims (28 per cent). This success rate is roughly half that of the success rate of the plea across all types of claim in our study. Again, statistically, this difference is very unlikely to be down to chance.[31] The reason for the close association between the

the null hypothesis. Hence, the lower the p-value, the more likely it is that the null hypothesis is false. The p-value in this instance is very low, which strongly suggests that the observed disparity is not attributable to chance (in the form of the sample of claims we happened to survey), so that the data provide strong evidence that the success rate of the plea does indeed vary across the different damage types. This evidence is reinforced by logistic regression analysis. This analysis showed that, when pure economic loss claims were compared with personal injury claims, the odds of a finding of contributory negligence were notably lower in pure economic loss claims ($p < 0.001$). In many academic disciplines, a p-value of less than 0.05 is regarded as statistically significant, but the appropriateness of the use of this test of statistical significance in legal contexts has been questioned, and properly so in our view: see NB Cohen, 'Confidence in Probability: Burdens of Persuasion in a World of Imperfect Knowledge' (1985) 60 *New York University Law Review* 385, 412; DH Kaye, 'Is Proof of Statistical Significance Relevant?' (1986) 61 *Washington Law Review* 1333, 1342–45; DW Vick, 'Statistical Significance and the Significance of Statistics' (2000) 116 *LQR* 575. Accordingly, in this paper we eschew the language of 'statistical significance' in this binary sense and instead provide the p-values themselves in the footnotes, and more general observations on the cogency of a given finding in the text.

[31] Pearson's chi-square test, $p < 0.001$. And logistic regression analysis showed that when professional negligence claims were compared with road accident claims (the largest category of claim), the odds of a finding of contributory negligence were markedly lower in professional negligence claims ($p < 0.001$).

success rate in pure economic loss claims and in professional negligence claims is not hard to find. Of the 55 pure economic loss claims, the vast majority (48 claims) fell into the professional negligence category; similarly, of the 57 professional negligence claims, the preponderance (48 claims) were for pure economic loss. Of the other nine professional negligence claims, three were for personal injury (unsurprisingly, these were the three medical negligence cases) and six were for property damage.

The success rates of the plea of contributory negligence in the other six categories of claim were all much closer to the overall success rate of the plea, as follows: road accident claims, 65 per cent; employers' liability claims, 60 per cent; occupiers' liability claims, 59 per cent; public liability claims, 51 per cent; sports injury claims, 69 per cent; and 'other' claims, 57 per cent.

C. Discount Where Contributory Negligence Found

In the 331 claims in the sample in which the claimant was found guilty of contributory negligence, the average amount by which the claimant's damages were reduced rounded up to 40 per cent.

Figure 5 Average discount by damage type

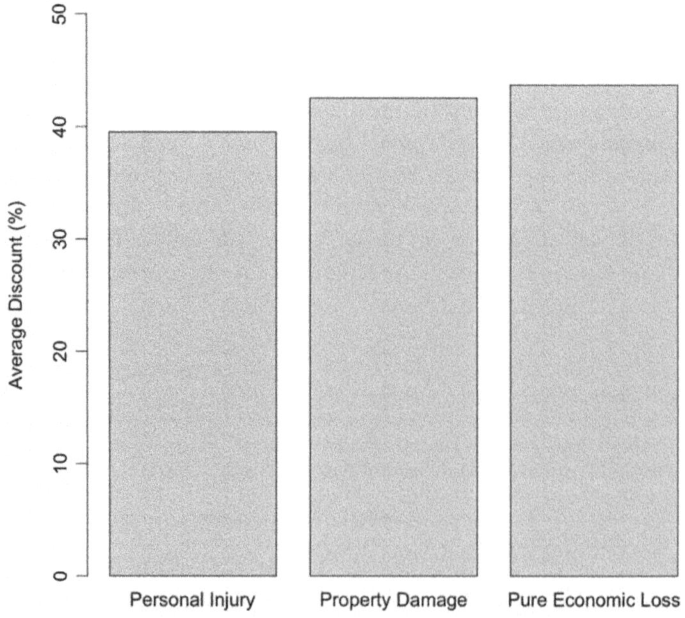

Figure 5 shows the average discount by damage type. The average discounts in property damage claims and pure economic loss claims were 43 per cent and

44 per cent respectively, somewhat higher than the average discount in personal injury claims (40 per cent). In relation to pure economic loss claims, this disparity is likely to be bound up with the higher discounts found in professional negligence claims,[32] as we have seen that most of the pure economic loss claims involved professional negligence (and vice versa). Further detail regarding the discounts made in respect of the three types of damage can be seen in Figure 6.

Figure 6 Discount by damage type[33]

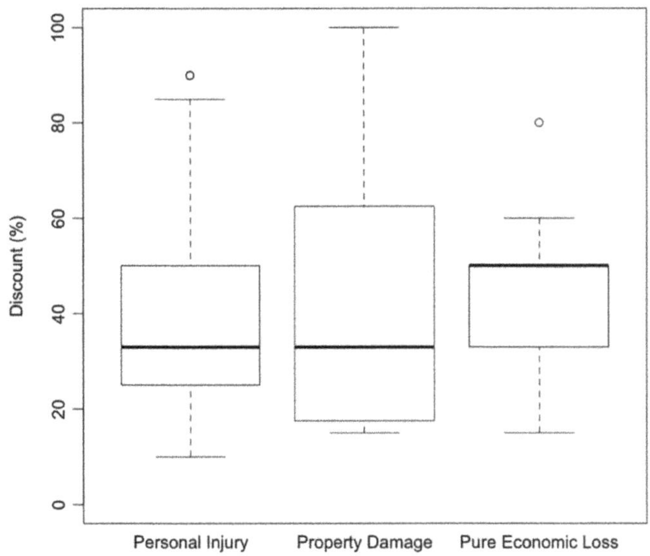

Turning from type of damage to type of claim, the average discount by type of claim is shown in Figure 7. As can be seen from this graph, the highest average discount (52 per cent) was found in professional negligence claims. The average discounts in the other types of claim were as follows: road accidents, 43 per cent; employers' liability, 32 per cent; occupiers' liability, 47 per cent; public liability, 35 per cent; sports injury, 38 per cent; 'other', 37 per cent. More detail on the interaction between discount and claim type is shown in Figure 8.

[32] See Figure 7 and accompanying text, below.

[33] The thick black line in the boxplot represents the median discount value, the box gives the first and third quartiles of the discount values, and the dotted lines extend out to 1.5 times the interquartile range (the range between the value at the first quartile and the third quartile). Outliers are drawn as dots.

Figure 7 Average discount by claim type

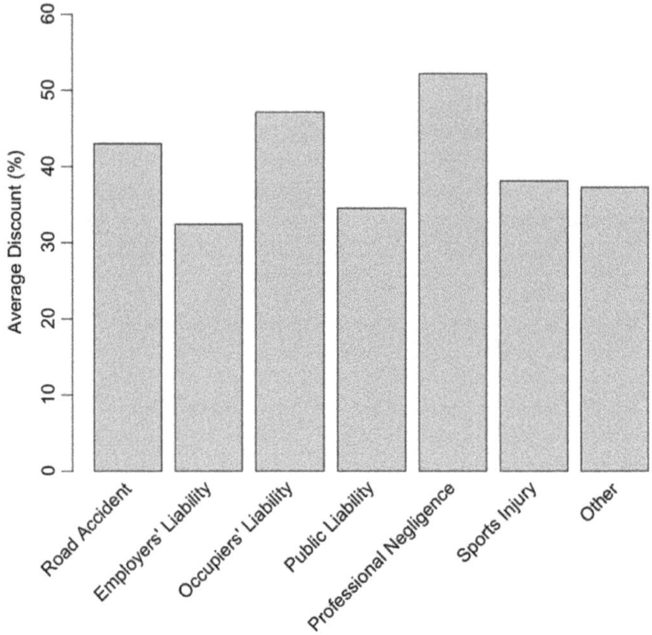

Figure 8 Discount by claim type

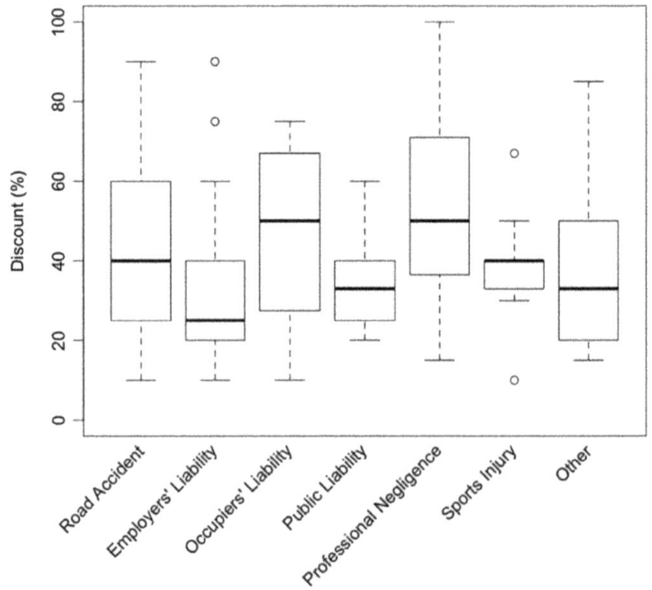

Even though there were only 16 professional negligence claims in the sample where a discount was made, statistical analysis suggests that the disparity between the average discount in professional negligence claims and in claims in three of the other categories of claim type (employers' liability, public liability and 'other') was very unlikely to be down to chance.[34] As for the disparity between the average discount in professional negligence claims and the average discount in road accident claims – the largest contextual category in terms of number of claims, and the one in which the average discount was closest to the average discount across all claims – there was a higher probability that this was down to chance.[35] Nevertheless, these results suggest that, while the courts are reluctant to find contributory negligence in professional negligence claims, when they do so the discount tends to be higher than in other types of claim.

Our study also reveals important facts about the range and frequency of discounts used by the courts in professional negligence cases. The lowest discount that we observed in such a case was 15 per cent,[36] while the highest was 100 per cent.[37] In *Speshal Investments Ltd v Corby Kane Howard Partnership Ltd*, Hart J referred to a discount below 20 per cent in the context of a claim against a valuer as being a 'token' one.[38] That perhaps suggests that he thought that discounts below that amount should not normally be made at all, and that the proper course to take in such circumstances is to find that there was no contributory negligence in the first place. The most popular discount was 50 per cent (five claims). Table 1 sets out all the discounts used in such cases. As can be seen from this table, there were more professional negligence claims (six) in which a discount greater than 50 per cent was imposed than there were such claims (five) where a discount of less than 50 per cent was imposed.

[34] Paired, two-sided t-tests of the differences between the average discounts in professional negligence claims and in these three claim types returned relatively low p-values, as follows: employers' liability claims (p = 0.005); public liability claims (p = 0.014); and 'other' (p = 0.036).

[35] A paired t-test of the average discount in professional negligence claims and in road accident claims returned a p-value of 0.154. The results of the paired t-tests of the average discount in professional negligence claims and the average discounts in other types of claim were broadly consistent with the results of Wilcoxon rank sum tests with continuity correction (eg, this test returned a p-value of 0.152 for the professional negligence/road accident pairing).

[36] *Playboy Club London Ltd v Banca Nazionale Del Lavoro SPA* [2014] EWHC 2613 (QB).

[37] *Six Continents Retail Ltd v Carford Catering Ltd* [2003] EWCA Civ 1790. In this case, a discount of 100 per cent was imposed as an alternative to a finding that the conduct of the claimants had broken the chain of causation between the defendant's negligence and the damage suffered by the claimant. On appeal, the finding on causation was overturned, and it was said that the finding of 100% contributory negligence must fall with it. This would suggest that the finding of 100% contributory negligence was really just another way of repackaging the finding on causation, a suggestion consistent with the view (shared by us) that findings of 100% contributory negligence are both incoherent and impermissible under the 1945 Act. See further on this issue, J Goudkamp, 'Rethinking Contributory Negligence' in E Chamberlain et al (eds), *Tort Law: Challenging Orthodoxy* (Oxford, Hart Publishing, 2013) 344–46. See *Brumder v Motornet Service and Repairs Ltd* [2013] EWCA Civ 195, [2013] 1 WLR 2783 [4] (Beatson LJ) for a recent decision in which it was said that findings of 100% contributory negligence are nonsensical.

[38] [2003] EWHC 390 (Ch) [69].

Table 1 Discounts used in professional negligence claims

Number of claims	Discount (%)
5	50
2	75
2	20
1	100
1	80
1	66.6
1	60
1	40
1	33.3
1	15

D. Further Details of Professional Negligence Claims

Of the 57 professional negligence claims, 51 were from England and Wales, four from Northern Ireland, and two from Scotland. Of the claims from England and Wales, all but one were decisions of the High Court. The exception was a medical negligence claim decided by the Sheffield County Court.[39] The four Northern Irish claims were decided by the High Court of Justice, and both the Scottish claims were decided by the Outer House of the Court of Session.

The types of professional who featured as defendants in the 57 professional negligence claims are shown, in decreasing order of frequency, in Table 2. The defendants in the seven claims where the defendant is classified as 'other' in this table were as follows: a financial adviser;[40] a supplier of fire suppression systems (two claims);[41] a company that provided a range of services – including assistance, testing and advice – in relation to leather products;[42] a company in the business of overhauling and reconditioning of parts used by the railway industry;[43] a company that (among other things) carried out searches in relation to property for potential purchasers;[44] and an IT firm hired to supply a company with an email system.[45]

[39] *Pidgeon v Doncaster HA* [2002] Lloyd's Rep Med 130.

[40] *Chrysalis Scotland Ltd v Clydesdale Bank Insurance Brokers Ltd* [2008] CSOH 144, 2008 GWD 38-578.

[41] *Trebor Bassett Holdings Ltd v ADT Fire & Security Plc* [2011] EWHC 1936 (TCC), [2011] BLR 661.

[42] *Argos Ltd v Leather Trade House Ltd* [2012] EWHC 1348 (QB), [2012] ECC 34.

[43] *Great North Eastern Railway Ltd v Railcare Ltd* [2003] EWHC 1608 (Comm).

[44] *Manorgate Ltd v First Scottish Property Services Ltd* [2013] CSOH 108, [2014] PNLR 1.

[45] *Logical Computer Supplies* (n 22).

Table 2 Defendants by profession

Number of claims	Profession of defendant
16	Legal Practitioner
9	Valuer/Surveyor
7	Insurance Broker
7	Other
4	Banker
3	Accountant
3	Architect
3	Engineer
3	Medical Practitioner
2	Project Manager

As can be seen from Table 2, the profession that features by far the most frequently in the contributory negligence case law is the legal profession, which accounts for 28 per cent of the professional negligence claims in the sample. The only two other professions that account for more than 10 per cent of the sample are valuers/surveyors (16 per cent) and insurance brokers (12 per cent). By contrast, there are only three claims in the sample where the defendant was a medical practitioner.[46] Our study therefore suggests that pleas of contributory negligence are rare in the medical negligence context, as might have been expected in the light of the fact that one of these three cases[47] is apparently the only reported English clinical negligence claim in which there was a finding of contributory negligence.[48]

Because the numbers of claims in each professional category are relatively low, a comparison of the success rate of the plea across these categories is of limited value. Nevertheless, it is perhaps noteworthy that in our sample pleas of contributory negligence almost never succeeded where the defendant was a lawyer or insurance broker, but that where the defendant was a valuer/surveyor, the plea succeeded more often than it failed. To be precise, the plea of contributory negligence succeeded in only two of the 16 claims against lawyers[49] (13 per cent), in only one of the seven claims against insurance brokers[50] (14 per cent), but

[46] The claims were *Pidgeon* (n 39); *Re P (deceased)* [2011] EWHC 1266 (QB); and *Spencer v Hillingdon Hospital NHS Trust* [2015] EWHC 1058 (QB). The plea of contributory negligence succeeded in *Pidgeon*, and failed in the other two cases.

[47] *Pidgeon* (n 39).

[48] Herring and Foster (n 2) 76.

[49] *Unicorn Consultancy Services Ltd* (n 18); *Alpha Credit Bank v Stephenson Harwood* [2002] EWHC 922 (Ch).

[50] *Dunlop Haywards* (n 23).

in four out of the nine claims against valuers/surveyors[51] (44 per cent). Discussion of possible causes for these disparities will be found in the next section of the chapter.

V. Discussion

Intriguing data emerge from our study concerning the operation of the contributory negligence doctrine in the professional negligence context. Three principal conclusions can be drawn: (1) contributory negligence is frequently pleaded in professional negligence litigation (10 per cent of the claims in our first instance sample were professional negligence claims); (2) pleas of contributory negligence are considerably less likely to succeed in professional negligence claims than in other types of claim; and (3) when claimants are found guilty of contributory negligence in professional negligence claims, the average discount is higher than in other types of claim. In the light of (2), (1) is perhaps unexpected, and it is possible that the lawyers acting for defendants in professional negligence claims are not aware of how unlikely a plea of professional negligence is to succeed in that context, with the notable exception of claims against valuers/surveyors. On the other hand, it is possible that these lawyers are aware of the low success rate of the plea, but also of the relatively high discounts that judges impose when they make a finding of contributory negligence in this context, and that this latter consideration proves decisive. It is also important to point out that defendants rarely have anything to lose by pleading contributory negligence, even if the prospects of success on the point are very slim,[52] and that a plea of contributory negligence may be a useful bargaining chip in settlement negotiations, even if it would be unlikely to succeed at trial. It is noteworthy in this connection that, in many of the professional negligence claims in our study where the court found against the defendant on this issue, it seems clear that the plea of contributory negligence was not put forward with any real force or enthusiasm.[53] In one case, for example, Tomlinson J began his discussion of the contributory negligence issue by saying:

> This defence [contributory negligence] was memorably described by Mr Railton [counsel for one defendant] at an early stage of the trial as 'limp'. Mr Railton was not of course

[51] *Speshal Investments* (n 38); *Webb Resolutions Ltd v E.Surv Ltd* [2012] EWHC 3653 (TCC), [2013] PNLR 15; *Aurora Leasing Ltd v Colliers International Belfast Ltd* [2013] NIQB 116; *Barclays Bank Plc v Christie Owen & Davies Ltd* [2016] EWHC 2351 (Ch), [2017] PNLR 8.

[52] However, defendants who unsuccessfully plead contributory negligence (or who succeed in the plea of contributory negligence, but abandon or lose on particular allegations of contributory negligence) may be required to pay the costs associated with that issue. For an indication that the courts might be relatively reluctant to require defendants to bear costs in these circumstances, see *The Governors and Company of the Bank of Ireland v Watts Group Plc* [2017] EWHC 2472 (TCC), [2017] BLR 625 [12] (Coulson J).

[53] It has been pointed out to us that defendants may not push a plea of contributory negligence very hard because it always needs to be argued on the footing that the defendant himself or herself was guilty of negligence, which is not a scenario that defendants will wish to emphasise.

> involved in this particular argument between Aon and SLAC, but his evaluation was in my view not uncharitable. To be fair to Mr Weitzman [counsel for Aon, a defendant which had pleaded contributory negligence] it was not an argument which he pursued with any more enthusiasm than his professional duty required.[54]

The second of our general conclusions is consistent with the commonly expressed view that it is difficult for a defendant in a professional negligence claim to make an allegation of contributory negligence stick.[55] There are obvious reasons why a professional will often face 'grave difficulty'[56] and will 'only rarely … be able to set up allegations of contributory negligence against their clients'.[57] These reasons include the fact that the professional will usually have greater expertise than the client in the relevant field, that the relationship between professional and client is often markedly asymmetrical in terms of power, and that it will often be reasonable for the client to follow professional advice and to rely on the professional to do properly the job that he or she has been engaged to do. These explanations are consistent with the differential treatment of human and corporate claimants in this context (since it might plausibly be supposed that corporate claimants are generally more capable of protecting their own interests in the context of professional advice than human claimants, so that the corporate/human claimant distinction can serve as a proxy for a sophisticated/unsophisticated claimant distinction). In our sample, only two out of 16 human claimants (13 per cent) were found guilty of contributory negligence in professional negligence claims,[58] while the equivalent figures for corporate claimants were 13 out of 40 claimants (33 per cent).[59] Clearly these figures are suggestive, although, admittedly, the relevant sample size is small and there might be alternative explanations for the differential treatment of human and corporate claimants. For example, it may be that judges are more willing to make discounts from the damages of corporations on the footing that it is usually easier for them to absorb and/or pass on losses than it is for individuals.[60]

[54] *Standard Life Assurance Ltd v Oak Dedicated Ltd* [2008] EWHC 222 (Comm), [2008] 2 All ER (Comm) 916 [109].

[55] See, eg, *Jackson & Powell on Professional Liability* (n 13) para 5.172 ('[i]n the context of professional negligence a successful plea of contributory negligence by the defendant is less common than in other areas of negligence'); S Walmsley et al, *Professional Liability in Australia*, 3rd edn (Sydney, Lawbook Co, 2016) para 1.2170 ('In claims against professionals by clients, it is often difficult for the professional to successfully plead contributory negligence').

[56] Marks (n 2) 226–27.

[57] *Unicorn Consultancy Services Ltd* (n 18) [128] (Rimer J).

[58] The two cases in which findings of contributory negligence were made against human claimants were *Pidgeon* (n 39), a medical negligence claim, and *Slattery v Moore Stephens* [2003] EWHC 1869 (Ch), [2004] PNLR 14, a claim by an investment banker against his tax advisers.

[59] Statistical analysis of this disparity by means of a Pearson's chi-square test gave a p-value of 0.175. We have excluded from this comparison one case in which the claimants were trustees of a rugby club (*Montlake v Lambert Smith Hampton Group Ltd* [2004] EWHC 938 (Comm), [2004] 3 EGLR 149), a scenario that does not neatly fit into the human/corporate claimant dichotomy.

[60] Statistical analysis of this disparity by means of a Pearson's chi-square test returned a p-value of 0.175, meaning that it could well be down to chance. It might be thought that the explanation for the disparity lies in the defendant's profession. As we have seen, pleas of contributory negligence were, on average, less likely to succeed when made by lawyers or insurance brokers than when made by

However, it is worth emphasising that, even in professional negligence claims involving corporate clients, the likelihood of a successful plea of contributory negligence is still considerably lower than in other types of claim, which suggests that the relative sophistication of the parties is only a partial explanation for the low success rate of pleas of contributory negligence in this context. Qualitative analysis of the claims in our sample suggests that a more powerful explanation for the low success rate of the plea in professional negligence claims is that judges are unimpressed by arguments to the effect that clients should have done more to check the work done, or advice given, by a professional. Put simply, in most cases the courts take the view that a client is entitled to rely on the expertise of a defendant who has (almost always) been paid to provide a professional service.[61]

In the light of these considerations, it is interesting to observe that while pleas of contributory negligence are less likely to succeed in professional negligence claims, when they do succeed the average discount is higher than in all other types of claim. Quite why this inverse relationship exists is unclear. One possible explanation is that claimants need to do something particularly unreasonable in order to be found guilty of contributory negligence in a professional negligence claim. If this is correct, then judges might conclude that claimants who have been found guilty of contributory negligence in professional negligence claims deserve to have their damages discounted by a sizeable amount. This explanation would suggest that in, say, a borderline road accident case (ie, a case involving relatively minor claimant fault), the typical response is a finding of contributory negligence but the imposition of a small discount, while in a borderline professional negligence case the typical response is a finding that there was no contributory negligence at all.

Another possible explanation for the relatively high discounts in professional negligence cases is that in other types of case, such as road accident claims, considerations of causative potency play a greater role in the apportionment decision, whereas in professional negligence claims the focus is often exclusively on the relative fault of the parties. Hence, where the relative fault of the parties is thought to be roughly equivalent in a professional negligence claim, an equal division of responsibility is likely to be considered appropriate, so that a relatively high discount of 50 per cent (or thereabouts) is likely to be made. By contrast, in a road accident claim where the relative fault of a pedestrian claimant and a motorist defendant is judged to be roughly equivalent, the fact that the defendant was

valuers/surveyors. It follows that if human claimants brought more claims against lawyers and insurance brokers than they did against valuers/surveyors that fact *might* explain (at least in part) why pleas of contributory negligence rarely succeeded against human claimants. However, this explanation is unconvincing in view of the fact that *corporate* claimants accounted for a higher proportion of the claims in our sample against lawyers and insurance brokers (69% and 100% respectively) than they did of the claims against valuers/surveyors (63%).

[61] We return to this theme throughout this section of the chapter. See also Marks (n 2) 219 ('in many factual circumstances, the client will reasonably rely so completely upon the professional's skills that the defence will not succeed'); *Jackson & Powell on Professional Liability* (n 13) para 10.234 (footnote omitted) ('it is often harder to establish contributory negligence against a claimant in a professional negligence context than it might be in other areas of negligence, because in many cases the client will be entitled simply to rely upon the advice he receives from the professional he has retained').

driving a motor vehicle will tend to mean that greater causative potency is judged to attach to the defendant's negligence,[62] so that a lower discount of, say, one-third, is more likely to be made.

Our study also suggests that a plea of contributory negligence is more likely to succeed when made by a valuer/surveyor than by a lawyer. There are several possible explanations for this disparity.[63] If we look first at the cases in our sample involving lawyers, the allegation of contributory negligence usually boils down to a failure on the part of the client to detect an error in draft work produced by the defendant, or to remember to do something which it is the responsibility of the defendant to remind the client to do.[64] The general attitude of the courts in such cases is that (in the words of a leading text on professional negligence) '[i]n most situations it would not be reasonable to expect a client to check on the advice given or service provided by a solicitor'.[65]

In *Credit Lyonnais SA v Russell Jones & Walker (a firm)*,[66] for example, the defendant had been negligent in not drawing to the client's attention the fact that time was of the essence in relation to a particular payment that needed to be made in order to exercise a break clause in a lease. The defendant's argument that the claimant (a major bank) had also been guilty of contributory negligence in not making the payment on time was rejected. Similarly, in *Akasuc Enterprise Ltd v Farmar & Shirreff*,[67] where the defendant's negligence consisted of failing to insert a mechanism into a conditional purchase agreement to protect an overage fee, the judge rejected the argument that the corporate client in question had been negligent in not noticing the omission. And in *Feakins v Burstow*,[68] it was said that it would be rare for a client alleging the negligence of a lawyer in the conduct of litigation to be found guilty of contributory fault. Finally, in a case where insurance underwriters had settled a claim in reliance on defective advice provided by their solicitors, Simon J gave short shrift to the defendant's allegation that the claimants had been guilty of contributory negligence in not realising that the advice it had given was flawed:

> The defendant was specifically instructed to consider the issue of coverage and it is difficult to see why the client, who has paid the solicitor to do the work, should check

[62] See, eg, the remarks in *Lightfoot v Go-Ahead Group Plc* [2011] EWHC 89 (QB), [2011] RTR 27 [50] (McCombe J).

[63] Another possible explanation (ie, additional to those set out in the following paragraphs) that has been suggested to us for this disparity is that judges tend to be relatively tough on lawyers in professional negligence cases because they have a good understanding of the nature of the work that lawyers do, and hence feel more comfortable making findings of negligence against lawyers than against other professionals. However, although this seems plausible, such a tendency would not necessarily carry through into a concomitant *reluctance* to find lawyers' clients guilty of *contributory* negligence.

[64] For general discussion of contributory negligence in claims against lawyers, see *Jackson & Powell on Professional Liability* (n 13) para 11.341ff, 12.043.

[65] Dugdale and Stanton (n 2) para 21.38.

[66] [2002] EWHC 1310 (Ch), [2003] PNLR 2.

[67] [2003] EWHC 1275 (Ch).

[68] [2005] EWHC 1931 (QB), [2006] PNLR 6.

> that the solicitor has done the task for which he has been employed … To put the matter more proverbially: if you hire a dog you do not expect to have to bark.[69]

By contrast, analysis of the case law involving valuers and surveyors suggests that claims against such defendants typically arise out of decisions made by institutional lenders which were based on several different considerations, only one of which was the valuation provided by the defendant. Such scenarios lend themselves to allegations of contributory negligence on the ground that the claimant's decision to lend was imprudent in the light of the other factors in play. In this context, failure by the claimant to act in accordance with prudent lending practices is readily interpreted by judges as a form of negligence on the claimant's part which played as much (if not more) of a causal role in the decision to make a loan to a third party against the security of a property than the negligent over-valuation of that property by the defendant valuer or surveyor.[70] As the leading practitioner text on professional negligence puts it:

> There are … areas where the client is a sophisticated entity retaining functions not delegated to the professional for which the client retains responsibility. One such area is that of a lending institution, and it is in this context that most of the contributory negligence cases relating to surveyors have been decided.[71]

Examples of such claims in our study include *Speshal Investments*,[72] *Webb Resolutions Ltd v E.Surv Ltd*,[73] *Barclays Bank Plc v Christie Owen & Davies Ltd*[74] and *Aurora Leasing Ltd v Colliers International Belfast Ltd*.[75] Considerable emphasis is placed in cases of this kind on the question of whether the claimant lending institution complied with common practice in the industry. According to Coulson J in *Webb Resolutions*, for example:

> In general terms, the approach is to see what was happening elsewhere in the lending market because, if the claimant was doing what its competitors were doing, negligence was unlikely, unless it could be shown that it was irrational or illogical.[76]

[69] *Newline Corporate Name Ltd v Morgan Cole (a firm)* [2007] EWHC 1628 (Comm), [2008] PNLR 2 [69]. For the same argument in respect of other types of professional adviser, see *Chrysalis Scotland* (n 40) [58] (Lord Glennie) (financial adviser); *Manorgate* (n 44) [58] (Lord Woolman) (property search company). See also the observation of Picard and Robertson (n 2) in the medical negligence context that 'as a general rule it is reasonable for a patient to rely on the professional opinion of their physician' (at 373).

[70] For general discussion of contributory negligence in claims against surveyors, see *Jackson & Powell on Professional Liability* (n 13) para 10-234ff.

[71] *Jackson & Powell on Professional Liability* (n 2) para 10.234.

[72] n 38.

[73] n 51.

[74] [2016] EWHC 2351 (Ch), [2017] PNLR 8.

[75] n 51. See also *Paratus AMC Ltd v Countrywide Surveyors Ltd* [2011] EWHC 3307 (Ch), [2012] PNLR 12, a case excluded from our study because the discussion of contributory negligence was hypothetical, where the judge held that if the defendant surveyors had been found liable, he would have reduced the damages by 60% for the contributory negligence of the claimant lender.

[76] *Webb Resolutions* (n 51) [71]. See also *Paratus* (n 75) [79]–[80] (HHJ Keyser); *Barclays Bank* (n 51) [232] (Richard Spearman QC) ('if a practice was accepted by a significant section of the banking

Failures to comply with the prudent lender standard have included not taking account of discrepancies between a borrower's statements as to his debts and those revealed by credit checks;[77] failing to make enquiries regarding a borrower's income and ability to service the loan;[78] and failing to take account of a borrower's misuse of an earlier loan.[79] Furthermore, in cases of this kind, a sophisticated lender may be held to have been at fault simply for not second-guessing the valuation provided by the defendant, though in such a scenario a lower discount can be expected.[80]

High discounts for contributory negligence can also be found in other types of professional negligence case, where the fault of the claimant is independent of the fault of the defendant (in that it does not lie in not checking or verifying the professional's work), or where the thing that the claimant ought to have done did not require technical competence. A good example of a case in which the claimant's fault was independent of that of the defendant is *Sahib Foods Ltd v Paskin KyriaKides Sands (a firm)*,[81] a case concerning fire damage to the claimant's factory, where liability was imposed on the defendant architects for the inadequate fireproofing of a food preparation room, but the damages were reduced by two-thirds because the claimant's employees had both caused the fire and contributed to its spreading by misinforming the defendants about the nature of the cooking process involved. Similarly, in *Logical Computer Supplies Ltd v Euro Car Parks Ltd*[82] the compensation awarded to a company for damage to its computer files that had been caused by employees of an IT firm hired to supply an email system was reduced by 50 per cent on account of the company's failure to apply 'business common sense and risk management'[83] by properly backing up its data.

Nevertheless, despite these broader trends, much still depends on the facts of the particular case, and the sophistication of the claimant is clearly a material consideration. In one claim against a law firm, for example, the judge took account, in finding that there was no contributory negligence, of the fact that the person who ran the claimant company had 'little or no experience' of property development and limited understanding of the 'intricacies of such agreements'.[84] By contrast, in one of the two instances in which a law firm successfully pleaded contributory negligence,[85] the claimant was a government department. The judge

market at the relevant time, it should not be held to fail to meet the standard of a reasonably competent bank unless plainly illogical').

[77] See, eg, *Paratus* (n 75); *Webb Resolutions* (n 51).

[78] See, eg, *Paratus* (n 75).

[79] See, eg, *Barclays Bank* (n 51) (40% discount).

[80] See, eg, *Speshal Investments* (n 38) (20% discount for not subjecting to critical analysis the disparity between the purchase price of the properties against which the loan was secured and the valuations provided by the defendants).

[81] [2003] EWCA Civ 1832, [2004] PNLR 22.

[82] n 22.

[83] ibid, [14] (Richard Fernyhough QC).

[84] *Akasuc* (n 67) [21], [80] (Peter Smith J).

[85] *Secretary of State for the Environment, Transport and Regions v Unicorn Consultancy Services* (n 18).

held that, as such, it should have had its own system in place for ensuring that it made a vital payment that would have enabled it to exercise a break clause in a lease on time, and ought not to have relied completely on its legal advisers to remind it.[86] It was, however, also a consideration in the latter case that the claimant knew that it was vital that the payment was made punctually, and that doing so required no special expertise.[87]

The sophistication of the client is also clearly relevant in claims against insurance brokers, where it is unlikely that a lay client will be found to have been at fault in not checking or failing to understand insurance documentation. To take one example, in *Arbory Group Ltd v West Craven Insurance Services*[88] it was held that a lay businessperson could not be expected to be familiar with the principles of computation of lost profits in the context of business interruption insurance, and that it was the duty of the defendant broker to explain its meaning to such a client.[89] However, such conduct is more likely to be considered negligent where the client is itself an insurance company, and, hence, 'as knowledgeable about insurance matters' as an insurance broker.[90] Overall, however, our finding that pleas of contributory negligence by insurance brokers succeeded in only 14 per cent of the claims in which they were made is consistent with the statement that in this context '[w]hile a reduction for contributory negligence is possible, in practice the courts show a good deal of indulgence towards assured who assume that their brokers have acted properly and do not take steps to double check'.[91]

Turning to the medical negligence context, the dearth of case law in our study provides further evidence that pleas (let alone successful pleas) of contributory negligence are most unusual in this area of law. It is also instructive to compare the facts of the only such case where a finding of contributory negligence was made, *Pidgeon v Doncaster HA*,[92] with the facts of one of the medical negligence cases in which the plea was unsuccessful, *Re P (deceased)*.[93] In *Pidgeon*, the claimant sought damages in respect of a cervical smear which was wrongly evaluated by the defendants as being negative. However, although the judge held that the defendants had indeed been negligent, he also held that two-thirds of the responsibility

[86] For similar reasoning in a Canadian case, see *Doiron v Caisse Populaire* (1985) 17 DLR (4th) 660, where the New Brunswick Court of Appeal held that a financial institution was guilty of contributory negligence for failing to check that the loan documents provided by the defendant solicitor complied with its instructions.

[87] *Secretary of State for the Environment, Transport and Regions* (n 18) [128] (Rimer J).

[88] [2007] Lloyd's Rep IR 491.

[89] For a similar analysis in the insurance context, see *Dunlop Haywards* (n 23) esp [224]–[225] (Hamblen J).

[90] *Jackson & Powell on Professional Liability* (n 13) para 16.182. For examples of the relative sophistication of the client affecting the contributory negligence analysis in claims against insurance brokers in claims not included in our study, see Dugdale and Stanton (n 2) para 21.37.

[91] M Jones (ed), *Clerk & Lindsell on Torts*, 22nd edn (London, Sweet & Maxwell, 2017) para 10.259.

[92] n 39.

[93] n 46.

for the failure to identify the claimant's cancerous condition lay with the claimant herself, who failed to have further smear tests, despite being repeatedly urged to do so in strong terms by several doctors. By contrast, in *Re P (deceased)*, where the judge described the facts of *Pidgeon* as 'extreme',[94] it was held that the deceased had not been negligent in failing to chase up hospital appointment letters that the defendant GP had sent to the wrong address, with the result that the deceased's breast cancer was incurable by the time it was diagnosed.

On one level, the lack of case law on contributory negligence in the medical malpractice context is unsurprising. As an Australian commentator has pointed out:

> The paternalistic model [of the doctor/patient relationship] places responsibility for the patient's health and medical treatment squarely on the shoulders of the doctor without reference to any responsibility the patient may have for his or her own health. It follows that contributory negligence principles have little application in a legal system that embodies the paternalistic model ….[95]

On the other hand, whatever model of the doctor-patient relationship is adopted, it is hard to see why clearly negligent conduct on the part of a patient who, for example, fails to attend a follow-up appointment should not be met with a modest reduction in damages. Furthermore, as common law legal systems move away from the paternalistic model of the doctor-patient relationship, courts may be more inclined to make findings of contributory negligence in medical malpractice litigation. In Canada, it has been said by commentators that 'the number of cases in which patients have been found contributorily negligent has increased significantly in recent years', a phenomenon linked to patients striving for (and achieving) 'a more equal role in … the doctor-patient relationship'.[96] Similarly, it has been argued that the shift away from a medical paternalism model towards a patient autonomy model in Australia following the decision of the High Court in *Rogers v Whitaker*[97] has led to increased reliance on the contributory negligence doctrine in medical malpractice litigation before the Australian courts.[98] As Harper says:

> The recognition of greater patient autonomy at law mandates that courts re-evaluate the foundational assumptions upon which the majority of medical law is premised. In the context of the defence of contributory negligence, this means that courts must

[94] ibid [61] (HHJ Mitchell).

[95] Harper (n 2) 3. See also Herring and Foster (n 2) 83 (under the traditional paternalistic model, '[t]he patients' role is essentially a passive one', with the result that 'there is little the patient can do that would be regarded as negligent').

[96] Picard and Robertson (n 2) 369. Nevertheless, even in Canada, the same authors say that the contributory negligence defence 'has been applied in relatively few medical negligence cases': ibid.

[97] (1992) 175 CLR 479.

[98] Harper (n 2) 17. It has also been said that the defence is frequently employed in medical malpractice litigation in the United States, where the courts have also embraced the patient autonomy model: see Herring and Foster (n 2) 76.

> move away from the implicit assumption of patient dependence, an assumption that, for decades, justified the preclusion of the defence of contributory negligence for defendant-physicians … There is an argument to be made that the movement for patients' rights demands reciprocity. For example, if patients have the 'right' to full disclosure by their physicians, then it can be argued that they also have the 'obligation' to reciprocate by fully and accurately disclosing to the physician all information that may be relevant to the patient's medical care.[99]

If increased patient autonomy also entails increased patient responsibility, then one by-product of the strong recent emphasis by the UK courts on patient autonomy in the medical non-disclosure context could be an increased focus on patient conduct in medical negligence litigation. After all, in *Montgomery v Lanarkshire Health Board* – where the Supreme Court replaced the *Bolam* test[100] with a patient-sided test of 'material risk' in medical non-disclosure cases – Lord Kerr and Lord Reed said, in the leading judgment, that:

> It would … be a mistake to view patients as uninformed, incapable of understanding medical matters, or wholly dependent on a flow of information from doctors. The idea that patients were medically uninformed and incapable of understanding medical matters was always a questionable generalisation … .[101]

Furthermore, their Lordships argued that certain the social and legal developments pointed away from a model of the relationship between doctor and patient based on medical paternalism towards an approach that treats them so far as possible as adults who are capable of understanding that medical treatment is uncertain of success and living with the consequences of their choices.[102]

Nevertheless, the judgment in *Montgomery* was handed down near the end of our study period, and so it remains to be seen whether this new-found emphasis on patient responsibility will mean that, in future, the contributory negligence doctrine will play a greater role in medical negligence litigation in the UK.

VI. Conclusion

Professional negligence cases are often thought of as rather different in certain important respects from other types of negligence proceedings.[103] It therefore

[99] Ventresca, Kryworuk and Chambers (n 2) 228. To similar effect, see Harper (n 2); SW Murphy, 'Contributory Negligence in Medical Malpractice: Are the Standards Changing to Reflect Society's Growing Health Care Consumerism?' (1991) 17 *University of Dayton Law Review* 151; Herring and Foster (n 2) 76.

[100] *Bolam v Friern Hospital Management Committee* [1957] 1 WLR 582, 587 (McNair J).

[101] [2015] UKSC 11, [2015] AC 1430 [76].

[102] ibid, [81].

[103] 'The nature and functions of the traditional professions have … resulted in certain significant distinctions in the application of basic tort rules to professionals. These distinctions have both restricted liability in some contexts and extended it in others': *Clerk & Lindsell on Torts* (n 91) para 10.02.

stands to reason that the contributory negligence doctrine might also operate in a distinctive way in that context. The burden of this chapter was, accordingly, to explore, employing both quantitative and qualitative analysis, how the doctrine functions in the professional negligence setting. Our findings suggest that the law of contributory negligence indeed adapts to the professional negligence environment. Thus, in our sample, the plea of contributory negligence succeeded much less frequently at first instance in the professional negligence context than in other types of case. However, when the plea did succeed, the average discount was higher than in any other category of case. Interesting differences were also observed in the way in which the contributory negligence doctrine applies to different types of professional. In our sample, the plea of contributory negligence was particularly unlikely to succeed where the defendant was a lawyer or insurance broker. By contrast, valuers and surveyors who alleged contributory negligence had more success in the plea. We identified sophistication of the claimant as an important factor in explaining the handling of the contributory negligence doctrine in this context, although we also observed that this was only one of several considerations to which significance was attached. One thing that is, however, clear, is that contributory negligence is regularly relied upon by defendants in professional negligence claims. That is unsurprising, given that it costs little or nothing to plead and yet significantly affects the quantum of recovery when the plea succeeds.

Appendix

Name of case	**Citation**	**Date of decision**	**Type of Professional**	**Type of Damage**	**Contributory negligence?**	**Discount (%)**
Cottingham v Attey Bower & Jones	[2000] PNLR 557	30 March 2000	Legal practitioner	Pure economic	No	
Cottingham v Attey Bower & Jones	[2000] PNLR 557	30 March 2000	Legal practitioner	Pure economic	No	
Secretary of State for the Environment, Transport and Regions v Unicorn Consultancy Services	[2000] NPC 108	19 October 2000	Legal practitioner	Pure economic	Yes	50

(*continued*)

(*Continued*)

Name of case	Citation	Date of decision	Type of Professional	Type of Damage	Contributory negligence?	Discount (%)
Logical Computer Supplies Ltd v Euro Car Parks Ltd	2001 WL 825094	19 June 2001	Other	Property	Yes	50
Pidgeon v Doncaster HA	[2002] Lloyd's Rep Med 130	9 October 2001	Medical practitioner	Personal injury	Yes	66.6
Alpha Credit Bank v Stephenson Harwood	[2002] EWHC 922 (Ch)	26 March 2002	Legal practitioner	Pure economic	Yes	60
Credit Lyonnais SA v Russell Jones & Walker	[2002] EWHC 1310 (Ch), [2003] PNLR 2	2 July 2002	Legal practitioner	Pure economic	No	
Alexander Forbes Europe Ltd v SBJ Ltd	[2002] EWHC 3121 (Comm), [2003] PNLR 15	20 December 2002	Insurance broker	Pure economic	No	
Sahib Foods Ltd v Paskin KyriaKides Sands	[2003] EWHC 142 (TCC), [2003] PNLR 30	3 March 2003	Architect	Property	No	
Speshal Investments Ltd v Corby Kane Howard Partnership Ltd	[2003] EWHC 390 (Ch)	5 March 2003	Valuer	Pure economic	Yes	20
Akasuc Enterprise Ltd v Farmar & Shirreff	[2003] EWHC 1275 (Ch)	5 June 2003	Legal practitioner	Pure economic	No	

(*Continued*)

Name of case	Citation	Date of decision	Type of Professional	Type of Damage	Contributory negligence?	Discount (%)
Great North Eastern Railway Ltd v Railcare Ltd	[2003] EWHC 1608 (Comm)	15 July 2003	Other	Property	No	
Six Continents Retail Ltd v Carford Catering Ltd	[2003] EWCA Civ 1790	29 July 2003	Project manager	Property	Yes	100
Slattery v Moore Stephens	[2003] EWHC 1869 (Ch), [2004] PNLR 14	31 July 2003	Accountant	Pure economic	Yes	50
Montlake v Lambert Smith Hampton Group Ltd	[2004] EWHC 938 (Comm)	6 May 2004	Surveyor and valuer	Pure economic	No	
Francis v Barclays Bank Plc	[2004] EWHC 2787 (Ch), [2005] PNLR 18	7 December 2004	Surveyor	Pure economic	No	
Hodson Development Ltd v CTA Civils	[2006] EWHC 1913 (TCC)	13 July 2005	Architect	Pure economic	No	
Feakins v Burstow	[2005] EWHC 1936 (QB), [2006] PNLR 6	8 September 2005	Legal practitioner	Pure economic	No	
Plymouth & South West Co-operative Society v Architecture Structure & Management Ltd	[2006] EWHC 5 (TCC), (2006) 108 Con LR 77	10 January 2006	Architect	Pure economic	No	

(*continued*)

(*Continued*)

Name of case	Citation	Date of decision	Type of Professional	Type of Damage	Contributory negligence?	Discount (%)
BP Plc v AON Ltd (No 2)	[2006] EWHC 424 (Comm), [2006] 1 CLC 881	13 March 2006	Insurance broker	Pure economic	No	
Arbory Group Ltd v West Craven Insurance Services	[2007] Lloyd's Rep IR 491	13 March 2007	Insurance broker	Pure economic	No	
Carleton (Earl of Malmesbury) v Strutt & Parker	[2007] EWHC 999 (QB), [2007] PNLR 29	11 May 2007	Surveyor	Pure economic	No	
Newline Corporate Name Ltd v Morgan Cole	[2007] EWHC 1628 (Comm), [2008] PNLR 2	10 July 2007	Legal practitioner	Pure economic	No	
Standard Life Assurance Ltd v Oak Dedicated Ltd	[2008] EWHC 222 (Comm), [2008] 2 All ER (Comm) 916	13 February 2008	Insurance broker	Pure economic	No	
Chrysalis Scotland Ltd v Clydesdale Bank Insurance Brokers Ltd	[2008] CSOH 144, 2008 GWD 38-578	14 October 2008	Other	Pure economic	No	
Devine v McAteer	[2008] NICh 18	18 December 2008	Accountant	Pure economic	No	

(*Continued*)

Name of case	Citation	Date of decision	Type of Professional	Type of Damage	Contributory negligence?	Discount (%)
Berry v Laytons	[2009] EWHC 1591 (QB), [2009] ECC 34	3 July 2009	Legal practitioner	Pure economic	No	
Martin v Triggs Turner Bartons	[2009] EWHC 1920 (Ch), [2010] PNLR 3	31 July 2009	Legal practitioner	Pure economic	No	
Dunlop Haywards Ltd v Barbon Insurance Group Ltd	[2009] EWHC 2900 (Comm), [2010] Lloyd's Rep IR 149	19 November 2009	Insurance broker	Pure economic	No	
Dunlop Haywards Ltd v Barbon Insurance Group Ltd	[2009] EWHC 2900 (Comm), [2010] Lloyd's Rep IR 149	19 November 2009	Insurance broker	Pure economic	Yes	80
Tom Hoskins Plc v EMR Law (a firm)	[2010] EWHC 479 (Ch), [2010] ECC 20	11 March 2010	Legal practitioner	Pure economic	No	
Scullion v Bank of Scotland Plc (t/a Colleys)	[2010] EWHC 2253 (Ch), [2011] PNLR 5	8 October 2010	Valuer	Pure economic	No	

(*continued*)

(*Continued*)

Name of case	Citation	Date of decision	Type of Professional	Type of Damage	Contributory negligence?	Discount (%)
Ground Gilbey Ltd v Jardine Lloyd Thompson UK Ltd	[2011] EWHC 124 (Comm), [2012] Lloyd's Rep IR 12	2 February 2011	Insurance broker	Pure economic	No	
Re P (deceased)	[2011] EWHC 1266 (QB)	11 March 2011	Medical practitioner	Personal injury	No	
Trebor Bassett Holdings Ltd v ADT Fire & Security Plc	[2011] EWHC 1936 (TCC), [2011] BLR 661	22 July 2011	Other	Property	Yes	75
Trebor Bassett Holdings Ltd v ADT Fire & Security Plc	[2011] EWHC 1936 (TCC), [2011] BLR 661	22 July 2011	Other	Property	Yes	75
Argos Ltd v Leather Trade House Ltd	[2012] EWHC 1348 (QB), [2012] ECC 34	22 May 2012	Other	Pure economic	No	
Webb Resolutions Ltd v E.Surv Ltd	[2012] EWHC 3653 (TCC), [2013] PNLR 15	20 December 2012	Surveyor	Pure economic	Yes	50
Blemain Finance Ltd v E.Surv Ltd	[2012] EWHC 3654 (TCC), [2014] 1 P & CR D44	20 December 2012	Valuer	Pure economic	No	

(*Continued*)

Name of case	Citation	Date of decision	Type of Professional	Type of Damage	Contributory negligence?	Discount (%)
Taylor v Bank of Ireland (UK) Plc	[2013] NIQB 50	19 March 2013	Banker	Pure economic	No	
Manorgate Ltd v First Scottish Property Services Ltd	[2013] CSOH 108, [2014] PNLR 1	4 July 2013	Other	Pure economic	No	
Aurora Leasing Ltd v Colliers International Belfast Ltd	[2013] NIQB 116	5 August 2013	Surveyor and valuer	Pure economic	Yes	20
Forsta AP-Fonden v Bank of New York Mellon SA/NV	[2013] EWHC 3127 (Comm)	16 October 2013	Banker	Pure economic	No	
The Law Society of Northern Ireland v Bank of Ireland	[2013] NIQB 130	18 December 2013	Banker	Pure economic	No	
Wellesley Partnership LLP v Withers LLP	[2014] EWHC 556 (Ch); [2014] PNLR 22	11 March 2014	Legal practitioner	Pure economic	No	
Playboy Club London Ltd v Banca Nazionale Del Lavoro SPA	[2014] EWHC 2613 (QB)	29 July 2014	Banker	Pure economic	Yes	15
Spencer v Hillingdon Hospital NHS Trust	[2015] EWHC 1058 (QB)	21 April 2015	Medical practitioner	Personal injury	No	

(*continued*)

(Continued)

Name of case	Citation	Date of decision	Type of Professional	Type of Damage	Contributory negligence?	Discount (%)
Orientfield Holdings Ltd v Bird & Bird LLP	[2015] EWHC 1963 (Ch), [2015] PNLR 33	26 June 2015	Legal practitioner	Pure economic	No	
Lloyds Bank Plc v McBains Cooper Consulting Ltd	[2015] EWHC 2372 (TCC)	2 October 2015	Project manager	Pure economic	Yes	33.3
Mansion Estates Ltd v Hayre and Co	[2016] EWHC 96 (Ch)	22 January 2016	Legal practitioner	Pure economic	No	
Commodities Research Unit International (Holdings) Ltd v King and Wood Mallesons LLP	[2016] EWHC 727 (QB)	5 April 2016	Legal practitioner	Pure economic	No	
Scott v EAR Sheppard Consulting Civil and Structural Engineers Ltd	[2016] EWHC 1949 (TCC)	27 July 2016	Engineer	Pure economic	No	
Scott v EAR Sheppard Consulting Civil and Structural Engineers Ltd	[2016] EWHC 1949 (TCC)	27 July 2016	Engineer	Pure economic	No	
Scott v EAR Sheppard Consulting Civil and Structural Engineers Ltd	[2016] EWHC 1949 (TCC)	27 July 2016	Engineer	Pure economic	No	

(*Continued*)

Name of case	Citation	Date of decision	Type of Professional	Type of Damage	Contributory negligence?	Discount (%)
Barclays Bank Plc v Christie Owen & Davies Ltd	[2016] EWHC 2351 (Ch), [2017] PNLR 8	30 September 2016	Valuer	Pure economic	Yes	40
Adams v Atlas International Property Services Ltd	[2016] EWHC 3120 (QB)	5 December 2016	Legal practitioner	Pure economic	No	
Harlequin Property (SVG) Ltd v Wilkins Kennedy	[2016] EWHC 3188 (TCC), [2017] 4 WLR 30	12 December 2016	Accountant	Pure economic	Yes	50

8

Allocating the Costs of Making Restitution: Change of Position

ROSS GRANTHAM

In an important sense, most claims based on the principle of unjust enrichment involve two innocent parties whose moral merits are finely balanced. In the paradigm case, where C mistakenly transfers to D $5,000 instead of the $500 he intended, the defect in C's intention removes the most obvious legal and moral basis upon which C should be held to be responsible for the consequences of the transfer. However, C is the author of his own misfortune. D did not cause or induce C's mistake and D bears no responsibility for C's mistake. On the other hand, where D still has the money and has done nothing with it, it does not seem right that D should be able to retain the money. Nor does it seem unduly onerous to ask D to return the money: D will not be left worse off and the burden of returning the money does not seem significant. Intuitively, however, the merits seem to shift where D has spent the funds on a lavish meal, or where D has booked a holiday next month for herself and her children. In a practical sense, the money that was initially transferred is now gone and, if D is to be asked to make restitution, it can only be from D's non-receipt resources. The obligation being imposed on D now seems much more onerous and the fact of C's mistake – for which D bears no responsibility – now seems insufficient as justification for the obligation: why should D have to dip into her own pocket (and disappoint her children) to bail C out of the consequences of C's self-inflicted misfortune?

The essential character and distinguishing feature of the law of unjust enrichment, which includes the defence of change of position as a core element, is usually understood to be its focus on gains, not losses. As Professor Peter Birks said: 'The law of restitution is the law of gain-based recovery, just as the law of compensation is the law of loss-based recovery.'[1] Nevertheless, in cases such as

[1] P Birks, *Unjust Enrichment*, 2nd edn (Oxford, Clarendon, 2005) 3. See also C Mitchell, P Mitchell, S Watterson, *Goff and Jones The Law of Unjust Enrichment*, 9th edn (London, Sweet & Maxwell, 2016) 1–17; A Burrows, *A Restatement of the English Law of Unjust Enrichment* (Oxford, OUP, 2012) 26; J Edelman and E Bant, *Unjust Enrichment*, 2nd edn (Oxford, Hart Publishing, 2016) 32.

the example above, the effect of the law is to apportion the losses arising out of the interaction of the parties.[2] If, as a result of C's transfer, D has dissipated[3] the money, then one or other of C or D will be left out of pocket. If C is entitled to restitution of the mistakenly transferred funds, then D will bear the losses of her dissipation of the funds received. If D is not required to make restitution, then C will bear the consequences of D's dissipation. In determining who bears the loss, the defence of change of position plays a key role. It is the defence that determines whether D's expenditure is to be brought into account in assessing whether (and how much) restitution is to be made and thus whether it is C, or D, who ultimately bears the cost of their joint misfortune.

The purpose of this chapter is to explore the defence of change of position from the perspective of loss allocation.[4] In the tradition of interpretative legal theory, the chapter will seek to construct an intelligible account of the defence of change of position as having not only a loss allocation *effect*, but as a doctrine that has loss allocation as its essential purpose or function. Such an account will incorporate the doctrinal landmarks identified by the authorities and will seek to articulate a rationale for the defence that explains and justifies its loss allocation function. That rationale will also cohere with the underlying justifications of the principle of unjust enrichment.

I. Development of the Defence of Change of Position

The structure of liability arising from claims based on the principle of unjust enrichment changed fundamentally with the decision of the House of Lords in *Lipkin Gorman (a firm) v Karpnale Ltd*.[5] In recognising for the first time a defence of change of position, their Lordships outlined a new strategy for the law of unjust enrichment. This strategy involved a significant liberalisation of the conditions of liability that were then balanced by expansive defences such as change of position.

[2] See generally, *Restatement of the Law Third, Restitution and Unjust Enrichment* (St Paul, Minn, American Law Institute, 2011) vol 2, § 65; H Dagan, *The Law and Ethics of Restitution* (Cambridge, CUP, 2004) 46–47; A Ratan, 'The Unity of Pre-receipt and Post-receipt Detriment' in A Dyson, J Goudkamp, F Wilmot-Smith (eds), *Defences in Unjust Enrichment* (Oxford, Hart Publishing, 2016) 87, 111.

[3] I use the word 'dissipate' as an encompassing and hopefully neutral term to capture the wide varieties of events and circumstances that may constitute a change in the defendant's position. This includes not only situations where the defendant has spent or committed the money received, but also those in which the defendant has forgone an opportunity to avoid a loss as a result of thinking the benefit received was hers to keep.

[4] E Bant, *The Change of Position Defence* (Oxford, Hart Publishing, 2009) ch 8 identifies the defence as being concerned with both the protection of the defendant from harm and the denial of protection where the defendant dissipates the benefits received while aware of the defect in the transfer. However, Bant is does not connect these ideas, or connect the rationale of the defence to the rationale of the principle of unjust enrichment.

[5] [1991] 2 AC 548 (HL).

As Lord Goff said, recognition of a change of position defence 'will enable a more generous approach to be taken to the recognition of the right to restitution, in the knowledge that the defence is, in appropriate cases, available …'.[6] The strategy outlined by the House of Lords was thus one in which a much greater burden was placed on the defences in determining the overall scope and extent of liability.[7] In recognition of this strategy, the law of unjust enrichment is now generally regarded as being reducible to four, fundamental elements:[8] benefit or enrichment; at the claimant's expense; the presence of an unjust factor in the transactional relationship between the parties; and whether there are defences, particularly the defence of change of position, open to the defendant.[9]

Despite the importance of the role assigned to change of position in this new strategy, Lord Goff declined to elaborate on the precise ingredients of the defence, its theoretical or conceptual role, or the circumstances that might justify denying the claimant's claim to restitution in full. He preferred instead that the defence develop on a case-by-case basis. His Lordship did, however, offer a broad description of the defence as being 'available to a person whose position has so changed that it would be inequitable in all the circumstances to require him to make restitution, or alternatively to make restitution in full'.[10] Lord Goff added that the defence would arise where 'an innocent defendant's position is so changed that he will suffer an injustice if called upon to repay or to repay in full, [so that] the injustice of requiring him so to repay outweighs the injustice of denying the claimant restitution'.[11]

Lord Goff's concern that 'nothing should be said at this stage to inhibit the development of the defence'[12] could not, however, do away with the need to understand the conceptual role of the defence if it were to develop in a principled fashion. Professor Peter Birks,[13] and later Professor Andrew Burrows,[14] conceptualised the defence in terms of the mechanism by which it defeated the prima facie

[6] *Lipkin* (n 5) 581.

[7] R Grantham and C Rickett, 'A Normative Account of Defences to Restitutionary Liability' [2008] 67 *CLJ* 92.

[8] *Banque Financière de la Cité v Parc (Battersea) Ltd* [1999] 1 AC 221 (HL), 227 (Lord Steyn): 'Four questions arise. (1) Has OOL benefited or been enriched? (2) Was the enrichment at the expense of BFC? (3) Was the enrichment unjust? (4) Are there any defences?' Generally, see Burrows, *The Law of Restitution* 3rd edn (Oxford, OUP, 2011) 27 and the authorities cited therein. See also Burrows, *Restatement* (n 1) 25; Edelman and Bant (n 1) 29–30.

[9] On the nature of change of position as a defence (a denial of prima facie liability) rather than a negation, see, D Klimchuk, 'What Kind of Defence of Change of Position?' in A Dyson, J Goudkamp, F Wilmot-Smith (eds), *Defences in Unjust Enrichment* (Oxford, Hart Publishing, 2016) ch 4. On the analysis presented here, the defence may be understood as a denial, but where that denial is an integral part of the normative basis of the liability imposed. In other words, change of position functions to deny liability as part of the basis of liability. It is, therefore, a defence, but an atypical one.

[10] *Lipkin* (n 5) 580.

[11] ibid, 579.

[12] ibid, 580.

[13] Birks (n 1) 208.

[14] Burrows, *Restitution* (n 8) 526.

liability in unjust enrichment. Although Lord Goff's broad description seemed to invoke worryingly vague notions of injustice and inequity, the judgments in *Lipkin* also suggested that change of position operated by allowing the defendant to show that she was enriched to an extent less than that of the initial receipt. In Burrows' view:[15]

> It is submitted that the essential justification for the change of position defence is that the defendant has lost the enrichment, ie, disenrichment. Although the defendant was initially enriched (or appeared to be initially enriched) the change of position defence responds to the fact that the enrichment has subsequently (or even in anticipation of the initial enrichment) been countered by causally related loss or detriment so that overall the defendant has not been enriched.

The 'disenrichment' account initially gained significant support from both courts and commentators.[16] This no doubt reflected the fact that it offered a clear and apparently logical connection between claims based on the principle of unjust enrichment and the defence.[17] If unjust enrichment seeks to restore the benefit received by the defendant from the claimant then, to the extent that the defendant has dissipated the benefit, there is simply nothing left to restore. In this way, the defence functioned to negate a core element of the cause of action.[18] Disenrichment also corralled the impetus towards treating the defence as an open-ended discretion that was inherent in Lord Goff's original formulation of the defence in terms of preventing an 'injustice' being done to the defendant. Determining whether the defendant had lost the enrichment seemed like an exercise that could be informed by clear principles, as opposed to a broad assessment of the relative merits of parties' positions, which in turn risked the epithet of palm tree justice.[19] However, although it offers a comparatively simple and certain basis for the defence, the disenrichment approach nevertheless has significant shortcomings. As a normative account, it is incomplete and, as a descriptive account, it has been rendered inaccurate by subsequent developments in the case law.

As a normative account of change of position, the disenrichment rationale relies on a bare causal connection between the defendant's receipt and the defendant's expenditure to justify bringing the expenditure into account.[20] However, it is difficult to see how causation alone can offer a reason why the later expenditure

[15] ibid.

[16] E Bant, 'Change of Position: Outstanding Issues' in A Dyson, J Goudkamp, F Wilmot-Smith (eds), *Defences in Unjust Enrichment* (Oxford, Hart Publishing, 2016) 139.

[17] Tang Hang Wu, 'Taking Stock of the Change of Position Defence' (2015) 27 *Singapore Academy LJ* 148, 150.

[18] The disenrichment analysis also has the tendency to treat change of position as an element of the cause of action rather than as a defence.

[19] A criticism to which the law of unjust enrichment is always sensitive. See P Watts, '"Unjust Enrichment" – the Potion that Induces Well-meaning Sloppiness of Thought' [2016] *Current Legal Problems* 289.

[20] Grantham and Rickett (n 7) 120.

should be brought into account against the initial receipt.[21] While the receipt by the defendant may have been a *necessary* condition, it is certainly not a *sufficient* condition of the defendant's subsequent expenditure. Moreover, the expenditure normally occurs some time after the receipt and – even then – only rarely involves the dissipation of the actual value received, as opposed to other assets of the defendant. The causal connection between receipt and expenditure is thus not a causal one in any physical sense. Nor need the connection between receipt and expenditure be a particularly strong one. In the example given by Lord Goff in *Lipkin* of a defendant who, upon receiving money, immediately makes a charitable gift,[22] there is little room for other causes to intrude. However, in most cases of change of position the expenditure is more likely to be the result of a complex matrix of causes and effects, of which the receipt is only one. The highly contingent nature of the expenditure is reflected in the relaxation of the standard of proof required of the expenditure in cases such as *Philip Collins Ltd v Davis*.[23] The causal justification is also incomplete at the conceptual level. Even where a strong causal link can be established as a matter of fact, the question remains as to why this link should defeat the claimant's claim. The expenditure was not a condition of the transfer and in many cases the defendant will be unaware of its occurrence. Also, in terms of the relationship between the claimant and defendant, while causation may offer a reason on the defendant's side to bring the expenditure into account, it is a reason that does not touch upon the claimant. Unlike estoppel, in the paradigmatic case of change of position the claimant does not induce, or encourage the defendant's detrimental reliance and thus there is no obvious reason to visit upon the claimant the consequences of the defendant's expenditure.

Disenrichment also struggles as a descriptive account.[24] As the defence has been developed in the authorities, the content of the defence has increasingly diverged from the predictions of a disenrichment analysis. First, the disenrichment analysis presumes that the circumstances that are to count as a change of position must mirror the concept of enrichment as it is understood for the purposes of the claim in unjust enrichment.[25] As Burrows says: 'As change of position is best justified as concerned with the disenrichment, it naturally follows that that there is a close link between establishing that the defendant is initially enriched and the defence of change of position.'[26] Therefore, insofar as the concept of enrichment as an element of the claim in unjust enrichment is largely limited to pecuniary benefits, the disenrichment approach predicts that it is only pecuniary changes in position that can, or should, count. However, development of change

[21] E Weinrib, *The Idea of Private Law* (Cambridge, Mass, Harvard University Press, 1995) ch 3.

[22] *Lipkin* (n 5) 579.

[23] [2000] 3 All ER 808, 829–30.

[24] For a more detailed critique of the descriptive accuracy of 'disenrichment' see, Bant (n 4) 126–30 and Bant (n 16) 140–46.

[25] Bant (n 16) 142.

[26] Burrows, *Restitution* (n 8) 532.

of position has not followed this logic and the courts have taken progressively wider views of what might count as a change of position. In *Philip Collins Ltd v Davis*,[27] Jonathon Parker J accepted that the defendants had changed their position by changing their life-styles: 'the overpayments caused a general change of position by the defendants in that they increased their level of outgoing by reference to the sums so paid'. In *Commerzbank AG v Price-Jones*,[28] the Court of Appeal held that a decision to forgo pursuing employment elsewhere would count as a change of position. In these cases the particular change of position, while not being a direct expenditure of money, nevertheless has clear financial implications. In other cases, however, the financial implications of the decision are even more remote. Thus in *Commerzbank*, Munby J gave as an example of what he thought would count as a change of position the decision to divorce.[29] In *Scottish Equitable plc v Derby*, Robert Walker LJ accepted that a 'breakdown in [the defendant's] health'[30] would, if causally attributable, constitute a relevant change of position.

Secondly, the extension of the defence to non-pecuniary changes in the defendant's position also strains the idea inherent in the disenrichment analysis, which involves the loss of the benefit received.[31] If non-pecuniary changes in position count, and indeed if changes of position in anticipation of the receipt of the benefit count, then it is only in the most attenuated sense that the defendant can be said to have lost the benefit received from the claimant. This attenuation is also reflected in the language the courts now use to describe the defence. In emphasising that change of position is a 'principle of justice'[32] that operates where it would be 'inequitable' for the defendant to be required to make restitution, the courts are seemingly less concerned with determining the defendant's net enrichment on a balance sheet basis, than with whether the defendant would be harmed, or be left worse off, by making restitution. Although Burrows seeks to elide these two issues,[33] they nevertheless suggest quite different rationales for the defence.

Thirdly, a pure disenrichment approach seems at odds with denial of the defence to a defendant who is not in 'good faith'. As Justice Edelman has noted extra-judicially, if 'the defence were based solely on the rationale of disenrichment, then the defence should be available regardless of whether the defendant acted in bad faith, or whether the defendant has knowledge of the claim or a liability to

[27] [2000] 3 All ER 808, 830.
[28] [2003] EWCA Civ 1663.
[29] ibid, [66]. See also *Goff and Jones* (n 1) 27–31.
[30] [2001] 3 All ER 818 [31].
[31] Burrows, *Restitution* (n 8) 526, quoted above at n 15.
[32] *Commerzbank* (n 28) [43].
[33] For example, Burrows, *Restitution* (n 8) 532, recognises that the defence 'is concerned with loss and detriment', but he tries to accommodate that observation within a disenrichment analysis by equating detriment with disenrichment: the defence 'is concerned with loss and detriment' (*and hence disenrichment*)'. Emphasis added.

repay the money'.[34] Where the defence is understood to rely simply on a causal link between receipt and expenditure, such that one can say that the benefit the defendant received is no longer in the defendant's hands, then as long as the receipt caused the expenditure (which is entirely consistent with the defendant knowing of the defect) then the defence is made out and it cannot matter that the defendant knew, except as a limitation imposed for reasons extrinsic to the supposed rationale of the defence.

Whether or not one finds the arguments above compelling, the disenrichment approach has been dealt a significant (and in Australia, a mortal)[35] blow by the recent decision of the High Court of Australia in *Australian Financial Services and Leasing Pty Ltd v Hills Industries Limited*.[36] Australian Financial Services and Leasing (AFSL) was defrauded into making payments to a number of companies, including Hills and Bosch, for the purchase of equipment that did not in fact exist. The fraudster told Hills and Bosch that the payments were being made in discharge of debts owed to them by companies he controlled (collectively referred to as TCP). Hills and Bosch applied the payments accordingly. On discovering the fraud, AFSL claimed restitution of the payments from Hills and Bosch on the ground of mistake. Hills and Bosch resisted that claim on the basis that they had changed their positions by discharging the debts owed to them by TCP, continuing to trade with TCP, abandoning existing proceedings to recover the debts from TCP, and foregoing opportunities to obtain security for the companies' debts from third parties. Before the High Court, AFSL argued that, in considering whether Hills and Bosch had made out a defence of change of position, the 'enquiry should be into the net enrichment of each recipient as a result of the receipt' and that the court 'must place a value on the debt which is repaid, or upon the lost opportunity to recover the debt, because the defence operates only pro tanto to the extent of that proven value'.[37] As the plurality noted, 'AFSL's approach focuses upon the extent to which Hills and Bosch have been "disenriched" subsequent to the receipt'.[38] On the facts, AFSL argued that the debts that Hills had discharged, and any opportunities to enforce or secure them were valueless, or of only minimal value, because the debtor companies were impecunious, with the result that neither Hills nor Bosch were disenriched.

[34] J Edelman, 'Change of Position: A Defence in Unjust Disenrichment' (2012) 92 *Boston ULR* 1009, 1021. See also Tang Hang Wu (n 17) 151.

[35] The authors of *Goff and Jones* (n 1) 27-03 adopt the High Court's approach as a statement of English law.

[36] [2014] HCA 14 (*AFSL v Hills*). The plurality consisted of Hayne, Crennan, Kiefel, Bell and Keane JJ. French CJ and Gageler J gave separate judgments. See generally, on this decision: Bant (n 16) 136; Tang Hang Wu (n 17); K Mason, 'Strong Coherence, Strong Fusion, Continuing Categorical Confusion: The High Court's Latest Contribution to the Law of Restitution' (2014) 39 *Australian Bar Rev* 284.

[37] *AFSL v Hills* (n 36) [61] (the plurality).

[38] ibid, [78].

Accepting Hill's and Bosch's arguments that precise valuation of the changes in their positions was not necessary, the High Court unanimously and unequivocally rejected the disenrichment analysis. In French CJ's view:[39]

> Consistently with the flexibility of its foundation standard, the defence could be applied pro tanto. Relevantly to the present appeal, that flexibility is not constrained by a global limitation based on a quantitative or pseudo-quantitative concept of disenrichment. As explained below, disenrichment, as propounded by the late Professor Birks, is at best a circumstance which may define a class of case in which recovery could be held to be inequitable. It is not a unifying rule for the change of position defence.

The plurality were equally clear in their rejection of disenrichment: 'More importantly, under Australian law, a mathematical assessment of enduring economic benefit does not determine the availability of restitutionary remedies'.[40]

Rather, in the High Court's view, the defence turned on whether the imposition of restitutionary liability would result in 'irreversible detriment'[41] to the defendant and that the defence sought to ensure that the imposition of restitutionary liability would not leave the defendant in a worse-off position than before the receipt of the benefit. In determining what matters might constitute detriment for the purposes of the defence, both the plurality and Gageler J saw the best analogy as being with the law of estoppel, which, in turn, was one species of the genus comprised by the 'equitable doctrine concerning detriment'.[42] This doctrine 'is concerned with the consequences that would enure to the disadvantage of a person who has been induced to change his or her position if the state of affairs so brought about were to be altered by the reversal of the assumption on which the change of position occurred'.[43] In the plurality's view, 'both estoppel and the defence are grounded in that body of equitable doctrine that prevents the unconscientious assertion of what are said to be legal rights'.[44]

The plurality also stressed that detriment was not to be 'considered to be a narrow or technical concept' and that, so long as it was 'substantial, it need not consist of expenditure of money or other quantifiable financial detriment …'.[45] Gageler J echoed this approach, saying that the 'detriment constituted by that difference in position need not, in every case, be financial or pecuniary. If financial or pecuniary, it need not, in every case, be established with precision. It can be an opportunity forgone. It must, in every case, be shown by the defendant to be substantial'.[46] On the facts of *AFSL v Hills*, the detriment consisted of a range of

[39] ibid, [17].
[40] ibid, [84].
[41] 'Irreversible' functions as part of the test for what constitutes detriment. In *Change of Position* (n 4) Bant seems to confuse an operational test for the application of the defence (irreversible detriment) with the rationale of the defence.
[42] *AFSL v Hills* (n 36) [84] (the plurality).
[43] ibid, [84] (the plurality).
[44] ibid, [86].
[45] ibid, [88].
[46] ibid, [157].

actions by Hills and Bosch that were non-pecuniary and almost impossible to value accurately, or precisely: a loss of the opportunity to engage lawyers and seek security for repayment of debts, and a loss of its opportunity to cease trading with the fraudster's companies.[47]

As Professor Elise Bant has noted, the emphasis on irreversible detriment, where the concept of detriment is broadly conceived and goes well beyond pecuniary expenditure, strongly suggests that the High Court saw the availability of the defence as turning on whether the defendant would be left in a worse-off position by being required to make restitution.[48] While all of the judgments invoke a concern with the defendant's position, this concern is perhaps stated most clearly by Gageler J. In his Honour's view, the circumstances in which the defence was available may be expressed in two conditions:[49]

> The first condition is that the defendant has acted (that is, done something the defendant would not otherwise have done) or refrained from acting (that is, not done something the defendant would otherwise have done) in good faith on the assumption that the defendant was entitled to deal with the payment which the defendant received. The defendant need not for the purpose of meeting this condition have acted on knowledge derived from the payer. Whether the defendant needs also to have acted reasonably is a question which does not now arise for determination. The second condition is that, by reason of having so acted or refrained from acting, the defendant would be placed in a worse position if ordered to make restitution of the payment than if the defendant had not received the payment at all.

The judgments in *AFSL v Hills* also suggest that the Court saw the ultimate rationale or purpose of the defence as being to determine who should bear the losses that have arisen out of the interaction of the parties.[50] Thus, in rejecting the disenrichment rationale, the plurality said that 'the enquiry undertaken in relation to restitutionary relief in Australia is directed to *who* should properly bear the loss and *why*'.[51] In support of this being the central enquiry, the plurality quoted § 65 of the *Restatement of the Law Third, Restitution and Unjust Enrichment*.[52] In the commentary to § 65, the Reporters state:[53]

> The affirmative defense of change of position gives effect to inherent limitations of a liability based on unjust enrichment, and it is an important device by which the law of restitution justifies the imposition of liability independent of fault. Seen from a slightly different perspective, the defense of change of position is frequently a means of accommodating primary rules of gain-based liability to transactions that involve a measure of economic loss. … The law of restitution, like the law of torts, assigns losses on the

[47] ibid, [95] (the plurality) and [166] (Gageler J).
[48] Bant (n 16) 148. See also Tang Hang Wu (n 17) 153.
[49] *AFSL v Hills* (n 36) [157].
[50] Bant (n 16) 149 also seems to accept this.
[51] *AFSL v Hills* (n 36) [78].
[52] *Restatement of Restitution* (n 2).
[53] ibid, 515.

basis of fault. Loss incurred as a result of the recipient's change of position may be allocated to the claimant by eliminating or reducing the recipient's liability in restitution, so long as the recipient is no more responsible than the claimant for the transaction the claimant seeks to reverse.

II. The Change of Position Defence as a Loss Allocation Mechanism

It is clear that the *practical effect* of the application of the change of position defence is to allocate the loss that arises from the benefit having been consumed or dissipated. The benefit that remains available to restore the parties is now less than the prima facie amount to be restored. Take the following example:

> C owed D $500, being a loan from D. C repaid the loan by way of an electronic funds transfer of $500. D had nominated as the bank account for repayment an account she used only for saving up for special things. The money sat in the account for some weeks. D decided on the spur of the moment to treat her family to a lavish meal. In fact, C had previously paid D $200 in cash in partial repayment some weeks ago.

Here, the relevant transaction that links C and D is comprised of a mistaken payment of $200 (by C) and a mistaken expenditure (by D). The justification for linking the payment and expenditure and treating both payment and expenditure as constitutive of the parties' transactional relationship is that they are causally connected – without the mistaken payment of $200 by C, D would not have had sufficient funds to have had the lavish meal. Viewed as a single transaction, the net result is that the $200 transferred from C to D has been consumed. Therefore, in terms of the transactional relationship between C and D there is a net loss ($200) and they cannot now both be restored to the *status quo ante* exclusively from the value that was initially transferred. To undo the effects of the transfer therefore requires either C, or D, to draw on his or her other resources. The availability or not of restitution for C will, at least in a practical sense, allocate that loss: if D is not required to make restitution, C will bear the loss; if D is to be required to make restitution, then D will bear the loss.

While the judgments in *AFSL v Hills* suggest that the rationale of change of position is intimately connected with the allocation of losses and a concern that the defendant must not be left in a worse position,[54] *AFSL v Hills* is nevertheless not complete as an account of the normative basis of change of position, or of its relationship with the normative basis of the principle of unjust enrichment. In particular, the judgments do not explain, first, why a defendant who has changed her position in good faith must not be left worse off and, secondly, why a defendant who has changed her position may properly be left worse off where the defendant

[54] Bant (n 16) 149.

is not in good faith. The remainder of this paper will seek to fill in the gaps in the High Court's account of change of position and to construct a principled account of the defence as a loss allocation mechanism that coheres, at least at the level of abstract normative justification, with the principle of unjust enrichment.

A. Claims Based on the Principle of Unjust Enrichment

A claim justified by the principle of unjust enrichment is characterised by three central conceptual features.[55] First, the liability which arises from a claim in unjust enrichment is restorative or rectificatory in its nature and objective. It seeks only to reverse a (defective) transaction between claimant and defendant thereby restoring both of the parties to the *status quo ante*.[56] Secondly, the liability justified by the principle of unjust enrichment is exclusively gain-focused. That is, liability is dependent on, and limited to, a benefit having been received by the defendant from the claimant. Unjust enrichment is not concerned with any loss suffered by the claimant (other than as a means of establishing that the benefit the defendant received was received from the claimant) and does not seek to compensate the claimant for consequential losses arising from the transaction in question.[57] Thirdly, the liability is *prima facie* strict in that in the paradigm case (a mistaken payment), liability does not depend on fault or wrongdoing by the defendant (or indeed the claimant) and liability is routinely imposed on a defendant who is wholly innocent.

The often passive, unknowing and blamelessness role that the defendant has in the defective transfer of wealth by the claimant means that the moral merits of the claimant and defendant are finely balanced.[58] Thus in *AFSL v Hills*, both the claimant and the defendant were innocent victims of a fraudster. The reasons for the claimant's claim to recover value that she did not really intend to part with are clear, but these reasons do not seem to touch on the defendant at all. The defendant has committed no wrong and, in the paradigm case, is not in any sense responsible for the claimant's misfortune. The normative force presented by the principle of unjust enrichment in favour of the claimant's restitution is, therefore, relatively weak (or perhaps better described as brittle) as compared with, say, the normative force underpinning a claim against a defendant who has deliberately or knowingly injured the claimant through the commission of a wrong. This brittleness

[55] D Klimchuk, 'The Structure of the Right to Restitution for Unjust Enrichment' (2007) 57 *University of Toronto LJ* 661, 663.

[56] See, eg, *Goff and Jones* (n 1) 1–17; Burrows, *Restatement* (n 1) 26; A Lodder, *Enrichment in the Law of Unjust Enrichment and Restitution* (Oxford, Hart Publishing, 2012) 206; M McInnes, *The Canadian Law of Unjust Enrichment and Restitution* (Toronto, LexisNexis, 2014) 8. See also Ratan's discussion of the choice of the baselines against which restoration is to be measured: (n 2) 89–94.

[57] Birks (n 1) 3, 7; *Goff and Jones* (n 1) 1–17; Bant (n 16) 149.

[58] J Penner, 'We All Make Mistakes: A "Duty of Virtue" Theory of Restitutionary Liability for Mistaken Payments' (2018) 81 *MLR* 222, 228.

is off-set by, or reflected in, the limited reach of unjust enrichment claims: unjust enrichment claims only ever seek to impose liability to restore the benefit received. The defendant is not being asked to dip into her own resources to make good harm that has been done to the claimant, or a loss suffered by the claimant.[59]

Far from being a weakness in the conceptualisation of unjust enrichment claims, as is often suggested, the brittleness of the justification presented by a claim in unjust enrichment may in fact be central to its explanation in terms of the principle of corrective justice. The principle of unjust enrichment is widely thought to instantiate the idea of corrective justice. In *Kingstreet Investments Ltd v New Brunswick (Department of Finance)*, the Supreme Court of Canada was clear that 'Restitution is a tool of corrective justice'.[60] However, there are problems accommodating unjust enrichment within the idea of corrective justice, at least as it is articulated by Professor Ernest Weinrib. The most challenging of these problems is that, in the paradigm case, not only is the defendant not the cause of the claimant's misfortune, but, as in the example above, the defendant may quite reasonably not even know that the benefit had been received. The limited reach of unjust enrichment may, however, supply an answer to this problem.

A claim in unjust enrichment is typically explained in terms of corrective justice by pointing to a defect in the claimant's decision to transfer the benefit. Certain defects in the claimant's thought processes are understood as being inconsistent with the claimant's decision being a genuine expression of the claimant's free will, and as autonomous agents we ought not to be deprived of our property except by way of a genuine expression of our free will.[61] However, the requirement of correlativity which is central to corrective justice demands that we give equal respect to the autonomy of the defendant. Therefore, if the defendant is to be deprived of (what is now prima facie) her property through the imposition of a legal liability to make restitution then the autonomy of the defendant and her interest in not being deprived of her property other than freely must also be implicated.[62] We must be able to point to a reason to undo the transfer that is applicable to both claimant and defendant and which links them as doer and sufferer of the same injustice. From this perspective, the strict liability which characterises the doctrinal formulation of unjust enrichment liability presents a problem, as there appears to be no reason which touches on the defendant. Weinrib's solution is to find the implication of the defendant's autonomy in an 'acceptance' by the defendant of a benefit that the defendant is imputed to know

[59] A Burrows, 'Good Consideration in the Law of Unjust Enrichment' (2013) 129 *LQR* 329, 330; *ASFL v Hills* (n 36) [17] (French CJ).

[60] [2007] 1 SCR 3 [32].

[61] E Weinrib, *Corrective Justice* (Oxford, OUP, 2012) 203 refers to this as the 'principle of justice in transfer'. See also A Drassinower, 'Unrequested Benefits in the Law of Unjust Enrichment' (1998) 48 *University of Toronto LJ* 459, 477; C Webb, 'Property, Unjust Enrichment, and Defective Transfers' in R Chambers, C Mitchell, J Penner (eds), *Philosophical Foundations of the Law of Unjust Enrichment* (Oxford, OUP, 2009) 102.

[62] E Weinrib, 'The Normative Structure of Unjust Enrichment' in C Rickett and R Grantham (eds), *Structure and Justification in Private Law – Essays for Peter Birks* (Oxford, Hart Publishing, 2008) ch 3.

is not given as a gift, and thus must be paid for.[63] Although highly sophisticated, Weinrib's analysis relies on a rather strained notion of 'acceptance'[64] and would seem to entail that, contrary to the positive law, the claim is not complete until sometime after the receipt.

Professor Birks claimed that the strict liability regime of restitutionary liability was justified by the fact that in a claim in unjust enrichment the claimant is:[65]

> not trying to make you worse off. He seeks only that you should give up the gain obtained … He asks that you return to the position you would all along have been in had you not received from the [claimant] money to which you were not entitled. The strict liability reflects this difference between a defendant who is being asked to bear a loss and a defendant who is only being required to surrender a gain. It takes very slight facts to justify the relocation of an extant gain, and fault on the part of the recipient is not one of them.

This justification for restitutionary liability rests crucially on being able to say that the defendant is not harmed, or left worse off by such liability. However, as Dr Wilmot-Smith has noted, prima facie, if the defendant is to be required to give back value received from the claimant, where D was entitled to treat that receipt as effective, then the defendant is in fact left worse off:[66]

> Had she (the payee) not made restitution, she would have had the enrichment – which *ex hypothesi* has value. Various projects would have been open to her which are now foreclosed. The no harm thesis looks in danger of failing to prove its crucial claim – that there is no harm in disenrichment.

Wilmot-Smith is correct to link the benefits received to our autonomy interest. From the perspective of corrective justice, our possession of and entitlement to what Kant called 'external objects of choice'[67] is relevant because these objects are the extension of our free will.[68] These objects allow us to actualise our purposiveness as autonomous agents in the physical world.[69] Our respect for the free will of the individual, therefore, entails that we must also respect the individual's choices and decision making in relation to those objects that have been integrated into and form part of the expression of the individual's purposiveness. Those 'external objects of choice' that actualise the autonomy and free will of the individual will

[63] Weinrib (n 61) 203–09.

[64] In Weinrib's account, the defendant's acceptance is essentially imputed to him as a matter of law. It is, therefore, a rather thin notion of acceptance and whether such a thin notion is sufficient to implicate the defendant's autonomy is far from clear.

[65] Birks (n 1) 7. See also Burrows (n 59) 330; Webb (n 61) 362; Bant (n 16) 149; P Cane, *Responsibility in Law and Morality* (Oxford, Hart Publishing, 2002) 221.

[66] F Wilmot-Smith, 'Should the Payee Pay?' (2017) 37 *OJLS* 844, 848.

[67] I Kant, *The Metaphysics of Morals* (Trans M McGregor, Cambridge, Cambridge University Press, 1996) [6.247].

[68] Weinrib (n 61) 223, 274–75; E Weinrib, 'The Rights of Corrective Justice', Obligations VI Conference, July 2012, University of Western Ontario, 12.

[69] J Nadler, 'What Right Does Unjust Enrichment Law Protect' (2008) 28 *OJLS* 245 262, suggests that it is our *capacity* for purposiveness that is relevant, not the particular exercise of it.

extend to most if not all things comprising the defendant's patrimony, as all of things which the defendant is entitled to regard as her own will shape and affect her plans, projects, and choices in one way or another.[70]

Where the defendant has integrated the 'objects' that were received by what turns out to have been a defective transfer into her purposiveness, such that these 'objects' now represent the actualisation of her agency, we can agree with Wilmot-Smith that to require the defendant to return those things is clearly to make the defendant worse off. However, there may be cases where the defendant has not integrated what was received into her purposiveness.[71] Suppose, that C has handed D a $50 note by mistake, but immediately realised her mistake and immediately asks for it back. In this case, it is not clear that requiring the defendant to simply hand the $50 back leaves the defendant worse off in the relevant sense. It is unlikely that, in the second or so that the defendant held the banknote, the defendant has integrated the banknote into her plans and projects, such that it represents the actualisation of her free will.[72] A similar conclusion seems possible in respect of the more likely scenario where C has caused an electronic funds transfer to be made to D but D has not checked her bank account and thus does not know about it.

If it is plausible to say in these situations that the defendant is not harmed by restitutionary liability because the receipt has had no impact on her purposiveness, then we are able to explain why a claimant's claim to restitution is normatively justified in cases where the defendant retains the benefit received and cannot be said to have otherwise dissipated it. One formulation of this explanation is that we can simply dismiss the cost as being the price of actualising the private rights of the parties as 'public rights'. The additional demands of transforming the 'justificatory structure latent in the relationship'[73] of the parties into a system of public rights necessitates and justifies some constraint on the autonomy of the parties.[74] An alternative formulation recognises that being required to make restitution does involve some coercion of the defendant's will (albeit still minimal) but that this coercion is justified on the basis that for the defendant to stand on her strict entitlement to freedom (in relation to her not being deprived of

[70] Weinrib (n 61) 275 notes that objects become relevant because they express our capacity for choice, even though they may not presently be the subject of choice. From this it follows that 'it must be possible for an object of choice to lie within the choosing subject's capacity for use even when no particular use is being made of it'. The corollary is that 'if an external object of choice could not rightfully be within a choosing subject's power the latter's freedom would be restricted …'.

[71] Kant (n 67) [6.248] seems to accept this in distinguishing between bare possession in fact ('empirical possession') and 'intelligible possession'. Intelligible possession refers to one's moral authority over the object.

[72] In the example above, if D had decided to splurge on a lavish meal while unaware of receipt or the balance of the account, we might also conclude that imposing liability on D to make restitution would not leave D worse off.

[73] Weinrib (n 21) 218.

[74] E Weinrib, 'Private Law and Public Right' (2011) 61 *University of Toronto LJ* 191, 204–06.

her property) in these circumstances would be an abuse of that freedom.[75] This idea is apparent in the reasoning of the High Court in *AFSL v Hills*, where the plurality says that 'both estoppel and the defence are grounded in that body of equitable doctrine that prevents the unconscientious assertion of what are said to be legal rights'.[76] Therefore, in terms of the correlativity problem and the need to find a reason on the defendant's side to justify restitution, we might say in this case that, because the bare possession of the object is not an actualisation of the defendant's free will, we either do not need to implicate the defendant's autonomy to justify restitution because there is no infringement of the defendant's autonomy, or some coercion of the defendant's autonomy is justified to prevent abuse.

B. Doctrinal Over-reach and Change of Position

As the law currently stands, a claim based on unjust enrichment measures the gain at the point of receipt. Prima facie liability is assessed without regard to any post-receipt dissipation by the defendant. To return to the example above, if D received $200 by mistake, then the prima facie liability imposed on D is to restore that $200. Therefore, as a matter of the positive law, a claim in unjust enrichment may give rise to a prima facie liability that is significantly greater than the enrichment remaining in D's hand at the date of trial. If D has dissipated some or all of the benefit, then D will be left in a worse-off position – D will be required, effectively, to use her own resources to make good C's error. If, however, as suggested above, the normative justification of a claim in unjust enrichment supports only restoration of the extant gain, and does not support imposing a loss on the defendant, how do we ensure that the doctrinal formulation of the claim does not over-reach its normative justification? The answer is the defence of change of position. Viewed from this perspective, the defence represents the doctrinal implementation of the inherent limitation on the normative justification provided by the principle of unjust enrichment. The defence ensures that the defendant is not left worse off (as we have articulated that notion). It does this by defeating the prima facie liability where, and to the extent that, the imposition of such liability would undermine or negate the choices, plans and projects the defendant made in reliance on or as a consequence of the receipt.[77] Where this is the case, such that the benefits now represent the actualisation of the defendant's agency, restitution of the prima

[75] D Jensen, 'Compensation for Breach of Trust – The Remoteness Impasse' in C Rickett (ed), *Justifying Private Law Remedies* (Oxford, Hart Publishing, 2008) 205, 210. Thus, Kant (n 67) [6.231], says: 'if a certain use of freedom is itself a hindrance to freedom in accordance with universal laws (that is, wrong), coercion that is opposed to this (as a hindering of a hindrance to freedom) is consistent with freedom in accordance with universal laws, that is, it is right'.

[76] *ASFL v Hills* (n 36) [86].

[77] Note that on this analysis the focus shifts from identifying items of expenditure to one of whether in imposing restitutionary liability the law would deny respect for the defendant's choices as to the use of the defendant's resources.

facie amount would leave the defendant worse off and extend beyond the normative justification of unjust enrichment liability. The defence functions, therefore, to prevent the liability at the doctrinal level over-reaching its normative justification and, accordingly, the defence must be understood to constitute an integral part of explanation of, and justification for, restitutionary liability.

The trial and error nature of the process by which the common law 'works itself pure'[78] means that we cannot expect perfect consistency. In the case of the defence of change of position, the decision to leave the defence to develop on a case-by-case basis with only the broadest of outlines has likely exacerbated any inconsistencies. However, the conceptualisation of the role and rationale of change of position suggested here is nevertheless broadly consistent with, and offers an explanation of, the core doctrinal elements of the defence as they have been developed by the courts. The core elements of the defence are that of detriment and causation.[79]

i. Detriment

An understanding of the defence as a means to protect the defendant from the harm associated with the impact on her autonomy implies a very broad concept of what should constitute detriment. It certainly cannot be limited to pecuniary losses. Rather, the criterion will be whether there is evidence that the defendant has integrated the benefits received into her plans and projects as an autonomous agent, such that allowing restitution would be to upset those plans and projects and falsify the defendant's decision-making processes. This approach to detriment is consistent with the trend in the cases that extends the idea of a 'change' or 'detriment' beyond purely pecuniary expenditure to matters that may broadly be described as 'life choices'. Three examples will suffice to illustrate the point. In *Gertsch v Atsas*,[80] the defendant had received a distribution under a will. This led the defendant to decide to further her education at university and to forgo opportunities to earn an income. Foster AJ held that the 'radical change' the defendant made in her life was sufficient to make out the defence:[81]

> Putting it broadly, she gave up paid employment and became a university student, existing on the pensions and grants referred to, together with rent from the flat, which she had created in her home. Undoubtedly she has changed her position on the faith of the receipt.

In terms of the present analysis, the defence was allowed because the benefits received under the will had been integrated into the D's plans and purposes – she had

[78] A Corbin, 'The Dead Hand of the Common Law' (1917–18) 27 *Yale LJ* 668, 672, n 15.

[79] The issue of matters that disqualify the defendant will be discussed further below as they raise different issues.

[80] [1999] NSWSC 898.

[81] ibid, [94].

changed her lifestyle and long-term goals. Whether or not there was a direct expenditure of the benefits was not to the point. To have required the defendant to make restitution in these circumstances would have been to deny respect for D's autonomy.

In *RBC Dominion Securities Inc v Dawson*,[82] the defendant had used money mistakenly paid to her to replace her furniture with new furniture of a better quality. The Newfoundland Court of Appeal held the purchase of the new furniture established the defence of change of position. This was so even though the Court accepted that the new furniture Mrs Dawson had purchased meant that she was still enriched: 'these assets replace the money'.[83] Mrs Dawson was nevertheless entitled to defeat the claim for restitution because she had 'changed her standard of living when she would not otherwise have done so'.[84] This finding, which is highly problematic on most conceptions of the defence, is consistent with the idea that the defence is about ensuring that the defendant is not left worse off, where 'worse off' is understood in terms of an impact on the defendant's autonomy. The decision to buy new, better quality furniture meant that Mrs Dawson has integrated the receipt into her plans and projects and the claim in unjust enrichment did not offer a reason to deny respect for her choices.

The final example is *Donis v Donis*.[85] Although the case is concerned with the doctrine of proprietary estoppel, similar comments in *Commerzbank AG v Price-Jones* and the approach of the High Court in *AFSL v Hills* suggest that these comments are equally applicable to change of position. In *Donis*, the Court held that the detriments that Mrs Donis was said to have suffered were the decisions to marry her husband and to have a child. In accepting Mrs Donis' arguments, Nettle JA said:[86]

> Where, however, as here, the detriment suffered is of a kind and extent that involves life-changing decisions with irreversible consequences of a profoundly personal nature, it is in my view beyond the measure of money and such that the equity raised by the promisor's conduct can only be accounted for by substantial fulfilment of the assumption upon which the respondent's actions were based.

The conclusion that the requirements of the defence are met by changes of this sort are impossible to reconcile with a disenrichment, money-in-money-out analysis. Marrying and having a child cannot plausibly be regarded as a cost or expenditure. Therefore, the only basis on which such matters can be considered relevant as a means of defeating a claim to restitution is that they are a clear expression of the defendant's purposiveness which the law must respect unless there are clear justifications for not doing so. A claim in unjust enrichment, being a

[82] (1994) 111 DLR 4th 230.
[83] ibid, 239.
[84] ibid.
[85] [2007] VSCA 89.
[86] ibid, [34].

claim justified only where D's autonomy is not constrained, does not offer such a reason.

ii. Causation

If change of position is properly understood as a means to protect the defendant from the harm associated with the impact on her autonomy, then the focus of the causal inquiry is not so much on whether there is a direct chain of cause-and-effect between the defendant's receipt of the benefit and an expenditure, but rather on whether the receipt has had an impact on the defendant's decision making and choices. Thus, in *Commerzbank*, the Court of Appeal rejected a narrow, technical approach to causation in favour of a much fuzzier standard where it is sufficient merely that the changes in the defendant's position were 'referable' to the receipt. In Mummery LJ's view:[87]

> it is neither necessary nor desirable to carry across to the issue whether it is inequitable to require restitution and to impose on it all the mass of learning on causation questions generated by the cases on the recoverability of damages for tort. Change of position is based on a principle of justice. It is a broad defence to a claim for restitution, which is itself based on a broad principle of unjust enrichment. In deciding whether the particular circumstances render it inequitable to require the recipient of an overpayment to make full restitution, the need for a sufficient causal link should not be narrowly applied. … As was said by Jonathan Parker J in the Philip Collins case at p. 827 the change of position must in some way be 'referable to' the actual or anticipated payment of money by which the recipient is enriched.

This suggests not only that the defendant need not have relied on the receipt, but that the connection between receipt and dissipation may be indirect and not susceptible to direct proof. Indeed, in *AFSL v Hills*, the High Court did not even discuss the issue of the nature of the link and seemed concerned only with whether being required to make restitution would harm the defendant.

The approach suggested here constructs change of position as a defence with a very broad scope. If the defence is to protect the defendant's autonomy, then it must extend to all those situations ('changes' in position) in which the benefit received has been integrated into the defendant's plans and projects, or has impacted on the defendant's choices. This is so even where those changes cannot be valued in money terms, or where the defendant remains enriched on a balance sheet approach. However, while broad, the defence will not extend to cases of 'ordinary expenditure'[88] or actions taken by the defendant for reasons not referable to the receipt. If the changes are ones the defendant would have undertaken anyway, then the defendant is not left worse off and thus requiring the defendant to make restitution is within the normative reach of the principle of unjust

[87] *Commerzbank* (n 28) [43].
[88] Generally, *Goff and Jones* (n 1) 27-08.

enrichment. If the expenditure is one made for reasons other than the receipt, then, in making the defendant bear the consequences of that choice through the imposition of restitutionary liability, the law continues to respect the defendant's autonomy. In *Commerzbank*, the Court of Appeal took a very broad approach to what constituted detriment and to the connection required between the receipt and the defendant's actions, but still denied the defence. The Court found that the defendant had acted for reasons unconnected with the receipt – the receipt had, therefore, not impacted on the defendant's decision-making process and thus imposing restitutionary liability did not deny the defendant's autonomy.

A focus on the impact of the receipt of the benefit on the defendant's decision making may also explain the court's acceptance of anticipatory changes in position. Although the Privy Council in *Dextra Bank & Trust Co Ltd v Bank of Jamaica*[89] dismissed the point as mere semantics,[90] on normal principles of causation used throughout the law, it is very difficult to understand how expenditure that occurred before the receipt can be said to have been caused by the receipt. If, however, the relevant connection is not between the receipt and the expenditure, but between the receipt and the defendant's decision making, then it is a relatively simple matter to say that the defendant's decision making was engaged by matters that preceded the receipt.[91]

Similarly, cases of an independent loss of the benefit received may be straightforwardly accounted for on this basis. Where, for example, the benefit received by the defendant is lost for reasons independent of the defendant (such as where the benefit received is stolen), it seems intuitively right that D be afforded the defence. Nevertheless, as many commentators have pointed out, on a strict reliance approach it cannot be said that the defendant's dissipation was in reliance on the receipt and the defendant is thus denied the defence. However, if change of position is understood as being concerned with ensuring the defendant is not left worse off (in the sense described above) by the imposition of restitution, because the principle of unjust enrichment does not justify imposing losses on the defendant, then it follows that the defence must be available in cases of independent loss of the enrichment. Although in such a case the benefit received from the claimant has clearly not become integrated into the defendant's plans and projects, if the defendant were required to make restitution she could necessarily do so only out of her own non-receipt resources. The imposition of restitutionary liability would, therefore, impact the defendant's choices, plans, and projects as regards those non-receipt recourses. Once it is accepted that the relevant connection is not between the receipt and expenditure of the benefit received, but rather between the receipt and the defendant's choices, it follows that the defendant's

[89] [2002] 1 All ER (Comm) 193.

[90] The Privy Council said: 'It is surely no abuse of language to say [in a case of anticipatory change of position] that the defendant has incurred the expenditure in reliance on the claimant's payment …': ibid, 204. With respect, even if it is not an abuse of language, it is surely an abuse of logic.

[91] Ratan (n 2) 91.

choices as regards her non-receipt recourses must also be protected by the defence, at least where there is a causal relationship between the receipt and the impact on the defendant's choices.

C. The 'Bad Faith' Defendant

In stating the broad outlines of the defence in *Lipkin*, Lord Goff said that '[i]t is, of course, plain that the defence is not open to one who has changed his position in bad faith, as where the defendant has paid away the money with knowledge of the facts entitling the claimant to restitution'.[92] Whether analysed as a disqualifying factor,[93] or a positive requirement of 'good faith',[94] the denial of the defence to defendants who know of the defect in the transfer, or who take the risk that the transfer might be un-done is a fixed feature of the defence. Thus, if in the example above, instead of D knowing only the total balance of the bank account, D had in fact reviewed each of the payments made into the account over the last month, including C's payment, before deciding to use the money on a lavish meal, we might well conclude that D knew of the mistake, or at least took the risk of the receipt being disputed. In such a case, the defence will not be available to D and D will be required to make restitution of the full amount received. The effect of this rule is that D will bear the loss arising from the parties' interaction. Any account of the defence of change of position must, therefore, explain why in this situation the defence is not available and why the loss is allocated to D.

On the analysis above, the principle of unjust enrichment does not offer a reason for the defendant to bear the loss arising from the interaction of the parties. The principle of unjust enrichment justifies making the defendant restore a gain received, but it does not justify making the defendant bear a loss. Where the defence of change of position operates, the defendant is protected from liability for loss and any liability is limited to the benefit remaining in the defendant's hands. However, where the defence is not available then, in effect, the loss arising from the interaction of the parties is allocated to the defendant.

The question posed by the denial of the defence to a defendant who is not in good faith is, therefore: how, or why, does the defendant's awareness of the defect in the transfer engage the defendant's interest in autonomy sufficiently to justify imposing the loss on the defendant? There seem to be two, possible answers. The first is that, where the defendant knows of the defect in the transfer, we can say that the defendant's dissipation of the benefit is not referable to the receipt: the defendant is taken to have accepted the risk that she would be spending her own money. However, this is a conclusion about factual causation and it is entirely conceivable that a defendant who knows that she has received a windfall

[92] *Lipkin* (n 5) 580.
[93] *Goff and Jones* (n 1) 27–40.
[94] Edelman and Bant (n 1) 342, 362.

by mistake will rush out and spend it precisely because she knows someone will ask for it back.[95] Therefore, the conclusion that the expenditure is not referable to the receipt can only be made as matter of 'legal causation': that is, we have decided that such expenditure *ought not to count*. We are then still left with a question as to *why* it ought not to count and *why* the defendant ought to bear the loss.[96]

An answer to the question why the defendant ought to bear the loss was hinted at by Thomas J in *National Bank of New Zealand Ltd v Waitaki National Processing (NI) Ltd*.[97] Once the defendant becomes aware of the defect in the transfer, the defendant comes under a duty broadly analogous to that owed by a voluntary bailee of goods to not dissipate the benefit.[98] The law of involuntary bailment is a somewhat obscure footnote to the law of bailment generally and authorities on whether the bailee owes any duties are in a far from satisfactory state. Nevertheless, the authorities are consistent with the bailee having a duty to take reasonable steps to preserve the property that has come into her possession. Thus, the bailee must not deliberately consume or destroy the goods,[99] and if the goods are lost she will incur liability only if she has failed to act reasonably in the circumstances.[100]

In the case of involuntary bailment, the duty, such as it is, rests on the claimant's continuing legal ownership and the defendant's possession of the claimant's goods. In the case of claims based on the principle of unjust enrichment, in contrast, ownership of the benefits received will usually have passed to the defendant. Nevertheless, we can say that once the defendant knows of the defect affecting the transfer, then the defendant's legal ownership is in dispute and is in a broad sense defeasible. In such a case, it is not unreasonable to suppose that the defendant should have some responsibility for the preservation of the benefits received pending resolution of the defeasibility. In that sense, the defendant who knows of the pending claim is in a position analogous to that of the involuntary bailee: in both cases the recipient has a limited duty not to dissipate the benefits in their custody.

[95] If the amount is large enough, it may cause one to flee the country: 'NZ's "runaway millionaire" pleads guilty', *The Australian*, 12 June 2012 (https://www.theaustralian.com.au/news/latest-news/nzs-runaway-millionaire-pleads-guilty/news-story/c6b6bb13f56ab7a32e7e5457fb4fb1a1?sv=107eb2433ad3854ff338a8521bd4ddfd).

[96] It is not possible simply to say that the defendant ought to bear the loss because the benefit did not belong to him. In the paradigm case of restitutionary liability, ownership of the benefit will have passed to the defendant at the point of receipt. Thus, at the point of expenditure, the benefit does belong to the defendant as a matter of the law of property. See also Ratan (n 2) 111.

[97] [1999] 2 NZLR 211, 226. See also Klimchuk (n 9) 83–84.

[98] The situation cannot be described as a bailment in the strict sense, as bailment presumes tangible property. In restitutionary claims the benefits are either intangible (choses in action), or the circumstances of the transfer operate to vest title to tangible property in the defendant.

[99] *Foster v Juniata Bridge Co* 16 P St 393 (1851).

[100] *Elvin and Powell Ltd v Plummer Roddis Ltd* (1933) TLR 158; *Scotland v Solomon* [2002] EWHC 1996 (Ch); *Taylor v Diamond* [2012] EWHC 2900 (Ch). There are older authorities, notably *Lethbridge v Phillips* (1819) 2 Stark 544; *Howard v Harris* (1884) Cababe & Ellis 253; *Neuwith v Over Darwen Co-operative Society* (1894) 63 LJQB 290, which say that the involuntary bailee is not liable for mere negligence in losing the goods. More recent authorities have held that the involuntary bailee is liable

Normatively, the existence of a fairly modest duty owed by the defendant not to dissipate a benefit that she knows she may not be entitled to keep serves to justify imposing responsibility – and thus the loss – on the defendant where the defendant does dissipate the benefits. A breach of this duty connects claimant and defendant together as doers and sufferers of the same wrong and supplies the missing reason on the defendant's side as to why the defendant may properly be left worse off as a result of restitution of the prima facie amount of the benefit received. In an economic sense, the defendant's liability to the claimant for the prima facie amount of the benefit received is effectively to require the defendant to compensate the claimant.[101]

The analysis of the liability of a 'bad faith' defendant for the full prima facie benefit in terms of a duty not to dissipate the benefit is supported by the fact that the circumstances in which the defendant is denied the defence of change of position for a want of good faith largely coincide with the circumstances in which there would be a breach of a duty of non-dissipation. Thus, just as an involuntary bailee is liable for knowingly consuming or destroying the goods, the defence is denied to a defendant who has dissipated the benefit where she knows, or has grounds to believe, that the benefit was not hers to dissipate. An involuntary bailee is not liable for mere negligence in losing the goods, but must still act reasonably. Similarly, the defence of change of position will continue to be available to a defendant who negligently failed to appreciate the transfer was defective, but the defence will be denied if, knowing of the defect, the benefit was lost because the defendant acted unreasonably in the circumstances. As the authors of *Goff and Jones* note:[102]

> In *Niru Battery Manufacturing Co v Milestone Trading Ltd (No.1)*, Moore-Bick J reviewed the degree of fault needed to disqualify a defendant, and his comments were approved by the Court of Appeal. … The judge also thought that bad faith is: '… capable of embracing a failure to act in a commercially acceptable way and sharp practice of a kind that falls short of outright dishonesty as well as dishonesty itself.'
>
> This formula does not include negligence, suggesting that a defendant can rely on the defence although he has negligently failed to recognise the flawed nature of the transfer by which he has been benefited. Defendants can also rely on the defence although they have changed their position by making foolish investment decisions which turn out badly: if they honestly believe that money is theirs to spend as they choose, they cannot be criticised for spending it unwisely.

for gross negligence: *JJD SA (a company) v Avon Tyres Ltd* (unreported, EWCA, 23 February 2000); *Taylor v Diamond* [2012] EWHC 2900 (Ch) [100]–[106]. In seeking to reconcile the cases, N Palmer, *Palmer on Bailment*, 3rd edn (London, Sweet & Maxwell, 2009) para 13-012, suggests that 'an acceptable compromise would be to exact from the involuntary bailee a variable standard of care according to what is reasonable in all the circumstances of the case.'

[101] *Restatement of Restitution* (n 2) identifies the defendant's fault as the reason why the defendant should bear the loss. However, merely labelling the defendant as the more at fault seems insufficient. We need a reason why the defendant's fault is relevant, especially when the claimant's fault in making the transfer in the first place is not relevant.

[102] *Goff and Jones* (n 1) 27–41.

The analysis of the liability of the bad faith defendant in terms of a duty not to dissipate the benefits may suggest that the claimant's recovery is not actually an award of restitution, but one of compensation. If that were the case, then the analysis would mis-describe a salient feature of the defence. However, this is not necessarily the case. Analytically, the duty not to dissipate the benefit must operate prior to the award of restitution of the benefit received. The primary obligation imposed by the duty is not to dissipate the benefit received and arises at the moment the defendant becomes aware of the defect in the transfer. When that primary obligation is breached the secondary obligation requires the defendant to make good any dissipation from his own resources. In other words, as in the case of a trustee,[103] the defendant is simply treated as though she still has the full amount of the benefit received. It is then on that basis that the liability to make restitution is imposed.

III. Conclusion

The analysis presented here has three important implications for the defence of change of position and the law of unjust enrichment more generally. First, the defence of change of position becomes an even more important element in the proper functioning of the law of unjust enrichment than we might previously have thought. Although in operational terms it may be properly characterised as a defence, change of position is nevertheless integral to the principle of unjust enrichment. That is, unlike many other claims in the private law, where the normative basis of liability is complete independent of any defences, the normative basis of unjust enrichment liability is only fully made out only when the defence is incorporated as an integral part of that normative account. This also explains why the defence must be understood in the same normative terms as the cause of action. Secondly, the defence must be understood to have an extremely broad scope. The defence must respond to any situation where the receipt of the benefit has influenced the defendant's choices and decision making. Crucially, this must encompass situations where the influence is merely indirect, does not involve any pecuniary expenditure, and cannot be precisely valued. Thirdly, the net effect of conceiving of the defence in these terms is that 'good faith defendants [will] never

[103] This is typically effected through the process of account. If the beneficiary is able to falsify the account, the trust property is deemed to be what it would have been had the dissipation not occurred. See, eg, *Libertarian Investments Ltd v Hall* (2013) 16 HKCFAR 681 [169] (Lord Millett NPJ): 'If he [the defendant] dissipated it or invested it at a loss, the plaintiff will naturally have the disbursement disallowed and disclaim any interest in the property in which it was invested by treating it as bought with the defendant's own money'; *Ultraframe (UK) Ltd v Fielding* [2005] EWHC (Ch) 1638 [1513] (Lewison J): 'The beneficiary falsifies the account when he alleges that the trustee has applied trust property in a way that he should not have done (eg, by making an unauthorised investment). If the allegation is proved, then the account will be taken as if the expenditure had not been made.'

have to put their hands in their own pockets'.[104] Doctrinally we may still be able to say that the measure of prima facie liability is the full value received. However, it may be a more accurate characterisation of the emphasis and quantum of unjust enrichment liability to say that liability is of the amount remaining in the defendant's hands at the date of trial, *unless* the benefit has not been integrated into the defendant's purposiveness, or the defendant knew of the defeasible nature of the receipt before its dissipation.

[104] Burrows (n 59) 330.

9

Certainty in Calculating Monetary Remedies for Breach of Fiduciary Duty

SIMONE DEGELING*

Breach of equity's proscriptive fiduciary duties against unauthorised profit or conflict between self-interest and duty or conflict(s) between duties owed to multiple principals may result in a profit in the hands of the defendant wrongdoer. In *Warman International Ltd v Dwyer*,[1] a unanimous High Court of Australia confirmed the 'stringent rule that the fiduciary cannot profit from his trust'[2] such that it is irrelevant that the fiduciary is in good faith, has acted honestly and reasonably or that the profit is one which the principal 'was unwilling, unlikely or unable' to make.[3] The claimant is entitled, subject to any discretionary factors such as laches and acquiescence, and any allowances,[4] to an account of profits.

* I am grateful for the comments of Jessica Hudson on an earlier draft and the research assistance of Maximus Jones. Any errors are mine.

[1] (1995) 182 CLR 544.

[2] ibid, 557 (the Court). There is a debate as to the true nature of this equitable liability, and whether in substance all fiduciary breaches amount to wrongdoing in the sense of breach of a primary obligation. Professor Lionel Smith in 'Fiduciary relationships: ensuring the loyal exercise of judgment on behalf of another' (2014) 130 *LQR* 608 differentiates between the no conflict rule and the no profit rule. He argues (at 625) that the no conflict rules '… tell a fiduciary when judgment cannot be safely exercised in relation to a fiduciary power'. Breach of the no conflict rules render a transaction, inter alia, voidable by the principal. Smith views (at 628) the no-profit rule as a rule of primary attribution pursuant to which profit obtained in breach of duty is attributed to the principal from the moment of acquisition. The no-conflict rule is thus about the vitiation of the principal's consent and the no-profit rule about the carrying out or enforcement of the principal's primary right to the profit. On Smith's view, therefore, any remedy associated with the no profit rule is not about equitable wrongdoing. It is not necessary for the analysis in this chapter to resolve the debate as to the true nature of equitable fiduciary obligations. To the extent that the analysis is concerned with accommodating *hypothetical* value as a matter of calculation, it is also potentially consistent with Smith's approach.

[3] ibid, 558 (the Court).

[4] The court may award an allowance: (i) for the skill and effort of the fiduciary in earning the profit: see *Warman* (n 1) 562 (the Court); *Boardman v Phipps* [1967] 2 AC 46, 104 (Lord Cohen), 112 (Lord Hodson); and (ii) for other expenses incurred in earning or realising the profit: see *Phipps v Boardman* [1964] 1 WLR 993, 1018 (Lord Wilberforce); *Paul A Davies (Australia) Pty Ltd (in liq) v Davies* [1983] 1 NSWLR 440, 451–52 (Hutley JA); *Short v Crawley (No 30)* [2007] NSWSC 1322, [753] (White J).

Subject to the doctrine of election,[5] the fiduciary's conduct also leaves her vulnerable to a claim for equitable compensation.[6] Relevantly, equity recognises as a head of loss the principal's lost commercial opportunity, where a real loss has been suffered, such as a lost opportunity to put funding to a profitable use.[7] In calculating the value of the lost chance, the court may make some adjustments to the value of the lost opportunity in recognition of the expenses which would have been incurred had the principal pursued the now lost opportunity.[8] For example, a court may permit an adjustment to the value of loss for which equitable compensation is awarded reflecting 'the notional salaries which would have been paid'[9] by the principal to the defaulting fiduciary had the commercial opportunity been pursued by the principal.

This chapter argues that in both the loss and the gain measures, equity must grapple with the task of bringing into the ledger hypothetical value. When considered through the lens of lost commercial opportunity, this issue arises since the value of the claimant's lost opportunity will include anticipated or as yet unearned profit, which might be cast as the claimant's future or past hypothetical loss. Similarly, when viewed through the lens of the fiduciary's unauthorised gains, the difficulty becomes one of determining the extent to which the fiduciary's future profit is incorporated and is vulnerable to return via an account of profits. In previous work, I have suggested that in awarding equitable compensation for breach of fiduciary duty, equity has employed techniques to make certain the claimant's loss.[10] Thus, the question arises: how does equity value and take account of the fiduciary's gains *expected* to be earned through the fiduciary's breach of duty? This chapter explores whether a parallel analysis may be required in relation to valuing gains made by the fiduciary. It asks whether a certainty principle operates on the gain side of the remedial menu. At the outset it must be conceded that the overall

[5] See generally *Grimaldi v Chameleon Mining NL (No 2)* (2012) 200 FCR 296, [183]–[187] (the Court); *Tang Man Sit v Capacious Investments Ltd* [1996] 1 AC 514.

[6] Drawing on the work of Dr Steven Elliott QC, equitable compensation may be understood as substitutive equitable compensation ('substitutive compensation') which is based on the common account and refers to orders of the court calculated by reference to the substituted value of assets dissipated by the custodial fiduciary or trustee without authority. Substitutive compensation therefore compels the custodial fiduciary or trustee to obey their duty to maintain the fund. Reparative equitable compensation ('reparative compensation') makes good a loss caused by the trustee or custodial fiduciary's breach of trust. This chapter deals with equitable compensation in the reparative measure. See *Agricultural Land Management v Jackson (No 2)* [2014] WASC 102, [348]–[349] (Edelman J); *AIB Group (UK) plc v Mark Redler & Co Solicitors* [2015] AC 1503 (SC(E)), [53]–[54] (Lord Toulson) ('*AIB*'); S Elliott and C Mitchell, 'Remedies for Dishonest Assistance' (2004) 67 *Modern Law Review* 16.

[7] See, eg, *Ramsay v BigTinCan* [2014] NSWCA 324; *O'Halloran v R T Thomas & Family Pty Ltd* (1998) 45 NSWLR 262; *Hart Security Australia Pty Ltd v Boucousis* [2016] NSWCA 307.

[8] *V Flow Pty Ltd v Holyoake Industries (Vic) Pty Ltd* [2013] FCAFC 16, [71] (the Court).

[9] ibid.

[10] S Degeling, 'Loss of a Chance and Breach of Fiduciary Duty: The Requirement of Certainty of Loss' (2016) 28 *Singapore Academy of Law Journal* 825; S Degeling, 'Discretion and Equitable Compensation' in S Degeling and J Varuhas (eds), *Equitable Compensation and Disgorgement of Profit* (Oxford, Hart Publishing, 2017) 324–26.

purpose of this chapter is exploratory rather than conclusive. In identifying this larger conceptual pattern of hypothetical value in both the loss and gain responses to breach of fiduciary duty, some tentative answers are proposed in suggesting a certainty principle for particular equitable monetary remedies. However, the analysis also identifies further lines of inquiry for future research. The general rules giving shape to monetary remedies in equity are still developing and further work is required satisfactorily to resolve the controversies and puzzles surrounding hypothetical value in both the loss and gain response. Some of these issues are highlighted in Section IV below, Implications.

I. What is Certainty?

Certainty is a concept most often associated with claims for compensatory damages at law. Pursuant to this principle, '[t]o justify an award of substantial damages where loss is asserted the claimant must satisfy the court both as to (i) the fact of damage, that is an adverse consequence; and (ii) as to its amount.'[11] However, consistent with the position that damages are 'an award in money for a civil wrong',[12] which traverse remedies in common law and in equity, certainty is a conceptual tool capable of applying to equitable money awards.

As discussed in Section II below, there is some evidence that in awarding equitable compensation for the claimant's lost commercial opportunity arising as a result a breach of fiduciary duty, courts make certain the claimant's loss. A lost commercial opportunity is an inherently uncertain loss. This is because the nature and extent of the loss depends on a number of contingencies. Thus, even when the court is satisfied that the chance or opportunity has been lost in a manner which is attributable to the conduct of the defendant, such that the relevant test of causation is satisfied, difficulties of calculation remain. Depending on the contingency involved, the court will discount the value of the lost commercial opportunity to reach a certain value of loss for the purpose of awarding compensation. For example, realising the commercial opportunity, and thus the nature and extent of the claimant's loss, may depend on the hypothetical conduct of a third party,[13] the hypothetical conduct of the claimant in deciding whether or

[11] J Edelman, *McGregor on Damages*, 20th edn (London, Sweet & Maxwell, 2018) [10-001]. See also K Barnett and S Harder, *Remedies in Australian Private Law* (Melbourne, Cambridge University Press, 2014) 32–39; M Tilbury, *Civil Remedies: Principles of Civil Remedies*, Vol 1 (Sydney, Butterworths, 1990) 149–56.

[12] Edelman (n 11) [1-001].

[13] *Sellars v Adelaide Petroleum NL* (1994) 179 CLR 332; *Heenan v Di Sisto* [2008] NSWCA 25, [28] (Giles JA with whom Mason P and Mathews AJA agreed); *Hendriks v McGeoch* [2009] NSWCA 53, [87]–[99] (Basten JA with whom Spigelman CJ and Giles JA agreed); *Falkingham v Hoffmans* [2014] WASCA 140, [44] (Pullin and Murphy JJA), [219] (Buss JA), special leave to the HCA refused [2015] HCATrans 066 (multiply by the degree of probability).

not to pursue the opportunity at all,[14] and the potential impact of the conduct of the defendant.[15]

II. Certainty of Loss: Equitable Compensation

In awarding equitable compensation for the loss of a chance, equity grapples with the need to make certain the claimant's loss. Equity arguably has two methods of making certain loss in awarding equitable compensation for the plaintiff's lost commercial opportunity arising on breach of fiduciary duty. The first employs a method of probabilistic reasoning. The second places certainty within equity's discretion and according to equity's assumed standards of conduct about the defendant. Each will be outlined in turn.

A. Probabilistic Reasoning in *Hart Security Australia Pty Ltd v Boucousis*

A probabilistic approach was adopted by the New South Wales Court of Appeal in *Hart Security Australia Pty Ltd v Boucousis*[16] in which Hart Security Australia ('HSA') alleged it had lost a 'valuable opportunity to negotiate a successful contract'[17] and sought equitable compensation. Boucousis was the sole director of HSA and, via intermediate companies, ultimately held a 37.5 per cent beneficial shareholding in HSA.[18] HSA wished to enter into a contract to provide security services to Northern Territory Airports Pty Ltd ('NTA'). In March 2008 HSA and NTA signed a non-binding letter of intent directed to the finalisation of a commercial agreement between them for the provision of security at Alice Springs and Darwin airports. However, NTA remained sceptical about the financial stability of HSA and indicated it would only enter the contract with HSA if a bank guarantee of at least $1 million was provided securing HSA's performance under the agreement. The other ultimate shareholder in HSA was Hart Cyprus which had beneficial interest of 62.5 per cent also held via intermediary companies. Hart Cyprus objected to the requirement for a bank guarantee and negotiations between HSA and NTA reached an impasse.

[14] *Heenan* (n 13) [28], [32] (Giles JA with whom Mason P and Mathews AJA agreed) (assess on a balance of probabilities).

[15] Contract cases include the following, which indicate support for both a balance of probabilities and a degree of probabilities method of making certain the loss: *Commonwealth v Amman Aviation Pty Ltd* (1991) 174 CLR 64; *Chaplin v Hicks* [1911] 2 KB 786.

[16] [2016] NSWCA 307.

[17] ibid, [165] (the Court).

[18] ibid, [12].

Faced with the likely collapse of the transaction, Boucousis pursued another option. Without the knowledge or consent of Hart Cyprus (relevantly the directors of Hart Cyprus),[19] HSA, Boucousis and ATMAAC agreed to make a rival bid with the necessary guarantee being given by Investec Bank, an existing financier to the ATMAAC group.[20] Pursuant to the proposal, a new entity ATMAAC Aviation would be incorporated, which would by a share issue become the holding company of HSA. ATMAAC Aviation would enter the security contract with NTA, thus displacing HSA. A by-product of this structure would be a dilution of the shareholding of Hart Cyprus. Boucousis was to receive a shareholding and directorship in ATMAAC Aviation and employment in the ATMAAC group. The Court noted that, in the event that HSA did not contract with NTA, Boucousis' role at HSA would doubtlessly end, as HSA would not likely remain solvent.[21] In the event, neither ATMAAC Aviation nor HSA entered into a contract with NTA. HSA brought proceedings against Boucousis for breaches of equitable fiduciary duties and statutory duties under sections 181(1), 182(1) and 183(1) of the Corporations Act 2001 (Cth).

This chapter focusses on HSA's equity for relief arising on breach of Boucousis' equitable fiduciary obligations. The New South Wales Court of Appeal found that Boucousis had breached his fiduciary obligation to HSA, as through his conduct there was an actual or substantial possibility of conflict between his fiduciary duty to HSA and his self-interest.[22] The Court demonstrated the fiduciary breach through exploring an alternative hypothetical course of action, in which HSA's intermediate shareholder

> … (and thereby Hart Cyprus) should be made aware of the proposed share issue so as to be given the opportunity, *in that context*, to provide funds or other financial support to enable [HSA] to pursue the NTA contract; or the opportunity to propose some other means of enabling that to occur which would not result in a change of control of [HSA] and the dilution of the value of [the majority shareholder's] shareholding to nil ….[23]

Such a course would not have been in Boucousis' personal interest.[24] Once HSA's shareholder (and, therefore, Hart Cyprus) had knowledge of the proposed ATMAAC transaction, 'steps might be taken to prevent or frustrate the issue of shares in pursuit of the ATMAAC proposal'.[25] In result, Boucousis would be denied the 'significant personal benefits',[26] including a directorship, shareholding and employment, entailed in the ATMAAC proposal. Given that Boucousis

[19] ibid, [12].
[20] ibid, [13].
[21] ibid, [112].
[22] ibid, [123].
[23] ibid, [121] (emphasis in original).
[24] ibid, [122].
[25] ibid, [122].
[26] ibid, [120].

had not obtained the informed consent of HSA's shareholder to the ATMAAC transaction, he had no defence to his breach of fiduciary duty.[27]

HSA sought equitable compensation for the loss of the opportunity to negotiate a successful contract with NTA.[28] Of relevance to this chapter is the following statement of principle, to the effect that in order to succeed, HSA had to make certain its loss:

> HSA had to establish to the required standard that the opportunity to continue to negotiate with NTA, in the absence of the pursuit by HSA of the ATMAAC proposal, had real value because the prospect of a successful outcome was substantial rather than speculative; and that it was lost by Mr Boucousis' conduct.[29]

On the facts, HSA failed to meet these elements. The New South Wales Court of Appeal relied on the trial judge's findings that, on the balance of probabilities, the trial judge was *not satisfied* that Hart Cyprus may have been prepared to support the $1 million bank guarantee required by NTA and *nor was the trial judge satisfied* that NTA would have been prepared to relax the requirement for a guarantee.[30] Therefore, the impasse between the parties would not have been resolved. HSA could not demonstrate that, by reason of Boucousis' breach of fiduciary duty, it had lost a valuable opportunity to negotiate a contract with NTA and equitable compensation was denied.

In requiring HSA to make certain its loss, the court referred to *Sellars v Adelaide Petroleum NL*.[31] *Sellars* establishes that when suing for the value of a lost commercial opportunity, where that opportunity is impacted by the potential conduct of a third party (in *Sellars*, Pagini), the compensation awarded must reflect the likelihood and value of the lost opportunity such that the plaintiff demonstrates that a 'real' loss has been suffered. *Sellars* concerned a claim for damages under section 82 of the Trade Practices Act 1974 (Cth). Adelaide Petroleum had entered into parallel negotiations with two companies, Pagini and Poseidon, with the object of persuading one of them to acquire as part of a corporate restructuring the directors' shareholding in Adelaide. As a result of the defendants' (Poseidon and Sellars, described as 'the executive responsible'[32]) misleading conduct in breach of section 52 of the Trade Practices Act, Adelaide temporarily abandoned negotiations with Pagini.[33] Negotiations with Pagini eventually resumed, and a contract was entered into, but Adelaide established that there was a 40 per cent chance that Pagini would have contracted on terms more favourable to Adelaide had their negotiations not been disrupted by the misleading conduct of the defendants.

[27] ibid, [123]. See also [12], [109].
[28] ibid, [165].
[29] ibid, [166].
[30] ibid, [168]–[169].
[31] (1994) 179 CLR 332.
[32] ibid, 341 (Mason CJ, Dawson, Toohey and Gaudron JJ).
[33] ibid, 342–43 (Mason CJ, Dawson, Toohey and Gaudron JJ).

A plurality of the High Court of Australia held that, in order to recover damages under the Trade Practices Act for the value of the lost opportunity, the applicant must show:

> ... on the balance of probabilities that he or she has sustained *some* loss or damage. However, in a case such as the present, the applicant shows *some* loss or damage was sustained by demonstrating that the contravening conduct caused the loss of a commercial opportunity which had *some* value (not being a negligible value), the value being ascertained by reference to the degree of probabilities or possibilities. It is no answer to that way of viewing an applicant's case to say that the commercial opportunity was valueless on the balance of probabilities because to say that is to value the commercial opportunity by reference to a standard of proof which is inapplicable.[34]

Thus, a percentage-based probabilities approach is employed to make certain the value of the lost commercial opportunity. Whilst *Sellars* has previously been applied in calculating the value of equitable compensation,[35] it is important to recognise an important limit to the discounting approach set out in *Sellars* when applied to equitable compensation for breach of fiduciary duty. Strictly understood, the above statement of principle directs us to take into account 'the degree of probabilities or possibilities' of the lost opportunity being sustained by the contravening conduct, thereby accommodating the impact of the hypothetical conduct of third parties. On the facts of *Sellars*, there was a 40 per cent chance that Pagini (a third party to the misleading conduct) would have agreed to terms more favourable to Adelaide had the initial negotiations not been broken off. Damages were therefore calculated by discounting or multiplying the value of the more generous hypothetical contract by 40 per cent.[36]

The approach in *Sellars*, when applied to statutory damages or compensatory damages for breach of contract, also permits a court to discount the value of the lost opportunity by reference to the hypothetical conduct of the *plaintiff*.[37] For example, by discounting the value of the lost opportunity for the risk that the plaintiff may not have taken up the opportunity or for other reasons decided not to complete the contract. However, when applied to the calculation of equitable compensation for breach of fiduciary duty, it is submitted that the same analysis should be impermissible, at least where the plaintiff is the principal in the fiduciary relationship. This is because the fiduciary owes a strict obligation of loyalty such that within the scope of the relationship, the fiduciary must not put herself in a position of conflict or possibility of conflict between duty and self-interest or conflicting duties owed to more than one principal, and must not make a profit by reason or use of her position.[38]

[34] ibid, 355 (Mason CJ, Dawson, Toohey and Gaudron JJ) (emphasis in original). See also 362–64 (Brennan J).

[35] See, eg, *Ramsay* (n 7).

[36] ibid, 350, 355 (Mason CJ, Dawson, Toohey and Gaudron JJ).

[37] *Heenan* (n 13) [32]–[33] (Giles JA with whom Mason P and Matthews AJA agreed).

[38] *Commonwealth Bank of Australia v Smith* (1991) 42 FCR 390, 392 (the Court); *Breen v Williams* (1996) 186 CLR 71, 135 (Gummow J); *Pilmer v Duke Group Ltd (in liq)* (2001) 207 CLR 165, [78]–[79]

Unless the breaching fiduciary has disclosed the nature and extent of the conflict or profit, and has obtained the informed consent of the principal as establishes the defence of informed consent, the principal will have an equity for relief. As will be further explored in Section III below, when considering the parallel category of account of profits, the absolute loyalty commanded by the fiduciary norm also means that in determining liability it is irrelevant that the profit is one which the principal 'was unwilling, unlikely or unable to make'.[39] Equity's normative commitment to a strict obligation of loyalty means that the fiduciary may not raise the hypothetical future conduct of the principal in escaping liability for a profit. This chapter argues that equity's settings in relation to conflict should also inform equity's method of making certain the fiduciary's loss when calculating equitable compensation for a lost commercial opportunity. Thus, the fiduciary's obligation of loyalty should inform this calculus such that the value of equitable compensation for the value of a lost commercial opportunity should not be altered to reflect the risk that the principal 'was unwilling, unlikely or unable'[40] to take it up and a court should not be permitted to discount the value of a lost commercial opportunity for the risk that the principal would not have pursued it.

Returning to *Hart Security v Boucousis*, the New South Wales Court of Appeal confirmed the trial judge's decision not to award equitable compensation.[41] The approach of the Court of Appeal, consistently with *Sellars*, was to require the plaintiff to establish the existence of the lost opportunity on a balance of probabilities and then establish that the lost opportunity 'had *some* value (not being a negligible value) … or which involved a "substantial, and not merely speculative" prospect of producing a benefit.'[42] It is in the latter calculus that *Sellars* invites a percentage probabilities based approach to reflect the likelihood and value of the lost opportunity.

As explained above, the evidential obstacles facing HSA were that NTA would not resile from its requirement for a guarantee and that Hart Cyprus, the majority shareholder in HSA, would not agree to the guarantee. In confirming the trial judge's decision not to award equitable compensation, it is not clear whether HSA failed to establish the causation element or, in addition, whether the Court discounted for the risk that the opportunity to negotiate a contract with NTA

(McHugh, Gummow, Hayne and Callinan JJ); *Birtchnell v Equity Trustees and Agency Co Ltd* (1929) 42 CLR 384, 408 (Dixon J); *Boardman* (n 4) 124 (Lord Upjohn); *Hospital Products v United States Surgical Corporation* (1984) 156 CLR 41, 103 (Mason J). See also *Maguire v Makaronis* (1997) 188 CLR 449, 461 (Brennan CJ, Gaudron, McHugh and Gummow JJ); *Howard v Commissioner of Taxation* (2014) 253 CLR 83, 107 [59] (Hayne and Crennan JJ). There is a debate as to whether the prohibitions against conflict and profit are separate principles or form part of the same principle: see, eg, *Chan v Zacharia* (1984) 154 CLR 178, 199 (Deane J); *Howard* (n 38) 106 [57] (Hayne and Crennan JJ); *FHR European Ventures LLP v Cedar Capital Partners LLC* [2014] UKSC 45, [5] (the Court). However, for the purposes of the arguments advanced in this chapter, nothing turns on this distinction.

[39] *Warman* (n 1) 558 (the Court).

[40] ibid.

[41] *Hart* (n 7) [170]–[172] (the Court).

[42] ibid, [141]. See also [170]–[171] (the Court).

would not in any case have been pursued by the principal (HSA). On the facts of *Hart Security v Boucousis*, it must be conceded that the facts as presented were capable of going to both causation and certainty of loss. However, if the analysis in this chapter is correct, it is submitted that *if*, but for Boucousis' breach of fiduciary duty, HSA would not have suffered any loss, causation will be satisfied.[43] However, in making certain the value of that loss, reflecting the likelihood and value of the lost opportunity, a court should not take into consideration whether or not the principal would have pursued the opportunity. To do so permits an argument running contrary to the fiduciary's strict obligation of loyalty.

B. Embed Certainty Within Equitable Discretion

There is some evidence of an alternative model of making certain loss for the purposes of awarding equitable compensation, which is to embed the inquiry within equitable discretion and according to equity's model of expected fiduciary conduct.[44] Consistent with an approach which requires that the plaintiff's equity for relief is met by the minimum remedy to meet the justice of the case, rather than having recourse to percentages and probabilities, the Court may 'be robust and do rough and ready justice without having to justify the amount of its award with any degree of precision'.[45] Adopting the approach of Handley JA in *Houghton v Immer (No 155) Pty Ltd*,[46] Ribeiro NPJ in *Libertarian Investments Ltd v Hall* stated:

> … in such circumstances, the Court adopts a robust approach. This was explained by Handley JA … as follows:
>
> 'In my judgment the Court should assess the compensation in a robust manner, relying on the presumption against wrongdoers, the onus of proof, and resolving doubtful questions against the party "whose actions have made an accurate determination so problematic". See *LPJ Investments Pty Ltd v Howard Chia Investments Pty Ltd* (1990) 24 NSWLR 499 at 508.'[47]

Libertarian similarly involved a breach of fiduciary duty. Woods wanted to acquire a 10 per cent share in an entity (TSE). Hall undertook to assist Wood to acquire the shareholding and towards the end of 2002 they used for this venture EUR 50 million (GBP 5,949,994) provided to Woods via his company Libertarian.

[43] *Youyang Pty Ltd v Minter Ellison Morris Fletcher* (2003) 212 CLR 484, [46] (Gleeson CJ, McHugh, Gummow, Kirby and Hayne JJ) quoting *Target Holdings Ltd v Redferns* [1996] AC 421, 436 (Lord Browne-Wilkinson). The 'but for' test is said to perform an exclusionary rule against a common-sense view of causation, so that the defendant is not made to pay for losses which would have been suffered even if the breach of duty had not occurred: see *Canson Enterprises Ltd v Boughton & Co* [1991] 3 SCR 534, 556 (McLachlin J). *Agricultural Land Management* (n 6) [394]–[395] (Edelman J).

[44] See also S Degeling, 'Loss of a Chance and Breach of Fiduciary Duty (n 10) 845–48.

[45] *Libertarian Investments Ltd v Hall* (2013) 16 HKCFAR 681, [174] (Millett NPJ).

[46] (1997) 44 NSWLR 46, 59 (Handley JA with whom Mason P and Beazley JA agreed).

[47] *Libertarian* (n 45) [138] (Ribeiro PJ). See also [123] (Ribeiro PJ), [174] (Millett NPJ).

Woods paid the money into a trust account set up by Hall at a firm of solicitors. Unbeknown to Woods or Libertarian, Hall had designated the trust account as the client account of Hall's company, Axdale. Hall transferred without authority substantial funds in and out of the trust account, and in October 2003 withdrew GBP 5,463,508 claiming that this money was to purchase 1,777,700 shares in TSE at GBP 3.11 per share. This was not true. No shares were purchased and no explanation was given as to how the money was used.[48]

Woods relied on a breach of fiduciary duty[49] to claim the loss suffered by Libertarian, which was said to be the opportunity to on-sell TSE shares in the market, which also assumed a notional hypothetical share purchase date by Libertarian/Woods. The court acknowledged the inherent difficulties in finding a basis for valuing the shares.[50] Principal amongst these were the 'guesswork' and 'evidential gaps' in ascribing a price a potential buyer would have been willing to pay for a hypothetical shareholding in a company whose share register was in a state of flux, the time of the hypothetical transaction being more than 10 years prior.

Despite these difficulties or uncertainties of valuation, the court awarded equitable compensation. The value of the lost opportunity was made certain by reference to equity's normative expectations of the fiduciary. As explained by Millett NPJ the court

> … may [first] be able to take the fiduciary at his own word and use his falsehoods to establish the facts as if they were true, even though they are known to be untrue. Secondly the court is entitled to make every assumption against the party whose conduct has deprived it of the necessary evidence.[51]

III. Certainty of Gain: Account of Profits

In *Warman v Dwyer*, the High Court of Australia stated that:

> A fiduciary must account for a profit or benefit if it was obtained either (1) when there was a conflict or possible conflict between his fiduciary duty and personal interest, or (2) by reason of his fiduciary position or by reason of his taking advantage of opportunity or knowledge derived from his fiduciary position.[52]

In parallel with the principle identified in relation to loss, this chapter argues that the speculative nature of the inquiry requires a court to apply a principle of certainty when valuing the fiduciary's future hypothetical gains for the purposes of an account of profits. In order to advance this argument, this chapter first turns to the position in relation to non-hypothetical profit. As has been said, consistently

[48] ibid, [30] (Ribeiro PJ).
[49] ibid, [35], [106], [111]–[112] (Ribeiro PJ).
[50] ibid, [137] (Ribeiro PJ).
[51] ibid, [174] (Millett NPJ).
[52] *Warman* (n 1) 557 (the Court). See also 563 (the Court).

with the fiduciary norm, in calculating the value of the defendant's gain following a breach of fiduciary duty or by reason of her fiduciary position,[53] the Court is *not* permitted to inquire as to the hypothetical conduct of the principal since 'it is no defence that the plaintiff was unwilling, unlikely or unable to make the profits for which an account is taken ….'[54]

The leading case is *Warman International Ltd v Dwyer* which concerned the exclusive Australian agency for the distribution of gear boxes manufactured in Italy by Bonfiglioni.[55] The agency for distribution was held by Warman International Ltd ('Warman'), the general manager of the Queensland branch of which was Brian Dwyer ('Dwyer'). The agency arrangement between Warman and Bonfiglioni was terminable by either party on three months' notice.[56] In August 1986, Bonfiglioni invited Warman to form a joint venture for assembly in Australia of its products. Warman declined. Dwyer was dissatisfied in his employment and by 1986 had become 'discontented and anxious', in part because of Warman's policies towards Bonfiglioni and the potentially negative impact this might have on his employment.[57] Between February and April 1988 Dwyer and Bonfiglioni discussed forming a joint venture for the supply of Bonfiglioni products in Australia and arranged for Dwyer's existing staff to work for the new venture. As it was entitled to do under the contract,[58] Bonfiglioni in June 1988 gave Warman the necessary three months' notice to terminate their agreement and Dwyer resigned from his position at Warman. Dwyer had earlier caused Bonfiglioni Transmission (Aust) Pty Ltd ('BTA') to be incorporated as the vehicle for his joint venture with Warman. In August 1988 shares in BTA were issued to Dwyer and his wife and also to Bonfiglioni. BTA and Bonfiglioni in September 1988 executed a joint venture agreement under which BTA took over the agency business in Australia which included the assembly and distribution of gearboxes. Dwyer and his wife were also the sole shareholders in Engineering Transmission Agencies Pty Ltd ('ETA') which distributed other Bonfiglioni products and some non-Bonfiglioni products.

Dwyer was clearly in breach of his fiduciary obligations to Warman[59] as Dwyer had used his 'knowledge and position as a senior executive officer of Warman to advance his own interests ….'[60] This use was in breach of Dwyer's obligation not to put himself in a position of conflict or the possibility of conflict with Warman, and

[53] ibid, 557, 563 (the Court).

[54] ibid, 558 (the Court).

[55] The Court points out that there were various companies in the group, variously managed by members of the Bonfiglioni family, but that it was unnecessary to distinguish between the companies, it sufficing to 'refer to them collectively as Bonfiglioni or Bonfiglioni interests': ibid, 549 (the Court).

[56] ibid, 551 (the Court).

[57] ibid, 550 (the Court).

[58] ibid, 565 (the Court).

[59] ibid, 554 (the Court). The Court of Appeal upheld the trial judge's conclusion that Dwyer had acted in breach of his fiduciary duty and that conclusion was not challenged on appeal to the High Court of Australia. See also 556. The existence and scope of Dwyer's fiduciary obligation is easily identifiable in his position as employee of Warman. See generally: *Hospital Products* (n 38) 96–97 (Mason J); *Harris v Digital Pulse* (2003) 56 NSWLR 298.

[60] *Warman* (n 1) 552 (the Court).

Dwyer also obtained a benefit by reason and/or use of his fiduciary position. ETA and BTA were held to be liable with Dwyer because the companies had 'knowingly and actively participated in Dwyer's breach of fiduciary obligation'.[61] No submission to the contrary was made on appeal to the High Court of Australia. Both BTA and ETA were successful businesses and Warman therefore sought equitable relief from Dwyer, ETA and BTA including an account of profits.[62]

Taken strictly, the facts of *Warman* disclose no uncertainty of calculation in the sense that there were no hypothetical profits. At the time of trial, the defendants' gains were capable of evidential proof as a matter of historical facts since the gains existed in Dwyer's hands in the form of the value of his shareholding in BTA and ETA[63] and presumably any dividends (if paid), and in the hands of the companies themselves in the profits of their business. The profit to be calculated related to 'the profits of BTA's and ETA's business for a limited initial period'.[64] There was thus no need to speculate, at least in relation to the remedy claimed,[65] about whether the defendants would make a profit from Dwyer's breach.

In calculating the value of the account of profit, the High Court of Australia confirmed that it was for Warman to establish that it was 'inequitable to order an account of the entire profits'.[66] Unless he could do so, Warman 'must bear the consequences of mingling the profits attributable to [his] breach of fiduciary duty and the profits attributable to those earned by the defendant's efforts and investment.'[67] On the facts, 'the relationship between Warman and Bonfiglioni was not mutually enthusiastic and … the association was destined to end'.[68] Although it was unclear precisely when this termination might have occurred, the Court supported the trial judge's conclusion that Warman's distributorship would have lasted for no more than a year beyond the date of Warman's breach of fiduciary duty.[69] The Court held that subject to allowances, the account should be valued at BTA's profits for its initial two-year period of operation commencing September 1988 (reduced from the four-year period ordered by the Queensland Court of Appeal).[70]

[61] ibid, 564–65 (the Court) citing *Consul Developments v DPC* (1975) 132 CLR 373, 397 (Gibbs J).

[62] As discussed in *Warman* (n 1) at 569, it was common ground between the parties that orders against one should be 'against all three'. Thus, any remedy against Dwyer would also be against ETA and BTA.

[63] Placing a value on the value of Dwyer's shareholding in ETA/BTA, and any gain made by Dwyer via any increase in the value of these shares or excess over the cost of the shareholding to him (ie a capital profit), may have raised the need to incorporate future value. This is because the present valuation of shares may in part be a function of the future performance of the company. However, as noted in *Warman* (n 1) at 563–64 (the Court), Warman did not pursue a claim in respect of Dwyer's shareholding in ETA and BTA.

[64] *Warman* (n 1) 567. See also 570.

[65] ibid, 564.

[66] ibid, 561.

[67] ibid, 562.

[68] ibid, 565.

[69] ibid, 565–66.

[70] ibid, 567, 570 (the Court). September 1988 was selected as the date on which the joint venture between Dwyer, Bonfiglioni and BTA was executed.

In inquiring about the date on which the agency between Warman and Bonfiglioni would have ended had Dwyer not been in breach of fiduciary duty,[71] the Court arguably permitted an inquiry running contrary, as stated by Arden LJ in *Murad v Al-Suraj*, to the position that 'for policy reasons … courts decline to investigate hypothetical situations as to what would have happened if the fiduciary had performed his duty.'[72] Whilst the plurality framed their deliberations as 'making full allowance for the limits of judicial discretion',[73] it is difficult to reconcile the High Court of Australia's inquiry as part of an exploration as to whether the profit was earned in a manner as would satisfy a test of causation which requires the breach to be *a* reason for the gain.[74] Certainly, subsequent academic and judicial commentary has suggested that the *but for* test of causation is the correct approach.[75] Alternatively, it may be possible to reconcile the High Court's approach by regarding it as an inquiry about remoteness, relevantly as to whether the profit is too remote from any breach of fiduciary duty.[76] For example, Mitchell argues that:

> a better approach is to say that the courts … [apply the *a reason*] causation test, but moderat[e] its effect by using a remoteness rule: they let the fiduciary keep part of

[71] ibid, 565–66, 567.

[72] [2005] EWCA Civ 959, [76] (Arden LJ).

[73] *Warman* (n 1) 567.

[74] ibid, 558. See also *Murad* (n 72) [59], [67], [76] (Arden LJ) [96], [111] (Jonathan Parker LJ); as discussed in C Mitchell, 'Causation, Remoteness and Fiduciary Gains' (2006) 17 *KCLJ* 325, 331–33, one view is that the breach of fiduciary duty must have been *a* reason, not *the* reason, for the gain. See also G Virgo, 'Restitutionary Remedies for Wrongs: Causation and Remoteness' in C Rickett (ed), *Justifying Private Law Remedies* (Oxford, Hart Publishing, 2008) 322–23. P Devonshire, 'Account of Profits for Breach of Fiduciary Duty' (2010) 32 *Sydney Law Review* 389, 401 supports a robust approach to causation stating that '[a]ccountability must be exacted, at least to the point that profits in the fiduciary's hands are unquestioningly the products of the breach' but does not specify the standard pursuant to which such a causation in inquiry should be satisfied. See also *Lifeplan Australia Friendly Society Ltd v Ancient Order of Foresters in Victoria* [2017] FCAFC 74 [64]–[68] (the Court) (on appeal to the High Court of Australia, judgment reserved) in which the Court emphasises at [64] that 'there is no call to require a strict, or direct or proximate relationship between each particular transaction from which the profit in a business is derived and some particular breach. There is no call to generalise about the adequacy or not of the so-called but for test. The facts should be examined to ascertain the causal relationship between the breaches and profits to assess whether it is sufficient to conform with the policy of the rule of responsibility to attribute a liability to account for those profits.'

[75] See, eg, *Murad* (n 72) [154]–[155], [160] (Clarke LJ) (in dissent); Virgo (n 74) at 326 also suggests that 'there is no justification for the rejection of the but for test of causation when accounting for profits following a breach of fiduciary duty.'

[76] Mitchell (n 74) 336–39. See generally: P Birks, *An Introduction to the Law of Restitution* (Oxford, Clarendon Press, 1984) 351–55; J Edelman, *Gain Based Damages: Contract, Tort, Equity and Intellectual Property* (Hart Publishing, 2002) 108–11; Virgo (n 74) 306. For a contrasting view, see K Barker, 'Riddles, Remedies and Restitution: Quantifying Gains in Unjust Enrichment Law' (2001) 54 *CLP* 255. Barker at 291 cautions against use of the language of remoteness of gain, since its heritage lies in loss-based contract and tort cases where the policy concerns are different.' In the case of breaching fiduciaries, Barker considers at 294 that any risk of a windfall or surplus to the principal is a lesser evil than leaving the gain in the hands of the breaching fiduciary and at 295 that all 'accretions in value which are attributable to the relevant injustice, as opposed to other incidental factors such as the defendant or a third party's labour, skill, property or business acumen, should in principle should be recoverable.'

> the gain because it [is] too remote a consequence of the breach to justify making her account for it.[77]

Whatever the correct position about the test of causation and the role of remoteness in account of profits for breach of fiduciary duty, a problem of certainty may nonetheless arise in respect of hypothetical value to be included in the valuation of an account of profits. *Dart Industries Inc v Decor Corporation Pty Ltd* states that '[a]n account of profits is confined to profits actually made'.[78] Assuming for one moment the general correctness of this position, an account of profits ordered against a fiduciary may be in respect of trading profit or capital profit. It is in the valuation of capital profit that the risk of uncertainty arises.

Capital profits are the gain on the disposal (or value on notional disposal) of an asset calculated by deducting the cost of the asset from the proceeds received on its disposal. For example, in *Warman*, the Court pointed out that the amount by which the value of shares held by Dwyer in BTA and ETA exceeded their cost to him would have represented a capital profit.[79] Similarly, the proceeds of sale of the trademarks and goodwill of a business whose success was in part due to a passing off were also regarded as a capital profit.[80] Depending on the asset in question, the calculation may require a court to bring into present value the estimated future value of the asset. This future value of the asset presently accrues to the defendant since the future value is reflected in the capital profit or capital value of the asset. However, it may also involve an appreciation of hypothetical future value. Thus, for example, where the asset is a business including its brand name and goodwill, sale of the business will mean that the vendor 'receives a capital sum from the buyer in return for a right to the future income stream which the buyer expects the property will generate'.[81]

Capital profits are understood to be in contrast to trading profits which are the profits of the company or entity before costs. Consistently with the position that '[a]n account of profits is confined to profits actually made',[82] capital profits and trading profits are both capable of being given up via an account of profits.[83] Fidelity with this position requires that the capital profit is viewed as an existing profit: '[i]n principle, there is nothing wrong with the court estimating the profit by drawing inferences, provided that there is some evidence of *actual* profit.'[84]

[77] Mitchell (n 74) 336.

[78] (1993) 179 CLR 101, 111 (the Court).

[79] *Warman* (n 1) 563. An account of profits for this value was not pursued, proceedings in the High Court focusing 'exclusively upon the businesses of BTA and ETA and the profits made by those companies': at 564.

[80] *Apand v Kettle Chip Co Pty Ltd* (1999) 88 FCR 568, [54], [58] (Beaumont J), [79], [81], [85] (Heerey J).

[81] ibid, [81] (Heerey J).

[82] *Dart Industries* (n 78) 111 (the Court).

[83] As to the availability of an account of profits for capital profits: *Warman* (n 1) 563 (the Court); *Apand* (n 80) [156] (Emmett J); *V-Flow Pty Ltd v Hollyoake Industries (Vic) Pty Ltd* [2013] FCAFC 16, [35] (the Court); *Lifeplan Australia Friendly Society* (n 74) [77], [85]–[89] (the Court).

[84] *V-Flow* (n 83) [35] (the Court), citing *Apand* (n 80) (emphasis in original).

An account of profits for capital profits was raised by the facts of *Lifeplan Australia Friendly Society Ltd v Ancient Order of Foresters Friendly Society*.[85] Lifeplan and Foresters were competitors in the funeral bond and pre-paid funeral market, albeit that Lifeplan was the larger business. These products were sold to consumers through Australian funeral directors and depended on a relationship with the funeral directors to reach potential customers. Woff and Corby were employees of Lifeplan. Whilst in Lifeplan's employ, and in breach of fiduciary duty to Lifeplan, Woff emailed confidential strategic business planning and financial intelligence planning documents to the board of Foresters. Woff and Corby also took steps to divert and solicit business from funeral directors (and hence the underlying customer base) to move from Lifeplan to Foresters.[86] In particular, Woff and Corby developed the Business Concept Plan ('BCP') which was:

> a comprehensive plan … prepared utilising valuable confidential information of their employer … that set out a detailed strategy to attach the commercial base of that employer in order to win as many clients as possible from the employer after they left it, and so to take as quickly as possible the business presently enjoyed by Lifeplan and replicate its success for the benefit of the new prospective employer.[87]

Foresters funeral product business became highly successful. Whilst there were variations on the specific features of the various products, the essential elements were that the funeral bonds were sold 'pre-need' to consumers and '[could] only be claimed following the death of the client and for the purposes of contributing to their funeral expenses.'[88] Once invested, consumers could not withdraw their funds (other than to pay for funeral expenses according to the terms of the product)[89] and Foresters received a fee calculated at 2 per cent of the funds under management for their services in managing the fund.[90] Foresters was found to have knowingly assisted Woff and Corby to breach their fiduciary duties to Lifeplan.[91] Lifeplan claimed an account of profits in the hands of Foresters, which raised the question as to the most appropriate method of quantifying the account. Although the equity in *Lifeplan* was in relation to the conduct of a dishonest participant in a breach of fiduciary duty, the Court's approach is of relevance to the quantification of an account for the associated and underlying breach of fiduciary duty.[92]

[85] [2017] FCAFC 74 (on appeal to the High Court of Australia, judgment reserved).
[86] ibid, [9]–[10].
[87] ibid, [32].
[88] *Lifeplan Australia Friendly Society v Woff* [2016] FCA 248, [76] (Besanko J).
[89] ibid, [469] (Besanko J).
[90] ibid, [77], [418] (Besanko J).
[91] *Lifeplan* (n 74) [11], [41], [52] (the Court).
[92] ibid, [67]–[68] (the Court) emphasised that the policy of equity in holding an accessory (to a breach of fiduciary duty) to account are no different to the policy holding the fiduciary to account. The same normative drivers, such as 'the enforcement and support of fidelity, conscience and trust and the stopping of the gain from infidelity, breach of trust and fraud' apply: at [67].

Informed by the position that:[93]

> [t]he choice of end point against which to make the valuation is not driven by any logical analysis beyond the recognition that it should support and fortify the underlying principles being vindicated: fidelity, trust and honesty. The causal connection is one that vindicates those considerations and one which might be seen to act as an encouragement against being swayed to participate for personal gain in the dishonest breaches of others in their duties of fidelity.

The Full Federal Court of Australia confirmed that the necessary causal link was established between the breach and the gain in the hands of Foresters.[94] In fashioning the remedy, the Court's task was to value the profit, with a particular challenge being how to how to give appropriate recognition to the fact that the breaches of duty did not transfer an existing business, but rather led to the development of a new business in the hands of Foresters from the ground up.[95] One possibility was to come to some valuation of Foresters business, with a degree of proportionality of response given that Woff and Coby were instrumental to the business success of Foresters and the 'business would not have been established without them'.[96] Alternatively, the Court could attribute the net present value of particular contracts entered into by Foresters up to a particular time. Swayed by the observation that the BCP contemplated a five-year plan,[97] and that the breaches commenced in 2010,[98] the Court ordered valuation to be on the basis the present value of contracts as at 30 June 2015, with a valuation date of 30 April 2015. This approach was expressed to capture:

> capital profits that would not have been made had the breaches in which the participation occurred not been committed. But the limitation to that date gives due recognition to the other factors to which we have made mention and which affect and assessment of the proportionate consequences of the breaches and the participation therein. The setting of the date at 30 June 2015 sets the account within the framework of the five-year business plan, with a modest deduction of six months.[99]

Implicit in the Court's valuation of Foresters' gain was therefore an incorporation of future value. The impact of the order was to require Foresters to account for the present value (as at 30 April 2015) of income earned *and to be earned* on each contract entered into up to 30 June 2015. So do the facts *Lifeplan* raise a problem of certainty? Assuming that causation is satisfied, is it necessary to consider the future, or hypothetical events, in order to determine the nature and extent of

[93] ibid, [87]. See also [62].
[94] ibid, [61], [64], [66]. It is unclear whether the Court applied the but for test, albeit that it is clear that on the facts the Court found this test to be satisfied.
[95] ibid, [85].
[96] ibid, [85].
[97] ibid, [17], [88].
[98] ibid, [6]–[8].
[99] ibid, [88].

Foresters' gain? This chapter tentatively answers the question in the affirmative. Contrary to the position in *Warman v Dwyer*, where the profits could be calculated on the basis of historical facts, *Lifeplan* apparently suggests the need to speculate about future hypothetical events. Implicit in the Court's reasoning in *Lifeplan* is a method of making certain the defendant's gain. The Court's approach rests on whatever accounting assumptions are inbuilt into the process of taking the 'net present value of contracts up to a particular date'. Some of these assumptions may have related to future or hypothetical events.[100] For example: the future underlying performance of the Lifeplan funds under management and the expected number of payments from the fund, given that funeral bonds could only be claimed for funeral expenses. Although these calculations are not as transparently probabilistic as the parallel process we identify in making certain a lost commercial opportunity, the discounting involved in taking the present value nonetheless takes account of the relevant uncertainty and associated contingencies to render the gain certain. It is difficult to unpack opaque reasoning, but if the argument in this chapter is correct, we should also be entitled to assume that these contingencies should *not* include the possibility that the Lifeplan as principal would not have pursued these contracts. Consistently with the position that the absolute loyalty required of the fiduciary means that it is irrelevant that the gain in their hands is one which the principal 'was unwilling, unlikely or unable to make'[101] the fiduciary ought not be permitted to ask when valuing the account, contra the interests of the principal, to discount the value of the profit to reflect this contingency. This conclusion also rests on the Court's position that the 'relevant remedy depends on the nature and character of the relevant rule of responsibility, and of the remedy sought'[102] and that there was little relevant normative distinction for the purposes of analysis between breach of fiduciary duty and the participatory liability of Foresters.[103]

IV. Implications of Certainty: Breach of Fiduciary Duty

The above discussion considers future hypothetical gain in the calculus of capital profit. The question arises whether, in the alternative, the principal might claim

[100] *Lifeplan* (n 74) [86] (the Court). The judgment at trial in *Lifeplan Australia Friendly Society v Woff* [2016] FCA 248, [418] (Besanko J) makes reference to the applicants' expert who 'adopted … a discounted cash flow methodology using a net present value calculation'. 'This model was constructed … having regard to the history of Lifeplan's Fund … and claims history from 1990 to 2010.' This appears to refer to a different time period. Nonetheless, it gives some indication of the assumptions underlying the net present valuation methods adopted.

[101] *Warman* (n 1) 558 (the Court).

[102] *Lifeplan* (n 74) [62].

[103] ibid, [67]–[68].

some measure of future gain. For example, using the facts of *Lifeplan*, an alternative basis of conceptualising Foresters' gain (bearing in mind that this was in reality the value of Foresters' business) may be one which looks not only to the value of existing funeral bond contracts, but also to the value of funeral bond contracts *yet to be written*.[104] An immediate obstacle to such an analysis may be the argument that if the fiduciary has made no profit, then the obligation to account for the profit is not engaged. As stated in *Warman*, 'A fiduciary must account for a profit or benefit if it was obtained [inter alia] … or (2) by reason of his fiduciary position or by reason of his taking advantage of opportunity or knowledge derived from his fiduciary position.'[105] However, such an argument ignores the possibility that the fiduciary's profit may arise because of the prohibition against conflict between duty and self-interest. Whilst there is a debate about the relationship between the no profit rule and the no conflict rule,[106] this analysis treats 'the obligations as if they are distinct, while recognising that both may, and often will, be engaged by the one set of facts.'[107] Thus, in *Warman*, Dwyer breached both his obligation not to obtain any unauthorised benefit and also not to be in a position of conflict. Subject to the satisfaction of causation, the analysis in this chapter suggests that in such a case of hypothetical gain, equity would also necessarily be required to establish the nature and extent of the defendant's gain in order to engage the obligation to account.

There are other implications which concern the adjustments to an equitable monetary award for breach of fiduciary duty. All equitable remedies are discretionary. In order to prevent the unjust enrichment of the principal which would otherwise remain, the court may award the breaching fiduciary a just allowance or equitable allowance for her care and skill in generating the gain.[108] Where the fiduciary has been guilty of 'any dishonesty or bad faith, or surreptitious dealing, [s]he might not be allowed any remuneration or reward'.[109] On the loss side, a court may permit an adjustment to the value of loss for which equitable compensation is awarded reflecting 'the notional salaries which would have been paid'[110] by the principal to the defaulting fiduciary had the commercial opportunity been pursued by the principal.[111] The question arises how these further adjustments to

[104] This possibility is averred to by the trial judge in *Lifeplan Australia Friendly Society v Woff* [2016] FCA 248, [455] (Besanko J).

[105] *Warman* (n 1) 557 (the Court). See also 563 (the Court).

[106] There is a debate beyond the scope of this chapter as to whether or not the profit principle stands separately to the conflict principle: see, eg, *Chan* (n 38) 198 (Deane J); *Warman* (n 1) 557–58 (the Court); M Conaglen, *Fiduciary Loyalty* (Oxford, Hart Publishing, 2010) 114–20; R Nolan, '*Regal (Hastings) v Gulliver*' in C Mitchell and P Mitchell (eds), *Landmark Cases in Equity* (Oxford, Hart Publishing, 2012) 519–27.

[107] *Howard* (n 38) 106 [57] (Hayne and Crennan JJ).

[108] *Boardman* (n 4) 104 (Lord Cohen), 112 (Lord Hodson); *Warman* (n 1) 568 (the Court).

[109] *Phipps v Boardman* [1965] 2 WLR 839, 861 (Denning LJ). As shown by *Warman*, in which the fiduciary was actively dishonest, yet an allowance was not withheld, the fiduciary allowance for care and skill has been controversial.

[110] *V-Flow* (n 83) [71] (The Court).

[111] See generally S Degeling, 'Discretion and Equitable Compensation' (n 10) 324–26.

value interact with any requirement that the nature and extent of the loss or gain be made certain.

Finally, this analysis has only been in relation to the equitable remedial response to a breach of fiduciary duty. However, it must be acknowledged that accounts of profits are also capable of being raised in response to a whole panoply of civil wrongs, including, for example, some breaches of contract,[112] infringement of intellectual property rights,[113] and breach of equitable obligations of confidence.[114] The analysis in this chapter has sought to align equity's normative settings in the fiduciary sphere and the applicable test for certainty. Relevantly, in the contingencies to be accounted for, that the fiduciary should not be permitted to speculate about the conduct of the principal since to do so would arguably run contrary to the conduct expected of the fiduciary. If this analysis is correct, then we should expect parallel inquiries in relation to the other civil wrongs for which an account of profits is available, informed by the respective normative concerns of those civil wrongs, in order to determine the ambit of any certainty principle.

V. Conclusion

The general rules giving shape to equitable monetary remedies are still developing. This chapter suggests that in addition to the more familiar requirement of causation, equity requires the claimant's hypothetical loss such as a lost commercial opportunity, and perhaps also the defendant's hypothetical gain, to be made certain. Whilst more familiar to legal analysis when considering compensatory damages at law for a lost chance, there is some evidence that equity already implements a requirement of certainty when awarding equitable compensation for a lost commercial opportunity. To the extent that hypothetical gain is incorporated into an account of profits, the court is implicitly making the gain certain such that it may be disgorged. In taking into account the past and future hypothetical events, this chapter suggests that, contrary to the position at law, the court should not be permitted to speculate about the hypothetical conduct of the claimant principal since to do so runs contrary to the underlying fiduciary obligation.

[112] *Attorney General v Blake* [2001] 1 AC 268.

[113] *Colbeam Palmer Ltd v Stock Affiliates Pty Ltd* (1968) 122 CLR 25; *Dart Industries* (n 78); *Apand* (n 80).

[114] See generally P Turner, 'Equitable Remedy of Compensation for Breach of Confidence' in S Degeling and J Varuhas (eds), *Equitable Compensation and Disgorgement of Profit* (Oxford, Hart Publishing, 2017) 260–61.

PART IV

Apportionment Between Defendants

10

Contribution Among Wrongdoers: Reducing the Risk of Contribution Recovery Shortfall and Other Issues

DAVID CHEIFETZ

I. Introduction

> Contribution is a simple concept but a complicated business – primarily because it involves three causes of action: the victim's claim against the contribution claimant, the victim's claim against the contribution defendant, and the contribution claim itself.[1]

Where solidary liability is the rule as between an injured person and the wrongdoers legally responsible for the injured person's harm, the injured person does not have to sue all of the wrongdoers to obtain full recovery.[2] All that the injured person risks by not suing all of the wrongdoers is the prospect that those sued will not have sufficient assets to cover the full loss. In modern terminology, wrongdoers who are responsible for the same damages[3] are usually described as being 'jointly and severally' liable. The term 'solidary liability,' is the proper label for the full, shared, liability of each wrongdoer for the 'joint liability' portion of what is commonly called 'joint and several' liability.[4]

[1] P Kutner, 'Contribution Among Wrongdoers: Liability Issues In Contribution Law' (1985) 63 *Canadian Bar Review* 1, 58. On contribution see generally C Mitchell, *The Law of Contribution and Reimbursement* (London, Oxford University Press, 2003). For United Kingdom law: D Cheifetz, *Apportionment of Fault in Tort* (Aurora, Canada Law Book, 1981). For Canadian common law jurisdictions: J Kleefeld, 'Concurrent Fault at 90: A History of Ontario's Negligence Act and Canada's Uniform Contributory Fault Act' in E Quill and RJ Friel (eds), *Damages and Compensation Culture: Comparative Perspectives* (Oxford, Hart Publishing, 2016) 217–99 and LN Klar, *Tort Law*, 6th edn (Toronto, Carswell, 2016) 656–76. Mitchell's monograph is the best Commonwealth text devoted to contribution issues.

[2] 'Wrongdoer' is used, for convenience only, as a label which includes both the actor and a person vicariously liable for the actor. The usage is not meant to suggest that a person who is only vicariously liable to the injured person has committed a wrong.

[3] I have intentionally used 'damages' rather than 'damage'. Liability is for 'damages' resulting from 'damage'. It is trite that the general rule in tort is that there is no liability if the harm – the damage – does not result in damages. The problem of the meaning of 'same damage' versus 'same damages' for contribution is not, on the whole, a Canadian problem. See Part IV(B) for further discussion.

[4] Kleefeld, (n 1) 227; Cheifetz (n 1) 7; The Ontario Law Reform Commission, *Report on Contribution Among Wrongdoers and Contributory Negligence* (Toronto, Ministry of the Attorney-General, 1988) 31–40;

The usual explanation for the injured person's choice of whom to sue is a combination of the likelihood of success and the likelihood of collection. As between the injured person and the wrongdoers, the consequence of solidary liability is that each wrongdoer is liable for all of the recoverable damages, even if there is another wrongdoer who is, or could also be held, liable. The accepted rationale for this approach is that it is better that the injured person be fully compensated without requiring him or her to attempt to sue all the wrongdoers; and that any injustice that results from this approach ought to be borne, as between injured person and wrongdoers, by the wrongdoers. The general rule is that the injured person cannot, though, collect the same loss more than once.[5]

To balance the potential for injustice as between wrongdoers implicit in a solidary liability system, modern common law jurisdictions tend to have some form of reimbursement remedy by which a wrongdoer who has paid more than the wrongdoer's 'share' of the injured person's loss may recover, from the other wrongdoers, some or all of that payment. As between the wrongdoers against whom the plaintiff could have obtained judgment, the remedy to ameliorate the potential for injustice as between the multiple wrongdoers, implicit in solidary liability to the injured person, is the right to contribution.[6]

Where there is more than one wrongdoer, there is always the potential that the wrongdoer who pays the injured person, whether voluntarily or after a judgment, will not be able to collect partial, or full contribution from the other wrongdoer(s). The potential for a 'contribution recovery shortfall' ('CRS')[7] is an inevitable consequence in any regime where the wrongdoer's liability to the injured person is for all of the damages (in modern terminology, 'joint' or 'solidary', meaning the wrongdoers are each potentially liable for the whole loss, even though others are also at fault) but contribution liability is 'several' (meaning separate and proportionate).[8] If contribution liability is several,[9] it is limited to the wrongdoer's share of the injured person's loss, however the share is defined. In cases where three or more

Glanville Williams, *Joint Torts and Contributory Negligence* (London, Stevens & Sons Ltd, 1951) 1. An older term for 'solidary' is '*in solidum*'.

[5] OLRC, *Report* (n 4) 31–40, 46–48; Cheifetz (n 1) 7; Mitchell (n 1) 172–73, paras 8.36–8.38.

[6] OLRC, *Report* (n 4) c 4; Cheifetz (n 1) 8–10; Mitchell (n 1) ch 3.

[7] This acronym will be used where grammar and sense permit. To illustrate the CRS problem, the chapter uses a modified version of the basic contribution scenario in tort: three wrongdoers, W1, W2 and W3, are legally responsible – meaning liable if sued timely in an claim adjudged correctly – for harm sustained by P. P is entitled to recover damages for the harm from any of them, but cannot collect the same damages more than once. The contribution claimant will be described as W1; and the contribution defendants as W2, W3, W4 … W*x*. I use contribution as the term for the remedy regardless of whether the amount sought or recovered is the full amount paid by the contribution claimant.

[8] D Cheifetz, 'Allocating Financial Responsibility Among Solvent Concurrent Wrongdoers' (2004) 28 *Advocates' Quarterly* 137, 194–98, 237. The OLRC, *Report* (n 4) 33 states: '[h]owever, a scheme of contribution can benefit one wrongdoer only where the other wrongdoer is available and capable of satisfying her portion of the liability. … The principle [of solidary liability] operates primarily to ensure full compensation to the injured person, to the occasional detriment of a solvent wrongdoer who is required to satisfy the entire liability, regardless of her degree of fault.'

[9] The orthodox position, at least at law in the common law, and under statute; but not necessarily in equity: see Mitchell (n 1) 71, para 4.11.

wrongdoers are potentially liable to the injured person and their contribution liability is several, the potential for contribution recovery shortfall exists if: (1) one or more of them does not have assets to pay that wrongdoer's contribution share; or (2) one or more of them is immune to a contribution judgment, and the share of the immune wrongdoer(s) cannot be distributed, in some appropriate fashion, among the wrongdoers with assets.[10]

In cases involving three or more wrongdoers, the CRS problem can potentially be resolved by re-allocating (redistributing) the amount of a third wrongdoer's contribution liability as between the contribution claimant and the contribution defendants who are able to pay.[11] This is the solution I propose in this chapter.

The only way to eliminate the CRS risk in instances of three or more wrongdoers is to allow, in appropriate circumstances, the allocation, as between the wrongdoers with assets, of the contribution amounts of the wrongdoer(s) from whom contribution is not available.[12] Depending on the formula used to determine the contribution amounts, the law must either: (1) calculate the amount of collectible contribution on a 'just and equitable' basis, meaning that the CSR risk is somehow taken into account in the calculation of the contribution amount; or (2) where the contribution formula specifically refers to percentages or degrees of fault, allow for the allocation of the share(s) of the immune wrongdoers on a basis that reflects the contribution claimant and defendants' blameworthiness *relative to one another*.[13] In either case, the effect is, in a sense, to create at least some amount of solidary liability for contribution.[14]

The CRS problem has been recognised in some Commonwealth jurisdictions.[15] It has been partially addressed in one Canadian jurisdiction by amendment to the contribution legislation.[16] The one, Canadian, judicial attempt of which I am aware that addressed a CRS problem caused by the insolvency of one of the wrongdoers was reversed on appeal.[17] I will show in this chapter that, even without specific

[10] 'Share' is the amount which corresponds to the wrongdoer's fault percentage, multiplied by the damages.

[11] There will be a contribution recovery shortfall in instances of only two wrongdoers where the contribution defendant lacks assets to pay; however, there is no contribution share *requiring redistribution* to do justice as between solvent wrongdoers. The contribution recovery shortfall problem in this instance is an unavoidable consequence of joint liability to the injured person rather than a result of contribution doctrine. The shortfall issue is eliminated if liability to the injured person is several but then there is no need for contribution.

[12] For the purpose of this article, unless otherwise mentioned, 'wrongdoers' includes only those wrongdoers who would have been held liable to the injured person if sued appropriately.

[13] This also means that, where the plaintiff is also at fault, the numerical percentage or degree of fault is irrelevant once used as part of the calculation to determine each of the wrongdoer's 'actual' share of fault. See below Part III(C).

[14] *Dubai Aluminium Company Ltd v Salaam* [2002] UKHL 48, [2002] 3 WLR 1913 [67] explicitly recognises that the effect is to create solidary liability for contribution.

[15] The United Kingdom situation is mentioned, briefly, below nn 54–55 and associated text.

[16] Saskatchewan: The Contributory Negligence Act, RSS 1978, c c-31, s 3.1(1) enacted in 2004. See J Kleefeld, 'The Contributory Negligence Act at Seventy' (2015) *Saskatchewan Law Review* 31, 102–05.

[17] *Renaissance Leisure Group Inc v Frazer* 2004 CanLII 21044, 242 DLR (4th) 229 (ONCA) varying *Renaissance Leisure Group Inc v Frazer* 2001 CanLII 28229, 197 DLR (4th) 336 (ONSC).

legislative solutions, contribution doctrine, properly understood, contains a practical and just solution for the CRS problem. The solution is available whether the amount of contribution is determined on the 'just and equitable basis', or 'relative degree of fault' basis, at least so long as the basis of apportionment is the comparative blameworthiness of the wrongdoers.[18] Relative (meaning comparative) blameworthiness is accepted as the governing principle of apportionment under both formulations.[19]

Part II of the chapter provides a brief survey of the law in the Canadian common law jurisdictions and of the solutions to a few of the more common issues in contribution jurisprudence. Part III outlines three solutions for the CRS problem: (1) either a new statutory solution, or (where possible) the reinterpretation of existing statutory criteria, for those who believe that that is the only, or the better, solution; (2) a better and different understanding of the meaning of the existing statutory contribution formulas; and (3) an argument from principle, that the better understanding of the equitable contribution remedy is that the ability to distribute the amount of contribution liability as between those required to and able to pay, is inherent in the principles of the remedy.

The position asserted is that, in principle, it does not matter, as between W1 and W2, why contribution is not recoverable from W3, so long as W3 could have been held liable to P for the damages which W1 paid P. That is, there is no difference in principle between the situations where: (1) W3 has no assets, so that a contribution judgment, existing or potential, will be uncollectible; (2) there is a relevant reason preventing the practical, valid, commencement of a contribution claim against W3, even assuming W3 has assets;[20] and (3) W3 has, since P's harm occurred, acquired a defence against P, so that W3 cannot be held liable to P.

Part IV addresses a potpourri of issues including the issue of whether, in principle, a still-existing potential for liability to the injured person is a necessary prerequisite for contribution. The chapter concludes in Part V with a few remarks offering a better explanation of contribution.

II. Brief Overview of Contribution in Common Law Canada

In practice, the situation in common law Canada is unremarkable, even if the law is not necessarily so. All of the Canadian common jurisdictions have legislation

[18] Cheifetz (n 1) 97–104; Klar (n 1) 674; Klar ch 6 in this text on the meaning of comparative blameworthiness. See also Mitchell (n 1) 192, para 10.19, and at 196–99.

[19] Klar (n 1) 674; Cheifetz (n 1), 99–104.

[20] I include here the situation where W3's assets are located in another jurisdiction and it would be unjust as between W1 and W2 to require W1 to attempt to collect from W3 in that jurisdiction.

that governs contribution claims in, at least, tort.[21] In some jurisdictions, the legislation has been interpreted to cover all claims for contribution arising out of harm caused by fault, regardless of the cause of action.[22] The first contribution statute was enacted in 1930 in Ontario. The other common law jurisdictions passed their own legislation in subsequent years.[23] In all cases, the statutes are still accurately and succinctly summarised as law reform in need of additional, if not necessarily universally urgent, law reform.[24]

To determine the amount of contribution payable, most of the common law jurisdictions use a formula referring to the 'amount that may be found by the court to be just and equitable having regard to the extent of that person's responsibility for the damage', with that formula being understood to require the court to determine the wrongdoers comparative blameworthiness.[25] The other common law jurisdictions use some version of a formula which specifically refers to the 'relative degrees of fault' of the wrongdoers. The original and basic form is that found in the Ontario legislation: 'as between themselves … each is liable to make contribution and indemnify each other in the degree in which they are respectively found to be at fault'.[26] A few jurisdictions have separate statutes for contribution and contributory fault (negligence) apportionment. While the contributory fault apportionment legislation is capable of being interpreted to create a statutory right of contribution, the case law holds that only the contribution-specific statute applies.[27]

A number of provincial law reform commissions have recommended that the apportionment statutes be repealed and replaced with new, allegedly better, legislation that responds to the concerns identified in case law and the reports of the commissions.[28] That has not occurred. There have been only two, significant amendments. One type allows the distribution, among solvent wrongdoers held liable to pay contribution, of the contribution shares of a wrongdoer against whom a contribution judgment is obtained, if the judgment cannot be collected.

[21] Quebec law has an analogous remedy under its Civil Code: see Civil Code of Québec, CQLR c CCQ-1991, Art 1536. See also *Bow Valley Husky (Bermuda) Ltd v Saint John Shipbuilding Ltd* [1997] 3 SCR 1210, 1267, 1997 CanLII 307 [101]. That remedy is outside the scope of this chapter.

[22] Cheifetz (n 8) 348–49.

[23] For a detailed review of the history of Canadian contribution legislation, see Kleefeld (n 1). See also Cheifetz (n 1) 10–11 (contribution after judgment) and 145 (contribution after settlement).

[24] *Bitumen & Oil Refineries (Aust) Ltd v Commissioner for Government Transport* [1995] HCA 1 [12]: 'a piece of law reform which seems itself to call somewhat urgently for reform'.

[25] See, eg, The Tort-Feasors Act, RSA 2000, c T-5 (Alberta) and the Tortfeasors Act, RSNB 2011, c 231 (New Brunswick). See Klar in this text.

[26] See, eg, Negligence Act, RSO 1990, c N 1, s 1 (Ontario) and the Negligence Act, RSBC 1996, c 333 (British Columbia).

[27] *Parkland (County of) v Stetar* 1974 CanLII 198, [1975] 2 SCR 884, 898; Cheifetz (n 1) 46; Kleefeld (n 1) 249.

[28] Alberta Institute of Research and Reform, *Contributory Negligence and Concurrent Wrongdoers* (Report No 31, 1979); Law Reform Commission of British Columbia, *Report on Shared Liability* (LRC 88, 1986); Manitoba Law Reform Commission, *Contributory Fault: The Tortfeasors and Contributory Negligence Act* (2013); OLRC, *Report* (n 4); Law Reform Commission of Saskatchewan, *Discussion Paper: The Insolidum Doctrine and Contributory Negligence* (Saskatoon, 1997); Uniform Law Conference of Canada, *Uniform Contributory Fault Act*.

'Collected' is not defined but the extra-statutory material relevant to the amendment process and interpretation requires the conclusion that amendments were intended only for the situation where a contribution judgment has been obtained but then cannot be collected because the contribution defendant is insolvent.[29] The other type of amendment clarifies the commencement and duration of the limitation periods governing contribution claims.[30]

The lack of statutory change is not surprising. On the whole, despite the brevity and ambiguity of the legislation, the results of Canadian common law decisions dealing with contribution have been sensible.[31] Apart from that? Contribution is usually a remedy that matters only to those with money, including their counsel. If one is not sued, or if one does not have assets to pay, then one does not need contribution. Generally, if one has assets, paying a bit to keep most or a significant portion of the assets – and to keep the issues away from lawyers and judges who might become confused, and so make the law even more confused – is a wise move. The result is that, at least in Canada, judges are rarely asked to decide difficult legal issues of contribution. When this happens, there is often good reason to doubt the merits of their analyses, even where the final decision seems the correct or, at least, an acceptable result.[32]

III. Solutions for CRS

A. Statutory Solution: Amendment

The various Commonwealth law reform bodies that have considered the redistribution of contribution liability issue since the 1970s have concluded that specific legislation is required to allow courts to calculate the amount of contribution liability in such a way as to include amounts resulting from the absence,

[29] Below Part III(A).

[30] In general, the orthodox rule, that the limitation periods start to run when the contribution cause of action arises, has been abolished. The Limitation Acts of most jurisdictions now provide that the contribution claim starts to run on the earlier of: (1) the date when the contribution claimant knows, or ought to know a contribution claim is required, and (2) the date on which the claimant is served with the injured person's court process. In some circumstances, this creates the risk of the contribution limitation period expiring before a wrongdoer knows enough to know that a contribution claim is appropriate; perhaps even that another concurrent wrongdoer exists. This potential is exacerbated by increased judicial willingness to find concurrent causation and 'indivisible' injury. Additional comment on the legislative amendments to contribution limitation periods is beyond the scope of this chapter. The issue is discussed in some detail, in the context of the Ontario legislation, in Kleefeld (n 1) 275–81.

[31] The small amount of academic scholarship in the area might be seen as some proof of that claim.

[32] See Cheifetz (n 8); D Cheifetz, 'Postscript: The Retreat Begins' (2004) 8 *Advocates' Quarterly* 389; 'Postscript 2: The Retreat Continues' (2004) 29 *Advocates' Quarterly* 276 (all on *Martin v Listowel Memorial Hospital* 51 OR (3d) 384, 2000 CanLII 16947 (ONCA) and *Renaissance* (n 17)); D Cheifetz, 'For Whom The Bell Tolled' (2007) 33 *Advocates' Quarterly* 45 (on *HSBC Securities (Canada) Inc v Davies, Ward & Beck* 74 OR (3d) 295, 2005 CanLII 1626 (ONCA)); D Cheifetz, 'Silk Purses and Silver Linings" (2011) 38 *Advocates' Quarterly* 371 (on *Waterloo Region District School Board v Truax Engineering Ltd* 103 OR (3d) 81, 2010 ONCA 838).

or impecuniosity of a third wrongdoer.[33] The law reform bodies, most likely in the light of the United Kingdom experience, did not think the 'just and equitable' form of legislation was clear enough on its own.[34] 'Redistribution' is a better term than 'reallocation' because the contribution share of the insolvent wrongdoer is distributed among the solvent wrongdoers. It is not 'reallocated' it the sense that the insolvent wrongdoer ceases to have it. The insolvent wrongdoer remains liable to the solvent wrongdoers.[35]

Only one common law jurisdiction in Canada has enacted a statutory solution, notwithstanding the recommendations of the Uniform Law Conference of Canada and various law reform bodies.[36] As enacted, the provision is probably limited to the CRS problem resulting from either the insolvency of W3, or instances where W3's assets are outside of Canada and not exigible through reasonable efforts. This can be divined from its reference to situations in which 'the court is satisfied that the contribution of a person found at fault cannot be collected';[37] and from the various law reform proposals that led to its enactment.[38] The text of the enactment is that proposed by the Saskatchewan Law Reform Commission in its 1997 discussion paper.[39] The brief discussion in that report of the reason for, and the form of, the amendment supports the conclusion that it was intended to apply only in cases where the wrongdoer lacks exigible assets.[40] The Commission's report summarises the need for the amendment in these words: 'the present scheme of contribution between defendants is potentially unfair because it does not reallocate responsibility between solvent defendants when a co-defendant is unable to contribute.'[41]

The text of the amendment proposed in the OLRC report expressly refers to collectability issues other than insolvency; however without providing any direction as to what those might be.[42] The OLRC wrote that it 'wished to address the issue of how the risk of insolvency or absence on the part of one concurrent wrongdoer should be shared among a number of solvent concurrent wrongdoers'.[43] The recommendation was that:[44]

> Where there are three or more concurrent wrongdoers and one cannot pay his or her due share of the liability because of insolvency or for any other reason, that share shall be allocated to the other concurrent wrongdoers proportionately to the degrees in

[33] See n 28.
[34] See below at text associated with nn 54–55.
[35] See, eg, text associated with n 44.
[36] Saskatchewan's The Contributory Negligence Act, RSS 1978, c c-31, s 3.1(1) enacted in 2004.
[37] See n 36 above.
[38] See Kleefeld, (n 16) 101–05; Saskatchewan, 'Report' (n 28) 14–15; Alberta, 'Report' (n 28) 84–86. See also the draft state recommended by the OLRC in it 1998 report (n 4) and the Uniform Law Conference of Canada, Uniform Contributory Fault Act, s 9: http://www.ulcc.ca/en/uniform-acts-new-order/older-uniform-acts/647-contributory-fault-act.
[39] ibid.
[40] Saskatchewan, 'Report' (n 28) 14–15.
[41] ibid, 14.
[42] OLRC, *Report* (n 4) 48, 285.
[43] ibid, 48.
[44] ibid, 285.

> which they are found responsible, without discharging the liability of the defaulting concurrent wrongdoer to contribute.

It is not clear what the OLRC meant by 'or for any other reason'. The report does not provide examples. In the related discussion, it describes the wrongdoer who does not pay as one who 'is insolvent or otherwise unavailable to satisfy her share of liability'.[45] Again, the OLRC did not explain what circumstances other than insolvency might be caught by 'unable to satisfy'. A wrongdoer who simply refuses to pay, short of a judgment, does not qualify as one who 'cannot pay,' or is 'unable to satisfy'. A situation in which a wrongdoer 'cannot pay' or is 'unable to satisfy', that is not due to insolvency, seems to be one where there is a valid reason that *prevents* the wrongdoer from paying; however that explanation does not make sense in context. Absent illegality, a wrongdoer who wants to pay that wrongdoer's share, and who has assets to do so, is able to do so, even if the wrongdoer has a good defence to an action for contribution. In any event, the Ontario legislature never enacted the proposal.

B. Solution from Principle: Statutory Interpretation without Amendment

Contribution remedies are based on corrective justice: they are designed to correct what would otherwise be an unjustified enrichment of one wrongdoer at the expense of another.[46] In most Commonwealth jurisdictions, contribution between wrongdoers is a statutory remedy. Apportionment legislation is remedial: '[t]he purpose of the legislation is to … provid[e] a mechanism for each of those who contributed to the loss to share the financial responsibility in the proportions of their respective degrees of fault.'[47] There is no good reason to interpret the enabling legislation in a manner that produces injustice between the wrongdoers, if the text of the legislation does not compel that interpretation. Rather, so long as the legislation permits, it should be interpreted in a manner which eliminates injustice between the wrongdoers and which is consistent with the principles of corrective justice.

In Canada, the mandated approach to statutory interpretation is: '[t]he words of an Act are to be read in their entire context and in their grammatical and ordinary sense harmoniously with the scheme of the Act, the object of the Act, and the intention of Parliament.'[48] In addition, all of the common law jurisdictions in Canada have statutes setting out basic rules regarding statutory interpretation.

[45] ibid, 47–48.

[46] E J Weinrib, 'Contribution in a Contractual Setting' (1976) 54 *Canadian Bar Review* 338, quoted in the text accompanying n 102.

[47] *Martin* (n 32) [34].

[48] *British Columbia Human Rights Tribunal v Schrenk* 2017 SCC 62 [30]; *Re Rizzo & Rizzo Shoes Ltd* 1998 CanLII 837, [1998] 1 SCR 27 [21] (SCC).

The statutes all contain provisions in the following or equivalent form: '[e]very enactment must be construed as being remedial, and must be given such fair, large and liberal construction and interpretation as best ensures the attainment of its objects.'[49] Finally:

> [t]he purpose of the [contributory fault and contribution] legislation is to facilitate full recovery of the loss for the plaintiff, while at the same time providing a mechanism for each of those who contributed to the loss to share the financial responsibility in the proportions of their respective degrees of fault.[50]

These principles of statutory interpretation require Canadian courts to interpret the contribution legislation in a just manner as between the contribution claimant and the contribution defendant.[51]

The one, Canadian, judicial attempt to reallocate an impecunious wrongdoer's share of liability to another wrongdoer using the Ontario 'relative degrees of fault' formula succeeded at trial, but was reversed on appeal.[52] However, the appellate decision specifically left open the possibility of such re-allocation in some circumstances. The court did not provide any guidelines.[53]

There are no reported Canadian cases involving contribution share redistribution under the 'just and equitable amount' form of legislation.

A long series of court decisions that started under the original United Kingdom contribution legislation and ended in a 2002 House of Lords decision under the Civil Liability (Contribution) Act[54] has established that, under the 'just and equitable' formula, the default rule in contribution claims is the distribution of the share of the impecunious wrongdoer among the solvent wrongdoers. *Dubai Aluminium* contains the following statements which are equally applicable to the Canadian legislation:[55]

> The object of contribution proceedings under the *Contribution Act* [*sic*] is to ensure that each party responsible for the damage makes an appropriate contribution to the cost of compensating the plaintiff, regardless of where that cost has fallen in the first instance.' …
>
> The plaintiff may well not proceed against him [the insolvent wrongdoer] at all; but whether he does or not the whole of the liability of meeting the judgment falls to be apportioned between the other defendants, as otherwise the deficiency arising from the insolvency is borne by whichever defendant happens to satisfy the judgment, a result which it is the purpose of the 1978 Act to avoid ….

[49] Interpretation Act, RSBC 1996, c 238, s 8. *Rizzo & Rizzo Shoes* (n 48) [22] states that the statutory requirement that all legislation is remedial is in addition to the general principle of interpretation. The provinces have equivalent legislation: see, eg, Legislation Act, 2006, SO 2006, c 21, Sch F, s 64(1) (Ontario) and Interpretation Act, RSA 2000, c I-8, s 10 (Alberta).

[50] *Martin* (n 32).

[51] See also *Dubai Aluminium* (n 14).

[52] *Renaissance* (ONCA) (n 17) [37]. The trial judge adopted the United Kingdom approach.

[53] ibid, [52]. The passage is quoted at n 70.

[54] *Dubai Aluminium* (n 14). See *Fisher v C H T Ltd (No 2)* [1966] 2 QB 475 (CA) on the prior legislation.

[55] *Dubai Aluminium* (n 14) [52], [167] (citation omitted).

It is reasonable to expect that the *final* result in Canada will be the same should a judge, informed of the United Kingdom case law, be asked to interpret the equivalent Canadian legislation.

The 'respectively to the plaintiff and one another' formula[56] is the approach that has been used in Ontario since 1930, when legislation was enacted. It is also the approach used in apportionment calculations under the analogous legislation of the other provinces, the United Kingdom, and Australia, where the award is to be the amount of contribution that is just and equitable taking into account the wrongdoers' responsibility for the damage.

The traditional interpretation of the 'respective degrees of fault' formula is that W2 pays W1 an amount calculated by applying W2's quantified degree of fault to the amount of P's judgment. W2's obligation to pay commences once W1 has paid more than W1's share. The most W2 has to pay is the amount that W1 has paid in excess of W1's share, up to the limit of W2's share.[57] This formula satisfies everybody, so long as all of the wrongdoers have assets to pay their allocations; that is, so long as there are no absent or impecunious wrongdoers. Otherwise, it produces the risk of the contribution recovery shortfall.

The question is: fault respective to whom? Respective to other wrongdoers, or to the injured person, P? The answer to that question produces different results. 'Relative degrees of fault' formulas need not be interpreted to mean that the court is to calculate the extent of W2's liability to pay contribution to W1 by using the amount which W2 was originally found to be responsible for the harm compared to P, should P also be at fault.

On its face, the text of the 'degrees of fault' formulas specifically relates the amount of contribution payable to a calculation of the claimant and defendant wrongdoers' *respective* degrees of fault. For example, the Ontario statute provides:

> … where two or more persons are found at fault … [towards the plaintiff then] … as between themselves … each [of the persons [found at fault] is liable to make contribution and indemnify each other in the degree in which *they are respectively found* to be at fault or negligent.[58]

The British Columbia wording is:

> if 2 or more persons are found at fault … they are liable to contribute to and indemnify each other in the degree to which they are respectively found to have been at fault.[59]

All versions of the apportionment legislation specifically provide that the wrongdoers' liability to the injured person is 'joint and several'. That provision is in the legislation dealing with contributory fault, where the jurisdiction has separate

[56] See n 26.

[57] *Renaissance* (ONCA) (n 17); *Ingles v Tutkaluk Construction Ltd* 2000 SCC 12, [2000] 1 SCR 298; Cheifetz (n 1) 60–61; OLRC, 'Report' (n 4) 188–90.

[58] Negligence Act (n 26) s 1 (emphasis added). There are now small, grammatical differences in the text of the formulas of some of the various statutes, but the substance is the same.

[59] Negligence Act, RSBC 1996, c 333 s 4(2).

statutes for contributory fault and contribution. It is not in the separate contribution statutes which do not have similar, express, provisions dealing with the nature of the liability for contribution.[60] None of the versions use any version of 'several' in referring to the amount of contribution payable. That fact is a difference which ought to have been taken into account in interpreting the sections; that is, as evidence against the several liability interpretation.[61]

The words 'joint' and 'several' both had procedural as well as substantive meanings. The procedural meaning referred to whether the multiple alleged wrongdoers could be sued jointly in one action, or had to be sued separately, that is, severally. Given that there was no right of contribution between tortfeasors at common law, the procedural aspect is irrelevant. As there was no existing 'extent' of contribution liability from which to start, and the rationale for allowing contribution at all was to rectify an injustice, there seems no good reason to have started from 'several' – partial – liability rather than solidary liability without some explanation.

To the extent that the answer to the question 'why does Canadian common law consider contribution liability to be several?' turns on the text of the statutes, we have to assume that the conclusion was based on the apparent meaning of the phrase 'as between themselves … each is liable to make contribution and indemnify each other in the degree in which they are respectively found to be at fault or negligent' (or its equivalents) *without* considering whether 'respectively' might mean something more in the context of a contribution claim between two wrongdoers, where there are other wrongdoers who will not contribute. When all of the fault is divided among only two wrongdoers, the contribution allocation will always be calculated using the 'actual' degree in which they are respectively found to be at fault. However, the situation changes where there are three or more wrongdoers.[62]

[60] See, eg, Contributory Negligence Act, RSA 2000, c C-27, s 2(2) (Alberta) and Tort-Feasors Act, RSA 2000, c T-5 (Alberta); Contributory Negligence Act, RSNB 2011, c 131, s 3 (New Brunswick) and Tortfeasors Act, RSNB 2011, c 231 (New Brunswick). Both forms of statute specifically provide for a right of contribution in the jurisdictions that have both. The 'contributory negligence' statutes use the 'respective degrees of fault' formula; the 'tortfeasor' statutes the 'just and equitable amount' formula. Case law has established that contribution in tort is governed by the 'tortfeasor' statutes.

[61] *Alberta (Information and Privacy Commissioner) v University of Calgary* 2016 SCC 53 [53], [2016] 2 SCR 555, and *Agraira v Canada (Public Safety and Emergency Preparedness)* 2013 SCC 36 [81], [2013] 2 SCR 559: '[f]irst, according to the presumption of consistent expression, when different terms are used in a single piece of legislation, they must be understood to have different meanings. If Parliament has chosen to use different terms, it must have done so intentionally in order to indicate different meanings.'

[62] The OLRC, *Report* (n 4), 48, recognised this. The situation to which its proposal applies is founded on there being three or more wrongdoers. It is also correct to say that, when contribution liability is being recalculated because a wrongdoer is unable to pay, the actual degrees of fault, or the comparative degrees of fault of the wrongdoers, as originally calculated, are not changed. All that is changed is the amount that each has to pay, because the total is divided among fewer people. The involvement of an at-fault injured person does not change the situation, because the plaintiff's share of fault is calculated as if there is only one wrongdoer. After that, the plaintiff's share is deducted, leaving the balance to be allocated among the wrongdoers. See *Ingles* (n 57) [55], [60].

I am not aware of any consideration of this issue in any Canadian decision before or after *Renaissance*.[63] I believe there are none. The most one can say is that, for whatever reason, the judges in the initial cases, proceeding from the comparative blameworthiness principle, must have been satisfied that the legislation should be interpreted to produce several liability for contribution, only, with the relevant degree of fault being that determined in the initial apportionment of the 100 per cent of fault.[64] The necessary implication of several liability in the result in *Ingles v Tutkaluk Construction Ltd* and the court's explanation of the calculations is a statement of the state of the current law without analysis as to its origins or adequacy.[65]

In *Apportionment*, I stated that contribution liability was several, referring only to the wording of the formula and comparing the situation to that of co-debtors, between whom contribution liability is also several.[66] I did not cite any cases in which the assertion was specifically made. It was a statement of what the practice was. The Ontario legislation was enacted in 1930. *Apportionment* was primarily an analysis of the Ontario legislation, but I would have looked for cases from the rest of Canada. I no longer have my research for the text, but I am satisfied that had I found a case, and realised what I had found, I would have cited it.

In any event, I still did not find a case when the issue next arose because of *Renaissance* – nor did the trial judge, or the Court of Appeal – and I wrote 'Allocating' and its two postscripts.[67] In *Renaissance*, the Ontario Court of Appeal treated the question of the nature of contribution liability as settled. The court stated, without referring to case law and without providing any analysis, that contribution liability 'is several, not joint, and a defendant [to a claim for contribution] cannot be required to pay more than his or her share of a tort victim's damage or loss in accordance with the apportionment of fault'.[68] The Court of Appeal set aside the trial judge's decision that the proper interpretation of the Ontario wording allowed him to distribute, as between W1 and W2, for contribution purposes, the insolvent W3's amount of contribution liability so that W1, alone, did not bear the burden of W3's share.[69] The Court of Appeal dealt with the issue in a summary fashion, holding the legislation did not permit it:[70]

> … [I]n its exhaustive study on the subject of contribution, *Report on Contribution Among Wrongdoers and Contributory Negligence*, (Toronto: Ministry of Attorney General, 1988)

[63] *Renaissance* (n 17).

[64] I have never found a contemporaneous case specifically considering that issue for the Canadian legislation.

[65] *Ingles* (n 57) [55], [60] applies that rule but does not cite case law or other scholarship. The specific passage is quoted at n 101.

[66] Cheifetz (n 1) 60.

[67] See n 8 above.

[68] *Renaissance* (ONCA) (n 17) [48].

[69] ibid. The trial judge's rationale, adopting the analysis of the United Kingdom legislation, was that this was the just and equitable interpretation of the Ontario legislation, notwithstanding the different wording.

[70] ibid, [52].

> at pp. 47–48, the Ontario Law Reform Commission concluded that it would be equitable to allow the court to divide the share of a wrongdoer 'insolvent or otherwise unavailable to satisfy her share of liability' between the remaining wrongdoers in proportion to their respective degrees of fault. However, the legislature has not yet acted on that recommendation. The situation as among wrongdoers who are all sued and all found to be jointly and severally liable to the plaintiff may be different but I can see no basis for dividing the share of an insolvent wrongdoer in the circumstances of the present case. As I have explained above, Frazer was never sued by Mellanby, and his exposure to liability is to Renaissance for contribution assessed according to his own degrees of fault or negligence.

The Court did not conduct its own analysis of the text of the legislation. It did not explain why it might make a difference if all of the wrongdoers had been sued. The last sentence is a non sequitur. The fact that the injured person never sued W2 is irrelevant. The extent of W2's liability for contribution was always a question of what the legislation means.

I am not aware of any decision since *Renaissance* in which a judge considered the suggestion in the Court Appeal's reasons that there might be circumstances in which the distribution of the contribution share of the insolvent wrongdoer among solvent wrongdoers is justified.

The principles of statutory interpretation in the context of contribution legislation set out, above, are applicable regardless of the form of the contribution legislation. The question is to what extent the principles allow distribution of an 'uncollectable' contribution share in the context of the contribution formula, which is: 'in the degree in which they [the wrongdoer claiming contribution and the wrongdoer from whom contribution is claimed] are respectively found to be at fault'. The claim in this chapter is that the interpretation rules reiterated by the Supreme Court of Canada in *Schrenk*[71] and the purpose of contribution legislation require the existence in both forms of legislation of some process for distribution, in appropriate circumstances, amongst wrongdoers with exigible assets, of the contribution share of wrongdoers from whom contribution cannot be obtained reasonably.

C. The Comparative Fault Reading

The standard for apportionment is comparative blameworthiness. What one does is compare the extent to which each wrongdoer has departed from the particular standard of care applicable to that person. The Commonwealth 'practice is to look at such causative conduct in terms of relative or comparative blameworthiness or culpability; that is, to see in what degrees the parties departed from the norm of reasonable conduct.'[72]

[71] *Schrenk* (n 48).

[72] Klar (n 1) 674. See also Klar, ch 6 in this text, above at 146–47; Cheifetz (n 1) 99–102 (contribution), 232–33 (contributory fault); *Heller v Martens* 2002 ABCA 122 [30]–[41], 4 Alta LR (4th) 51.

Recall that contribution is a remedy for allocating the responsibility for damages among those in the group at fault who are able to pay, so as to bring about fairness in the allocation of the cost of indemnifying the injured person for the harm for which all are responsible. Recall, as well, that in a solidary liability regime, absent agreement or other specific exception, all wrongdoers are liable for all of the injured person's recoverable damages, not just a portion. So, as between the wrongdoers, it cannot be a basic principle of contribution that the extent of contribution liability be several. Rather, a basic principle of contribution liability is that the apportionment between the wrongdoers must be just, or just and equitable, if one believes that equitable adds something.[73]

The comparative fault reading of the 'degrees of fault' formulas means that contribution legislation is to be understood to allow the calculation of the amount of contribution liability to be based on the ratio of the degrees of fault assigned to the contribution claimant and contribution defendant(s), not based on their actual percentages.[74] That difference does not produce a different result in instances of only two wrongdoers, or instances of three or more, where all have assets and are prepared to contribute. It produces a different result *only* in the situation where there are three or more wrongdoers and some, but not all contribute. The difference is that the 'shares' of the wrongdoers not contributing are divided amongst the wrongdoers contributing, in accordance with the ratios of the latter's respective degrees of fault. The result is that none of the contributing wrongdoers, alone, absorb the shares of the wrongdoers who have not contributed. This is the just result required by the principles of contribution, regardless of the taxonomic category in which one places contribution.[75]

The consequences of the comparative fault reading are entirely consistent with the purpose of the contribution remedy: 'a mechanism for each of those who contributed to the loss to share the financial responsibility in the proportions of their respective degrees of fault'.[76]

This redistribution of the amount of contribution liability will be done *after* the initial 'true' allocation of fault as between all of the persons found to be at fault.[77] The initial allocation establishes their actual relative or comparative blameworthiness. A subsequent distribution of the financial share of a wrongdoer who is unable to pay, where the distribution of the share is in accordance with the comparative blameworthiness of the contribution claimant(s) and contribution defendant(s),

[73] Common law contribution between co-debtors was several; but equitable contribution could be solidary: Mitchell (n 1) 71, para 4.11.

[74] Cheifetz (n 8) 198–204.

[75] See Part V, below.

[76] *Martin* (n 32) [34].

[77] The approach in *Martin*, ibid, is to ignore persons not at fault who are not party to the action if their only relevance is to degrees of fault, rather than the question of whether the person was at fault at all. Ignoring the presence of others who are at fault, at the initial stage, is contrary to principle and creates a legion of unnecessary, intractable apportionment issues which are beyond the scope of this chapter. I reviewed the issues in some detail in Cheifetz (n 8) 31, and its two postscripts (n 32).

does not change their comparative blameworthiness. The redistribution of the 'uncollectable' contribution share eliminates the contribution recovery shortfall, regardless of how fault shares are calculated initially. The result amounts to a form of solidary liability for contribution.[78] If, for contribution purposes only, all of the wrongdoers' fault is allocated to those wrongdoers involved in the action and who have assets, the result could be seen as a just allocation of responsibility as between those wrongdoers, regardless of whether it is, or is not, just as between them and any other wrongdoer.

The 'respectively to one another' interpretation – which compares the fault of the wrongdoers for the purposes of calculating the amount of contribution liability – provides a just solution to the risk of a contribution recovery shortfall. It is, at least, equally consistent with the text of the contribution formula as the traditional interpretation. It is the better interpretation because it provides a just solution to a problem created by the traditional interpretation. Contribution is an issue of how much one wrongdoer should reimburse another, so it makes more sense to base the amount payable on the comparative blameworthiness of the contribution claimant and contribution defendant to one another, rather than to the injured person. If 'respectively' in the formula is interpreted to mean 'respectively to one another' then the formula becomes 'in the degree in which they are *respectively to one another* found to be at fault' and not 'in the degree in which they are *respectively to the injured person and one another* found to be at fault.'

D. Solution from Principle: Basic Contribution Principle

Ernest Weinrib wrote, decades ago, that contribution 'provides a mechanism for the achievement of the fundamental policy which Aristotle termed corrective justice.'[79] If we accept that statement, as we should, then the default rule should be that succinctly stated in *Dubai Aluminium*:

> [t]he object of contribution proceedings … is to ensure that each party responsible for the damage makes an appropriate contribution to the cost of compensating the plaintiff, regardless of where that cost has fallen in the first instance.[80]

Assuming solidary liability to the injured person, then, as between the wrongdoers, there is no reason in principle to require the wrongdoer(s) sued by P to

[78] Cheifetz (n 8) 198–204. The statement in *Martin* (n 32) [34] that the purpose of apportionment legislation in the contribution context is to provide 'a mechanism for each of those who contributed to the loss to share the financial responsibility in the proportions of *their respective degrees of fault*' should be seen as an invitation to adopt the comparative fault interpretation of the contribution formula. (Emphasis added.) The *Martin* statement of purpose is the same as that in *Dubai Aluminium* (n 14) [167] quoted at the text associated with n 80.

[79] Weinrib (n 46) 349–50.

[80] *Dubai Aluminium* (n 14) [52].

bear the entire risk as the starting principle. In any contribution claim, it should always be possible (but not required) for the court to distribute, between the contribution claimant and contribution defendants, the contribution shares of the wrongdoers from whom contribution is not available, so that the burden of payment is shared fairly between those able to pay, regardless of who first paid the injured person. The considerations will be justice between the parties to the contribution claim and, where appropriate, the broader concerns of the justice system.

In principle, it seems that, in the usual instance, there is a good argument that redistribution ought to be unjust where the contribution defendant has previously settled with the injured person for a fair estimate of only the contribution defendant's 'basic' share, even where the contribution defendant knew, or ought to have known, that one or more of the other wrongdoers lacked assets. This suggestion is based on the accepted premise that solutions which foster settlements are desirable.

IV. Other Issues in Contribution Jurisprudence

This part addresses two significant issues:

(1) is contribution available from a contribution defendant who, since the occurrence of the harm, has acquired a defence to any claim by the injured person, other than one that asserts that the contribution defendant has already paid the injured person the contribution defendant's share? This is also described as the 'no benefit to the contribution defendant' issue; a problem seemingly requiring an exception to basic principle, or statutory amendment, if contribution is a remedy in unjust enrichment;[81] and

(2) the meaning of the requirement that (actual or potential) liability of the contribution claimant and contribution defendant to the injured person be in respect of 'same damage' or 'same damages' as a precondition to contribution.

[81] Orthodox unjust enrichment doctrine in Canada and the United Kingdom requires the payment that the claimant seeks to recover to have created a loss to the claimant and a corresponding gain to the recipient. See Mitchell (n 1) 51–52, paras 3.13–3.16 and 122, para 6.05 specifically on contribution understood as an unjust enrichment remedy. Mitchell (n 1) para 6.05: 'Claims for contribution … are claims in unjust enrichment and a claim in unjust enrichment will not lie unless the defendant has been enriched.' (Internal footnotes omitted.) See also D Cheifetz, 'Contribution Between Negligent Tortfeasors and Unjust Enrichment: An Outline of a Solution to the "No Benefit to B" Issue' (2016) 53 *Alberta Law Review* 879. In that article, I outlined how existing unjust enrichment principle can be used to justify an exception to the requirement of an actual benefit to W2 from W1's payment to P, so that once-existing liability of W2 to P is, in principle, sufficient. That is, it becomes the reason for – but not the fact of – the now-existing immunity that W2 has to P, that determines whether the contribution claim may succeed.

A. Contribution from a Wrongdoer Who has Become Immune to P

A contribution defendant who would have been liable to an injured person for the amount paid by the contribution claimant wrongdoer has received a benefit as a result of that payment. Any potential liability the contribution defendant might have had to the injured person for that amount has been extinguished.[82] That point, alone, should be sufficient to make the courts re-think any analysis of contribution doctrine that produces unjust results as between contribution claimants and contribution defendants, subject to the proper interpretation of applicable legislation.

In most cases, W1's payment, when made to the injured person P, reduces the potential liability of W2 (or W3, W4, etc) to P by some portion. However, in a few cases, W1's payment will not reduce W2's potential liability to P, because W2 will not have any. This might be because: (1) W2 acquired immunity to P *after* the event that injured P; or (2) there was a pre-existing relationship between W2 and P which provided W2 with an immunity that W2 would not otherwise have had, in relation to P's harm, which would otherwise have been actionable against W2; or (3) for some other reason, under the legal system that governs, P never could have had a cause of action against W2 in relation to the particular harm. There is disagreement in the scholarship about whether it is a core requirement of the right that the payment in fact reduce W2's potential liability to P, or whether the requirement is merely that it could and would have done so, but for some event that occurred after the injured person sustained the harm.[83]

I have consistently argued for the latter position; that, in justice and principle, the sufficiency of once-existing potential for liability to the injured person is the better and correct position.[84] Others, however, disagree, essentially on the basis that, as the remedy is in unjust enrichment, a benefit to the wrongdoer from whom contribution is sought is a necessary condition of the existence of the contribution right.[85] My current, albeit only somewhat reluctant, belief is that, if contribution is an unjust enrichment remedy, as unjust enrichment is currently explained in United Kingdom and Canadian law, then, in principle: (1) the existing benefit requirement (which becomes the still-existing potential for liability principle in contribution) will have to govern, (2) absent a specific exception in unjust enrichment principle for contribution on the grounds of justice, or (3) a different rule by statute.[86] I believe that a better, more coherent, principled approach is to recognise

[82] The premise, here, is that the situation is not one where, for some reason, the injured person is allowed double recovery.

[83] See n 81 and the text associated with nn 84–85.

[84] See, eg, Cheifetz (n 1) and Cheifetz (n 8).

[85] See, eg, Mitchell (n 1) paras 3.13–3.15, 6.05.

[86] This is not the case, however, if contribution is not a remedy in unjust enrichment. See the text associated with nn 87–90 and Part V – hence my 'only somewhat reluctant belief'. Taking contribution

that the contribution right is not a right in unjust enrichment, notwithstanding that its application corrects an injustice.[87]

Some of the Canadian jurisdictions have dealt with what I have called the 'no benefit to the contribution defendant' problem by statute, if only for the instance where W2's immunity to P is the result of the expiration of the limitation period governing P's action against W2. The statutes provide, in effect, that the mere fact that the P's limitation period for suing W2 has expired does not of itself provide W2 with a defence to the contribution claim.[88] In some jurisdictions where there

out of unjust enrichment allows me to avoid the need to challenge, or distinguish the foundations of unjust enrichment scholarship.

[87] The common approach in unjust enrichment scholarship is to include contribution between wrongdoers: see, eg, A Burrows, *The Law of Restitution*, 3rd edn (Oxford, Oxford University Press, 2011) 459 ('contribution is concerned to effect restitution of an unjust enrichment') and generally c 17 especially 455–59; also C Mitchell, P Mitchell, S Watterson (eds), *Goff & Jones The Law of Unjust Enrichment*, 9th edn (London, Sweet & Maxwell, 2016) c 19–20. Mitchell left the taxonomic issue open in Mitchell (n 1), para 3.03. He wrote: the analysis 'proceed[s] on the basis that claims for contribution … should be classified as claims in unjust enrichment, regardless of whether they can also be classified as equitable claims, statutory claims, or claims at common law because '[i]n principle … there is no necessary opposition between the categories of equitable claim and claim in unjust enrichment' (internal quotation marks omitted). Instances of contribution do involve an injustice which needs to be corrected. However, the remedy for that injustice does not fall within the current doctrinal explanation of unjust enrichment, at least as it is explained in United Kingdom or Canadian law; nor could it if one accepts Peter Birks' summary of the defining characteristics. Peter Birks wrote in *Unjust Enrichment*, 2nd edn (Oxford, Oxford University Press, 2005) 38: 'Every case of unjust enrichment is materially identical to mistaken payment of a non-existent debt.' Whatever the essential elements of contribution between wrongdoers might be, they cannot be construed, validly, as equivalent to instances of mistaken payment for non-existent debt. Even if one does not accept this restriction – so including claims founded on legal compulsion or necessity, or if one uses unjust enrichment as an explanation for subrogation – there are other reasons why including contribution within the unjust enrichment remedy is problematic. For the most part, instances to which the unjust enrichment remedy is applicable are in some sense flawed. It is that flaw that, in the appropriate case, allows, but does not require, the application of the remedy. The 'restitutionary' order that is made if the claim is successful may be seen as either reversing or preventing the unjust enrichment by requiring the return of something of value (usually money) to the claimant. The effect of the order is to 'undo' the transaction that created the 'unjust enrichment'. It is as if it never happened (in law). There is no analogous reversal or prevention in contribution. No part of the events that are the source of the contribution right are flawed. The contribution claimant's recovery of contribution is not as a result of the reversal of the transaction in which the contribution claimant paid the injured person. The payment to the injured person is not 'undone'. The contribution claimant is reimbursed some amount – up to the value of W2's share: so in that sense there is a reversal of the claimant's 'loss' – if the contribution claim is allowed but that reversal or prevention (of W2's unjust enrichment) is not because W2 should never have received (the benefit of) the payment to P. A more comprehensive explanation is outside the scope of this chapter.

[88] See, eg, Limitations Act, RSA 2000, c L-12, ss 3(1.1) and 3(1.2) and *Whitecourt Power Limited Partnership v Elliott Turbomachinery Canada Inc* 2015 ABCA 252, [33]–[36]. Jurisdictions in which the contribution statute has been held to mean that still existing liability is a precondition, at least where W2 (the contribution defendant) has been held not to be liable to P on the basis of a defence such as a limitation or notice provision: Alberta – see *Parkland* (n 27) and *Howalta Electrical Services Inc v CDI Career Development Institutes Ltd* 2011 ABCA 234, 515 AR 163. Jurisdictions in which once-existing potential for liability has been held to be the governing principle, absent statute: British Columbia – *The Owners, Strata Plan LMS 1751 v Scott Management Ltd* 2010 BCCA 192, 318 DLR (4th) 567, leave to appeal denied 2010 CanLII 69205 (SCC); Nova Scotia – *MacKenzie v Vance* 1977 CanLII 1868, 74 DLR (3d) 383 (NSCA). See the discussion in Klar (n 1) 672–73 especially n 257. Ontario has legislation. The Ontario Negligence Act once had a specific provision dealing with the effect of the

is no statutory answer, the modern conclusion seems to be that, in principle, the mere fact that W2 is no longer liable to P does not provide W2 a defence to W1's contribution claim.[89] If and when the expiration of P's limitation period for suing W2 will be held to provide W2 with a defence to W1's contribution claim is a normative issue requiring evidence as to what is just between the parties and in the administration of justice.[90]

B. Same Damage or Same Damages and Related Issues

On the whole, Canadian jurisprudence does not struggle with the issue of the meaning of the 'same damage' or 'same damages' requirement, regardless of the form of the legislation.[91] The cases consider whether there could be concurrent liability amongst the wrongdoers for the loss alleged by the injured person in respect of which contribution is claimed without framing the issue in terms of the taxonomy of the liability that the contribution claimants and defendants may have to the injured person.

On the whole, Canadian judges seem to understand that, in principle, contribution cannot be available in 'one or the other' instances of liability to the injured person; that is, where the contribution defendant cannot, as a matter of law, be liable to the injured person for the damages in respect of which contribution is claimed.[92]

This 'one or the other' explanation is *not* how the 'same damage' or 'same damages' requirement is usually expressed in the Canadian jurisprudence, but it

expiration of the limitation period governing P's action against W2. That provision was repealed. It was not re-enacted or replaced by any analogous provision in any other statute. Nonetheless, in *Waterloo v Truax* (n 32) the Ontario Court of Appeal that the new Ontario Limitations Act was to be understood as having continued the law as it existed before the repeal of the specific provision in the Negligence Act. This decision is discussed in Cheifetz, 'Silk Purses' (n 32).

[89] Cheifetz (n 81).

[90] ibid.

[91] At least, most Canadian judges do not: see the cases listed in n 92 and associated text. The Ontario form does not have the 'same damage' or 'same damages' phrase in the section that creates the contribution right; however, the section has been interpreted as if it does in older cases: Cheifetz (n 1) 11.

[92] Contribution claims dismissed: *Lawson v Viersen* 2012 ONCA 25, 108 OR (3d) 771; *Davy Estate v CIBC World Markets Inc* 2009 ONCA 763, 97 OR (3d) 401. See however, *Wallace v Litwiniuk* 2001 ABCA 118, 92 Alta LR (3d) 249, which seems to stand for the proposition that, if the causes of action are taxonomically different, then the claims are not for the 'same damage'. In *Wallace*, P was injured in a motor vehicle accident. His lawyers did not commence P's action before the limitation period expired. P sued his lawyers. The lawyers claimed contribution from the other driver in the accident, alleging that the accident was caused or also caused by that driver's fault. The contribution claim was dismissed on the basis that P's claim against the lawyers and the claim P had against the driver were not for the same damage, because the causes of action were different. That analysis is not applicable to the reasoning in the Ontario decisions. *Wallace* should be understood as an 'either or' case, if one assumes that P's action against the negligent driver would have succeeded if commenced in time. If the action against the driver could succeed, the action against the lawyers had to fail. Conversely, the action against the lawyers could succeed if, and only if, the action against the driver was out of time.

seems to be what it means. There is both a factual and legal causation aspect to this issue, which is usually overlooked, or misunderstood, when decisions assert that contribution is available only as between concurrent wrongdoers. While we do have concurrent wrongdoers where the wrongful conduct of one or the other, but not both, may have been a cause of the harm, we do not have concurrent causation. The choices are alternatives. We have alternative causation. At the level of *factual causation*, 'one or the other' means that, if there is a finding that the conduct of one wrongdoer is a factual cause of the loss, then the conduct of the other wrongdoer cannot be a factual clause.

The situation is different (and conclusions regarding the availability of contribution may be more difficult) where the issue is concurrency at only the legal causation stage. Here, there is factual concurrency – the facts permit a finding of more than one person whose conduct was a factual cause – so the issue becomes whether there is a legal bar precluding the conclusion that the factually causal wrongful conduct of the contribution defendant is a legal cause. For example, the basis for a conclusion that some loss is too remote (not proximate) to be compensable in P's claim against W2 might not be applicable to P's claim against W1. If, as a matter of law, W2 may never be held liable to P for a particular loss, even if it was factually caused by W2's wrongdoing, then W2 is still a concurrent wrongdoer. However, W2's immunity to the claim by P provides a defence to the contribution claim.[93] It might be said that, since the purpose of determining cause in law is to determine legally responsibility, the wrongful act of W2 does not amount to a legal factual cause but is merely a condition of the loss.[94] Then, because W2 was *never* (even potentially) liable to P for this loss, it follows that as a matter of *current* contribution principle, W2 cannot be held liable to W1 for contribution.[95]

It is a question of contribution principle whether the law should distinguish between: (1) instances where W2 was 'never liable' as a result of some transaction between P and W2 predating the harm where W1 was not involved in the transaction in any relevant sense, and (2) instances in which W2 was never liable as a consequence of a rule of law that exists independently of the conduct of P and W2. It should be conceded that there is merit in the position that, in principle, W1 should not be prejudiced by the pre-loss conduct of W2 and P that is independent of W1 any more than by post-loss conduct of P and W2. That position would allow the law to decide, in the particular case, whether the factual basis for W2's defence is one that allows the conclusion that it should be preferred

[93] *Giffels v Eastern Construction* 1978 CanLII 39, [1978] 2 SCR 1346, 1354–56.

[94] C Sappideen and P Vines, *Fleming's The Law of Torts*, 10th edn (Sydney, Law Book Co, 2011) 229, para 9.30, and Klar (n 1) 523 and the text associated with footnotes 22–24, and especially n 22, on the explanations of law's distinctions between mere conditions and causes. This might be one way in which to make sense of the House of Lords decision in *Royal Brompton Hospital National Health Service Trust v Hammond and Others* [2002] UKHL 14, [2002] 1 WLR 1397; that is, the conduct of the contractor (W2) was a condition but not a legal cause of the employer's loss for which the architect (W1) was liable, and in respect of which the architect claimed contribution.

[95] *Giffels* (n 93).

over W1's contribution right. However, that argument in respect of W2's immunity to P acquired before the harm occurred is, in principle, contrary to *Giffels*, at least where W2's immunity arises out of a contract with P.[96] On its face, and in principle, the discussion in *Giffels* is not limited to immunity to P's claim acquired in a pre-harm contract.[97] This is not the same as a defence to P's claim acquired by W2 *after* the occurrence of the harm.[98]

In any event, *Giffels* is likely to govern all instances where W2 asserts an immunity to P's claim based on pre-loss events. *Giffels*, on strict stare decisis principles, is binding only on Ontario courts and only in relation to immunity acquired under a pre-harm contract. However, it is unlikely to be distinguished and limited on the disingenuous basis of different wording in the statutes.

C. The Mechanics (Process) of Apportionment and Other Issues

The jurisdictions which have separate contributory fault (negligence) and contribution statutes use the explicit 'respective degrees of fault' formula for contributory fault apportionment and the 'just and equitable' formula for contribution apportionment. The comparative blameworthiness principle governs both.[99] There is no logical basis for suggesting that the basic principles governing apportionment of fault as between wrongdoers should be different from those governing apportionment as between injured persons and wrongdoers. In principle, a person's status as an injured person or wrongdoer is irrelevant to the issues concerning the allocation and apportionment of fault. If a jurisdiction chooses to have different principles, that decision has to be seen as a normative decision to create an exception to principle.

The principles governing the manner by which shares of fault are to be determined and allocated are the same for contribution as for contributory fault: relative (meaning comparative) blameworthiness:

> Under negligence statutes, the basis of apportionment between concurrent tortfeasors is the same as in contributory negligence .... '[A]ssessing degrees of fault or the extent of a person's responsibility must relate to the relative culpability or blameworthiness of

[96] ibid.

[97] *Giffels* (n 93) 1354–56. Even if it were, the Supreme Court of Canada's decision in *R v Imperial Tobacco Canada Ltd* 2011 SCC 42, [2011] 3 SCR 45 is not, albeit without discussion of this issue. See [135]–[139].

[98] *Strata Plan* (n 88). See also *Howalta* (n 88) [70]: 'My concern is that we not interpret that legislation such that we replace the old rule with another one which likewise prevents a proper sharing of liability especially because the legislation was enacted for the express purpose of getting rid of the rule which prevented apportionment of liability.'

[99] *Heller v Martens* (n 72) (both formulas); *Parent v Janandee Management Inc* 2017 ONCA 922 [15] (relative degrees) citing and applying Klar (n 1) 674; additional cases listed in Klar (n 1) 674, fn 260.

> the parties. The apportionment decision depends upon which of the defendants failed most markedly to live up to the standards of conduct expected.[100]

That situation, which has to be correct in principle, has been accepted without reported discussion in the case law. I am not aware of any case in which a court considered whether the different formulas in the statutes of the same jurisdiction required the court to decide whether the legislature meant there to be different principles; nor the related issue of whether there ought to be some difference in the apportionment rules for contribution.

The decision to restrict redistribution of the contribution share of a wrongdoer from whom contribution is not available to the other wrongdoers, and not to include the injured person by allocating some portion of the 'immune to contribution' wrongdoer's fault share to the latter where the injured person is also at fault, is the logical consequence of the reason for maintaining solidary (joint) liability of wrongdoers to the injured person. It is a normative decision that is consistent with the principle of solidary liability. It is not a decision to have different principles governing apportionment, even where the injured person is in some relevant sense responsible for the contribution defendant's 'immunity'.

Where the injured person is at also at fault and there is more than one wrongdoer, the wrongdoers are treated as a unit for the contributory fault allocation; hence the total amount of the wrongdoers' fault to be apportioned among the wrongdoers is 100 per cent less the percentage of fault assigned to the injured person(s).[101]

> When there are two or more tortfeasors, and a plaintiff has also been found negligent, the proper approach to apportionment is to first reduce the extent of the recoverable damages in proportion with the plaintiff's negligence, and then to apportion the remaining damages between the defendants, in accordance with their fault … (citations omitted).

V. Conclusion

Weinrib wrote that contribution:

> provides a mechanism for the achievement of the fundamental policy which Aristotle termed corrective justice. It thus transcends, or should transcend, the individual compartments of tort and contract into which we have fragmented our conceptualization of the law.[102]

I have added unjust enrichment to the mix. Contribution, although it corrects an injustice and results in an award which is restitutionary in the sense that it

[100] Klar (n 1) 674.
[101] *Ingles* (n 57) [55]. See also Cheifetz (n 8) 324–26.
[102] Weinrib (n 46) 349–50.

results in reimbursement, is not a remedy in unjust enrichment. It is a remedy based on corrective justice with its own criteria. The fact that there may be 'no benefit to W2' in consequence of W2's acquired immunity to P, is not a bar to the remedy, but merely one factor to be taken into account in deciding whether it will be allowed in the particular case.[103]

The CRS solution does not create a problem of principle when contribution is understood as an equitable remedy which requires justice as between contribution claimant and contribution defendant. At the least, it should be conceded, though, that taking contribution out of the strictures of unjust enrichment might provide more flexible, non-statutory, judge-made, solutions. In any event, the correct answer to that issue is not required for this chapter to be complete. The premise is that contribution is available from the wrongdoers from whom it is sought. The issue is how fairly to apportion the contribution liability amongst the wrongdoers with assets to pay.

Where a wrongdoer has a *useful* contribution remedy, the wrongdoer may be more inclined to settle with an injured person or, at least, assuming liability, to pay fair compensation. As such, the contribution remedy, by providing a mechanism for each of those who caused the loss to share the financial responsibility in the proportion required by justice, may be said to help to facilitate full recovery of the loss for the injured person.[104]

[103] See n 87 and associated text.
[104] *Martin* (n 32); *Howalta* (n 88) [70]; *Dubai Aluminium* (n 14) [52], [167].

11

Reforming a Reform: Why Has It Been So Hard to Reform Proportionate Liability Reforms?

BARBARA McDONALD

I. Introduction

Proportionate liability has now been part of the litigation landscape in Australia for more than a decade. Where it applies – in tort, contract or statutory claims for economic loss or property damage arising from negligence or statutory claims for misleading or deceptive conduct – it replaces the common law approach of solidary, or joint and/or several, liability for wrongs. It was soon appreciated that this significant reform affects not just those involved in disputes and litigation. The regime also affects and sometimes even limits freedom of contract and the contractual imposition and restriction of liability in transactions, joint ventures and multi-party arrangements in a range of commercial and private contexts, including construction and infra-structure projects and the supply of professional services. It has thus become part of the landscape of commercial risk allocation as well.

In itself, the switch from several, or solidary, liability to proportionate liability is a relatively simple concept. Where several wrongdoers have contributed to a claimant's loss, each should only be liable for its just proportion of the loss, rather than being potentially 100 per cent liable under the system of joint and several liability and left to pursue any available contribution claims against other wrongdoers.

However, such a simple concept hides a number of issues of substance and practicality which add to the complexity of the scheme and its relationship to the existing contribution regimes, while the overall justice of the regime belies the simplistic notion of a defendant being liable only for its 'just proportion', which underpins much of the argument in favour of the regime. As Professor Andrew Burrows, former Law Commissioner for England and Wales, has put it:[1]

> [w]hile perhaps at first looking and sounding eminently reasonable, closer investigation reveals that proportionate liability would be contrary to both principle and sound policy. It would, in essence, replace harshness for defendants with glaring unfairness for plaintiffs.

Law reform bodies and many commentators were unconvinced of any pressing need, or convincing rationale for the proportionate liability regime before it was introduced and many tend to remain sceptical that its introduction has achieved any significant reduction in litigation or insurance costs, or improved efficiency or overall fairness in outcome. The expressed justifications for the regime – usually most stridently offered by parties who stand to benefit from it – have recently been thoroughly and convincingly debunked in Barker and Steele's analysis.[2] It is telling that the New Zealand Law Commission in its 2014 report was clearly unconvinced by the Australian experience that proportionate liability was better overall, as a matter of policy, than joint and several liability:[3]

> [The] Commission is of the view that fundamentally the policy issue comes down to a choice between a blameless plaintiff taking on the risk of an absent defendant, or a wrongdoer co-defendant taking on that risk. On this issue, the Commission comes down in favour of the innocent party. Unless there is some substantial reason of public policy that demands some adjustment, parties who have actually caused the harm are the parties who should bear that risk.

The Australian experience hardly provides a model: the most noticeable feature of proportionate liability in Australia is the variation in the regimes in different states and territories. This has added an undesirable, additional layer of complexity to an already complex regime, particularly for entities operating nationally across state boundaries, or for anyone caught up in intra-state transactions or disputes. It has meant there may be real advantages for one party if the applicable law is that of one state, rather than another: this may happen by accident, as in tort, or it may happen by design in contract. These variations between the regimes are thus a problem in themselves for parties, but they also inevitably invite the question: which of these regimes is the best?

The problems raised by the lack of uniformity or consistency across the country quickly saw a review of the proportionate liability regime come on to

[1] A Burrows, 'Improving Contract and Tort', in A Burrows (ed), *Understanding the Law of Obligations: Essays on Contracts, Tort and Restitution* (Oxford, Hart Publishing, 2000) 176, referring to the Law Commission of Great Britain's *Feasibility Investigation of Joint and Several Liability* (London, HMSO, 1996).

[2] K Barker and J Steele, 'Drifting Towards Proportionate Liability: Ethics and Pragmatics' [2015] 74 *CLJ* 49.

[3] New Zealand Law Commission, *Liability of Multiple Defendants* (Report 132, June 2014) 3.37.

the agenda of the Standing Committee of Attorneys-General (SCAG), which was subsequently renamed as, or replaced by, the Standing Committee of Law and Justice (SCIL). Yet the item itself became a standing item, as years went by without significant progress in reaching consensus. Reports were provided to SCAG by lawyer Tony Horan in 2007[4] and by Professor JLR Davis in 2008,[5] with consultation draft model provisions and regulatory impact statements released for discussion in 2011[6] and 2013.[7] 22 submissions were received in response to the 2013 draft model provisions.[8] In 2014, the Standing Committee of Law and Justice was replaced by the Law, Crime and Community Safety Council (LCCSC). However, it appears that the project on proportionate liability has been forgotten and in 2018 certainly no consensus for reform is apparent.

Over the same period, as cases dealing with interpretation of the statutes slowly made their way through the courts – as far as the High Court of Australia on two occasions[9] – litigants and commentators began to grapple with the practical impact of the reforms on defendants' liabilities and claimants' remedies. Those practical impacts can be measured against the predictions of fairness and unfairness that were argued by leading commentators at the outset.[10]

II. Overview

This chapter will look at the need for reform and the hurdles to uniformity, with emphasis on two issues on which there is an important variation between states, or on which there is a lack of consensus for further reform where reform is warranted.

It will then – briefly – consider whether some of the warnings as to potential unfairness in such a regime have proved true. In the author's view, the outcome of *Hunt & Hunt Lawyers v Mitchell Morgan Nominees Pty Ltd*,[11] while, with respect,

[4] T Horan, 'Proportionate Liability: Towards National Consistency', Report to the National Justice CEOs, September 2007, http://www.justice.tas.gov.au/__data/assets/pdf_file/0017/113624/Horan_Report.pdf.

[5] J Davis, 'Proportionate Liability: Proposals to Achieve National Uniformity', Report to the National Justice CEOs (2008) http://www.justice.tas.gov.au/__data/assets/pdf_file/0016/113623/Davis_Report.pdf.

[6] See SCIL archive on the LCCSC website: http://webarchive.nla.gov.au/gov/20141215123639/http://www.lccsc.gov.au/sclj/archive/former_sclj.html.

[7] *Proportionate Liability Model Provisions* (PCC-386, 26 September 2013, prepared on behalf of Parliamentary Council Committee of SCLJ by the ACT office): http://www.justice.nsw.gov.au/justice-policy/Documents/proportionate_liability_model_provisions.pdf.

[8] http://www.justice.nsw.gov.au/justicepolicy/Pages/lpclrd/lpclrd_consultation/lpclrd_bills.aspx.

[9] *Hunt & Hunt Lawyers v Mitchell Morgan Nominees Pty Ltd* [2013] HCA 10, (2013) 247 CLR 613; *Selig v Wealthsure Pty Ltd* [2015] HCA 18, (2015) 255 CLR 661.

[10] A Rogers 'Fairness or Joint and Several Liability' (2000) 8 *Torts LJ* 107; M Tilbury, 'Fairness Indeed?: A Reply to Andrew Rogers' (2000) 8 *Torts LJ* 113; Burrows (n 1) 175.

[11] *Hunt & Hunt* (n 9).

probably correct, clearly demonstrates the failings of the regime as a matter of fairness, justice and policy.

First, however, for the assistance of those who may wonder why Australian law on this point is in such a legal morass, the chapter will provide a brief introduction, explaining how and why proportionate liability was introduced into Australia.

III. The Proportionate Liability Legislation: Why and How it was Enacted

As Barker and Steele describe, despite the appeals to the economics of insurance viability and affordability, the regime is more appropriately seen as a political or policy choice than as an ethical, or economic one.[12] It was introduced at the urging of certain professional and other entities, typically potential defendants in proceedings where multiple actors were to blame for a claimants' loss yet whom, it was complained, were targeted as sole defendants due to their deep pockets, whether from professional indemnity insurance, tax or ratepayers' funds, or simply their corporate coffers of profits.

This is not the first, or the last time that these powerful lobby groups have been able to push the executive and the legislature into law reform for their own benefit. Surely the quickest legislative response in the Australian private law context to an inconvenient High Court of Australia decision was the reform of the contributory negligence apportionment legislation after the High Court in *Astley v Austrust Ltd*[13] took the words of the existing statute to mean what they said: that apportionment for contributory negligence only operated where contributory negligence would have been a complete defence before the statute, that is, in tort claims for negligence. The legislation thus did not assist defendants where the plaintiffs relied, as they could at their choice, on a breach of a concurrent contractual duty of care, even if this was co-extensive with the tort duty. After successful lobbying by the insurance and accountants' lobbies, the apportionment legislation around the country was amended in 2000 to allow apportionment for contributory negligence in such contractual claims.[14] Another example is the Australian Consumer Law, where, without explanation and somewhat inexplicably, there is an exception for qualified architects and engineers from the 'fit for purpose' guarantees for the supply of services.[15]

Proportionate liability was first proposed as a regime of limited application by the Davis Committee in 1995. The committee was headed by Professor JLR Davis

[12] Barker and Steele (n 2) 59.
[13] [1999] HCA 6, (1999) 197 CLR 1.
[14] See, eg, Law Reform (Miscellaneous Provisions) Act 1965 (NSW), s 9.
[15] Australian Consumer Law, Sch 2, Competition and Consumer Act 2010 (Cth), s 61.

of the Australian National University, and included former Justice Andrew Rogers QC, who had presided over the long-running *AWA Ltd v Daniels, t/a Deloitte, Haskins and Sells*[16] case, in which claims were brought against auditors. In his judgment Rogers J had stated:

> A well insured defendant, who may perhaps be responsible for only a minor fault, in comparison with the fault of the other persons, may nonetheless, be made liable, at least in the first instance, for the entirety of the damage by the plaintiff. The defendant may indeed seek contribution from other persons responsible for the major damage. Why should the whole of the burden of possibly insolvent wrongdoers, fall entirely on a well insured, or deep pocket defendant?[17]

The Committee's Stage Two Report in 1995 proposed that 'joint and several liability for negligence which causes only property damage or economic loss be replaced by liability which apportions fault, in all the circumstances, among those responsible for the damage or loss'.[18] In 1996, draft model provisions were released, but, because the model as a whole was opposed by law reform bodies in both New South Wales and Victoria, there was no discussion at all at the time of the detail of the proposed legislation. The push for reform, and open discussion of it, stalled.

However, come 2002 and the desire by Federal and State governments to be seen to be doing something about the so-called crisis relating to personal injury liability insurance at the time, large scale legislative tort reform was introduced to counteract apparently overgenerous 'Santa Claus' judges and, it was implied, unmeritorious victims blaming others for their self-inflicted misfortunes.[19] Despite the reforms being trumpeted as enacting greater 'personal responsibility' for one's own risk-taking activities and personal injuries, the legislators also slipped in proportionate liability for property damage and economic loss. One can imagine that it may only have been the refusal of the Ipp Committee which conducted the *Review of the Law of Negligence*[20] to recommend proportionate liability for personal injury that prevented the government from applying this defendant-friendly regime to all negligence claims. While the government was prepared to accept the rejection for personal injury claims, it did not think the Ipp Committee's

[16] (1992) 10 ACLC 993.

[17] ibid, 1022.

[18] JLR Davis, *Inquiry into the Law of Joint and Several Liability: Report of Stage Two* (Attorney-General's Department, Commonwealth of Australia, 1995) 32 (the Davis Report): http://138.25.65.17/au/journals/AUConstrLawNlr/1995/26.pdf.

[19] It was no coincidence that New South Wales Premier Robert Carr announced the new raft of 'personal responsibility' reforms at iconic Bondi Beach in Sydney. This had been the scene of the accident in *Swain v Waverley Council* (2005) 220 CLR 517, in which the High Court of Australia had upheld a jury verdict finding the local council liable for injuries Mr Swain received when he dived into shallow waves, between the flags set up by council lifesavers, and hit his head on a sandbank, causing paralysis.

[20] *Review of the Law of Negligence – Final Report* (September 2002) 173–79: https://treasury.gov.au/review/review-of-the-law-of-negligence/ (the Ipp Report).

criticisms held such force in relation to property damage and economic loss.[21] Yet recent events, such as the awful fatal fires from flammable cladding on apartment blocks and the ongoing risk in buildings where such cladding has been installed, show that there can be no easy or stark demarcation between liability for personal injury and liability for property damage or economic loss from defective construction work. There may be powerful reasons for imposing solidary responsibility for dangerous defects on any of those who had a necessary role in creating, or not preventing, this shocking risk to life.

The immediate explanation for the regime was that professional liability insurance was becoming unaffordable and that this was due to certain classes of defendants being targeted as deep pockets, rendered 100 per cent liable and being left to seek contribution, if they could, from others also responsible. Defendants thus bore the risk of the other, sometimes more culpable, wrongdoers being insolvent, wound up, or dead, or of their having absconded from the jurisdiction – the more likely scenario in cases involving corporate frauds which auditors had negligently failed to detect.

There are, of course, two issues here: one is the economic, or practical reality of insurance viability and affordability, and the impact on that of solidary, or proportionate liability. In very basic terms, insurance affordability through the setting of premiums is not merely a matter of 'funds in' and 'claims out'. It is also governed by the management of funds in between these two events and successful management, in turn, depends largely on local and global investment markets. In 2002, there had been two shocks to the system affecting returns on invested funds for Australian insurance companies: the impact on investor confidence from the terrorist events of September 11, 2001, and the collapse of re-insurer HIH Insurance Ltd through a combination of fraud and mismanagement. In addition, medical insurers were feeling the same heat of the global downturn and record levels of compensation being awarded for the life-time costs resulting from negligent obstetric care.[22] Of course, potential defendants in property and economic loss claims – and their insurers – will benefit, if they can reduce their primary liability by shifting the blame to others. But the trumpeted economic benefit of proportionate liability assumes that defendants will always be able to find some other wrongdoer to blame and that insurance premiums will reduce. Yet potential defendants still need to insure themselves against being solely responsible, and premiums no doubt are set to reflect this risk.

A concern for providing incentives for insurers to remain in particular insurance markets can be seen in a comment by the relevant minister of the government

[21] R Debus, 'Tort Reform in New South Wales: State and Federal Interactions' (2002) 25 *University of New South Wales LJ* 825, picking up a point made in the *Davis Report* (n 18) 32–33. Tilbury (n 10) 118, describes the distinction as 'completely unprincipled' and as not recognising the very real vulnerability of some victims of negligently-caused 'pure economic loss.'

[22] See, eg, *Diamond v Simpson (No 1)* [2003] NSWCA 67.

in Victoria, when joint and several liability was replaced by proportionate liability in the building and construction industry:[23]

> This reform is one of the major factors that will give insurers the incentive to stay in the construction industry. Together with the new compulsory insurance requirement, the measures will establish a fair and responsible liability regime.

It was apparently the case that insurers were refusing to insure some builders, or would do so only at an exorbitant price, which was said to make it difficult for the builders to compete.[24] With great respect, one would have thought that the measure of requiring compulsory insurance by builders, alone, would guarantee a very ready and profitable market for insurers, and steadier premiums. However, it also illustrates that proportionate liability would operate much more beneficially for a plaintiff if it formed part of a regime where all relevant actors were covered by compulsory insurance.

As Barker and Steele point out,[25] and as the New Zealand Law Commission noted, there is no actual evidence of the impact on insurance affordability of either system:[26]

> The appeal of proportionate liability rests on supporting industry or commerce by promoting economic efficiency. When there is no sound evidence that it would be more efficient within the wider economy for our country as a whole to move this risk to the innocent party [the plaintiff] via a proportionate liability regime, the Commission finds that there can be no justification to depart from our current rule of joint and several liability.

In the absence of evidence, reliance on economic arguments appears theoretical, or mere assertion (or optimism) at best.

The other issue that was at the heart of the justification of the regime was the matter of fairness: defendants argued that it was not fair that they should bear the risk of other, often more culpable, defendants not paying up. Even if all equally to blame, why should one be 100 per cent liable when it had only been one of, say, four entities responsible? The two sides of the fairness argument had been keenly and concisely debated two years before the Civil Liability Acts reforms in the *Torts Law Journal* by Andrew Rogers QC, a member of the Davis Committee and a strong proponent of proportionate liability, on the one hand, and by Professor Michael Tilbury, then head of the NSW Law Reform Commission, which had opposed the scheme, on the other.[27]

[23] Second Reading Speech, Building Bill 1993, the Hon RR MacLellan, Victorian Parliament, Hansard, 11 November 1993, quoted by Rogers (n 10) 110.

[24] *Boral Resources Pty Ltd v Robak Engineering & Construction Pty Ltd* [1999] VSCA 66 [12] (Batt JA), [71] (Chernov J).

[25] Barker and Steele (n 2) 70–72.

[26] NZ Law Commission (n 3) 3.38.

[27] Tilbury (n 10). As Rogers noted in his comment (n 10) 108, the New Zealand Law Reform Commission and the English Law Commission (sic) had already also opposed such reforms.

Rogers' views were particularly influenced by what he had seen, as the judge in *AWA v Daniels*, as the unfairly heavy burden placed on auditors by joint and several liability after the 'excesses of the 1980s in the financial and corporate world',[28] although he recognised that any regime would be of general application.

Rogers was responding to a report of the New South Wales Law Reform Commission on contribution between persons liable for the same damage.[29] He noted, first, that there had been a worldwide tendency to focus on comparative fault in determining compensation, in the sense of making reductions for contributory negligence of a plaintiff and saw no reason why this trend should not progress to look at comparative fault of multiple defendants at a primary stage of the proceedings, rather than 'further down the chain in the contribution proceedings'.[30] He then relied heavily on the repeated 'economic' insurance-based arguments found in the justifications for the Victorian building industry scheme quoted above and concluded that, therefore, the reform was as warranted for auditors as it had been for builders. In fact, he argued it was warranted 'right across the commercial world' and even in the case of doctors, who needed an adjustment of insurance premiums as much as construction workers.[31] There was no recognition of the critical part played by the compulsory insurance requirement in achieving the affordability, viability and loss-spreading impacts of the Victorian building scheme.

Rogers' then re-iterated the oft-repeated assertions made by stakeholders on fairness. However, what is striking about the 'fairness' arguments put up by proponents of proportionate liability is that none admits to the just and basic rationale for joint and several liability that can be found in causation principles: before any of these hard-done-by defendants could be liable, their negligence must have been a necessary cause of the *whole of the plaintiff's loss*.[32] 'But for' the negligence of each one of them, the plaintiff would not have suffered *any* of *that* loss. Putting it another way for emphasis, if any one of them had carried out their functions with due care, the plaintiff could not have suffered *any of the loss claimed at all*. Even leaving to one side the cases where a particular, deep-pocketed defendant had voluntarily taken on a supervisory, or gatekeeper role[33] – auditors, supervising architects or builders, lawyers – the basic causation requirement of liability provides a powerful justification, without more, for joint and several liability.

[28] Rogers (n 10) 107.

[29] New South Wales Law Reform Commission, *Contribution Between Persons Liable for the Same Damage* (Report 89, 1999).

[30] Rogers (n 10) 108. Barker and Steele (n 2) 56, explain the flaw in this argument and the drawing of an unsupportable link between the two doctrines: the reasoning behind the introduction of apportionment for contributory negligence was to *relieve* plaintiffs from the harshness of the defence which had excused defendants from liability entirely. It does not follow that plaintiffs should be *unable* to recover in full from defendants who are liable to them, simply because someone else happens to also be at fault.

[31] Rogers (n 10) 110.

[32] The situation is of course quite different if the plaintiff's loss is divisible into parts, each of which was separately caused by a different defendant who will be solely liable for that part. In one sense, proportionate liability is trying to treat all losses as if they were divisible.

[33] As will be discussed below in relation to the decision in *Hunt & Hunt* (n 9).

Professor Tilbury, a Commissioner (part-time) at the New South Wales Law Reform Commission and Academic Secretary of the Victorian Attorney-General's Law Reform Advisory Council, replied strongly to Rogers' criticisms and assertions, describing them as fallacious. Noting the causal requirements for liability, Tilbury asks:[34]

> What possible relevance is the existence of other defendants to liability between the instant defendant and the instant plaintiff where, ex hypothesi, the instant defendant has caused the damage? A fortiori, if the blunt operation of the law is mitigated by giving the instant defendant … a right of contribution against others who have caused the same damage.

Moving on to the fairness arguments of only holding defendants liable for their 'share', Tilbury notes that:[35]

> The problem is that this identifies fairness or justice only from the defendant's point of view. Generalised rules of law cannot be formulated on so narrow a basis. The interests of the plaintiff must be taken into account.

Tilbury identifies three arguments in favour of joint and several liability: full liability on each defendant promotes efficient deterrence by promoting compliance with standards; the defendant can absorb the loss through insurance while the plaintiff is unlikely to be able to obtain insurance against others' wrongdoing; and the wrongdoer should bear the burden of complexity of legal proceedings, not the innocent plaintiff. He notes that there is little evidence that the increase in insurance costs in the 1980s and 1990s inhibited economic, business, or entrepreneurial activity.

Somewhat surprisingly, Tilbury takes seriously an argument that was not raised by Rogers, but which was raised by stakeholders in consultations with the New South Wales Law Reform Commission: what Tilbury describes as a 'very genuine concern' of defendants with 'the moral condemnation which is perceived to be inherent in a judgment against them for full liability' and its reputational effect. He notes that this 'constitutes a real unfairness for defendants in the regime of joint and several liability'. However, it is hard to see the unfairness here. In the case, for example, of auditors picking up the bill for losses wrought by fraudulent employees or directors which the auditors should have detected, the judgment rests on causative negligence, but not fraud or moral wrongdoing. The inference from the judgment is supported by the truth: the defendant *was* negligent when reasonable care would have avoided *all* the loss for which it is held liable. Has not the defendant 'earned' this dint in its reputation? Nevertheless, despite his sympathy for the reputational argument, Tilbury noted the range of situations involving multiple wrongdoers and concluded that this factor alone was not

[34] Tilbury (n 10) 114.
[35] ibid, 116.

sufficient to warrant a generalised system of proportionate liability that would often operate in a manifestly unfair way.

Tilbury was, like most academics and all current judges, a disinterested commentator, but the New Zealand Law Commission notes:

> Not surprisingly, views on which rule is better, fairer or more efficient tend to divide neatly according to whether a person is more likely to be a plaintiff or a defendant. The views on either side are often strongly entrenched, and there is no consensus on which system is fairer.[36]

So, with no reference to the law reform bodies which had rejected the proposals, proportionate liability was introduced into the legislative programme of tort reform in the New South Wales Parliament in October 2002, without explanation.

The lack of uniformity in the Australian regime can be partly explained by the piecemeal and independent introduction of the regime that then followed across the country. It did not commence as a uniform programme of legislation across the States and Territories, such as that which gave rise to the uniform Defamation Acts of 2005 or (across federal and state levels) the Australian Consumer Law. While the second round of tort reform, of which it was part, passed through New South Wales Parliament in October 2002, the proportionate liability provisions did not come into effect until the then Trade Practices Act 1974 (Cth) (the 'TPA') was amended to apply proportionate liability also into claims for misleading or deceptive conduct. This was because it had been recognised that most claims for professional negligence – a specific concern of the Davis Committee – were accompanied by a claim of misleading or deceptive conduct (for example, based on implied representations that due care and skill had been exercised), so that proportionate liability in tort or contract claims would be useless to the defendant, if a plaintiff could get around the regime by suing under the TPA on the same facts. The new TPA provisions and the NSW provisions commenced in 2004. But in the meantime, Victoria's scheme, under amendments to the Wrongs Act 1958, had already commenced in 2002, while Queensland's Civil Liability Act was enacted, with less haste and seemingly more careful thought on statutory wording, in 2003. Other states and territories followed, with variations.

IV. Hurdles to Uniformity

There are several aspects on which the regimes differ in the various states and which have proved contentious in the push for uniformity. This chapter will concentrate on two aspects:[37]

(1) Which claims, or causes of action, should be subject to proportionate liability, that is, 'apportionable'?

[36] NZ Law Commission (n 3) iv, Foreword.

[37] One question is whether courts should consider only the contribution of parties to the action when determining the apportionment of each defendant. In essence, the issue is whose responsibility

(2) Whether or not parties should be free to 'contract out' of the regime. To determine this, and to determine the effect of any prohibition, it is necessary also to identify what types of contractual arrangements amount to 'contracting out'.

A. Which Claims Should Be Apportionable?

While there is not a wide variation in Australian legislation on this issue, the application of the regime remains contentious. There are in fact two questions here. The first question is: given the intent of Parliament, how should apportionable claims best be defined in the legislation? This is partly a matter of drafting but, unfortunately, infelicitous drafting has a way of effecting substantive change by over-literal, or tendentious interpretation. The substantive change then becomes the status quo, which is hard to shift, particularly if it benefits influential stakeholders. The second question is openly substantive: if we were taking the opportunity to start afresh, which causes of action *should* be apportionable?

Professor Tilbury in his response to Rogers' critique, pointed out that there was nothing in the terms of reference for the Davis Report of 1995 that required the recommendations be limited to actions in negligence.[38] Further, somewhat oddly (or disingenuously?) for someone who opposed proportionate liability so strenuously, he stated: 'There is absolutely no reason why proportionate liability should be restricted to claims in negligence'.[39]

Nevertheless, as Tilbury admits, the Davis Report shows that the concern of that committee was with claims in the tort of *negligence*, or for breach of contractual duties of *care*, and statutory claims for misleading or deceptive conduct. There is simply no discussion on other causes of action. Auditors, for example, are sued for failing to exercise reasonable care in carrying out their auditing role for a company: the claim is both contractual and tortious. Auditors do not have a strict liability at common law to provide accurate reports which would arise regardless of lack of fault on their part. Negligence would need to be proven by the plaintiffs. Auditors would probably also be liable for misleading or deceptive conduct under Australian statute law for loss caused by inaccuracies in their audit report.

Similarly, we see that the proportionate liability reforms were introduced into the New South Wales Parliament as part of the 'the most fundamental changes to the law of *negligence* ever made' (emphasis added).[40] There was absolutely no discussion of any possible impact on strict contractual undertakings or rights, or

it should be, in terms of legal work and costs, to ensure that all possible, legally-liable contributors to the loss are brought to court in a particular matter. It should not be assumed that it will always be more efficient and more just to put that burden on the plaintiff. Another question is whether proportionate liability should benefit wrongdoers who are jointly liable to the plaintiff. A positive answer to the latter notion effectively destroys joint liability and would significantly reduce the rights of plaintiffs.

[38] Tilbury (n 10) 115.

[39] ibid.

[40] Second Reading, Civil Liability (Personal Responsibility) Act 2002, New South Wales Legislative Assembly, Premier Robert Carr, Hansard, 23 October 2002.

other forms of strict liability, such as indemnities or claims in equity. There was no discussion that freedom of contract would be restricted: if anything, the thrust of other reforms in the tort reform packages was to allow parties to limit liabilities in negligence by contract, for example, in the context of recreational services.

So too in Queensland, when the then Attorney-General, the Hon RJ Welford, delivered the Second Reading Speech for the Civil Liability Bill 2003, he spoke of the need for reform of the law of *negligence*, with particular emphasis on personal injury damages and the amendments to the general law on breach of duty, causation, inherent risks, contributory negligence and other defences. With respect to proportionate liability, he went on:[41]

> The bill provides a major change to the apportionment of loss between parties to an action for property damage or economic loss. In these categories of claim and liability, the bill abolishes joint and several liability for property damage or economic loss in actions involving more than one defendant. In such actions, a court will now assess the proportionate liability of each defendant party, taking into account any contributory negligence and then each defendant will be responsible only for payment of their respective portion of the damages. This is in response to the concerns raised by professional bodies about excessive professional indemnity premiums and the potential for unlimited liability from large claims. It should be pointed out that the principle of proportionate liability, introduced in this way, will not apply to personal injury claims.
>
> The bill has been carefully framed to ensure that average consumers are protected in claims for negligent professional advice, giving rise to damages for which compensation might be apportioned. The scheme of proportionate liability will apply only where damages are assessed in excess of $500,000, thus protecting smaller-scale claims involving consumers of lesser commercial sophistication. Proportionate liability will also not apply:
>
> - where multiple defendants form a common intention to cause the loss; or
> - where one defendant is the agent of another; or
> - where one defendant was engaged to provide professional advice for the express purpose of preventing the loss actually incurred due to action by another party; or
> - where the defendant was fraudulent.
>
> In these cases, the defendant will be held liable for the entire damages suffered and liability for damages will not be apportioned. These measures will ensure that average consumers are protected in their dealings with professionals and with corporations.

It can be seen that there is no discussion of what actions are captured, but the speech as a whole is about liability in *negligence*. It must be assumed then that the intent of the parliaments was to introduce proportionate liability only for *negligence* claims, at least as far as the common law was concerned.

[41] Legislative Assembly, Parliament of Queensland, Hansard, 11 March 2003, 368: https://www.parliament.qld.gov.au/documents/hansard/2003/030311HA.PDF.

i. Which Legislative Model Best Encapsulates That Intent?

Leaving to one side, for the moment, claims based on breaches of federal and state statutory prohibitions of misleading or deceptive conduct, most States and Territories follow the New South Wales model, which defines an 'apportionable claim' as including 'a claim for economic loss or damage to property in an action for damages (whether in contract, tort or otherwise) arising from a failure to take reasonable care, but not including any claim arising out of personal injury.'[42] In contrast, in Queensland, an apportionable claim is defined as 'a claim for economic loss or damage to property in an action for damages arising from a breach of a duty of care.'[43]

The Queensland definition is certainly the most consistent with the original intent of the regime, as implied by the extrinsic materials referred to above, that, as far as the common law was concerned, proportionate liability should apply to claims *for negligence*. It was well-accepted by that time that claims for negligence could rest on a tortious or a contractual duty of care.[44] Although most statutory obligations, prohibitions or liabilities are couched in strict terms, it may also be the case that a statutory duty requires merely reasonable care for compliance, and thus the claim would be one for negligence.

The problem with the NSW provision is the ambiguity of its drafting. The specific ambiguities are: do the words 'arising from a failure to take reasonable care' qualify the word 'claim' or 'action', or the words 'economic loss or damage to property'? What is meant by 'arising from'? Does the section require that the action or claim must arise from a failure to take reasonable care, in the sense that the failure to take care is an essential element of the action or claim? Or does it merely mean that the action or claim, whatever its elements, must have come about because the defendant failed to take reasonable care?

Professor John Carter and this author have argued that the first interpretation is the only sensible interpretation.[45] It is a matter of what in substance is the plaintiff's claim. Is it one for negligence – the failure to take care, in breach of a duty of care – or is it one based on some other cause of action? There are many other causes of action which support a claim for pure economic loss or property damage.

[42] Civil Liability Act 2002 (NSW), s 34(1)(a); Civil Law (Wrongs) Act 2002 (ACT), s 107B; Wrongs Act 1958 (Vic), s 24AF(1)(a); Proportionate Liability Act (NT), s 4(2)(a); Civil Liability Act 2002 (Tas), s 43A(1)(a); Civil Liability Act 2002 (WA), s 5AI(a).

[43] Civil Liability Act 2003 (Qld), s 28(1)(a); cf Law Reform (Contributory Negligence and Apportionment of Liability) Act 2001 (SA), s 3(2).

[44] *Henderson v Merrett Syndicates Ltd* [1995] 2 AC 145 (HL); *Hawkins v Clayton* (1988) 164 CLR 539 (HCA).

[45] B McDonald and JW Carter, 'The Lottery of Contractual Risk Allocation and Proportionate Liability' (2009) 26 *Journal of Contract Law* 1.

This is not merely a matter of pleading. We agree that whether a cause of action is made out on particular facts depends, not on the pleading of facts, but on the facts as proved. So we have no argument with the view that a plaintiff cannot, just by pleading certain facts which cannot be supported on the evidence, succeed in dressing up an apportionable claim as a non-apportionable claim.[46] We agree that this also means that it may only be after evidence is heard that it will be settled, by the findings of the judge, whether the facts support a cause of action which is not apportionable.[47] The plaintiff may then rely on that action, at his or her election.

However, we have argued that it is quite a different conclusion to say, as was decided in *Reinhold v New South Wales Lotteries (No 2)*,[48] that a claim becomes an apportionable claim merely because it is proved that the relevant defendant was negligent. Such a conclusion ignores the elements of the causes of action on which the plaintiff may rely, on the facts as proved. If, for example, the plaintiff proves that he or she has the benefit of a strict contractual obligation or warranty, or of a strict statutory duty[49] or warranty, the breach of which caused the relevant loss of a type which was not too remote[50] or within the contemplation of the statute,[51] then the plaintiff has proved all the facts necessary for recovery. Any finding of, or dispute as to, negligence is irrelevant. The claim is not an apportionable claim: it does not arise out of negligence when negligence is no part of the cause of action.

That approach has some judicial support. As Macfarlan JA stated in *Perpetual Trustee Company Ltd v CTC Group Party Ltd (No 2)*:[52]

> For a successful action for damages to have arisen from a failure to take reasonable care, it is in my view necessary that the absence of reasonable care was an element of the, or a, cause of action upon which the plaintiff succeeded.

To decide otherwise is to turn every claim into a negligence claim, which dramatically expands the already imperial march of negligence law, undermines the role and existence of other centuries-old legal and equitable causes of actions and obligations, and undermines the ability of parties to protect themselves by negotiating the benefit of strict obligation.

[46] *Dartberg Pty Ltd v Wealthcare Financial Planning Pty Ltd* [2007] FCA 1216 (Middleton J); *Chandra v Perpetual Trustees Victoria Ltd* [2007] NSWSC 694 (Bryson AJ).

[47] *Reinhold v NSW Lotteries Corporation (No 2)* [2008] NSWSC 187 (Barrett J); *Dartberg Pty Ltd v Wealthcare Financial Planning Pty Ltd* [2007] FCA 1216 [30] (Middleton J).

[48] *Reinhold* (n 47).

[49] M Davies and I Malkin, *Focus Torts*, 7th edn (Sydney, LexisNexis Butterworths, 2015) 13.36.

[50] *Hadley v Baxendale* (1854) 156 ER 145, 151.

[51] *Travel Compensation Fund v Tambree* [2005] HCA 69, (2005) 224 CLR 627.

[52] *Perpetual Trustee Company Ltd v CTC Group Party Ltd* (No 2) [2013] NSWCA 58 [22]. Meagher JA [36] found it unnecessary to decide the issue, while Barrett JA [43] suggested it was necessary to engage in a wider enquiry, as he had done in *Reinhold* (n 47). There have been several cases by single judges in the Supreme Court since the 2013 judgment, but none has had to decide the issue: *Pfizer Australia Pty Ltd v Probiotec Pharma Pty Ltd* [2010] NSWSC 532 [8] (Biscoe J); *Dunn v Hanson Australasia Pty Ltd* [2017] ACTSC 169 [612]. *Monaghan Surveyors Pty Ltd v Stratford Glen-Avon Pty Ltd* [2012] NSWCA

The courts have not been prepared to extend proportionate liability to claims for breach of trust,[53] or for knowing receipt of property subject to a fiduciary duty.[54] It is to be hoped that the same logic is in future applied to strict contractual claims. But at present, we still await an authoritative review at appellate level of the 'strenuous debate'[55] as to the arguably flawed interpretation in *Reinhold (No 2)* of the New South Wales legislation in its application to strict contractual duties. It is surprising that no review has occurred, given the enormous impact such an interpretation has on contractual allocation of risk. It is hoped that the dearth of authority is not because this interpretation has been accepted by litigants and industry as correct beyond doubt.

As a matter of drafting, and assuming the intent of the legislature to be directed at negligence-based claims and breaches of statutory prohibitions on misleading or deceptive conduct, the Queensland wording is to be preferred. Alternative, suitable wording for 'an apportionable claim', as it applies to common law claims, was suggested by Professor Davis in his 2008 Report to the SCLJ. It is similar to what can be found in the Law Reform Miscellaneous Provisions Act 1965 (NSW), or the Law Reform Act 1995 (Qld), and so has the attraction of consistency: 'a) A breach of tortious duty of care, or from a breach of a contractual obligation which is concurrent and co-extensive with such a tortious duty …'.

But, while this wording was in the consultation drafting instructions for the model provisions, stakeholders, in their submissions on the 2011 model, Draft 7, objected to such a narrow definition and argued either for the existing NSW/Victorian/Western Australian model, or an even broader definition.[56] It appears that, as far as they were concerned, the more claims that are apportionable the better and an ambiguous definition which can be (and has been) interpreted to their advantage is better than a clear one that cannot.

94 [76]ff and *Perpetual Trustee Co Ltd v Milanex Pty Ltd (In liq)* [2011] NSWCA 367 illustrate that similarly ambiguous drafting also appears in other application sections of the Civil Liability Act 2002 (NSW). Basten JA comments, in obiter dicta, that '[t]he logic of [Macfarlan JA's] reasoning is undeniable, in terms of the language of the statute' although in relation to the particular incidental issue at hand he then delves into the legislative history.

[53] *George v Webb & Ors* [2011] NSWSC 1608 [325] (Ward J): '[t]his breach of trust would have occurred (and the liability arises) whether or not there had been a failure on the part of the solicitors to take sufficient care in complying with the directions that were given to them. Therefore I consider that the liability, as found, is not one predicated on or arising from a failure to take reasonable care and this is not an apportionable claim'.

[54] *Cassegrain v Cassegrain* [2016] NSWCA 71. Both this judgment and that of *George v Webb* (n 43) also discussed the issue of whether equitable claims could be considered to be claims for 'damages' in the terms of the application section.

[55] *Cassegrain* (n 54) [20] (Basten JA). However, the judge stated: 'Whatever the strength or weakness of the critique, it has no application in the present case. The conduct of the appellant in the present case, as a knowing recipient of property transferred in breach of fiduciary duties, involved neither strict liability nor negligence, but a higher level of moral responsibility.' At [23] Basten JA pointed out that the liability of the defendant in equity rested on her proven knowledge, not on her failure to make reasonable enquiry.

[56] SCAG Proportionate Liability Regulation Impact Statement September 2011, SCIL archive (n 6) 17.

The 2013 Proportionate Liability Model Provisions appear to be the latest model released by the joint government committee. The relevant section about common law claims is as follows:[57]

> 2 Application – pt 1
>
> (2) A claim is an *apportionable claim* if it is for economic loss or damage to property in—
>
> (a) an action for damages (in contract, in tort, under statute or otherwise) where a failure to take reasonable care is an element of the claimant's action; or
>
> **Examples – actions that are apportionable claims**
> 1 breach of duty of care
> 2 breach of express contractual term to take reasonable care
> 3 breach of implied contractual term to take reasonable care
> 4 breach of director's civil obligation to act with reasonable care and diligence
> 5 breach of statutory warranty to render services with due care and skill
> 6 breach of implied warranty to render services with due care and skill
>
> **Examples – actions that are not apportionable claims**
> 1. breach of strict contractual duty
> 2. breach of absolute contractual duty
>
> *Note* An example is part of the Act, is not exhaustive and may extend, but does not limit, the meaning of the provision in which it appears (see Legislation Act, s 126 and s 132).

Of the 22 submissions on this model, one was from the Chief Justice of New South Wales, the Hon TF Bathurst.[58] The Chief Justice noted that the new definition was, presumably, to cure the ambiguity in the drafting of the current New South Wales model, which could 'arguably' render a breach of a strict contractual term apportionable, if it results from a failure to take care. However, he noted that there would also be ambiguity in the word 'element', which would only achieve its purpose of curing the current problem if 'element' is understood to mean 'essential part' of the cause of action. He also commented on the inclusion of examples relating to a director's duties, pointing out that, for the breach of some directors' duties, civil penalties may be imposed by legislation, and on a number of other details in the drafting of the current Act and the proposed model. With respect, these comments

[57] https://www.pcc.gov.au/uniform/proportionate%20liability%20model%20provisions.pdf.
[58] http://www.justice.nsw.gov.au/justicepolicy/Documents/supreme_court_of_nsw.pdf.

are especially valuable, coming as they do from a highly experienced and impartial leading participant in the legal system. They show that care must be given to every word and example, to ensure that the words used say what they are intended to say and that what they intend to say is clear and justified.

Other stakeholders made somewhat predictable submissions in protection of their own interests. The Law Society of New South Wales[59] (which on this topic, represents lawyers and law firms, rather than being impartial) in its submission preferred the current definition of an apportionable claim which they stated was 'well understood'. It repeated the point that pleadings should not determine apportionability of a claim, without dealing with the more substantive point that the different essential elements of different causes of action should determine apportionability. It did not want to restrict the operation of proportionate liability.

Perhaps surprisingly, the Insurance Council of Australia[60] supported the narrow definition in the proposed model, limiting proportionate liability to claims where failure to take reasonable care is an element of the claim. One might have thought that, given their support for proportionate liability, they would support a more general application of the scheme to all liabilities. However, they agreed with the Regulatory Impact Statement which has suggested that this narrow definition can be expected to provide greater certainty in risk allocation for commercial contracts.

Thus, the debate as to what claims should be apportionable has moved beyond the mere question of drafting and interpretation to capture the original intent of the Parliament, to a broader question. Perhaps because potential defendants have seen the very real benefits of proportionate liability in one legal context, they are calling for it to be extended to others. So this leads to the second question.

ii. If We Had a Clean Slate, Which Causes of Action Should Be Apportionable?

The answers to that question among stakeholders seem, generally, to be strongly motivated by self-interest. It is clearly in the interests of potential defendants, usually providers of services or products, but also of others on whom liability may fall, such as occupiers of property, that as many claims as possible, against them, be apportionable. Why be 100 per cent liable – for any type of liability – if one can apportion some of the primary liability to another? Why not apply proportionate liability to strict contractual obligations, or to breaches of fiduciary or other equitable duties and liabilities, or to the ever-increasing gamut of statutory liabilities for loss, if someone else is also to blame for the plaintiff's losses?

[59] http://www.justice.nsw.gov.au/justicepolicy/Documents/law_society_of_nsw.pdf.

[60] Letter from Robert Whelan, ED & CEO, Insurance Council of Australia, 17 April, 2014: http://www.justice.nsw.gov.au/justicepolicy/Documents/insurance_council_of_australia.pdf. Consistently, perhaps, with its support for a narrow application of the legislation to negligence claims only, it objected to contracting out by potential plaintiffs.

A simple answer is that such a wide regime, particularly if coupled with a prohibition on contracting out as discussed below, totally undermines both *freedom* of contract and the obvious *efficiency* of advance contractual allocation of risks, both of which are large ideals that it is beyond the scope of this chapter to defend. What is objectionable in independent parties agreeing, in advance, on who will bear the risk if things do not proceed as planned and loss is caused? What will be the value of a strict promise, or a guarantee, or indemnity, if its enforceability is subject to apportionment? How can a court make a 'just' reduction – based on fault – of the liability of someone who has made a strict promise, as to which fault is irrelevant?

For potential claimants – clients, or consumers of services and products, or third parties to some transaction or activity – there are significant disadvantages in having a wide definition of 'apportionable claims'. For disinterested commentators, the answer to the question depends both on the potential impact on the rights and liabilities of different types of parties in an enormously wide range of situations, in terms of fairness, and on the whole order, coherence and justification for well-established rules of private law, in terms of logic. The essential question is the legal basis of a defendant's liability: whether it is imposed by law or agreement, whether it is strict, whether it based on intention, on negligence, on knowledge, or on unconscionable conduct. The private law of rights, obligations and liabilities is not just an amorphous mass of indistinguishable examples. Despite Tilbury's statement, quoted above,[61] it would be a major shift in civil liability to abandon all forms of several and joint liability for wrongs in favour of proportionate liability, and one that should be based on solid evidence of economic value and convincing ethical grounds.

It should not be assumed that government agencies, who no doubt influence legislators, are always disinterested commentators in this debate: government departments and agencies are routinely both potential defendants for breaches of their contractual and tort obligations to citizens and entities, but also potential claimants. They may be clients of a wide range of external service providers, for example, legal, accounting or technology services, or in building, construction and infrastructure projects, as illustrated below.

Whether or not more *statutory* claims, or claims for breach of other statutory provisions, should be apportionable, is another issue. As the High Court decided in *Selig v Wealthsure*,[62] proportionate liability application sections in Federal statutes are specific and will be strictly construed: a court has no basis for widening the application sections by treating as analogous claims based on sections *not specified*. Why proportionate liability applies to some statutory breaches, but not others in the same Act, is not always easy to discern. It seems to be a matter of

[61] Tilbury (n 10) 115: 'There is absolutely no reason why proportionate liability should be restricted to claims in negligence'.
[62] *Selig* (n 9).

the legislature reacting to certain trends: proportionate liability was extended to claims for misleading or deceptive conduct in breach of section 52 of the Trade Practices Act 1974 (now section 18 of the Australian Consumer Law), and claims under parallel sections of the Corporations Act 2001 (Cth)[63] and the Australian Securities and Investment Commission Act 2001 (Cth),[64] as they usually accompanied tort and contract claims. Now plaintiffs rely, if they can, on claims under different sections to avoid proportionate liability. What is clear is that, if plaintiffs can avoid a hurdle in one sort of claim by relying on a different claim, they will do so. There seems to be no reason why, *if* proportionate liability is appropriate at all, it should not be enacted for other substantially similar statutory claims.

B. Contracting Out of Proportionate Liability

A highly contentious issue in the discussions for uniformity, is whether parties should be free to make contractual arrangements overriding the proportionate liability provisions. For short, we will call this 'contracting out,' although it is not entirely clear which types of contractual arrangements would actually come within any prohibition on contracting out and which would not.

There are various ways a party could override the legislation, if free to do so. One is an express term that the relevant legislation does not apply. Another would be an express term that the liability of the parties is joint and several, or several. Another would be an express term that the liability to the plaintiff would not be reduced due to the liability of any other person or entity for the same damage. These are all obvious ways to contract out of the regime and probably what most commentators have in mind when they discuss the issue.

There may be other ways to achieve the same effect, or to override the court's apportionment of primary liability. One or more parties could agree with the plaintiff in advance as to their respective share of any loss suffered by the plaintiff. This would seem quite efficient in avoiding recourse to the courts, much like an agreed damages clause.[65] Another way would be an indemnity agreement in favour of the plaintiff with the defendant. Here, the parties are creating a strict liability to indemnify. Such was the case in *Perpetual Trustee Company Ltd v CTC Group Pty Ltd (No 2)*,[66] where the New South Wales Court of Appeal upheld the right of Perpetual to enforce CTC's indemnity, rather than have its claim against CTC limited by proportionate liability.

More uncertain is whether imposing a contractual cap on liability is also, in effect, contracting out of the court's ability to determine a defendant's fair share

[63] Claims under s 1041I for contravention of s 1041H.

[64] Claims under s 12GF for conduct in contravention of s 12DA.

[65] Hopefully avoiding any dispute that the arrangement amounted to a penalty upon any party.

[66] *Perpetual Trustee v CTC* (n 52).

of liability.[67] Given that contractual limits on liability are often suggested as more just and effective, alternative ways to limit defendants' liability, support industry and economic activity and maintain insurance availability and viability[68] (which are the professed objectives of many supporters of proportionate liability), it would be ironic if capping were treated as contracting out. Yet capping undoubtedly limits the court's allocation of liability and requires the parties to have some freedom of contract to achieve it.

The Insurance Council of Australia, for example, in its response to the 2013 model provisions, stated that it supported the model provisions (option 5) 'which ensure that: "contracting out is prohibited for all contracts except an agreement by a concurrent wrongdoer to contribute to indemnify [sic] another concurrent wrongdoer"'.[69] Would 'all contracts' include terms capping liability below the level a court would have apportioned to the wrongdoer?

There appear to be three legislative models currently in use across Australia which affect the parties' rights to contract out. The first is to allow unrestricted contracting out of the proportionate liability provisions. The Civil Liability Act 2002 (NSW), which is followed in Tasmania[70] and Western Australia,[71] has a very broad contracting out provision:[72]

> This Act (except Part 2) does not prevent the parties to a contract from making express provision for their rights, obligations and liabilities under the contract with respect to any matter to which this Act applies and does not limit or otherwise affect the operation of any such express provision.

In CTC's unsuccessful special leave application to the High Court of Australia, the Court noted:[73]

> [The New South Wales legislation] operates to ensure that the apportionment provisions of the Act yield to the express intention of the parties. That this should be so, as the Court of Appeal held, is hardly surprising. *The contrary view would attribute to the legislature an intention to interfere with freedom of contract where it is not possible to discern in the Act any hint of an intention to do so.*

This provision should allow parties to restrict a defendant's ability to use the proportionate liability legislation either to limit its primary liability, or to avoid

[67] How a cap arranged with one potential defendant affects the responsibility of other potential wrongdoers is also uncertain, but it should arguably not affect the apportionment, applying the same logic as in *James Hardie v Selstam* (1998) 73 ALJR 238 [87] (Kirby J): 'It is clearly contrary to principle to place a plaintiff and a tortfeasor, against whom contribution has been, or may be, sought in a position where they can, between themselves, deprive another tortfeasor of its statutory right to contribution.'

[68] NZ Law Commission (n 3); Tilbury (n 10).

[69] Above n 60. Emphasis in the original.

[70] Civil Liability Act 2002 (Tas), s 3A(3).

[71] Civil Liability Act 2002 (WA), s 4A.

[72] Civil Liability Act 2002 (NSW), s 3A(2), a general clause allowing contracting out of the Act, except for the restrictions on personal injury damages.

[73] *CTC Group Pty Ltd v Perpetual Trustee Company Ltd* [2013] HCATrans 248 (emphasis added). See also *Aquagenics Pty Ltd v Break O'Day Council* [2010] TASFC 3 [16].

pre-existing contractual indemnities or arrangements with other defendants. It appears that sometimes parties, who could have taken advantage of it, have overlooked reliance on section 3A, perhaps because it is a general provision rather than one found within Part 4 dealing with proportionate liability.[74]

The second model is to prohibit parties from excluding the application of the proportionate liability provisions. The Queensland legislation expressly excludes Chapter 2 Part 2 (enacting proportionate liability) from any 'freedom of contract' provision similar to that which exists in New South Wales.[75]

The third model is for the legislation to be silent as to the ability of parties to contract out of its provisions generally, or out of the proportionate liability regime. This is the situation in Victoria, South Australia, the Northern Territory and the Australian Capital Territory. The assumption appears to be that contracting-out is not allowable in those states or territories, unless the statute specifically authorises it. It is not clear on what authority this assumption is based.[76] If a client could extract from a service provider a promise that the latter would not raise contributory negligence, it may exceed the cover provided by insurers, but would such a clause be struck down? It would be preferable for the situation as to contracting out of proportionate liability at least to be made clear by the legislation.

In submissions to the Standing Committee of Law and Justice in 2011 and 2013, industry and professional proponents of proportionate liability were strongly opposed to allowing parties to contract out. They argued that it undermines the purpose and effectiveness of the scheme because those with greater bargaining or market power (for example, government departments, or large corporate clients, like banks) unfairly use it to pressure service providers into giving up the benefits of proportionate liability if they want the lucrative work on offer. It is said to be the exercise of unequal bargaining power by the large powerful clients. Paradoxically, this sudden concern for unequal bargaining power manifests itself for the benefit of defendants in this context of dealings between well-advised commercial entities, but not for the benefit of individuals, or small businesses, who have no bargaining power against deep-pocketed providers and find themselves unable to recover in full from negligent actors because some other actor also happened to be to blame.

It certainly seems to be the case that in New South Wales, where contracting-out is allowed, it is common for deep-pocketed clients to demand the exclusion of proportionate liability in their contracts. Indeed, it is deeply ironic that the New South Wales Government, whose then Attorney-General's Department was at the forefront of the push for proportionate liability, routinely insists on contracting

[74] This seems the best explanation for the fact that, in *Reinhold v New South Wales Lotteries (No 2)* [2008] NSWSC 187, the defendants were held to be prevented by Civil Liability Act 2002 (NSW), s 36 from pursuing any breaches of their pre-existing contractual rights against each other; breaches which may have caused their respective liability to the plaintiff.

[75] Civil Liability Act 2003 (Qld), s 7(3).

[76] A similar issue would be whether parties may contract out of the defence of, or the statutory apportionment for, contributory negligence.

out of the regime when it is a client in infrastructure and other construction projects. Furthermore, it requires counterparties to include the contracting out clause in their subcontracts. A current example can be seen in the New South Wales Government's Sydney Light Rail Project Deed template.[77]

Insisting on contracting out is also, it appears, what large corporate clients in New South Wales do for their copious quantities of lucrative legal work, which law firms want to attract. It is argued that their ability to insist on such provisions, as the 'price' for the work and under threat that they will go elsewhere, undermines one of the primary rationales and objectives of the scheme: reducing the cost of professional liability insurance.

Nevertheless, there seems to be no shortage of either builders, or professionals willing to do work on these terms in New South Wales or Western Australia. In the absence of real evidence that the freedom to contract out in New South Wales and Western Australia is reducing the availability and viability of insurance, or increasing the cost of premiums and thus the cost of services, or restricting industry or professional services in those States when compared to Queensland or Victoria, it is difficult to see why parties' ability to negotiate terms should be restricted. Further, given the extent to which the New South Wales government, as a client and user of services, is itself firmly wedded to contracting out, this seems to be a substantial block to uniformity among the Australian States and Territories.

V. The Fairness of the Regime – Is It Demonstrated by the Case Law?

Proportionate liability was promoted and introduced by governments as a fairer system of allocating responsibility for harm caused by negligence, or certain statutory breaches: defendants should not be held wholly responsible when others are also to blame for the plaintiff's loss.

In New South Wales, it was enacted as part of legislation with the overriding object of promoting 'personal responsibility';[78] the general rubric of the Ipp *Review of the Law of Negligence* which led to wholesale tort reform throughout Australia.[79] But to what extent does proportionate liability really reflect, or promote, 'personal responsibility' on a plaintiff's part? It *might* do so if the plaintiff had always been free to choose – and thus take responsibility for choosing – the various people, or entities, which were to provide goods or services, the negligent delivery of which caused the plaintiff's loss. For example, the plaintiff might have selected a lawyer, an accountant, a surveyor and an IT specialist, all of whom

[77] At Clause 60: https://www.transport.nsw.gov.au/sites/default/files/media/documents/2017/slr-project-deed-redacted.pdf.

[78] Civil Liability Amendment (Personal Responsibility) Act 2002 (NSW).

[79] Above n 20.

were to have a role in some project, or transaction. In such cases, it may be appropriate to argue that the plaintiff should, by reason of proportionate liability, bear the risk of non-recovery from one of the advisors the plaintiff chose.

However, there will be many situations where the plaintiff had no role in selecting the various entities who ended up, by negligent accident, causing his or her loss. For example, the plaintiff's property might be damaged by several actors, with all, or with some of whom, the plaintiff had no prior relationship. Vehicles could run off the road into the plaintiff's property after a collision caused by several, negligent drivers. One or more of them might have been brought into the mix by another wrongdoer, as in the case of a negligent contractor who subcontracts aspects of the work to another. Both would be liable to the plaintiff for negligent property damage, or negligent professional work,[80] but it is hard to see why the plaintiff should have the burden of chasing another person's sub-contractor to recover the full loss.

Even when the plaintiff has chosen both actors whose separate wrongs caused the plaintiff's loss, the outcomes produced by proportionate liability may seem skewed. While the decision in *Hunt & Hunt Lawyers v Mitchell Morgan Nominees Pty Ltd*[81] was correct in terms of the intent and interpretation of the legislation, the result epitomises what is potentially unfair about the proportionate liability regime. The plaintiff financiers sued their lawyers for negligently failing to protect them from the fraud of some shady characters to whom the plaintiffs had advanced moneys. The defendant lawyers were clearly negligent. Some might call their error a basic legal or professional error in drafting a mortgage that would effectively secure moneys advanced by their client. Yet, because the fraudulent parties were clearly more culpable in causing the loss when compared with the merely negligent lawyers, the clients were unable to recover more than 10 per cent of their loss from the defendants, even though they had gone to them, as professionals, *for protection from the very kind of loss that eventuated.* To this author, this seems intuitively wrong as a legal outcome.

The unease with the result persists even though the plaintiff was a commercial profit-making entity – not a usual object of concern – rather than a mere individual, and had reportedly chosen to deal with some shady characters. A fortiori, if the plaintiff were an individual of modest means and with little bargaining power, who had relied on professional advisors to protect him or her from fraud: are we really saying that such a person does not deserve protection by a system in which the professional advisers have to – presumptively at least – bear a very substantial proportion of the loss?

[80] The liability of the sub-contractor to the head client is less obvious in the case of negligently-caused pure economic loss in construction contexts: *Rail Corp NSW v Fluor Australia Pty Ltd* [2009] NSWCA 344, esp [2], [5]–[6] and [126]–[133].

[81] *Hunt & Hunt* (n 9).

So what is the problem at the heart of proportionate liability? *Hunt & Hunt* illustrates that the apportionment process, as directed by the legislation, currently only considers the relative fault and causative contribution of the wrongdoers *as between each other.* It was assumed by the legislators and the proponents of proportionate liability that the same percentage apportionment that would take place between wrongdoers in a contribution claim should simply be transposed to the plaintiff's primary claim against defendants. It assumes that the percentages allocated to each wrongdoer must add up to 100 per cent for the plaintiff and no more. Of course, a plaintiff should not recover more than 100 per cent of its loss from all wrongdoers, but it does not necessarily follow that, as a matter of justice, each wrongdoer should only be liable for a fraction of 100 per cent. This is the misconception that underlies simple proportionate liability. Such a one-size-fits-all approach takes no account of the nuances of the circumstances in the *plaintiff's relationships with* the various wrongdoers.[82] Of course, any contributory negligence of the plaintiffs in choosing to deal with shady characters, if they were, would be taken into account to reduce the liability of the defendants. The question for the court in this case should have been: what is a fair allocation of responsibility for the defendant's negligence in failing to protect their client from potential fraud, against which the clients had sought protection by seeking advice and proper documentation?

To quote again Professor Tilbury:[83]

> The problem is that [arguments in favour of proportionate liability identify] fairness or justice only from the defendant's point of view. Generalised rules of law cannot be formulated on so narrow a basis. The interests of the plaintiff must be taken into account.

If we are to persist with a regime of proportionate liability, how can the legislation make appropriate allowance for circumstances where it is clearly unfair that a wrongdoer should be able to hide its own negligence behind another's wrongdoing? One way perhaps would be for the legislation to specify that, while a plaintiff cannot recover more than its actual loss from all wrongdoers, some wrongdoers may, where the court thinks it just and equitable, be concurrently liable with other wrongdoers for a proportion of the plaintiff's loss. While this may add more complexity to the regime, and keep alive the need for defendants to use contribution claims to recoup their liability, it would give the courts more discretion to avoid the heavy and potentially unfair burden which proportionate liability may impose on some plaintiffs while unjustifiably excusing defendants from liability for their own wrongdoing.

[82] For further discussion of a more nuanced approach, see S Harder, 'Advisor Liability; Claims for Contribution or Reimbursement between an Advisor and the Advisee's Contract-Partner' in K Barker, R Grantham and W Swain (eds), *The Law of Misstatements: 50 years on from Hedley Byrne v Heller* (Oxford, Hart Publishing, 2015) 202ff.

[83] Tilbury (n 10) 116.

VI. Conclusion

Looking back over the more-than-a-decade of the operation of proportionate liability, we can hardly say that its introduction has been smooth, or convincingly just. It has also raised many questions challenging the established legal order, even prompting the question of whether all multi-party obligations should be apportionable. There is nothing wrong with challenging the legal order, but we do need to be honest that this is what we are doing, rather than slipping major changes in under the cover of other reforms, or leaving the door open to unintended consequences by ambiguous drafting.

It is a reform that has been remarkably hard to review and correct. While it is a good thing that we have been cautious about corrections until we are sure we have the right replacement, perhaps the snail-paced progress to find the right model simply shows how unwise was the initial rush. Other jurisdictions have taken, and should continue to take note.

12

Causation and Proportional Recovery

ROB MERKIN AND JENNY STEELE

I. The Impact of *Fairchild*

The decision of the House of Lords in *Fairchild v Glenhaven Funeral Services Ltd*,[1] though on the face of it not concerned with apportionment at all, has ultimately led to the introduction into the English law of tort, and of insurance, of novel forms of proportional liability. The challenge for tort law was that rules on causation, as they then stood, precluded recovery in the absence of proof of a link between a given exposure to a harmful substance and consequent injury suffered at a much later date. In the case of mesothelioma, such proof was regarded as impossible where there was a chain of potential defendants. The challenge for insurance law was how policies were to respond to this gap. The practical outcome for both areas of law (tort, and insurance) has been the adoption of proportionality.[2] It should be said at the outset that there was nothing new, in practice, about a degree of proportionality in either tort, or insurance. Joint or cumulative tortfeasors are, through the Civil Liability (Contribution) Act 1978 (UK), ultimately required to bear a degree of liability broadly proportional to their respective contribution,[3] whichever of them is the initial target of the victim's action. Two or more insurers whose *concurrent* policies happen to overlap in respect of a single loss are, through the mechanism of contribution and following a successful claim against any of them,

[1] [2002] UKHL 22; [2003] 1 AC 32 ('*Fairchild*').

[2] A bizarre fact of academic life in the common law world is the virtual dearth of scholars researching into both tort and insurance. The issues that arise are frequently common to both, particularly in the spheres of causation and loss, but the solution reached in one rarely refers to the other. By way of example, both tort and insurance agree that an event causing unrepaired damage is for liability purposes to be left out of account if, by the time of the trial, there has been a supervening subsuming loss, but the bumpy journeys to that conclusion in tort (*Jobling v Associated Dairies* [1982] AC 794, effectively undermining *Baker v Willoughby* [1970] AC 467) and in insurance (*QBE Insurance (International) Ltd v Wild South Holdings Ltd* [2014] NZCA 447, effectively undermining *Ridgecrest NZ Ltd v IAG New Zealand Ltd* [2014] NZSC 117) have been endured quite independently.

[3] A variety of factors is relevant in making the decision on quantum of contribution. In arriving at proportional solutions, the criteria applied in different contexts may vary considerably.

ultimately required to carry only a proportionate share of the loss,[4] generally based upon a comparison of the amounts for which each insurer would independently have been liable to the assured.[5] *Fairchild*, however, particularly as it has been later interpreted, takes the law into new territory.

We argue here that, given the problems with which *Fairchild* deals, some form of proportional liability solution was more or less inevitable, not only at the level of tort law, but – if the tort judgments on the incidence of liability were to be meaningful – also at the level of insurance. A majority of the House of Lords in *Barker v Corus*[6] effectively retrenched on what was thought to be the outcome of *Fairchild*, by rejecting 100 per cent tortfeasor liability in favour of proportionality based on – presumably, but this is yet to be articulated fully – time on risk and intensity of exposure. In addition, the decision has already had a transformative effect on the question of proportional liability in employers liability insurance, first in *Durham v BAI (The Trigger Litigation)*[7] by causing the courts to construe such policies as responding to the year of exposure, rather than the year of injury; and then in *International Energy Group v Zurich Insurance plc UK*,[8] by allowing contribution between *consecutive* insurers on an entirely novel 'time on risk' rather than the established 'independent liability' basis.[9] It is apparent that, had conventional contribution been applied, an insurer on risk for one year but nevertheless facing 100 per cent liability for mesothelioma claims based on exposures in that year would have been required to contribute 50 per cent to an insurer on risk for 20 years of exposure and similarly facing 100 per cent liability.

We do not argue that, but for *Fairchild*, none of this would have happened. To the contrary, the argument developed in what follows is that the problem was latent and indeed would have arisen independently of *Fairchild*. Neither do we argue that proportionality is a better reflection of a particular defendant's 'share' of responsibility. Rather, we see proportionality in the *Fairchild* scenario as indicating a set of rough and ready practical solutions to a range of practical difficulties which faced not only tort law, but also the underlying insurance arrangements. Our view is that, for both tort and insurance law, a solution resembling *Fairchild* in one form or another – in which proportional liability was effected either through the adaptation of tort law itself, or through the creation of full

[4] Marine Insurance Act 1906 (UK), ss 32 and 80, codifying the common law on marine insurance and subsequently adopted in the non-marine context. The same sections appear in the legislation of virtually all common law jurisdictions.

[5] There are various measures of apportionment in this situation, notably 'maximum liability,' which focuses on the sum insured by each policy, and 'independent liability' which focuses on the liability of each insurer for the amount of the specific claim. In most cases both formulae give rise to a 50:50 outcome. It will be assumed for the purposes only of what follows, that independent liability is the correct analysis.

[6] [2006] UKHL 20; [2006] 2 AC 572 ('*Barker*').

[7] [2012] UKSC 14; [2012] 1 WLR 867 ('*Durham*').

[8] [2015] UKSC 33; [2016] AC 509 ('*IEG*').

[9] A suggestion put forward by the present authors in R Merkin and J Steele, *Insurance and the Law of Obligations* (Oxford, Oxford University Press, 2013), 378 and adopted by Lord Mance in *IEG* (n 8) [63].

liability with contribution – was more or less necessary because the problems with which the decision deals are real problems and not confined to one particular social and political issue.[10] Strong though the influence of the social context of industrial mesothelioma undoubtedly was, *Fairchild* is not to be dismissed as a one-off reaction to a particular social problem.

Given that *Fairchild* has taken us into new territory, the real question is exactly how far *Fairchild* is going to lead. Much ink has been spilt over the shock that *Fairchild* has created in the English law of tort, one that many advocate should be confined as closely as possible to the 'enclave' of mesothelioma, the fatal disease with which it dealt: this often builds on an argument that it is best seen as dealing with a particular social problem.[11] Similarly, on the face of things, the principles laid down in the authorities on consequential insurance claims arising out of the *Fairchild* ruling are limited to that context. Earlier authority on the liability of insurers for exposure claims had reached the 'date of injury' solution for exposure injuries in the context of public liability insurance: *Bolton Metropolitan Borough Council v Municipal Mutual Insurance Ltd.*[12] It is an open secret that the claim in *Bolton* was designed as a stalking horse for the many thousands of similarly-worded employers liability policies, and the extension of *Bolton* to such policies would have removed virtually all insurance liability, given that cover would then have existed only for injuries suffered in the policy year by *current* employees and not ex-employees. The outcome in *Durham* was a major shock to the small number of insurers who faced long-tail liability under employers liability policies in force up to 40 years earlier. It is to be stressed that *Fairchild* was concerned only with employers liability, and Lord Mance, on the opening of the arguments in *Durham*, expressed some relief that the Supreme Court was not being called upon to consider the correctness of *Bolton*.

It is apparent that the ultimate effect of *Fairchild* has been to adopt an approach under which rough proportionality was substituted for established principles of causation where proof of nexus between the negligence of any one among a group of potential defendants, and injuries later suffered, was an impossibility.[13]

[10] Note the wide range of comparative common law and civilian solutions canvassed in Lord Bingham's opinion in *Fairchild* itself (n 1) [23]–[32], concluding that if 'a decision is given in this country which offends one's basic sense of justice, and if consideration of international sources suggests that a different and more acceptable decision would be given in most other jurisdictions, whatever their legal tradition, this must prompt anxious review of the decision in question'.

[11] This, ultimately, seems to have been the view of Lord Hoffmann: had the House of Lords rejected liability in *Fairchild*, Parliament would have created a bespoke solution for mesothelioma claims, so that the experiment was unnecessary: L Hoffmann, '*Fairchild* in Retrospect' (2012) 39 *The Advocates Quarterly* 257–71. Lord Hoffmann, however, did not adopt the view that *Fairchild* went wrong in meddling with orthodox causation doctrine, since his view of causation is that the law can properly adapt the notion to its own ends.

[12] [2006] EWCA Civ 50; [2006] 1 WLR 1492 ('*Bolton*').

[13] It may be presented, of course, as a new route to establishing causation, in a limited range of circumstances; but the proportional nature of *Fairchild* liability after *Barker* (n 6) has made this hard to rationalise with coherence, particularly given that the route of arguing that what is caused is *risk* rather than injury – apparently espoused by Lord Hoffmann in *Barker* – has been closed off by the

That then followed through to insurance claims. Could *Fairchild* become the default outcome in other situations where it is not possible to identify the responsible tortfeasor in a group of tortfeasors? More importantly, could *Fairchild* become the default solution to impossibility of proof where there is only one potential tortfeasor but there are other potential causes of the loss? In either case, what are the parameters of this? Pushing things further still, could insurance and reinsurance[14] claims abandon causation as presently understood and replace it with proportionality, and, if so, in which circumstances?[15] We expand on these points as the chapter proceeds. In the following section, Section II, we defend *Fairchild*, and illustrate that a solution like it would have been needed at the insurance level quite independently of its precedential influence. In Section III, we explore the potential for *Fairchild*'s influence to expand, showing the way to a range of solutions to the problems we have just indicated.

II. In Defence of *Fairchild*

A. Introduction

The right of a claimant who has suffered loss to recover damages from a defendant for a tortious act traditionally rests upon causation in the form of the 'but for' test. The basic 'but for' test is easily stated: if the conduct of the defendant is left out of account, would the claimant have suffered loss? The claimant must prove that 'but for' causation is established on the balance of probabilities. Refinements of the 'but for' test have been proposed, which nevertheless continue to rest on identification

Supreme Court's decision in *Durham* (n 7), in which the issue was crucial. Lord Dyson's comments in *Heneghan v Manchester Dry Docks* [2016] EWCA Civ 86, [2016] 1 WLR 2036 ('*Heneghan*'), citing Lord Hoffmann's approach in order to justify proportional rather than full liability on the part of defendants, are to this extent problematic.

[14] The market decided to resolve the question whether *IEG* (n 8) is to be applied at the reinsurance level, ie whether an insurer liable under *IEG* principles is entitled to 'spike' claims into the most favourable year of reinsurance cover, in arbitration, under the cover of confidentiality. Flaux LJ was appointed as judge-arbitrator for the purpose. His confidential award was issued in April 2017 but, by virtue of a successful application to the Court of Appeal for permission to appeal on points of law under s 69 of the Arbitration Act 1996, in *Equitas Insurance Ltd v Municipal Mutual Insurance Ltd* [2018] EWCA Civ 991, his conclusions (but not yet his reasoning) have become public. Flaux LJ concluded that *IEG* should apply, that spiking was permissible and that an insurer with an entitlement to spike was not under any contractual or general law duty of utmost good faith to spread claims proportionately. The Court of Appeal, granting permission to appeal, ruled that these conclusions satisfied the appeal threshold test of being 'open to serious doubt'.

[15] Note also the decision in *The Cultural Foundation v Beazley Furlonge Ltd* [2018] EWHC 1083 (Comm), where the court considered the possibility that a loss fell within each of two consecutive years of insurance cover and held it to be arguable that the assured would, based on *IEG* (n 8), have the right to choose the appropriate year of cover. The point arose in the context of 'claims made' liability insurance, where cover is triggered by the notification to the insurer of circumstances that may give rise to a claim against the assured, or the making of a claim against the assured. Most policies provide that a notification of circumstances prevents notification in a later year, but in the absence of such a clause the possibility of two different notifications can arise.

of whether the defendant's conduct was a 'necessary' factor.[16] In a case where two or more defendants potentially face liability for their respective acts or omissions, causation determines whether each of them is responsible; and if the loss is a result of the acts of a defendant and external forces, causation determines if there is any recoverability at all.

In applying causation rules to concurrent causes, three quite different scenarios have to be distinguished. These can be explained by examples inspired by the comments of Baroness Hale in *Barker*.[17] The first involves independent concurrent causes: D1 and D2 simultaneously shoot C. The second involves indeterminate concurrent causes: D1 and D2 simultaneously shoot C, but only one of the guns is loaded, and it is not possible to show which gun it was. The third involves interdependent concurrent causes not amounting to a joint enterprise: D1, pursuing his own purposes, injures C, enabling D2 to make a simultaneous fatal shot which, without the intervention of D1, would have missed its target. The issues raised by each are quite different. Independent concurrent causes throw into doubt the efficacy of the 'but for' test, because each of the defendants can justifiably say that, if his own conduct is disregarded, C would still have been shot by the other and the result would have been the same. Indeterminate concurrent causes are essentially a question of proof, in that it is impossible to say which of the defendants caused the loss. Putting the matter in terms of standard of proof, neither D1 nor D2 can be said on the balance of probabilities to have been more likely than the other to have caused C's loss. Interdependent concurrent causes give rise to an allocation issue, in that there would have been no loss (in our example, no fatality) without the acts of both D1 and D2. Both pass the 'but for' test, and both attract liability. In English tort law, this remains full liability. However, through contribution proceedings, a liable defendant is able to seek the court's quantification of the appropriate liability of each defendant, producing a proportional outcome.[18]

It would seem, therefore, that traditional causation principles, combined with contribution, give a satisfactory solution only in the case of interdependent concurrent causes, although even there the task of apportioning responsibility is probably little more than a combination of best guess based on common sense. If mathematical criteria are applied at all, they are generally applied to elusive facts. Indeed the broad-brush nature of the exercise is in no sense disguised or avoided by the legislation.[19] The broad-brush character of this assessment is similar to

[16] An influential variation in academic debate is the 'NESS' test, which considers whether the defendant's breach was a 'necessary element in a sufficient set' of factors, or a necessary element of a set of conditions jointly sufficient for the result: see initially HLA Hart and T Honoré, *Causation in the Law* (Oxford, Clarendon Press, 1959), and more recently R Wright, 'Causation in Tort Law' (1985) 73 *Cal L Rev* 1735.

[17] *Barker* (n 6) [30].

[18] Civil Liability (Contribution) Act 1978 (UK). This allows a liable party to recover contribution from any other person who is liable in respect of 'the same damage'.

[19] The amount of contribution recoverable 'shall be such as may be found by the court to be just and equitable having regard to that person's responsibility for the damage' (Civil Liability (Contribution) Act 1978 (UK), s 2(1)).

the nature of the decision required of courts determining questions of contributory negligence in its proportionate form. One of the present authors has argued elsewhere that this proportionate form of contributory negligence (comparative negligence, as it is known in some jurisdictions) does not lend itself to the precise logic attributed to proportionate liability by some of its proponents.[20] Where contribution legislation is concerned, the rough and ready nature of the assessment is still more evident, and it is plain that relevant considerations go far beyond the relative causal responsibility of the parties (with which contributory negligence deals) to embrace non-causative factors such as the fact that one party holds un-disgorged profits resulting from the wrong,[21] or even the manner in which a party conducts proceedings.[22] But, at least there is a mechanism. The question to be posed is whether a proportional approach of some sort can resolve the difficulties in the other scenarios.

It is, to say the least, counter-intuitive that if both D1 and D2 have fired shots at C then they should both be able to walk away free of liability essentially because they can blame each other for the consequences. Without liability, there can be no contribution. Applying extended proportional liability, either D1 and D2 are each to be regarded as 50 per cent to blame for the purposes of a claim on behalf of C, or alternatively D1 and D2 are each to be regarded as 100 per cent to blame and the allocation takes effect between them in separate subsequent proceedings under the Civil Liability (Contribution) Act 1978. As with interdependent concurrent causes, the latter offers a proportional result, while removing the cost of additional proceedings and the risk of non-payment for the claimant. Proportional liability is conceptually more attractive where both D1 and D2 have fired loaded guns, because although it cannot really be said that each has caused half the loss, at least the result produces broad equity between them. However, if there is one loaded and one unloaded gun, so that the problem is one of indeterminacy, then under proportionality (of one form or the other) one or other of the defendants is going to be held 50 per cent responsible for a loss in which he had no part.[23]

B. Exposure Injuries

The range of possibilities becomes clearer if we transpose the scenario from exposure to bullets to exposure to harmful substances, thus also changing the time frame. C is negligently exposed to a carcinogen by D1 in year 1 and by D2 in year 2. C discovers in year 30 that he has suffered personal injury. The results of

[20] K Barker and J Steele, 'Drifting Towards Proportional Liability: Ethics and Pragmatics' (2015) 74 *CLJ* 49–77.

[21] *Dubai Aluminium v Salaam* [2003] 2 AC 366 (HL).

[22] *Re-Source America v Platt Site Services* [2004] EWCA Civ 665.

[23] It has been suggested that this may be justified on the basis that all defendants have, through their breaches, contributed to the impossibility of proof with which the claimant is faced: S Steel, 'On When Fairchild Applies' (2015) 131 *LQR* 363.

the medical evidence may be that: (1) each of the exposures by D1 and D2 would independently have caused the injury; or (2) one or other of the exposures has caused the injury, but it is not possible to ascertain which; or (3) the exposures had a cumulative effect and together gave rise to the injury. In case (3), if the injury is a divisible one, liability can clearly be apportioned by the law of tort.[24] In the case of an indivisible injury resulting from cumulative causes, there is some authority that each exposure making a material contribution is capable of giving rise to liability in full, but the fit between this conclusion, and principles of causation, is far from obvious, and the authority in question appears to involve a departure from 'but for' causation.[25] To the extent that more than one such exposure is tortious, one would expect contribution to operate. In case (1) it would seem that D1 has to carry the can, as D2 has merely exposed to risk a person who has already suffered the relevant outcome. Case (2) is the difficult one, and this is of course the problem arising specifically from exposure to asbestos. The difficulty exists because, in respect of asbestos, medical evidence: (i) cannot ascertain which of the potentially many thousands of exposures over a lengthy period led to injury 30 or so years later; and (ii) whilst it no longer supports the 'single strand' theory,[26] it continues to hold that some exposures will be causative, and others not,[27] rather than illness being the result of a cumulative effect from all exposures.[28] In short, we are faced with the equivalent of D1 and D2 each firing guns at C but only one of the guns being loaded. There are four possible responses.

[24] *Holtby v Brigham and Cowan* [2000] 3 All ER 423 (asbestosis); *Thompson v Smiths Shiprepairers* [1984] QB 405 (progressive hearing loss). *Bonnington Castings v Wardlaw* [1956] AC 613, where a breach of duty made a 'material contribution' to development of a progressive disease, is now understood to be such a case, though no question of proportionality was raised in that case.

[25] *Bailey v Ministry of Defence* [2008] EWCA Civ 883; [2009] 1 WLR 1052 – a controversial decision: S Green, 'Contributing to the Risk of Confusion? Causation in the Court of Appeal' (2009) 125 *LQR* 44–48; S Bailey, 'What is a Material Contribution?' (2010) 30 *LS* 167. In *Williams v Bermuda Hospital Board* [2016] UKPC 4; [2016] AC 888, the Privy Council regarded *Bailey* as merely applying the traditional 'but for' test, as proposed by Foskett J at first instance, but this was not the view of the Court of Appeal deciding the case.

[26] Lord Phillips described the theory as 'discredited' in *Sienkiewicz v Greif* [2011] UKSC 10; [2011] 2 AC 229, at [102]. The theory was rejected by the High Court of Australia in *Amaca Properties v Booth* [2011] HCA 53.

[27] For example, it is understood that once a cell is cancerous, further exposures will have no causative effect: *Sienkiewicz* (n 26) [103].

[28] Compare comments from the same expert for claimants in *Jones v Secretary of State for Energy and Climate Change* [2012] EWHC 2936 (QB) (occupational lung and bladder cancer, the 'Phurnacite case') and *Heneghan* (n 13) (lung cancer). The expert argued in *Jones* that, if he were to be asked the same question that had been asked in *Fairchild*, he would say that all exposures had probably contributed to the carcinogenic process. This, however, did not sway either Court. In *Heneghan*, the Court of Appeal applied a proportionate version of *Fairchild* to the development of a lung cancer after occupational exposure to asbestos. The claimant had argued for full liability based on a material contribution. The judge below, like the judge in *Jones*, the Court of Appeal argued, was right to reject the opinion of Dr Rudd that every period of exposure in fact contributed to the development of the deceased's cancer: 'This was not a medical opinion. It was an opinion that an inference of causation could be drawn from the epidemiological evidence. But for the reasons stated in the Phurnacite case and by the judge in this case, it was wrong to draw this inference. The epidemiological evidence permitted the contribution to the risk of cancer attributable to an individual defendant to be quantified. But it went no further than that.'

First, the traditional tortious 'but for' test of causation may be applied. C has to show on the balance of probabilities that the injuries were caused either by D1 or by D2. On our scenario he cannot do either, and so C bears his own financial loss (other than to the extent that, in the unlikely event, he has first party insurance) and D1 and D2 escape liability. It may be that there is evidence that one or other of the defendants is more likely to have caused the injury, by reason of intensity or duration of exposure, so that the balance of probabilities test is satisfied in respect of that defendant. Lord Phillips considered this kind of point in *Sienkiewicz v Greif*,[29] questioning why, if such issues could be used to define what proportion of risk was contributed by a particular defendant, they could not also be used to determine who was liable on balance of probabilities. He and the other members of the UK Supreme Court rejected this kind of reliance on epidemiological evidence, proposing that it was not sufficiently probative.[30]

Secondly, the law may adopt an artificial allocation of responsibility. Australian state workers' compensation legislation, based upon the English Workmen's Compensation Acts 1897 and 1906, arbitrarily lumps the entire liability on D2 as the last employer in the chain.

Thirdly, the law may take a robust approach to compensation, scrap proof of causation as a requirement for the imposition of liability and treat every tortious act by D1 or D2 capable of giving rise to the injury as having actually done so. This is the approach adopted by section 3 of the English Compensation Act 2006, although only in respect of mesothelioma claims. There is apportionment between D1 and D2, but in indemnity or contribution proceedings as provided for by the 2006 Act and not at the point of claim by C.

Fourthly, a less robust approach, but also adopting the abandonment of proof of causation, is proportionality. This proved to be the common law solution to the problem in *Barker*,[31] following what had earlier been perceived as an initial flirtation with the third solution in *Fairchild v Glenhaven Funeral Services*. The House of Lords in *Fairchild* did not make any finding that the liability of each defendant should be restricted to a 'share' of damages, and indeed was not invited by the parties to consider apportionment – a fact that was mentioned by Lord Bingham.[32] In the absence of any such discussion, it was concluded by most, not unreasonably, that liability was in full. Presumably, settlement of the claims would have proceeded on this basis, and mesothelioma is, after all, an indivisible disease. It seems likely that the defendants were unwilling to urge the court to accept the notion of proportional liability, since liability insurers were at the same time

[29] *Sienkiewicz* (n 26).

[30] According to Lord Dyson (ibid [216]), a 'claimant who seeks to prove his case on the balance of probability in reliance entirely on statistical evidence will inevitably fail, since he is able to do no more than prove on the balance of probability that the defendant probably injured him.' The Justices were persuaded by S Gold, 'Causation in Toxic Torts: Burdens of Proof, Standards of Causation, and Statistical Evidence' (1986) 96 *Yale LJ* 376.

[31] *Barker* (n 6).

[32] *Fairchild* (n 1) [34].

defending claims in the pleural plaques litigation, their defence resting firmly on the position that causation of a risk of injury is not causation of injury. In the end, it turned out that the insurers could have it both ways: *Fairchild* could be interpreted as a proportional solution, while pleural plaques which merely act as a marker for the risk of serious injury could not themselves amount to an injury.[33] English law was not ready to edge closer to recovery for 'loss of chance' in this form, but was ready to adopt proportional liability in the circumstances of *Fairchild*.

Certainly, it appeared from *Fairchild* that the liability of each defendant was for causation of mesothelioma, given the impossibility of proving which exposures were fatal, and which were not. The subsequent decision of the House of Lords in *Barker v Corus* took a further controversial step because, although it restricted the impact of *Fairchild* on defendants (an outcome which in practical terms was reversed in mesothelioma cases by the Compensation Act 2006),[34] in terms of legal principle it struck out afresh. *Barker* could be read as either: (a) the first English decision to endorse proportionate liability for an indivisible disease, or (b) the first English decision awarding damages for exposure to risk, rather than for causation of injury. Nothing in the Compensation Act 2006 alters the impact of *Barker* on common law principles, so this choice of interpretation remains significant.

In *Durham*,[35] the Supreme Court made clear that liability in both *Fairchild* and *Barker* is liability for the fatal mesothelioma incurred, and not for exposure to risk. Interpretation (b) therefore was ruled out. While it might have been thought that this implied the correctness of Lord Rodger's dissenting opinion in *Barker* (supporting liability in full on the part of each tortfeasor), the possibility of proportional recovery was not in issue in *Durham*, since section 3 of the Compensation Act 2006 applied, and the question therefore did not arise. Subsequently however, in *International Energy Group v Zurich Insurance Plc UK*, interpretation (a) was adopted: under *Barker*, each exposure is a tortious act, and the tort (it was clearly determined in *Trigger*) is complete when injury is sustained; however, each tortfeasor is liable only for a proportion of the loss, reflecting the extent to which his own misconduct might be thought to have contributed to it. This will reflect the degree to which the defendant contributed to the *risk* of development of mesothelioma. If we were to assume consistency of intensity of exposure over the relevant period (unrealistic though this may be in many instances), each tortfeasor faces liability for his own proportion of the total exposure period. But many other variables may be in play.

What is notable is that the common law here has sought to produce, between claimant and defendant, a result which appears to be akin to the one achieved in the Civil Liability (Contribution) Act 1978 between tortfeasors. However, the latter statutory approach is openly based on broad-brushed principles of equity

[33] *Rothwell v Chemical and Insulating Co Limited* [2007] UKHL 39, [2008] 1 AC 281.
[34] Section 3.
[35] *Durham* (n 7).

as we have seen, evidently allowing for impressionistic judgement and allowing for consideration of factors that are not causative where appropriate. Like the contributory negligence legislation, it makes no spurious claim to exactness.[36] The common law, on the other hand, tends to operate through – or at least with – appeals to principle. The embrace of proportionate liability in *Barker*, as confirmed by *IEG*, is likely a somewhat different beast from the Civil Liability (Contribution) Act 1978; and, to the extent that it operates beyond the disease of mesothelioma, or outside the operation of the Compensation Act,[37] it certainly has different implications for claimants.

Returning to our exposure problem and its possible solutions, we can see that only the first response deprives C of compensation altogether. All the others allow C to recover, but, leaving aside the case of divisible injury,[38] each of them does so at the cost of the traditional need to establish 'but for' causation. So, traditional causation rules must take a bow if it is thought appropriate for C to be compensated. Of course, what is being abandoned would appear to be merely the need to *prove* causation, since this is considered impossible. The solutions would not apply to a defendant who could be proven not to be a cause. But in the face of impossibility of proof, selecting the relevant approach necessarily involves appeal to something other than causation.

Leaving aside the specific public policy issues arising from asbestos and mesothelioma – and the existence of a special statutory scheme in the UK for compensation in such cases[39] demonstrates that wider considerations are at play in this context – the question is whether the sacrifice of causal principles is warranted. It may be that each of the underpinning purposes of tort – deterrence, punishment, compensation, risk-spreading – point towards the victim's right to recover: victims typically do not have any or adequate first party insurance; few can bear the financial burdens of what may be inflicted on them; and state support is unlikely to be adequate, even in the most enlightened of nations. Alternatively, a fairness-based approach may be adopted: each party who breaches their duty leading to exposure to risk also contributes to the impossibility of proving causation, and it is better that these wrongdoers bear the cost of this impossibility.

[36] Underlining this, see J Goudkamp and D Nolan, 'Contributory Negligence in the Twenty-First Century: An Empirical Study of First Instance Decisions' (2016) 79 *MLR* 575; and *Jackson v Murray* [2015] UKSC 5 [27]: 'It is not possible for a court to arrive at an apportionment which is demonstrably correct' (Lord Reed).

[37] *IEG* itself was a mesothelioma case, but arose in Guernsey, to which the Compensation Act 2006 did not apply.

[38] Apportionment of liability for divisible injury is an application of traditional causation principles, rather than a departure from them.

[39] The Diffuse Mesothelioma Payment Scheme (DMPS) was launched in April 2014 and began taking applications from July 2014. It was set up to provide payments to sufferers of mesothelioma who were negligently exposed to asbestos at work but unable to pursue a civil claim because their former employer no longer exists and their former employer's insurer cannot be traced. The insurance industry acknowledged their failure to keep adequate records and this was a factor in its agreement to fund the DMPS via a levy on active employers' liability insurers.

Though this may appear principled, it is nevertheless a novel principle for tort law to adopt. It reaches for a pragmatic solution on principled (fairness) grounds. Tort scholars have been mixed in their response, but there have been distinguished and loud condemnatory voices ranged against the *Fairchild* and *Barker* line of cases. Yes, compensation has been achieved, but at too high a price to established legal principle. The argument runs that *Fairchild* is an anomaly and should not be extended any further.[40] Nevertheless, *Fairchild* has been extended to occupational lung cancer resulting (on balance of probabilities) from exposure to asbestos.[41] The Court of Appeal stated that *Fairchild* would apply wherever its preconditions were present. As Lord Dyson put it:

> I can see no reason not to apply the *Fairchild* exception to the facts of the present case. There can be no objection in principle to extending it to situations which are not materially different from Fairchild's case. Indeed, principle requires that in a situation which is truly analogous to that considered in that case, the Fairchild exception should be applied. Otherwise, the law in this area would be inconsistent and incoherent.

The search is on therefore for a principled interpretation of *Fairchild*, which would not treat it as a narrow response to a particular problem – although certain of the preconditions of *Fairchild* spelt out by the Court of Appeal in *Heneghan* (such as the insistence that the rival causes involve a 'single agent'), may be resistant in the end to principled explanation. This search for principle is not however the key focus of this chapter. We adopt the alternative view that *Fairchild* is a pragmatic response to inevitable issues. Whether on the principled approach, or on our more pragmatic, problem-driven approach, *Fairchild* would tend to resist containment. The implications for its extent, however, would be different.

In our view, the pragmatic arguments for compensation are overwhelming. Not adopting a solution of some sort to the problems posed to claimants would be almost unthinkable. At the level of tort law and of insurance law, this may be addressed by considering the broad purposes of the law. There are differences, but the two deeply influence one another.[42] Securing compensation for those harmed by breaches of duty in a fair and efficient manner is an aspiration of the law of tort and liability insurance together. In insurance law, based as it is in contracting, we may add the necessity of reflecting commercial sense. On this premise, we move from a debate about causation to a debate about apportionment and allocation. But we will return, as appropriate, to the arguments of fairness and principle which are hinted at by Lord Dyson, when we consider the likely limits to the application of *Fairchild*.

What is apparent from the above scenarios is that, assuming that neither D1 nor D2 is insolvent or does not have insurance, all recovery responses for C lead

[40] Lord Brown expressed this view clearly in *Sienkiewicz* (n 26) [186]: 'mesothelioma claims must now be considered from the defendant's standpoint a lost cause, there is to my mind a lesson to be learned from losing it: the law tampers with the 'but for' test of causation at its peril'.

[41] *Heneghan* (n 13).

[42] We have argued this point at length elsewhere, most comprehensively in Merkin and Steele (n 9).

to an ultimate proportional sharing by D1 and D2. The second, artificial response leaves the loss entirely in the hands of D2, although D2 may well have a contribution claim against D1. The fourth response applies proportionality at the point of recovery by C, although, under this scenario, C may have to bear a proportion of the loss himself if there are self-inflicted exposures, or exposures from atmospheric conditions. The third response contemplates an initial 100 per cent payment by whichever of D1 and D2 is called upon to pay, but tempered by a contribution claim against the other. One theoretical problem arises from the third response where there have been exposures from other sources. It is far from clear who bears the loss for such exposures ie, whether it is borne entirely by the paying defendant or whether that defendant can recover some proportion from others liable to contribute.[43] We refer to this point below.

It cannot be questioned that *Fairchild* has highlighted a range of problems that were not contemplated when it was decided, and at time of writing those problems have yet to be fully resolved. But does that mean that *Fairchild* was either responsible for those problems, or wrongly decided? We take the view that there cannot be a proper analysis if tort issues are isolated from the underpinning insurance arrangements. If attention is focused not on tort law, which may be considered the 'gatekeeper' to compensation, but rather on how tort losses inflicted by multiple defendants are actually to be paid for, a series of entirely different and potentially more complex legal questions are exposed. Those issues are not just raised under liability policies providing indemnity for claims in tort, but are replicated in first party insurance. A further contention that we make is that insurance law in general has a lot to learn from *Fairchild*, and that there is a good case to align tort law and insurance law in a regime which includes elements of proportional liability in response to otherwise intractable problems. These problems are otherwise inclined to create problems of unfairness, with a particularly heavy impact on claimants. In short, causation has been unable to adapt to produce acceptable results in the situations under consideration.

C. Putting *Fairchild* to the Test: Life Without *Fairchild*

Without *Fairchild*, a victim of exposure in the conditions of uncertainty to which the decision applies by two or more defendants would have no tort claim, so, to that extent, the case is of crucial importance. However, it is our contention that in other respects the decision in *Fairchild* has contributed relatively little to the complexities of paying for mesothelioma claims and that such complexities arise wholly independently of *Fairchild*. To illustrate the point, let it be supposed that C has been exposed to asbestos by D1 alone for a period of 20 years and that there has been no self-exposure or atmospheric exposure. C would easily be able to satisfy a court that, on the balance of probabilities, his disease was caused by

[43] The 2006 Act precludes a contribution claim against the victim for any period of self-exposure.

negligent exposure, and there is no need to engage *Fairchild*. At that point, tort law, manning the gate to compensation, can lift the barrier and relax in the knowledge that nobody has played fast and loose with sacred causation principles. C's claim against D1 does not need to identify any individual exposure in the 20-year period as giving rise to his injuries, and C's claim cannot be time-barred unless he delays for more than three years after the discoverability of his injuries. It matters not whether liability is based upon an established tort per individual exposure or whether it flows from a course of conduct.

What, then, of D1's employers' liability insurance, which has been compulsory in the UK since 1 January 1972? The initial question is necessarily whether those policies actually respond to mesothelioma claims. In *Durham* the Supreme Court held that policies issued both in the pre-compulsory period and thereafter are to be construed as responding to exposure, rather than to injury. The latter finding would have, in all but exceptional cases, rendered the insurance devoid of value: injury-based policies apply to injuries inflicted upon a current employee, and mesothelioma injury – kicking in 30–40 years or so after exposure – is more likely to affect employees who have moved on to other employment, or who have retired. The Supreme Court's finding of exposure cover filled the 'black hole'. So we are off first base, and at this point in the reasoning we remain in a *Fairchild*-free zone. But for no longer; once there is more than one insurer involved,[44] proportionality and allocation necessarily raise their heads. It is to be remembered that the scenario with which we are concerned is one where single exposures do not contribute equally to injury: where that is the case, it may be possible to prove – by evidence or at least inference – a uniform regularity of exposure, so that each can be regarded as contributing to the loss at identifiable times. The problem is the one previously captured starkly in terms of the 'single strand', and now more generally present in the scientific – or at least legal – consensus that not all fibres are involved in the causation of mesothelioma.

Let us assume that for a 20-year period of exposure, D1 was insured by U1 for the first 15 years and U2 for the final 5 years. Can D1 recover from one or other of his insurers? There is a range of possible responses, reflecting those discussed earlier in respect to tortious liability. Outcome (a): D1 cannot, on the balance of probabilities, identify the year in which the killing exposure took place, because every year has an equal chance, and so can recover nothing. Outcome (b): D1 can show that, because U1 was on risk for 75 per cent of the period, on the balance of probabilities the killing exposure took place during U1's time on risk. It follows that U1 must bear the entire loss without contribution from U2, because, on the balance of probabilities, the damage did not occur during U2's five years on risk. That does not of course mean that D1 has identified which of the 15 years is the relevant years, just that it is more likely than not to have been one of them. Outcome (c): the loss is to be allocated 75:25 as between U1 and U2.

[44] And even if there is only one insurer, what follows will arise where that insurer seeks to bring claims against the various reinsurers on risk during its period of exposure.

The difficulty with Outcome (c) is that there is no insurance authority for it. To the contrary, apportionment of loss does not form a part of English insurance law, other than in the limited context of policies subject to average under which the assured is deemed to be his own insurer for the proportion of underinsurance: the result is that losses are divided between assured and insurer in their respective proportions.[45]

The final possibility is Outcome (d): each exposure is to be regarded as giving rise to a tort in its own right, so that liability can be pinned onto any exposure in any year. On that basis, each of U1 and U2 is liable for 100 per cent, but because there is concurrent liability then there is a right of contribution in the paying insurer from the non-paying insurer. At that point, as we noted in Section I above, a further complication arises, because the right of contribution is generally determined on an independent liability basis, ie, on the basis that the liability of each insurer is ascertained and the loss is allocated accordingly.[46] Adopting Outcome (d) in an unmodified form means that U1 and U2 are each liable for 100 per cent, so that whichever pays can claim 50 per cent back from the other despite the disparity in time on risk.

The point here being made is that, even where *Fairchild* has no part to play in pinning tort liability on D1, the allocation issue becomes live, albeit at one remove. Since we are now in the realms of insurance, we should ask which of the four outcomes produces the solution making the most commercial sense? Outcome (a) is plainly nonsensical, given that D1 has paid premiums for 20 years. Outcome (b) has two drawbacks. First, the insurer with the shorter period of cover is relieved of liability, even if the difference is a matter of minutes. Secondly, varying the facts and assuming that U1 and U2 are on risk for ten years each means that it is impossible to satisfy the burden of proof in respect of either and there is no recovery. Outcome (c) has the benefit of rough and ready justice and probably reflects the outcome that conforms with the risks undertaken by U1 and U2, but it has no legal basis. Outcome (d) achieves much the same as (c), with the additional benefit for D1 that the paying insurer bears the risk of the other's insolvency but with the downside that it is necessary to tinker with the rules on contribution between insurers to ensure that the loss is divided proportionately to time on risk and not equally.

We know how the Supreme Court actually dealt with this very problem, as the facts of *IEG v Zurich* are in essence those set out above. The minority of three opted for (c) and the majority of four opted for (d), but with the modification that it was necessary to vary the contribution principle to a proportional rather than independent liability approach, so that whoever paid was entitled to contribution based on time on risk.

The majority view in *IEG* was clearly based on the principle that, *Fairchild* having been decided for better or worse, it was necessary to extend *Fairchild* to the

[45] Marine Insurance Act 1906 (UK), s 81.

[46] *Commercial Union Assurance Co Ltd v Hayden* [1977] QB 804.

underlying insurance to maintain consistency. The minority view was that *Fairchild* was to be disregarded at the insurance stage and that proportionality was the appropriate solution. However, if we assume that *Barker* and *Fairchild* had not been decided and that the allocation problem had arisen only at the insurance stage, there is a powerful argument that the outcome in *IEG* would have been the same. With no *Fairchild*, the principle upon which the majority judgment proceeded is cut away, but that does not mean that it would not be reached by some other route. It is to be noted that nobody in *IEG* argued for (a) or (b). However, there is authority in favour of (a). In *Kelly v Norwich Union Fire Insurance Ltd*[47] Mr Kelly insured his bungalow with Norwich Union under a 12-month policy incepting on 29 October 1977. The relevant cover was for '[l]oss or damage to the buildings caused by any of the insured perils' and the insurers were to pay 'in respect of events occurring during the period of insurance.' The policy was renewed on the anniversary date for a further year on terms for all material purposes identical, and renewals continued until 28 October 1981. As a consequence of effects of the long, hot summer of 1976 on the subsoil, before the 1977 policy incepted there was a break in the mains water pipe leading to the bungalow, leading to an escape of water into the underlying soil and repairs were effected. A further break occurred at the repaired point in 1978. By April 1981 cracks appeared in the bungalow's walls, and a claim was made against Norwich Union. Further investigation showed that there had been a further escape of water in 1980 and that the water had caused the soil to 'heave'. The result, therefore, was that the two possible causes of water causing heave were the pre-policy escape in 1977 and the post-policy escape in 1980. Each side appointed experts, and it proved impossible for either of them to apportion the relative contribution of the two causes. For that reason, the claim was not pressed, on the basis that Norwich Union should be liable for a proportional part of the loss, and the judge noted that:

> In appropriate circumstances I would have thought it right to adopt such an approach, although I have been referred to no English case where this has been done. Indeed, I was never invited by counsel for Mr. Kelly so to apportion, and there has been no argument about it.

Instead, Mr Kelly had to argue that both bursts were covered by the insurance. On that he failed. The insurance by its terms covered events and not damage, so it was necessary to show that the events giving rise to the damage occurred during the currency of the policy. However, because he could not show which of the events gave rise to the damage – one before the insurance incepted and one after the insurance incepted – the claim had to fail.

Kelly can of course be distinguished as applying to a property policy, rather than a liability policy, but there seems nothing of substance in that point. In *Kelly* and *IEG* the policies covered exposure rather than damage. The lesson from

[47] [1989] 2 All ER 888 ('*Kelly*').

Kelly is that, if there are two exposures, each of which is capable of causing the loss but it is not possible to show which of them actually did so, then there is no recovery. Apportionment is precluded for the very reason that there is no relevant evidence.

Had the facts of *IEG* come before the Supreme Court in a *Fairchild*-free world, *Kelly* would surely have featured in the arguments. There is no way of knowing whether *Kelly* would have survived, but it is a reasonable guess that the absurdity of Outcome (a) and the arbitrary nature of Outcome (b) would have led the Court to ditch *Kelly* and to alight on either (c) or (d). In the mesothelioma context, Outcome (d) secures full payment for D1 and throws upon the paying insurer the risk of insolvencies of potential contributors. Outcome (c) secures as much payment for D1 as is available from those insurers who are solvent. Outcome (c) has at first sight an important advantage over (d), in that it removes to a limited extent a reinsurance problem. Under Outcome (c), the paying insurer need look to his reinsurers only for his own proportion of liabilities, whereas under Outcome (d) the paying insurer may well have to claim from his reinsurers both its own liabilities and those of any other insurer irrecoverable by reason of that insurer's insolvency. But even that potential advantage is only partly of assistance. Every year of insurance will be reinsured, and there will almost certainly be some variation in the identities of participating reinsurers at each renewal. The paying insurer will therefore be required to show that the loss falls into a given reinsurance year. As we know, that is impossible. The issues in *IEG* thus arise at the reinsurance level, if anything in a more acute form, and potential contribution recoveries are just one further complexity.

It is perhaps too far-fetched to suggest that Outcome (d), the solution adopted in *Fairchild*, is close to inevitable. However, it is at the very least one of two – and in our view the only two – plausible alternatives.

III. In Support of *Fairchild*: Causation in the Insurance Context

A. The Doctrine of Proximate Cause in Insurance Law

We have already established that, although the insurance cases arising in the wake of *Fairchild* have required novel solutions, these solutions might have been seized upon as a matter of common sense, irrespective of any felt need to replicate *Fairchild* at the insurance level. The alternative solutions would not have commended themselves. But how far could the influence of this extend?

Established insurance law principles require the assured to prove on the balance of probabilities that the loss was proximately caused by an insured peril occurring in the period of cover. Absence of any evidence means that the claim will be lost even though there was undoubtedly insurance coverage from one or other source in every eventuality. In the following paragraphs, we first outline the derivation of these principles and illustrate their effect. We then consider whether *Fairchild*, or at least its example, does or should pose a challenge to these established principles. Is the absence of evidence the same as the impossibility of proof?

Causation principles in insurance law were relatively late to develop. Until the growth of other forms of insurance in the 1850s, the courts were concerned almost exclusively with marine disputes, and the overwhelming bulk of the decided cases between 1756 and 1815 – the formative period of the law under Lords Mansfield and Ellenborough – were concerned with wartime conditions. Enemy warships and armed merchant vessels (privateers) derived a good living from seizing British merchant vessels and selling both vessel and cargo following condemnation by a prize court. Virtually all of the principles of law subsequently codified in the Marine Insurance Act 1906 were developed in seizure cases. The Lloyd's SG Policy, formally adopted in 1779 but based on wordings in use for the previous 150 years,[48] generally insured war and marine risks alike, and relevant exceptions related not to the cause of loss, but rather to the amount recoverable. However, war conditions led to increasing use of the 'FCS Warranty', an exclusion stating that the subject matter was 'warranted free of capture and seizure'.[49] This first appeared in the reported cases in 1743,[50] was pressed into greater use during the American War of Independence and became commonplace in the Napoleonic period. The FCS Warranty was the most important source of causation disputes.

Causation questions were resolved on an 'immediate' or 'direct' basis. That was generally taken to point to the last thing to happen to the subject matter, unless there was a clean break between events. Thus a vessel driven aground by bad weather and then confiscated by the enemy was lost by the latter cause,[51] and a vessel taken by the enemy and then lost by sea perils en route to an enemy port was regarded as the victim of a sea peril rather than capture.[52] It was only where the loss was complete at the time of enemy intervention that sea perils were to be regarded as the 'proximate cause'.[53] These and similar cases were reconsidered by the House of Lords in the landmark ruling *Leyland Shipping Co* v *Norwich Union Fire Insurance Society*,[54] where a vessel holed by a torpedo limped into Le Havre, only to be ordered out lest she sank in a coming storm. She was lost at sea in the storm. Their Lordships rejected the earlier case law pointing at the storm, and, in holding that the proximate cause of the loss was the torpedo rather than sea perils, each of the Law Lords used various terms to confirm the concept that the proximate cause was the effective, rather than the last, cause.

[48] It was not abandoned until 1983.

[49] The risk to merchant vessels was that of capture, not destruction. There was no profit to be made from burning or sinking merchant vessels.

[50] *Green v Brown* (1743) 2 Str 1199.

[51] *Green v Elmslie* (1794) Peake 279; *Livie v Janson* (1807).

[52] *Hagedorn v Whitmore* (1816) 1 Stark 157.

[53] *Bondrett v Hentigg* (1816) Holt 149; *Hahn v Corbett* (1824) 2 Bing 205. Unlike the position in English tort law, insurance law continues to work with the terminology of 'proximate cause', despite significant developments in the principles applied.

[54] [1918] AC 350 (HL).

Leyland Shipping was taken a step further in *Rhesa Shipping v Edmunds, The Popi M*.[55] In that case a fishing vessel disappeared without explanation off the coast of Scotland. Competing contentions were put forward: that of the insurers was unseaworthiness; that of the assured was the possibility of the nets having been snared by a Russian submarine. Neither could be proven, and at first instance Bingham J found for the assured on the basis of 'the least unlikely' cause. The House of Lords rejected that concept and instead confirmed that the assured bears the burden of proving that the loss was proximately caused by an insured peril. It was argued in *The Popi M* that, where competing causes of loss were put forward, it was appropriate to apply the Sherlock Holmes dictum that 'once you eliminate the impossible, whatever remains, no matter how improbable, must be the truth'.[56] That suggestion was viewed with deep suspicion, although not entirely ruled out in *The Popi M*, but it is now clear from later cases that the choice between two competing suggestions is not binary and that there is always a third possibility, namely that nothing has been proved to the standard of the balance of probabilities.[57]

B. Proving the Time of Loss: Reassessing *Kelly*

In *Kelly v Norwich Union*, as we have seen, Mr Kelly was plainly the victim of an insured peril, and suffered consequent damage, in the life of the insurance. What stopped him recovering was the possibility that the same peril occurring at an earlier point was also the potential cause of the damage. Minor changes to the facts demonstrate the weakness in the reasoning. Let it be supposed that, in year 1, Mr Kelly was insured by IA, and there was an underground leak arising from an insured peril. In year 2, Mr Kelly was insured by IB and there was another underground leak arising from an insured peril. In year 3, Mr Kelly discovered damage. It does not matter for our purposes whether the insurer in year 3 is IA, IB or non-existent: there cannot be a claim in year 3 because there is no insured peril in year 3, only damage. So Mr Kelly's claim has to be brought against IA and IB, and each claim inevitably fails because IA and IB can both point their respective fingers at each other and Mr Kelly can prove nothing either way. A related problem has arisen in the aftermath of the consecutive earthquakes in Christchurch in September 2010, February 2011 and June 2011, causing cumulative damage and frequently ultimate total loss. Many policyholders have been faced with the scenario of a change of insurers between the earthquakes, and there have been disputes as to the allocation of damage and repair costs to successive events.

[55] [1983] 2 Lloyd's Rep 235 ('*The Popi M*').

[56] A quote that appears in *The Adventure of the Blanched Soldier* (1926).

[57] *Nulty v Milton Keynes BC* [2013] EWCA Civ 15; *Ace European Group Ltd v Chartis Insurance UK Ltd* [2013] EWCA Civ 224; *Contact (Print And Packaging) Ltd v Travelers Insurance Co Ltd* [2018] EWHC 83 (TCC).

The issue has not been as acute as that in *Kelly* and indeed *Fairchild*, because it has proved possible to apply science to allow the assured to jump the balance of probabilities hurdle, although there has been interesting analysis of the credibility of modelling used as evidence for the purpose.[58]

But assume that the insurer in both year 1 and year 2 was IA. Can IA escape liability by arguing that unless someone in Mr Kelly's position can place his claim in either year 1 or year 2 there is no liability? From Mr Kelly's point of view that outcome is bizarre: he was insured for a two year period, and insured perils occurred in the two-year period, but he recovers nothing. From IA's point of view, the position is potentially somewhat different. Policy terms may have changed between the two years: a long hot summer before the year 1 insurance incepted has given rise to a mass of claims in year 1, and IA decides that with effect from year 2 the deductible for heave or subsidence damage should be raised from £100 to £1000. Additionally, in the light of the long hot summer, reinsurers decide to exclude heave and subsidence damage from the renewed casualty treaty issued to IA in respect of claims for perils occurring in year 2. So the year of coverage matters both to Mr Kelly and to IA, albeit in different degrees. Whose problem should this be? We suggest that it is contrary to sense to deprive Mr Kelly of all cover, that some proportional solution is called for and that, as far as he is concerned, the loss can be treated as occurring equally in each year: it is then a matter of taste as to whether he has to bear the full amount of each deductible or perhaps only half of each deductible, but that is a relatively trivial matter in the scale of things. As far as IA's outward claim against reinsurers is concerned, that follows IA's liability to Mr Kelly, so that IA cannot arbitrarily place the loss in year 1 and the reinsurers cannot insist that it is treated as a year 2 loss and consequently not reinsured.

An issue of this type arose in *MMI Ltd v Sea Insurance Co Ltd*,[59] where the Court of Appeal was satisfied on the balance of probabilities that a series of thefts at a dockyard over a period of 18 months, straddling three policy periods, had occurred with uniform regularity and could be allocated proportionately to each period of insurance. It is of interest to note that a single insurer was on risk for the entire period, and the question was how the losses were to be allocated to the three successive years of reinsurance coverage: there is nothing in the report to indicate an issue between assured and insurers whereby the assured was put to proof of loss

[58] *Vero Insurance New Zealand Ltd v Morrison* [2015] NZCA 246, where it was held that a model based on earthquake intensity was unreliable and to be taken into account only if there was no better evidence. Intensity modelling was similarly regarded with scepticism in *Prattley Enterprises Ltd v Vero Insurance New Zealand Ltd* [2016] NZCA 67, on the basis that it said nothing about repair costs following each event, and in *Sadat v Tower Insurance Ltd* [2017] NZHC 1550 such evidence was rejected entirely.

[59] [1998] Lloyd's Rep IR 421(CA). But contrast *Ted Baker Ltd v Axa Insurance* [2017] EWCA Civ 4097, where the policy imposed a £5000 per loss deductible in a scenario where there had been regular thefts over a five-year period. There was simply no evidence as to the size or frequency of losses to enable the Court to determine whether and how often thefts exceeded the deductible, with the outcome that the assured recovered nothing despite suffering losses of around £2 million in that period.

per year, as demanded by *Kelly*. However, it is hardly satisfactory to say that just because the point is not always taken in practice then there is no problem.

The proportional approach that we have suggested could resolve the *Kelly* problem owes a great deal to the example of *Fairchild*, and arises from a similar problem in a different context. We know the general cause of the damage suffered, but do not know which policy period it fell within, nor can we know. Essentially, each potential claim (against IA in period 1 or against IA in period 2) is, under *Fairchild*, now capable of being successful (though precisely what this means needs further articulation). If it is right that *Fairchild* provides a workable solution to the *Kelly* problem, then, at risk of letting the tail wag the dog, it must surely be appropriate to apply the same analysis to the scenario in which IA is on risk in year 1 and IB is on risk in year two. The number of cases is likely to be very small, as there will generally be enough evidence for the court to reach a conclusion on the balance of probabilities, but, where that is not the case, then the loss could perfectly easily be split. The *Fairchild* analysis, as adopted by the majority ruling in *IEG*, would allow Mr Kelly to sue either IA or IB for the full amount, leaving the paying insurer to recover what it can by way of contribution. The minority ruling in *IEG* would require Mr Kelly to claim half from each insurer. Given the current, tight prudential regulation of insurers, which of the approaches is adopted is probably of no great significance, at least other than for the reinsurers involved. *Fairchild* seems to us to point to either of two perfectly good solutions. Far from condemning the decision, this suggests that it is worthy of wider application.

C. Proving the Cause of Loss

We have thus far argued, in the context of *Kelly*, that an application of apportionment under an approach resembling *Fairchild* is appropriate where a claim is defeated because the time of the loss cannot be pinned down, even though there was insurance in place whenever the loss occurred. We would go further and suggest that apportionment may be appropriate where there is undoubtedly insurance in place but the cause of loss, and thus the appropriate insurer, cannot be identified. This however takes our discussion into new territory. In *Heneghan* as we have seen, the Court of Appeal ruled that *Fairchild* should apply in any case where its preconditions were fulfilled, to avoid incoherence in the law. The case was clearly and closely concerned with difficulties of evidence and proof in relation to industrial disease, and the preconditions of *Fairchild* as stated by the Court of Appeal included the (problematic) 'single agent' criterion. In *Heneghan* itself, it was treated as established on the balance of probabilities that the deceased's cancer was caused by exposure to asbestos. There were other potential causes (the deceased was a smoker), but the exposure to asbestos more than 'doubled the risk' that cancer would develop. The insurance cases we consider next cannot fit the single agent criterion. They are cases concerning unexplained losses, where sufficient evidence is impossible. Our argument is that the problems raised are equivalent to those problems with which *Fairchild* dealt; and that, far from confining the *Fairchild* approach to its enclave, it should be expanded as providing a more rational solution to the issues raised. This is not surprising. Outside the insurance field, in the law of tort, notions of 'proximate cause' were developed in all their gory complexity in order to deal with the injustice of the complete defence of contributory negligence. The reformed, proportional form of contributory negligence was devised precisely in order to supercede all of this. Can common law now achieve similar results to deal with continued problems in the application of the doctrine of proximate cause in insurance, in the particular context of impossibility of proof?

The Popi M and subsequent cases deny recovery for unexplained loss, on the basis that no contention can be proved or disproved. There may or may not be insurance coverage, but it cannot be demonstrated either way. In those circumstances there cannot be a claim, and the *Fairchild* principle has not been extended so far. *Fairchild* itself dealt with a case where it has been proved that there is a loss for which someone is responsible, but irresolvable doubt as to who that person might be; and the extensions of this to deal with cases where there are alternative, non-tortious causes have insisted on the 'single agent' criterion. However, we suggest that *The Popi M* does come into conflict with the spirit of *Fairchild*, raising very similar problems to the ones it was designed to ameliorate, where it is clear that one or other policy does respond to the loss.[60] Consider Malaysian Airlines flight MH370, which disappeared on 8 March 2014. Four years on, there is still no clear evidence as to why it was lost. Let us suppose – not unreasonably – that the aircraft's liability to passengers was insured by separate insurers against respectively aviation risks and terrorism risks. One or other of the insurers is plainly liable, but there is no way of knowing whether the cause of the loss was mechanical fault, or hostile action. This scenario differs from that in *The Popi M*, in that here there is insurance coverage whatever the cause of the loss but the insurer cannot be identified, whereas in *The Popi M* there may or may not be insurance coverage: nobody knows. Applying *The Popi M* to MH370, the assured will fail because the assured cannot establish a proximate cause on the balance of probabilities against either insurer.[61] Even if we alter the scenario in a minor fashion by assuming a single insurer covering all losses, the problem does not disappear if the insurer has separate reinsurances for aviation and terrorism: the insurer pays, but which of the reinsurers can be called upon for indemnification? The law points to no recovery, but this does not seem to be a logical outcome when there was plainly cover in place. In such a case, *The Popi M* can be distinguished, using *Fairchild* as the means to distinguish the problems for solution. In the tort context, if scientific evidence cannot establish which of two defendants is liable, *Fairchild* requires them to apportion the loss. Arguably, *Fairchild* may be applied by analogy where

[60] This may also be the case where it is shown on balance of probabilities that the loss was covered by one policy or another, and we return to this shortly.

[61] It is understood that insurers did in fact pay for this loss, but the basis of the settlement is unknown.

it is not clear which insurance policy should respond either where the alternative causes are themselves insured (all potential causes ought to give rise to liability, but are prevented by the existence of an alternative cause); or, by extension, to the cases where there is an alternative uninsured cause, provided it can be shown that, on the balance of probabilities, the loss arose from one of the insured causes.[62] The latter will be inherently difficult in the absence of evidence, but the former should hold good, resembling the problems of over-determination on which some of the reasoning in *Fairchild* was based. This reflects our problem-based approach to *Fairchild*: that it showed a pragmatic route to dealing with an inherent problem which is not confined to mesothelioma, nor even to industrial disease, and can point the way to suitable solutions for a range of similar issues.

D. Concurrent, Interdependent Causes of Loss

Where there are two or more possible causes of loss, the general approach of the courts is to strive to identify one or other of the causes as the proximate cause. However, that is not always possible, and where one of the causes is insured but the other excluded the position is governed by the ruling of the Court of Appeal in *Wayne Tank v Employers Liability Association*.[63] Here, the assured installed equipment for storing and conveying liquid wax used in the manufacture of the modelling clay 'plasticine'. A major fire occurred at the premises, and, in successful proceedings brought against the assured by the owners, two separate forms of negligence were identified: using dangerous materials; and leaving the equipment unattended but in operation before it had been tested. The assured sought indemnification under a liability policy that excluded 'damage caused by the nature or condition of any goods … sold or supplied by or on behalf of the assured'. The Court of Appeal concluded that the proximate cause of the loss was the nature of the goods so that the exclusion operated, but ruled obiter that, had it not been possible to split the two causes, there would have been judgment for the insurers. The rationale for giving priority to the exclusion is far from obvious. The decision turned on contract interpretation, Lord Denning being of the view that, if the underwriters 'have stipulated for freedom, the only way of giving effect to it is by exempting them altogether'.[64] Lord Denning added that the generality of an insuring clause should give way to the specificity of an exclusion, a comment that is far from convincing and indeed frequently an inaccurate representation of how policies are drafted.

[62] We have here stated the *Heneghan* decision (n 13), in effect, without recourse to the 'single agent' notion.

[63] [1974] QB 57 ('*Wayne Tank*').

[64] If one cause is insured and the other uninsured but not excluded, then Lord Denning's principle is inapplicable, in that the insurers have not stipulated for freedom, and there is full recovery because the insurers have been unable to prove the operation of an exclusion: *Global Process Systems Inc v Berhad, The Cendor Mopu* [2011] UKSC 5.

The proposition put forward in *Wayne Tank* has received general acceptance in England[65] and other common law jurisdictions. A recent decision in Australia is *Sheehan v Lloyd's Underwriters*,[66] where the Federal Court was faced with fatal damage to an engine of the assured's motor vessel. Within minutes of leaving berth, the engine suffered a loss of oil pressure, but the assured – who had neglected to read the manual and thus was unaware of the significance of the various alarms flashing and sounding – wrongly thought that it would be safe to return to berth at the automatically reduced speed. The policy covered 'accident' but excluded 'faulty design …' Allsop J held that the assured's conduct constituted an accident, but that the claim was defeated because proximate cause of the loss was faulty design in the form of defective oil seals. Allsop J ruled in the alternative that, had the two causes been interdependent and concurrent, the outcome would have been the same.

Wayne Tank has also been recently reaffirmed in New Zealand. In *AMI Insurance Ltd v Legg*[67] the assured operated both a farming business and a landscaping business from his lifestyle block. The assured's liability policy extended to farming but excluded 'legal liability arising out of or in connection with any retail shop'. The assured burned rubbish from both businesses on a single heap. The fire was thought to have been extinguished, but flared up as a result of weather conditions and caused substantial damage to neighbouring property. The Court of Appeal held that the insurers were not responsible for the loss, by reference to the evidence and to the precise terms of the coverage clause. The Court of Appeal nevertheless added that, had the point arisen, *Wayne Tank* would have been applied: it had been recognised in earlier New Zealand authorities[68] and to reject the principle as a matter of the construction of the words used would be to take contra proferentem beyond its acceptable limits.

E. Critique of the Concurrent Causes Rule

Wayne Tank bites in two different situations. The first is where the assured has a single policy: the assured must initially bring himself within the insuring clause on the balance of probabilities, and if that can be done then it is open to the insurers to demonstrate the operation of an exclusion on the balance of probabilities. It has not been suggested in the cases that if the assured gets home on the first point then that automatically defeats any possible reliance on an exclusion,[69] nor

[65] *Kuwait Airways Corp SAK v Kuwait Insurance Co SA* [1999] Lloyd's Rep IR 803; *Midland Mainline Ltd v Commercial Union Assurance Co Ltd* [2004] Lloyd's Rep IR 239; *Tektrol Ltd v International Insurance Co of Hanover Ltd* [2006] Lloyd's Rep IR 38; *UK Insurance v Farrow* [2016] EWHC 1090 (Comm).

[66] [2017] FCA 1340. See also *Wiesac Pty Ltd v Insurance Australia Ltd* [2018] QSC 123.

[67] [2017] NZCA 321.

[68] *State Insurance Office Manager v Bettany* (1990) 6 ANZ Insurances Cases 76,818; *Countryside Finance Ltd v State Insurance Ltd* [1993] 3 NZLR 745; *Body Corporate 326421 v Auckland Council* [2015] NZHC 862.

[69] There is an exception in marine insurance, where it has been held that perils of the seas (insured) and inherent vice (excluded) are mutually exclusive, so that if the assured proves the former then

has it been suggested that there is a 50 per cent prospect that the assured is covered and should therefore have a claim for 50 per cent of the proceeds.

The second situation in which *Wayne Tank* has an impact, bringing us closer to *Fairchild*, is where the assured has two or more policies potentially covering the loss. Many business activities take out insurance covering specific risks on a mutually exclusive basis. By way of illustration: a supplier of products will carry product liability insurance and public liability insurance (generally as separate sections of the same policy); an integrated construction company will carry professional indemnity insurance for the design stage and construction insurance for the building stage; and a shipowner will carry marine risks insurance and separate war risks insurance. Each form of insurance will exclude the other, so – assuming no gaps in coverage or overlaps – the assumption is that one or other of the policies will respond to any loss. If there is evidence as to what has occurred,[70] and the claim has elements that trigger both the insuring clause and the exclusion, there will be no recovery by virtue of the exclusions even though the assured can prove that each policy responds to the loss. Here we have a similarly absurd solution to the one featuring two hunters, with which *Fairchild* initially grappled. Here, each insurer can point to the existence of the other, and the assured bears the consequences.

Wayne Tank has not gone entirely unchallenged. In *Derksen v 539938 Ontario Ltd*[71] the assured had mutually exclusive employers liability and motor insurance policies. An employee was injured in a work-related motor accident, with the result that the employer's liability insurer denied liability by reference to the exclusion. Plainly a claim under the motor policy would have met with the same response. The assured was held by the Supreme Court of Canada to be entitled to an indemnity under the employer's liability policy, and *Wayne Tank* was rejected. *Derkson* was seized upon by Nation J at first instance in the *Legg* case, *New Zealand Fire Service Commission v Legg*,[72] the judge stating that 'the *Wayne Tank* principle should not be extended to apply to a situation where liability has been caused by an event or circumstances which the insurer agreed to cover but there is some connection with circumstances, not causative of the insured's loss, which the insurer argues should exclude its liability.' *Legg* was itself a case in which there was separate insurance for non-farming activities but separate defences were raised to the claim, and it is clear that Nation J thought that an assured who had two policies apparently providing comprehensive coverage should be able to recover from at least one of the insurers. As we have seen, the Court of Appeal thought otherwise.[73]

the latter is automatically discounted: *Global Process Systems Inc v Syarikat Takaful Malaysia Berhad, The Cendor Mopu* [2011] UKSC 5.

[70] We have already discussed the position where there is no such evidence.

[71] [2001] SCC 72 ('*Derksen*').

[72] [2016] NZHC 1492.

[73] The first instance decision in *Legg* was, before the Court of Appeal's reversal of it, questioned in *Sadat v Tower Insurance Ltd* [2017] NZHC 1550.

Authority against *Wayne Tank* is presently slender, and the authority of the case has recently been reaffirmed by the UK Supreme Court. In *Atlasnavios-Navegacao Lda v Navigators Insurance Co Ltd*[74] the assured's vessel was seized by Venezuelan customs authorities following the discovery of a quantity of cocaine strapped to the underside of her hull. The policy afforded coverage for malicious acts, but excluded loss caused by infringement of customs or trading regulations. The Court of Appeal held that the loss had been concurrently caused by these perils, and that *Wayne Tank* precluded recovery. The Supreme Court upheld the appeal on the alternative ground that there was no malicious act and the only peril was infringement of customs or trading regulations, so the concurrent cause point did not arise, but Lord Mance – speaking for the entire Court – noted that any doubts as to *Wayne Tank* did not in the present case 'have traction in relation to the present careful exclusion of the peril of loss arising from detainment by reason of infringement of customs regulations from cover'.[75] It is nevertheless our suggestion that the example of *Fairchild* shows the way to avoiding the absurd conclusion that each effective policy can successfully exclude the other.

F. Concurrent, Independent Causes of Loss

One, final scenario merits brief mention. *Wayne Tank* is concerned with the situation where two events, one insured and one excluded, have contributed to the loss. It may also be possible that two events operating at the same time were independently capable of causing the loss. The position here is somewhat different, because if the assured is able to prove that the loss was proximately caused by an insured peril operating, the insurer's only defence can be that, had the claim been brought on the basis of the other insured peril, there would have been no cover. The distinction between the two situations was noted by Hamblen J in *Orient-Express Hotels Ltd v Assicurazioni General SpA*,[76] a case arising out of the New Orleans hurricane in 2007, where a hotel suffered loss of business by reason of damage to its building and also by reason of administrative action which effectively shut down entire parts of the city until general repairs had been effected. The decision, largely in favour of the insurers, turned upon the express wording of the policy, but Hamblen J noted that none of the decided cases applying *Wayne Tank* had involved independent concurrent causes.

The same point had earlier been made, in more detail, by Kiefel J in *McCarthy v St Paul International Insurance Co Ltd*.[77] Her Honour noted that the outcome rested upon the proper construction of the policy, and that the question was whether the parties had agreed that there would be no cover if the loss was

[74] [2018] UKSC 26.
[75] ibid, [49].
[76] [2010] EWHC 1186 (Comm).
[77] (2007) 14 ANZ Insurance Cases 61–725.

caused by the excluded peril, or if the loss was *solely* caused by the excluded peril. Plainly Her Honour's sympathies were in favour of the latter. The same distinction, without the need for any decision, was drawn in *Baulderstone Hornibrook Engineering Pty Ltd v Gordian Runoff Ltd*[78] and *Limit (No.3) Ltd v ACE Insurance Ltd*.[79] Most recently, in *The Cultural Foundation v Beazley Furlonge Ltd*,[80] Simon Henshaw QC, sitting as a High Court Judge, commented that *Wayne Tank* and the other English cases were not concerned with the situation in which the loss arose from two causes operating independently, although the comments were obiter and the point was not developed.

IV. Conclusion

Here, we have taken a problem-based approach to *Fairchild*, suggesting that its pragmatic solution – which is rooted ultimately in proportionality – is not something to be feared, but to be appreciated. Attempts to confine *Fairchild* have turned on concerns about its disruptive effect on legal principle, and its potential unfairness to certain categories of defendant (particularly those making a minimal contribution to the risk of injury). The latter has been dealt with, in *Barker v Corus*, by bringing a degree of proportionality into the law of tort, rather than leaving it to contribution proceedings. The former can be largely avoided by regarding *Fairchild* not as stating revised principles so much as practical solutions to particular, but generalisable, problems of evidence and proof. A start was made in those insurance decisions which were made necessary by *Fairchild* liability – most notably *Durham (The Trigger Litigation)* and *IEG* – but we have argued that these are not the only cases in which a *Fairchild*-style solution would benefit the law. Indeed without the close connection to *Fairchild*, we suggest these cases would most likely have been decided in the same way.

The proportionality of *Fairchild* as it is now applied and understood is based ultimately on compromise, just as the proportionate form of contributory negligence (which rescued the law of tort from convoluted notions attached to proximate cause, and claimants from the effect of a harsh 'all or nothing' rule) is also based on compromise.[81] It avoids placing the burden of impossibility on claimants alone. The initial, full liability version of *Fairchild* passed that burden entirely to the class of defendants, a result now confined (by statute) to mesothelioma. But the resulting position spelled out in *Barker* is a robust and broad-brush solution, not to be confused with a principled statement that the share of exposure to risk is a measure of true responsibility. In the problems with which we have dealt, it is proof that is lacking, and in the absence of proof, a proportional solution

[78] [2008] NSWCA 243.
[79] [2009] NSWSC 51.
[80] [2018] EWHC 1083 (Comm).
[81] Barker and Steele (n 20).

cannot claim to precision. The further risk, that one defendant or another will prove to be insolvent, is now carried by claimants outside the area governed by section 3 of the Compensation Act. In the insurance context, as we have argued, this is a lesser risk.

We have therefore interpreted *Fairchild* as a pragmatic solution. It does not 'peg back' liability on the basis of some appropriate share of global responsibility for an outcome, as *Heneghan* shows, but apportions the burden of impossibility of proof. A similar solution is mandated at the insurance level in circumstances which are analogous in appropriate ways, in order similarly to avoid absurdity. This is not necessarily motivated by a need to replicate 'principles' derived from *Fairchild*: it is the existence of similar problems which suggests the appropriateness of similar solutions. We have had some years to appreciate the difficulties thrown up by *Fairchild*, and to begin to deal with them. Our argument is that we should now learn from *Fairchild*, rather than attempting to treat it as confined to a special enclave of its own.

As a concluding comment we would note that, in the UK, 'all-or-nothing' responses are gradually falling out of favour in contract law in general and insurance law in particular. Although the sharing of liability and the adoption of proportional remedies are different in nature, they have in common the overriding objective that losses should not necessarily lie where they fall where there is the possibility of a more nuanced approach. The majority of the Supreme Court in *Patel v Mirza*[82] rejected the previous, formalistic approach to the enforcement of illegal contracts and replaced it with proportionality criteria in this broader sense. It was recognised by a majority of the Supreme Court in *Versloot Dredging BV v HDI Industrie Versicherung AG*[83] that allowing an insurer to refuse to pay a genuine claim by reason of false statements made in the negotiation process was a disproportionate response to fraud. Finally, the Insurance Act 2015, following the lead of the non-marine regime in Australia in the Insurance Contracts Act 1984, has eschewed the all-or-nothing approach of avoidance to non-disclosure and misrepresentation and instead has adopted proportional remedies based upon what the insurer would have done, had there been a fair presentation. None of this could have been predicted five years ago, and our suggestion of an extension into the world of causation is far from a heresy.

[82] [2016] UKSC 42, [2016] 3 WLR 399.
[83] [2016] UKSC 45, [2017] AC 1.

13

Justice Between Defendants: A New Zealand Note on (non) Law Reform

GEOFF McLAY

I. Introduction

A. What is this Chapter About?

This chapter examines the persistent calls over the last four decades for statutory change to the contribution[1] of joint tortfeasors provision in New Zealand.[2] The New Zealand Law Commission, and its predecessor the Contracts and Commercial Law Reform Committee,[3] rejected any general change in the law towards the acceptance of proportionate liability, but recommended (in 1998 and 2014) statutory modernisation similar to that carried out in other countries. The Law Commission also recently (2014) proposed that 'minor defendants' should only have to pay a proportionate amount of a plaintiff's loss, and suggested that liability be capped for local authorities and auditors.[4]

In the absence of statutory change resulting from the Commission's recommendations, the New Zealand Supreme Court has, in two cases in the last decade, ended up achieving the modernisation reform to allow plaintiffs, and co-defendants, to better seek contribution. First, the Court has used the doctrine of equitable contribution to allow the joining of tortfeasors to contract claims;[5] and secondly,

[1] 'Contribution' is used generally to deal with issues that relates to the determination of the liability of co-defendants, and includes what others might label 'apportionment'.

[2] Law Reform Act 1936 (NZ), s 17. This is New Zealand's version of the Law Reform Act 1935 (UK). This chapter does not purport to be a general account of the law of contribution in New Zealand. For such accounts, see A Beck, 'Contribution' in P Blanchard (ed), *Civil Remedies in New Zealand* (Wellington, Thomson Reuters, 2011) 605–22.

[3] Contracts and Commercial Law Reform Committee, 'Working Paper on Contribution in Civil Cases' (1983). The Committee was one of a number of part-time law reform committee that existed before the Law Commission was established in 1986: see G Hammond, 'The Part-time Law Reform Committees: An Overview' (1988) 13 *New Zealand Universities LR* 135.

[4] New Zealand Law Commission, *Apportionment of Civil Liability* (NZLC R47, 1998) ('1998 Report') and *Liability of Multiple Defendants* (NZLC R132, 2014) ('2014 Report').

[5] *Marlborough District Council v Altimarloch Joint Venture Ltd* [2012] NZSC 11, [2012] 2 NZLR 726 ('*Altimarloch*').

it has liberally interpreted the statute's 'same damage' requirement to allow coordinate liability.[6] Despite the building industry's claims that some are exposed to too disproportionate a liability, New Zealand has not acted on calls to institute proportionate liability to control the extent of its liability. The Government also looks unlikely to adopt the minor defendant regime, and is yet to determine the fate of the recommended liability caps. The debate in New Zealand has been increasingly focused on contribution as a way of dealing with expanded negligence claims for economic loss, particularly in the building industry and in regard to liability for the 'leaky homes' crisis.

B. Why Be Interested in What Has Happened (Or Did Not Happen) in New Zealand?

As with many of the jurisdictions discussed in this book, New Zealand adopted the 1935 English law reform legislation, which enabled contribution between joint tortfeasors. There was a minor change in 1950 to enable contribution when the joint tortfeasor's liability might have been time-limited. New Zealand has not, however, adopted subsequent English changes enacted in 1978, which expanded the law beyond joint tortfeasors. Readers from other jurisdictions should be interested in the New Zealand contribution debates for a number of reasons.

First, the failure of the Law Commission's reform attempts may illustrate some of the difficulties of private law reform in a small jurisdiction. Secondly, the New Zealand Supreme Court presents a case study of the response of courts to the failure of law reformers to be successful, and possibly points to some of the limitations of judicial law reform. Thirdly and finally, in the last decade, the contribution debate in New Zealand has occurred in the context of economic loss and regulatory failure, rather than personal injury or property damage. This chapter suggests that the differences between New Zealand's new negligence law and the traditional negligence law in which contribution developed might have been better examined.

C. Some New Zealand Context

i. A Little Legal Background – New Zealand: The Land of Ever-expanding Economic Loss

Claims

It is impossible to understand New Zealand's contribution to tort debates without some understanding of its negligence law. In a number of important decisions in

[6] *Hotchin v New Zealand Guardian Trust Company Ltd* [2016] NZSC 24, [2016] 1 NZLR 906 ('*Hotchin*').

the late 1970s and 1980s, the New Zealand Court of Appeal adopted what now seems to be an expansive view of the law of negligence. The most significant cases were: the 1977 decision *Bowen v Paramount Builders (Hamilton) Ltd*,[7] holding that builders might owe a duty of care to subsequent purchasers of defective homes; *Scott Group Ltd v McFarlane*,[8] holding that auditors owe duties to subsequent purchasers of shares in the audited company; and a 1986 trilogy of cases which confirmed that local authorities might be liable for negligent building inspections,[9] for failing to notify of potential natural hazards when there had been a practice of doing so,[10] and for failing to correctly follow planning processes.[11] In deciding negligence cases, New Zealand courts talk about whether it is just and fair to impose duties.[12]

In the 1994 case of *Hamlin*,[13] the New Zealand Court of Appeal rejected the House of Lords' own rejection of the expansive *Anns*[14] test in its decision in *Murphy*.[15] The Court in *Hamlin* held that a local authority could owe a duty of care when inspecting the foundations of a relatively modest residential house. New Zealand courts subsequently applied *Hamlin* to negligent building approvals and inspections that lead to weathertight failings,[16] and have refused to limit *Hamlin* to domestic dwellings or to owner-occupiers, preferring to focus on the purpose of the building rather than the sophistication of the owner.[17] The case law, at least at the appellate level, has seen the constant expansion of potential liability. While changes to the Building Act 1994 have sought to reinforce the responsibility of builders rather than Councils for the fitness of buildings, Councils have found themselves owing duties of care to a large number of building owners, including owners of commercial buildings.[18] Although the most recent changes under the Building Act might limit liability to the owners of commercial buildings, that this is the case has yet to be established in the courts. Most recently, in *Southland Indoor Leisure Centre Charitable Trust v Invercargill City Council*,[19] the Supreme Court held that the local authority owed a duty to the owner of the centre after

[7] [1977] 1 NZLR 394 (CA).
[8] [1978] 1 NZLR 553 (CA).
[9] *Stieller v Porirua City Council* [1986] 1 NZLR 84 (CA).
[10] *Brown v Heathcote County Council* [1986] 1 NZLR 76 (CA), affirmed by the Privy Council in *Brown v Heathcote County Council* [1987] 1 NZLR 20 (PC).
[11] *Craig v East Coast Bays City Council* [1986] 1 NZLR 99 (CA).
[12] *Attorney-General v Carter* [2003] 2 NZLR 160 (CA).
[13] *Invercargill City Council v Hamlin* [1994] 3 NZLR 513 (CA), affirmed by the Privy Council in *Invercargill City Council v Hamlin* [1996] 1 NZLR 513 (PC).
[14] *Anns v Merton London Borough Council* [1978] AC 728 (HL).
[15] *Murphy v Brentwood District Council* [1991] 1 AC 398 (HL).
[16] See the account in G McLay 'Legal Doctrine, the Leaky Homes Crisis and the Limits of Judicial Law-making' in S Alexander et al, *The Leaky Buildings Crisis: Understanding the Issues* (Wellington, Brookers, 2011) ch 1.
[17] *North Shore City Council v Body Corporate 188529* [2010] NZSC 158, [2011] 2 NZLR 289 and *Carter Holt Harvey Ltd v Minister of Education* [2016] NZSC 95, [2017] 1 NZLR 78.
[18] *Body Corporate No 207624 v North Shore City Council* [2012] NZSC 83, [2013] 2 NZLR 297.
[19] [2017] NZSC 190.

the roof collapsed under snow, even though it was the owner's agents who had failed to build the centre as it had been permitted. The Supreme Court held that the plaintiff had been contributorily negligent in having failed to follow the recommendations of another design report, which might have avoided the collapse.

ii. The Leaky Homes Crisis: Some Factual Background

The failure of 'leaky homes' or 'weathertight buildings' has been a major policy problem. A combination of factors led to the failure of a large number of buildings: changes to the regulatory regime, pressures to build houses, failure to train the workforce to build those houses, and changing consumer tastes from traditional New Zealand timber houses to mono-clad buildings that were not suited to the New Zealand climate.[20] In the absence of a private or public building guarantee scheme that would otherwise compensate owners, local authorities came to be perceived as insurers, liable under the *Hamlin* doctrine. Local authorities are imperfect insurers, though, as their liability depends on claimants being able to establish the local authority breached its obligations either to approve buildings or to inspect them, and that the breaches were causative of the losses suffered.

In 2009, PricewaterhouseCoopers estimated that the total cost of the crisis was in the order of NZ$11.3 billion.[21] 'Leaky buildings' have cost the Auckland City Council, New Zealand's largest, $600 million so far.[22] Central government's response has been to provide a special Weathertight Homes Dispute Resolution Tribunal and a five-year settlement fund. Owners who agreed not to pursue claims against local authorities were entitled to claim 50 per cent of their losses, 25 per cent provided by central and local government. There has been considerable concern over the uptake of the settlement package, with many of those affected preferring the uncertainty of litigation and its potentially higher returns.[23]

Quite often, local authorities are not responsible for the entire losses suffered.[24] Most critically for this chapter, judges most often assess their responsibility as around 20 per cent for the losses that they might have prevented, and builders, engineers or architects as responsible for the remainder. Nevertheless, local authorities often pay the full loss because others are unavailable.

[20] See generally McLay (n 16).

[21] PricewaterhouseCoopers, *Weathertightness – Estimating the Cost* (Report for the Department of Building and Housing, Wellington, 29 July 2009).

[22] A Gibson, 'Leaky Buildings Cost Auckland Ratepayers $600m' *The New Zealand Herald*, online edn (Auckland, 5 November 2017).

[23] For an evaluation of the take-up of the scheme, see Ministry of Economic Development, *Evaluation of the Financial Assistance Package* (October 2013).

[24] A leading example is *Three Meade Street Ltd v Rotorua District Council* [2005] 1 NZLR 504 (HC).

II. Contribution in the Law Commission

A. Why Did the Commission Consider Contribution Twice?

The reasons behind 2012–2014 review were quite different from the 1992–1998 review. The earlier review was one of a number of classic 'lawyers' law' reform projects that the Commission referred to itself. The 1978 English improvement to the Law Reform Act 1935 contribution model formed the essential frame of reference for both the Contract and Commercial Law Reform Committee in the 1980s and the Law Commission in the 1990s. Their essential case for reform was one often made by lawyers arguing for change: that the 1936 New Zealand statute had become out of date, and lacked flexibility.

In referring joint and several liability to the Commission in 2012, though, the Government was not concerned with updating an old law, but rather with how the Government ought to deal with claims that local authorities and others in the building industry were exposed to liability that was out of proportion to their responsibility. The Department of Building and Housing had commissioned a report from a major law firm and an economic consulting firm in 2011, the *Sapere Report*.[25] The building industry presented joint and several liability to that review as the source of the industry's ills.[26] The report concluded that – taking into account the difficulties of proportionate liability and the shifting of the burden to plaintiffs of uncollected shares – it was not clear that proportionate liability would produce better results in the industry, unless the Government were to institute a compulsory insurance regime for new homes. The *Sapere Report* did not, however, end the debate either within the industry, or within Cabinet.[27] The Minister for Building and Construction authored a Cabinet paper to refer the issue to the Commission, seemingly as a way of settling the debate.[28]

B. The Law Commission's Recommendations

i. *The 1980s and 1990s: Pure Procedural Reform*

In 1998, the Law Commission recommended a new Civil Liability and Contribution Act. The Commission's draft Act was essentially a tidying and modernisation of the

[25] Buddle Findlay and Sapere Research Group, *Final Report to the Department of Building and Housing: Review of the Application of Joint and Several Liability to the Building and Construction Section* (26 April 2011).

[26] There has been persistent litigation in New Zealand about 'piercing the veil' of building and development companies, that depends on the degree of personal involvement that a particular individual might have had. See, eg, *Body Corporate 202254 v Taylor* [2008] NZCA 317, [2009] 2 NZLR 17.

[27] *Sapere Report* (n 25) [12.5].

[28] Minister for Building and Construction *Building Act Review: Review of Joint and Several Liability* (undated, 2012) available at www.mbie.govt.nz.

law of contribution and contributory negligence.[29] The reform would have brought New Zealand into line with the 1978 English Act. The draft Act would have clearly allowed responsibility to be apportioned to those who had breached contract. A new definition of 'wrongdoer' as a 'person whose acts or omissions give rise, wholly or partly, to a loss' would have been adopted, rather than just tortfeasors. Better apportionment of uncollected contributions from those unavailable (most likely through insolvency) to pay their shares of responsibility was to be accomplished through a new procedure that would have allowed a court to reapportion the uncollected shares. It would also have explicitly enabled contribution when there had been settlements.

ii. Rejecting Proportionate Liability Again, and Again

In both 1998 and 2014 the Commission rejected proportionate liability. The 1998 Report had been delayed to consider Australian rumblings for proportionate liability.[30] By 1998, the Commission had 'a firm view that no compelling case for departure from the solidary rule has been made' and that, if there was excessive liability for professional firms, that was a matter for the substantive law. It wrote:[31]

> If there is injustice in substantial sums being recoverable from a professional firm whose error is very small when measured against the heinousness of the conduct of a now insolvent wrongdoer who has also caused the loss, the remedy for such injustice must lie either in an examination of the duty imposed by the law on the professional firm or in the rules of causation applied.

In the Commission's view, there were also procedural disadvantages in abolishing the rule:[32]

> If there are 100 persons polluting a river, must P to recover damages join them all as defendants, and if P does not and chooses to join only D1 and D2 how does the judge determine apportionment among them and the absent 98? How binding is such an apportionment on the absent defendants?

In the Commission's 2014 Report, the choice remained as being between leaving plaintiffs, or defendants, with the risk of uncollected shares. The report rejected proportionate liability:[33]

> The proportionate system, which limits the liability of a liable defendant to the proportion of the loss they have been judged responsible for, means that if liable defendants

[29] The *1998 Report* (n 4) essentially mirrored a 1992 preliminary paper: New Zealand Law Commission, *Apportionment of Civil Liability* (NZLC PP19, 1992). The delay in reporting was explained by other priorities, but also by the need to consider Australian moves (which by 1998 had been rejected by the Commission) to introduce proportionate liability.

[30] See *1998 Report* (n 4) [2], referring in particular to JLR Davis, *Inquiry into the Law of Joint and Several Liability: Report of Stage One* (Commonwealth of Australia, 1994) and *Draft Model Provisions to Implement the Recommendations of the Inquiry into the Law of Joint and Several Liability* (Commonwealth of Australia, 1996).

[31] *1998 Report* (n 4) [7].

[32] ibid, [8].

[33] *2014 Report* (n 4) [3.34].

are absent or insolvent, it is the blameless plaintiff who will be out of pocket. It is imperative to note that proportionate liability is not a case of the plaintiff sharing some of the risk that there may be insolvent liable defendants. Under straight proportionate liability, that risk is allocated purely to the plaintiff.

iii. The 2014 Law Commission's Approach to Minor Defendants: Preventing the Injustice of Doing Too Much Justice?

The Commission remained concerned, as it had been in its *Issues Paper*,[34] that, for some defendants, being potentially liable for uncollected shares might create liability out of proportion to what might actually be just:[35]

> In the course of this review, many consultation participants argued that joint and several liability is unfair because it could result in a very minor party bearing the full amount of a loss. It was difficult to assess whether this is predominantly a theoretical problem or fear, or whether such results occur reasonably often in practice.

The Commission gave the following example to illustrate the concern:[36]

> The minor defendant issue may be more readily apparent in the usual situation where the contribution of each liable defendant is determined at the same time as judgment is given in the main proceeding. For example, in a leaky building claim a judge gives judgment against a number of defendants for the whole loss, making them all liable defendants. The judge then determines how responsibility should be apportioned between liable defendants and makes contribution orders accordingly. One of the liable defendants, a subcontractor, is adjudged to have a five per cent share of responsibility and gets the benefit of a contribution order for any amount he pays above that level. Under joint and several liability the plaintiff is not concerned with the contribution order and is entitled to demand the full amount of damages from the subcontractor. If the subcontractor pays as demanded he can then use the contribution order to seek contributions from the other liable defendants, subject to their respective maximum obligations to contribute. If one or more of the other liable defendants is insolvent or has absconded, the subcontractor may be left bearing the cost of most or even all the plaintiff's damages.

A minor defendant exception was about reducing a perception that joint and several liability produced unfairness in extreme cases.[37]

iv. Capping Local Authorities' and Auditors' Liability: Solving Specific Problems with Targeted Solutions

The 2014 Report recommended liability caps for local authorities and auditors. The Commission identified unique factors for each, but those revolved around the perception that both have become 'deep pocket' targets for plaintiffs.

[34] New Zealand Law Commission, *Review of Joint and Several Liability* (NZLC IP23, 2012) [3.26].
[35] *2014 Report* (n 4) [5.5].
[36] ibid, [5.6].
[37] ibid, [5.9].

Local authorities are required to be building certifiers, and they cannot withdraw from the market. The intention of the cap was to provide results similar to those that would have been achieved by proportionate liability. The amounts set under the cap ($300,000 per single dwelling, $150,000 per unit within a development, with a total cap of $3 million for a whole development) were calculated as estimates of the sums that might be awarded against local authorities as their contribution to the overall damage that had occurred.[38] The cap was to apply to buildings completed after the legislation might come into effect. The justice claims of the plaintiffs to full compensation might then perhaps give way to their knowledge, actual or presumed, that the local authority did not have responsibility for the full damage that might occur. The recommendation might be seen as dealing with the problem faced by the courts that their decisions had given rise to an expectation that Councils would provide insurance, and that this could not be changed ex post by a court restricting liability.

Unlike the tort liability of local authorities, which has been constantly expanded, the Commission recommended capping auditor liability in an area where there was basic uncertainty as to what the auditors' tort liability was. The Court of Appeal decided *Scott Group* in 1978, but New Zealand courts have not had the occasion to determine whether New Zealand would follow overseas cases to reject tort duties.[39] The leading Court of Appeal decision *Boyd Knight*, itself decided in 1999, was resolved not as a matter of whether there was a duty of care, but was rather based on whether investors could properly be said to have relied on accounts in a prospectus they had not read.[40]

The case for reform revolved very much around the difficulties for New Zealand firms in competition with Australian auditors, the latter of which might benefit from the caps allowed for by Australian law. The Commission argued that there was a trans-Tasman market for auditing, and the Closer Economic Relationship (CER) necessitated treating New Zealand-based auditors in the same way that Australian-based auditors were treated. Otherwise, the situation would create a potentially unfair advantage for Australian firms competing in a trans-Tasman market. This was the only area in relation to contribution in which CER considerations led to a recommendation for the reform of New Zealand law.[41] As a result, the Commission recommended a scale for caps on liability, depending on income received by the firm for the auditing of large companies, to mirror those in Australia.[42]

[38] ibid, [7.33]–[7.45].

[39] *Caparo Industries plc v Dickman* [1990] 2 AC 605 (HL); *Esanda Finance Corporation Ltd v Peat Marwick Hungerfords (Reg)* [1997] HCA 8, (1997) 188 CLR 241; *Hercules Managements Ltd v Ernst & Young* [1997] 2 SCR 165.

[40] *Boyd Knight v Purdue* [1999] 2 NZLR 278 (CA).

[41] *2014 Report* (n 4) [8.40].

[42] $2.5 million for $10 million income per annum; $25 million where income was between $10 and $20 million per annum; and $80 million where income was over $20 million per annum: *2014 Report* (n 4) [8.49].

C. Why Limited, Rather than Radical Recommendations?

i. Procedural Justice is About Plaintiffs, Not Defendants?

An interesting feature of both of the Law Commission's final reports was the privilege that was given to the concern that plaintiffs receive 'justice'. Concern about whether defendants might face too much liability because of joint and several liability shifted to a matter of whether the substantive law was correct – something outside the terms of reference. The trouble for the Commission was that, although the problems of local authority liability were clearly the reason for the reference, the reference itself had been expressly about joint and several liability, which was the name given to the problem by the industry and then adopted by Cabinet. It might have been better if the reference had in fact been more explicitly about appropriate liability regimes in the building industry, rather than about the problem identified by the industry.

ii. The Lack of a Persuasive Law and Economics Case

The Law Commission's reviews gave prominence to law and economics literature. Despite the Law Commission viewing an economic approach as important, though, it was not decisive. One frustration of the law reformers was the lack of a clear answer in the law and economics literature as to whether joint and several, or proportionate liability, would be more efficient, as the amount of care that a potential defendant would be likely to take would always be shaped by the total liability to which it could be exposed, rather than by the chance that it might be able to offload some of that liability to another party. In the first Law Commission project, two economists recommended proportionate liability as potentially helpful[43] because of concerns about the disadvantage at which joint and several liability placed those who have 'deeper pockets', such as local authorities or auditors. However, the Commission did not accept that shifting the risk of defaulting co-defendants to plaintiffs would provide better incentives for those plaintiffs to themselves take care:[44]

> We are not, however, persuaded by the further conclusion that, where there is a 'deep pocket', the adoption of a proportionate liability rule would be economically beneficial because it would have the effect of increasing the care undertaken by the claimant (We think this is an unproven assumption. Can it really be suggested that a result of proportionate liability would be a second-guessing of auditors by creditors or shareholders present or potential of a company? Or that owners or potential owners of residences would hover around breathing down the necks of builders to ensure that the building's foundations were properly laid?

[43] See C Blyth and B Sharpe, 'The Rules of Liability and the Economics of Care' (1996) 26 *Victoria University of Wellington LR* 91.
[44] *1998 Report* (n 4) [4].

Both the *Sapere Report* of 2011 and the Law Commission 2014 report concluded that there was no clear efficiency case for switching regimes. In its 2012 *Issues Paper*, the Commission had re-examined the general conclusion that both regimes were efficient in the sense of promoting an adequate amount of care. The Commission referred to a literature review conducted by two Wellington barristers that again re-enforced the ambivalence of economic analysis, but which also again accepted that the reality that other defendants might not pay could create an incentive for over-deterrence on the part of those with deep pockets.[45] The Commission's conclusion in the 2012 *Issues Paper* was that:[46]

> It is … [a] reasonable consensus in New Zealand that the combination of joint and several liability and a deep pocket is one situation that may lead to inefficiency. It is also the case, however, that the analysis predicts that this result is not inevitable, and inefficiencies from deep pockets can be controlled in other ways.

Nevertheless, not much came of this consensus, except perhaps a recommendation for the capping of local authorities' and auditors' liability. It did not lead to a general recognition of a need to reform the law. In its subsequent Report, the Commission argued that a clearer economic justification was needed to expose plaintiffs to the risk of defendants not being able to pay their shares. Justice was more important than economics.

iii. The (Non-)Effect of Australian Reforms

Once significant change between the 1998 report and the 2012 reference was the Australian switch to proportionate liability. An important justification in 1998 for not switching to proportionate liability was the consensus against it in the Commonwealth at the time. Both the 1983 Committee Paper and the 1992 Law Commission Preliminary Paper referred to the various rejections of proportionate liability made by Commonwealth Law Reforms bodies,[47] while noting the United States switches to proportionate liability as curiosities.[48]

The Australian change to proportionate liability regimes since the 1998 Report and the allowing of caps on auditor liability created a major alteration in the context. Not only had those reforms punctured the Commonwealth consensus against proportionate liability, even more importantly, a different Australian

[45] D Goddard and L Theron, *Joint and Several Liability: Literature Review* (Ministry of Economic Development, Draft Memorandum, 2004) referred to by the New Zealand Law Commission, *Review of Joint and Several Liability* (NZLC IP32, 2012) ('2012 Issues Paper') [8.11]–[8.14].

[46] *2012 Issues Paper* (n 45) [8.16].

[47] New Zealand Law Commission, *Apportionment of Civil Liability* (NZLC PP19, 1992) [94], citing Ontario Law Reform Commission, *Report on Contribution Among Wrongdoers and Contributory Negligence* (1988) and the New South Wales Law Reform Commission, *Report on Contribution Among Wrongdoers: Interim Report on Solidary Liability* (Report LRC 65, 1990), but contrasting the then position of British Columbian Courts.

[48] New Zealand Law Commission, *Apportionment of Civil Liability* (n 47) [96].

regime raised the question of whether New Zealand should harmonise with it under the CER banner.[49] In the 2013 *Issues Paper*, there is almost a sense that the Commission's default view was that the change in the Australian law ought to lead to a change in the New Zealand law. In the first chapter of the *Issues Paper*, the Commission wrote:[50]

> One of the key issues for New Zealand in any law reform is whether or not the laws of New Zealand and Australia should be aligned as a result of the Closer Economic Relations Trade Agreement (CER). … This harmonisation objective will be more easily achieved when the underlying economic circumstances of the two countries are very similar, and also where there is substantial Trans-Tasman activity in the field. In these cases it is desirable that the legal framework in both countries should be sufficiently similar to enable the efficient operation of a market, especially for those companies operating on both sides of the Tasman.

But, by the time of the final report, a greater scepticism of the Australian reforms (except perhaps in relation to the caps on auditor liability) had taken hold in the Commission. This may have been fuelled by the rather staunch opposition to proportionate liability by the New Zealand Law Society, amongst others. Proportional liability just did not apply to the New Zealand lawyer. In its final report, the Commission had become more concerned about the procedural and justice issues created by proportionate liability, and pointed to the origins of the Australian reforms in the insurance crisis of the 2000s.[51]

D. Explaining Why the Recommendations Have Not Been Adopted

There has been no attempt to legislate based on the 1998 Report, either in relation to contribution, or in relation to contributory negligence. This failure does not necessarily reflect the merits of the Report. There are other explanations. First, there was a relatively low uptake of Law Commission reports before the new procedure (which requires a government response) was adopted in 2006.[52] Secondly, the Commission had 'self-referred' the project. Geoffrey Palmer, in his 2001 review of the operation of the Law Commission, observed that the chances of a self-referred project being adopted were considerably less than one that had

[49] Closer Economic Relations is both the name of a 1983 trading agreement between New Zealand and Australia (the Australia-New Zealand Closer Economic Relations Trade Agreement, Australia-New Zealand (signed 14 December 1982, entered into force 1 January 1983) [ANZCERTA]), and also a name symbolic of attempts to eliminate trade and barriers between the two countries.

[50] *2012 Issues Paper* (n 45) [1.8]–[1.9].

[51] *2014 Report* (n 4) [3.16].

[52] Cabinet Office Circular, 'Law Commission: Processes for Setting the Work Programme and Government Response to Reports' (9 April 2009) CO 09/1, which requires the Government to report to Parliament if it does not intend to adopt the Commission's recommendations.

been requested by the Minister, simply because the Minister and his or her department would have some buy-in to the Report that was produced.[53] Thirdly, and perhaps most importantly, the 1998 Report and its legally earnest recommendations did not present a political case for why these reforms, as opposed to others, ought to attract the Minister's attention and crucial departmental resources. The Report had recommended clarifying the legal infrastructure, a task that arguably might be left to the courts themselves. In other jurisdictions, tort remains principally about personal injury, something that politicians cannot ignore. Indeed, as *Altimarloch* and *Hotchin* show, the courts had indeed some capacity to achieve some of these reforms themselves.

Government is now required to report to Parliament within six months of a Law Commission Report if it is not going to adopt the recommendations contained in the report. The Government's response to the 2014 Report was lukewarm. On the one hand, it accepted the overall conclusion against proportionate liability:[54]

> The Government accepts the Law Commission's recommendation to retain joint and several liability across the legal system, including for the building sector and professional services markets. The Government also notes that the Law Commission's recommendation to retain joint and several liability accords with previous Law Commission reports on this issue and independent advice to the Department of Building and Housing.

However, the response suggested that more work needed to be done on the Commission's more positive proposals:[55]

> The Law Commission has identified some potential issues around the operation of joint and several liability and recommended the changes to joint and several liability described above. Further analysis of the issues raised, as well as of the regulatory impact of those proposed changes is required. The Government also notes that the Law Commission's specific proposals have not been the subject of public consultation.

The Government then instructed the Ministry of Business, Innovation and Employment (in the case of caps on local authority and building and auditor liability) and the Ministry of Justice (regarding proposals relating to minor defendants) to do that work. The results of the reviews have not been made public despite an initial deadline of 20 November 2015.[56]

Some sense as to the Government's final approach to the cap issues may be able to be drawn from a very sceptical Cabinet Paper prepared by the Ministry of Business Innovation and Employment leading to the Government response,

[53] G Palmer, 'Evaluation of the Law Commission: Report for the Associate Minister of Justice and Attorney-General Hon Margaret Wilson' (April 2000) [301].

[54] *Liability of Multiple Defendants* (Government Response to Law Commission Report, presented to the House of Representatives 11 November, 2011) 5.

[55] ibid, 5–6.

[56] The Ministry of Business Innovation and Employment has established a webpage for its review of Auditors Liability: http://www.mbie.govt.nz/info-services/business/business-law/auditor-liability.

that pointed to the Commission's lack of industry evidence that New Zealand auditors were in fact disadvantaged in a trans-Tasman market and its failure to address the risks that caps themselves might create.[57]

The Commission's difficulty in regard to the minor defendant rule, perhaps reflected in a certain lack of precision in the Report, was how to articulate when someone might be a minor defendant, but could nevertheless be said to have been a cause of the harm that the plaintiff had suffered, and considered otherwise legally responsible for it. The Commission supplied an indicative statutory draft as to who might be a minor defendant that was more empowering for the court's discretion, rather than setting parameters for it:[58]

> In this section minor defendant means a party held liable in a civil action but which or whom the court or tribunal determines bears only a minor and limited responsibility for the plaintiff's loss.
>
> A liable party is not a minor defendant only because:
>
> (a) the party's share of responsibility falls below a particular percentage or proportion, or is less than any other party's share of responsibility, or both;
> (b) the party's involvement in relevant events was largely or completely restricted to providing verification, certification or other independent services required to facilitate the events or elements of them; or
> (c) the party was under a statutory obligation to provide relevant services or take relevant actions.

But this was not, seemingly, enough. The Ministry of Justice, as part of its evaluation of the recommendation, sought the New Zealand Law Society's view about the minor defendant proposal. The Society had submitted to the Commission in opposition to the proposal in the issues paper, and now doubled down on its criticisms.[59]

The minor defendant proposal had been misconceived, as any party that had been held liable must have caused reasonably foreseeable harm, and that such a result was 'completely fair'. Moreover, the Society was concerned about the procedural implications of the proposal and the effect that it might have on prolonging litigation, and making it more complex: the two-stage procedure under which a minor defendant might seek that status before trial added an unpredictable layer to the proceedings. Under the two-stage procedure, a minor defendant would have to establish the solvency of the other defendants, something of which it does not have evidence In the Society's view, any extra litigation cost imposed on the plaintiffs could not be justified unless there was a convincing case for change. Similarly, the 12-month period during which a minor might make an application to have the

[57] Cabinet Paper *Government Response to Law Commission Report: Liability of Multiple Defendants* (undated, available at www.mbie.govt.nz/).

[58] *2014 Report* (n 4) Appendix A.

[59] Letter from New Zealand Law Society to Ministry of Justice regarding 'Minor Defendants' – Law Commission Proposal (21 August 2015).

judgment reduced might undermine the security of payment, especially if the minor defendant was allowed to claw back payments that might have been made to the plaintiff on the assumption that there were other solvent and liable defendants.

The Commission – at least in the view of a major stakeholder, whose opposition might prevent any Minister from introducing a reform to an area that the Society might argue it knew best – had clearly struggled to make the case that there were gains to be made in reducing the exposure of one defendant, that overweighed the potential difficulties for all plaintiffs. It was the Commission's view that the application of such a provision would be rare, but the trouble, ultimately, from a law reform perspective was that it was extremely difficult to articulate ex ante the cases in which it might appropriately be applied.

Perhaps even more significant, in terms of whether the minor defendant rule might be adopted, was the fact that it did not solve the basic policy problem that had led Cabinet to refer the issue to the Commission in the first place. The Commission rejected the idea that gatekeepers, like local authorities inspecting buildings or auditors, should be automatically treated as minor defendants, as the extent of gatekeeper liability was properly a matter of the substantive legal regime. Moreover, as a practical matter, gatekeepers would most likely not satisfy the minor contribution threshold to qualify for the exception:[60]

> In any case, we doubt that gatekeepers will necessarily or regularly incur a low enough share of responsibility to qualify as minor defendants. Auditors, building consent authorities, valuers and solicitors may have a lesser share of responsibility in an impugned transaction than a principal actor. However, the gatekeeper's actions may be a strong 'but for' cause to the extent that it is difficult to say their responsibility is minor or limited. The relief provision should therefore require that each case must be examined on its merits, with no presumption that certain behaviours or responsibilities are likely to fall in the 'minor' range. …, it is still necessary to determine whether the gatekeeper's responsibility can be characterised as minor, taking into account all relevant factors. Such factors should include but not be limited to their responsibilities and level of responsibility, the nature of their negligence or other fault and the consequences of their actions.

E. Was the Law Commission Asked/Answering the Wrong Question?

On reflection, it seems to me that concluding that joint and several liability ought to apply to economic loss cases does not necessarily follow as it does in physical loss cases. Perhaps the high public interest in physical loss cases to ensure that, as far as possible, a person's position is restored to the position that he or she would have been in, but for the defendant's negligence means that the risk of the default of another defendant should remain with the defendant, rather than switch to the

[60] *2014 Report* (n 4) [5.19].

plaintiff whose physical condition or property needs to be restored. The same high public interest possibly does not exist with economic loss cases. Interestingly, it appears from the New Zealand law reform process that changes in substantive legal doctrine have also affected the way in which lawyers might see the justice of limiting a particular defendant's liability. The decision by the New Zealand courts that local authorities owed a duty of care in tort law was translated in submissions made by New Zealand Law Society, for instance, to an insistence that it is a matter of justice to plaintiffs that local authorities be required to cover the entirety of the plaintiff's loss to which they might be said to have contributed.[61] In some ways, the reference for the 2012–2014 review had focused on the wrong thing. The better question for the Commission was not so much ultimately about joint and several liability – the name that the building industry had given to their problems – but really about the proper shape of liability in the first place.

F. Why No Statutory Reform? The Reality of Arguing for Private Law Reform in New Zealand

Each of the law reform attempts discussed suggested relatively minor changes to the existing law. These changes have not been acted upon by the Government, but neither have they necessarily been rejected. This points to one of the persistent difficulties of law reform for a jurisdiction like New Zealand, where it is difficult to get government priority for what might be regarded as lawyers' law reform. While these reforms might seem significant to lawyers, or their individual clients, they are not seen as solving a major policy problem. At the time that the then National (conservative) Government referred joint and several liability to the Law Commission in 2012, it appeared that the leaky homes crisis had created a significant government priority in changing the law. Once the Law Commission had decided against proportionate liability, though, it became clear that it was not enough of a priority to pursue more minor reform. Indeed, one might argue that the purpose of the reference was to resolve persistent calls from the building industry for proportionate liability, rather than engage in the kind of private law reform that might make the job of lawyers or judges easier in court, or produce greater individual justice for clients.

III. The New Zealand Supreme Court as a Law Reformer

In the absence of legislative change, the Supreme Court has, in fact, achieved significant reform. The first case, *Altimarloch*, is suggestive of using equitable

[61] See New Zealand Law Society, 'Submission on the Review of Joint and Several Liability to the Law Commission' (21 February 2013).

contribution as a way of getting around the requirement that there be joint tortfeasors under the Act. Ultimately, because of the facts of the case, the Supreme Court did not award contribution by the tortfeasor because the measures of harm caused by the breach of contract and that caused by the tortfeasor were just too disparate. But the case showed the possibility that the Court would not wait for Parliament to act. If *Altimarloch* had hinted at the possibilities of judicial law reform to deal with the failure of the legislature, and partially accepted that it was possible, *Hotchin* confronted that possibility straight on, and, through a wider interpretative approach, appeared to endorse very significant change both to the Law Reform Act 1936 and the parallel equitable contribution. Indeed, after the case, it is possible to argue that New Zealand has now achieved much of the United Kingdom reform without having passed a statute.[62]

A. *Altimarloch*: Judicial Law Reform to Deal with Technical Issues Preventing Justice

i. Facts

Altimarloch was a complicated case.[63] The complications in the facts can, at first reading, obscure that the Court was expanding New Zealand notions of when contribution might be recovered. This is especially so, given the majority's decision that contribution was not appropriate, as the difference between the contract expectation approach that they had adopted in relation to one defendant was just too different from the tort measure applicable to the other.

The case involved a real estate agent's unauthorised misrepresentation about the water rights that were being purchased with a vineyard in Marlborough, New Zealand's premier wine region. The purchaser had paid $2.657 million, but in fact it was worth $2.55 million at the time it had been purchased. The purchaser brought a claim in contract against the vendor of $1,055,907, the amount needed to acquire water rights and build a pumping station to enable year-round water supply, which would have been available had the agent's representation been true. The purchaser also brought a claim against the local authority for negligently preparing the Land Information Memorandum (LIM). Much of the Supreme Court's consideration of the matter was about the substantive issues of what damages the vendor ought to be required to pay, and whether the Council ought to be held liable in tort. Elias CJ would have held that the correct contractual measure of damage was

[62] V Stace 'When Can One Defendant Claim Contribution from Another?' [2016] *New Zealand Law Journal* 425.

[63] *Altimarloch* (n 5). For a more detailed analysis, see D McLauchlan, 'Liability under Hedley Byrne for "Pre-Contract" Negligent Misrepresentation: A New Zealand Perspective' in K Barker, R Grantham, W Swain (eds), *The Law of Misstatements: 50 Years on from Hedley Byrne v Heller* (Oxford, Hart Publishing, 2015) 291.

$400,000 (the cost of providing the promised water rights), while the majority, led by Tipping and Blanchard JJ, held that the full $1,055,907 should be recovered.

There was also a dispute amongst the Court as to whether the Council could really be said to have caused the purchaser's loss, as the purchaser could sue the vendors for expectation damages far greater than the $110,000 difference in what was paid, and what the land might have been worth. Elias CJ and Tipping J agreed. Tipping J held that the Council had not contributed to the contractual remedies being diminished.[64] Blanchard J differentiated the right to receive damages from the actual performance of the contract.[65] McGrath J similarly thought that Tipping J had taken a 'narrow' view of causation.[66]

ii. Using Equity to Bypass the Act (Well, Almost)

Section 17 of Law Reform Act 1936 only allows contribution between joint tortfeasors.[67] The question, therefore, was whether equitable contribution, which all members of the Court considered was essentially a common law parallel contribution regime to the 1936 Act, could be adapted to allow contribution to a contractual damages claim. The result was to allow something close what the Law Commission had recommended in 1998, but which Parliament had failed to adopt. McGrath J adopted language from Australian cases like *Burke*[68] that looked to coordinate liability. He would have preferred the approach of Kirby J that would have removed all technical barriers to contribution, but ultimately considered that result could only be achieved by Parliament. But, in reality, his Honour's approach might have effectively done so, in allowing equitable contribution when '[t]he liabilities arose from different facts, occurring at different times and giving rise to different causes of action.'[69] It was enough that both parties had made errors that had led the plaintiff into entering in a contract that they otherwise would not have.

Tipping J, with whom Blanchard J agreed, also accepted the need in equitable contribution for 'coordinate' liability but argued that liability here was not coordinate because of the 'distinctly dissimilar' nature of the losses,[70] and that allowing contribution would extend the principles of equitable contribution. Elias CJ, with whom Anderson J agreed, denied that there could be contribution on the facts.[71] Importantly for the later case of *Hotchin*, Her Honour emphasised that it was the difference in the nature of the loss suffered, rather than any more technical

[64] *Altimarloch* (n 5) [120]–[121].
[65] ibid, [69].
[66] ibid, [207].
[67] The Council had argued that, since the claim was under s 6 of the Contractual Remedies Act 1979, liability was statutory and hence tortious in liability. Tipping J rejected this at [127].
[68] *Burke v LFOT Pty Ltd* [2002] HCA 17, (2002) 209 CLR 282, [103].
[69] *Altimarloch* (n 5) [225]–[227].
[70] ibid, [129].
[71] ibid, [57]–[58].

restriction on what might be the subject of contribution, which prevented contribution. She stated that the result might be different when 'the liability of each is properly seen as coordinate or of the same nature'.

B. *Hotchin*: Completing the Work of the 1998 Report?

i. *The Facts and the Narrow Legal Issue*

Hotchin was sued by the New Zealand Securities Commission[72] for incorrect representations made in prospectuses of the failed Hanover Finance. Hotchin had settled a statutory claim, but now sought to make the trustee company, Guardian Trust, which had been employed (as was required by the statute) to supervise the company's operations. Had Guardian Trust done a better job, Hotchin argued, Hanover's investors would have suffered less loss.

In both the High Court and the Court of Appeal, this attempt had foundered on the requirement in section 17 of the Law Reform Act 1936 that the party from whom contribution is sought be liable for the 'same damage' as the other defendant. In the Supreme Court, O'Regan and Arnold JJ would have agreed, but the majority of Elias CJ and Glazebrook and William Young JJ held there was a close enough connection between the investors' losses through the misrepresentations in the prospectus and the alleged negligence of Guardian Trust in supervising the Hanover business.

Victoria Stace has subjected the majority's holding to substantial criticism. She argues that the majority takes an overly broad view of the 'same damage' requirement,[73] and potentially opens up the use of contribution in situations that it previously would not have been available. In Stace's view, there are fundamental problems with treating the liability as giving rise to the same damage: the prospectus had overvalued the investments at the time that they were made, but Guardian Trust's responsibility, if any, was to preserve the value of the investments rather than the amount invested. While there might have been some crossover, Stace argues that the legal basis for the recovery was different. This focus on the conceptual difference was essentially the minority's view.[74] The minority contended that a similar claim for lost money was not enough, rather it required the same basis for the claim. The minority considered that cases from the United Kingdom or Australia that suggested a broader approach had been influenced by the wording of the reformed statutes.

There is an appeal in the logic of the minority and of Victoria Stace. But from a policy perspective, one wonders if this does overplay the need for the same

[72] Now the Financial Markets Conduct Authority.
[73] See V Stace, 'Contribution Rights Between Tortfeasors – What is the "Same Damage?"' (2016) 24 *Tort Law Rev* 145.
[74] *Hotchin* (n 6) [260].

damage, as opposed to coordinate damage. Surely, there may also be merit in simply allowing similar enough claims to be heard together.

ii. Hotchin *as Removing Technical Barriers*

Blanchard, Tipping and McGrath JJ had all retired and did not have to reconsider what they might have meant by their respective judgments in *Altimarloch*. But the Chief Justice's *Hotchin* judgment is much more expansive in terms of both statutory contribution and its equitable counterpart. In considering whether there was the 'same damage', what counted was the policy behind contribution: that 'it is unjust for the burden of meeting a loss for which others share responsibility to be borne by one party, to the benefit of those who escape liability'. The Chief Justice proposed that '[i]t is enough that the responsibility for the harm is shared'. She expressly agreed with Kirby J in *Burke* that 'the [contribution] cases rest on more general principles of justice',[75] and she rejected the narrow approach of Tipping J in *Altimarloch* as having effectively brought back a 'cause of action' requirement, despite having agreed that it was inappropriate. The expansive approach did not require legislation.[76] Glazebrook J took a similar approach to the Chief Justice in *Altimarloch*. She acknowledged that her more expansive approach to equitable compensation was different from that accepted from Tipping and Blanchard JJ's approach, but argued that there had been no majority in *Altimarloch*.

iii. Hotchin: *A Wrongdoer Seeking Contribution from His Own Guard?*

Hotchin was not a usual case, though. Guardian Trust was essentially acting as regulatory gatekeeper, and Hotchin was the person guarded. The trouble, ultimately, with the focus being on the interpretative issue was that the policy of potentially allowing Hotchin to essentially sue those who were supposed to prevent him from causing others harm does not come into the consideration of whether there is jurisdiction under section 17 of the 1936 Act to award contribution.

It might be the facts of the case that make one somewhat suspicious of the contribution claim. There is perhaps nothing intrinsically wrong with such contribution claims, so long as they are in line with the policy of the underlying substantive liability. William Young J pointed out earlier in his judgment that contribution was commonly sought in defective building cases, despite there being fundamentally different actions against the builder for negligent building and the council for negligent approval or inspection.[77] His Honour contrasted an

[75] ibid, [152].
[76] ibid, [153]–[157].
[77] ibid, [198]–[199].

English case, *Birse*,[78] in which a claim for contribution was not allowed against a consulting engineer by the builder of a defective reservoir, concluding:[79]

> To New Zealand eyes that result seems a little odd. Let us assume a defectively constructed and leaky complex building … a New Zealand court would conclude that the builder, its construction engineer and the building owner's employed engineer were concurrent tortfeasors all of whom were, or could be, liable in relation to the same damage (being the defective state of the building as constructed) and therefore able to seek contribution inter se.

William Young J's explanation was that it was the substantive law that brought the English and New Zealand courts to different conclusions on contribution.

In many ways *Hotchin* was a more extreme case, but it is a useful one to test whether the Court achieved a balanced law reform from the perspective not just of a Court trying to do justice, but also from the perspective of a defendant faced with what it believes is an unmeritorious contribution claim. Glazebrook J thought that the answer might come from exercising the Court's discretion that contribution awards should be 'just and equitable', to exempt a defendant if that was appropriate in the circumstances.[80] William Young J was equally sceptical, but suggested that it did not necessarily tell against jurisdiction.[81]

There is a question, though, whether an unbounded judicial discretion, which will only develop in a case-by-case way, gives sufficient guidance to parties, or indeed avoids unfair litigation burdens at trial, regardless of how remote, or unmeritorious the contribution claim might be. The minority was concerned about the effect of uncertainty on the settling of cases.[82]

What all of this might mean obviously needs to be left to future cases to consider. Having essentially removed the constraints around contribution actions provided by the 'same damage' requirement and thus having given greater scope for plaintiffs, the question for future courts will be the degree to which they are prepared to expand upon the justice and fairness requirement. How similar might such a pro-defendant consideration be to the Law Commission's minor defendant proposal, and how tempted might a lower court judge be to use it as a way of recognising something like proportionate liability? The 'justice and equity approach' only goes so far: if it were the plaintiff who had originally sued both defendants, it is not clear that the discretion would be used to prevent the plaintiff from being able to recover against a defendant who can be said to have caused loss. The trouble, ultimately, with the justice factors pointed to by Glazebook J may be that it is not so difficult to fit a similar argument about a builder seeking contribution from

[78] *Birse Construction Ltd v Haiste Ltd* [1996] 1 WLR 675 (CA).
[79] *Hotchin* (n 6) [201].
[80] ibid, [99], referring to s 17(2) of the 1936 Act, but Her Honour accepted that the same would be apply under equitable contribution.
[81] ibid, [234].
[82] ibid, [317].

a local authority into the same rubric of seeking to pass on responsibility to that local authority for a job that was properly the builder's.

C. Conclusions on Judicial Law Reform

The result of these two cases has been potentially to leave New Zealand with an expansive approach to contribution that jumps over many of the technicalities, but which leaves the ultimate determination of what is an appropriate contribution to judicial discretion. Glazebrook and William Young JJ clearly contemplated that there might be no contribution in *Hotchin* at all, as it would not be just and fair. While my colleague Victoria Stace has suggested that statutory law reform is not necessary,[83] in my view there has to be some concern that the Supreme Court may not have been best placed to conclude this reform. As McGrath J suggested in *Altimarloch*, the courts have limitations as to what reform might be accomplished. Either the reform might be too bound by past precedent, as one might critique the majority decision in *Altimarloch* as being, or too wide, giving an unbounded judicial discretion, as one might critique the decision in *Hotchin*.

IV. Overall Conclusion

This chapter has laid out the rather chequered history of New Zealand contribution law reform. If looked at simply as a matter of legislative reform, the debate has not led to much. But if we look at judicial reform as well, it is arguable that much procedural reform may have been accomplished, although we await other cases to tell us how far the Courts will take the expansive impulse in *Hotchin*. Leaving Courts to get on with reform is not such a bad thing, but it does leave the actual New Zealand law of contribution unwritten, and one wonders whether the fact that the Courts can fix up procedural issues if, or when, they occur, really ought to excuse the legislature's failure to fix them up itself. It also remains to be seen what the Courts make of the new possibilities that *Hotchin* may have created for a justice and fairness dispensation for some defendants. Overall, the New Zealand contribution debate has failed to resolve general problems with liability. But that may have been expecting too much for procedural reform. Interestingly the Law Reform Act 1936 has now been scheduled for 'revision'– a process that involves rewriting to make the provisions more modern but which is not supposed to change the underlying effect of the provisions.[84] Rewriting is, however, not the same as rethinking.

[83] See Stace (n 73) 157.

[84] Revision Bill Programme 2018 to 2020, presented to the House of Representatives under s 30(4) of the Legislation Act 2012 (4 April 2018).

INDEX

Introductory Note

References such as '178–79' indicate (not necessarily continuous) discussion of a topic across a range of pages. Wherever possible in the case of topics with many references, these have either been divided into sub-topics or only the most significant discussions of the topic are listed. Because the entire work is about 'apportionment' and 'private law', the use of these terms (and certain others which occur constantly throughout the book) as entry points has been minimised. Information will be found under the corresponding detailed topics.

www.ingramcontent.com/pod-product-compliance
Ingram Content Group UK Ltd.
Pitfield, Milton Keynes, MK11 3LW, UK
UKHW021811250926
475826UK00008B/54

9 781509 917501